Death and the Afterlife in Modern France

_____

INTRODUCTION

DEATH AND DYING have become fashionable topics in recent years. Although most people may not be inclined to discuss their mortal condition in casual conversation, medical and religious professionals, philosophers, and social scientists have dealt at length with the problems of defining death, treating the terminally ill, and understanding grief and mourning.[1] Concern about these issues, however, extends far beyond an audience of professionals and scholars. When the editors of *Time* chose "The Right to Die" as a cover story in 1990, they understood the popular interest in a feature on families and doctors who agonized over how to deal with patients in comas.[2] Current debates have centered on what *Time* refers to as "untamed medical technology" and on the need for doctors and hospitals to take into account the desires of individuals and families as they make decisions about the treatment of the terminally ill. The focus of the debate on the medicalization of death owes a great deal to the work of Elizabeth Kübler-Ross.[3] Drawing on her clinical experience, Kübler-Ross emphasized the importance of maintaining human relationships with the dying—a point of view that may seem self-evident to us partly because of the influence that her ideas have had over the past twenty years.

If there is any rival to Kübler-Ross in the shaping recent ideas about death and dying, however, it would probably be the French historian Philippe Ariès. For Kübler-Ross, death in the contemporary world has become an alienating experience during which the individual is too often deprived of the support of his or her family and is subjected to intrusive medical technology that sustains life only as it is defined in narrow medical terms. Although Ariès shares this critical perspective on the dangers of medicalization, his analysis of contemporary death is situated in a historical framework going back to the early Middle Ages.[4] According to Ariès, the "tame death" of the first millennium of the Christian era was a public event controlled by the dying, who saw their lives end with regret and resignation, but not with any great fear. During the Middle Ages the dying became increasingly concerned with their fate in the afterlife, a concentration on the self and its salvation that Ariès sees as enduring, although in different modes, through the eighteenth century. During the nineteenth century, the focus shifted from self to other; the separation from loved ones, especially from spouses and children, preoccupied the living, and only the expectation of a heavenly reunion made such losses bearable. In Ariès's scheme the shift from self to other is accompanied by a new aesthetic response in which the dying person and then the corpse are perceived as physically beautiful, a contrast with the baroque and classical perception that emphasized physical corruption and anonymous bones. This shift suggests that in the nineteenth century there was already a move toward the denial of death and of its consequences—a development that became manifest in the twentieth century, when death has been hidden in hospitals and stripped of the moral significance that it bore in earlier times.

Historians have criticized Ariès's evidence and methods (or lack thereof), and it is true that reading his work can be a frustrating experience.[5] A single memoir of the La Ferronnays family, for example, bears much of the weight for his interpretation of the nineteenth century, and evidence from one period is sometimes used to demonstrate a pattern ostensibly characteristic of another era. Ariès's synthesis is nonetheless of great importance, for it provides a much-needed historical context for the current debates about death and dying. Kübler-Ross and other critics are certainly correct in arguing for more humane treatment of the dying and for greater sensitivity on the part of families and doctors. These prescriptions, however, may focus too narrowly on the act of dying and on the power of the medical profession. As important as these issues are, they are informed by more general cultural patterns that shape the ways in which people think about their lives and deaths. For example, changes in religious belief and religious pluralism are clearly relevant for any understanding of how death is interpreted in the modern world. Ariès's achievement has been to call attention to the importance of considering the historical and cultural context as we seek to deepen our understanding of the current choices that we face when approaching death.

For Ariès the nineteenth century represents a crucial transition, a time when anxieties about death were transferred from a concern about the self to a fear of separation from the other. This central insight is compelling, and no one who reads Ariès can remain unaffected by the sensitivity with which he treats the emotions of those who struggled with their sense of loss. The relationship between family affection and the new sensibility both dominates Ariès's account and links it to his own earlier work on childhood.[6] But his focus on family feeling is at times so exclusive that it is easy to lose sight of what was happening outside the domestic circle, beyond the shades drawn to protect the dying and their families from scrutiny. Families did play a central role in mediating death, but Ariès neglects for the most part the poor who died alone in hospitals even before the full impact of medicalization was felt in the twentieth century. Even for middle-class families that tried to insulate themselves from the outside world, death was more an intruder than a welcome guest, bringing with it into the home a number of problems that forced the family to look outside as well as to themselves for solutions. Death was a civil and religious as well as a family affair, and both the State and the Church influenced and even controlled what people could and could not do as they separated themselves from their dead. Death could also be expensive, as new professionals emerged to provide an expanding quantity of decorations and services to families concerned that their dead be buried with the solemnity appropriate to their social station. Anyone who thinks and writes about death must be grateful to Ariès for calling our attention to the importance of broad cultural changes. However, by operating so consistently on a high level of generalization he made death into a domestic drama, isolated from other developments in the nineteenth century.

In the chapters that follow, my intention is to show how the attitudes toward death that emerged in nineteenth-century France were rooted in a specific social, religious, and political context. In a society marked by urbanization, declining levels of religious practice, the development of capitalist modes of production and consumption, increasing class stratification, and intense political and intellectual debate about all these issues, decisions about death inevitably bore public as well as private meanings. Montaigne knew in the sixteenth century that a man's character would be read once and for all in the way he died. In the nineteenth century death still provided a final occasion for the expression of personal character, but this was now a more complex composite of religious and political loyalties, family and social position. Trying to determine these in the fluid and contentious atmosphere of the nineteenth century could impose painful choices on individuals and families. When should the priest be called, if at all? How much should be spent on the funeral? Where should the burial take place, and what kind of monument should be raised on the grave? As Lawrence Taylor has noted, in answering such questions "we should examine changing forms in the discourse and material culture of death not simply as evidence of changing 'attitudes,' but as cultural forms which sought to reframe death, to assert new structures of experience and the moral authority of those who stood behind these forms."[7] The conditions that shaped these cultural forms and the meanings that they bore are the subject matter for my study.

Although death is a topic that extends too far and in too many directions to be dealt with comprehensively in a single book, the areas I have chosen to cover bear directly on the cult of the dead as it was experienced and understood in the nineteenth century. I begin by looking at the experience of death based on research in the discipline of demography. The shifts in mortality rates that accompanied the population growth and urbanization of the nineteenth century did not lead simply and inevitably to changes in the ways that death was dealt with and interpreted. But as Michel Vovelle and Lawrence Stone have pointed out, a knowledge of demographic change must inform any treatment of the cultural history of death.[8] I do not, however, approach demography simply as a convenient data bank for the historian. Demography emerged as a discipline in the nineteenth century, and the timing of its appearance and the questions it raised illustrate how contemporary anxieties about death were linked to social change. During the last century, studies of mortality became a principal index for measuring social problems—a technique that had ambiguous consequences. Although demographers were able to demonstrate an overall decline in mortality, their studies focused on particular problems such as suicide and tuberculosis that grew more severe, thus undercutting the optimism implicit in the general trend.

In the second part of my study I will analyze the models of death and the afterlife that were available in the folk, official, and alternative cultures of the nineteenth century. Ethnographic studies, which developed rapidly in the late nineteenth century, yield a rich vein of proverbial wisdom and domestic rituals that are invaluable for understanding how death was managed and interpreted in rural France. The fact that sayings and stories from the nineteenth century are still being published in France suggests their continuing importance. By the end of nineteenth century, and in our time as well, folk beliefs sometimes provide nostalgic relief from contemporary confusion about death.

Folk religious practices and beliefs existed alongside those of orthodox religion. Catholicism's map of the afterworld and its directions for reaching it were familiar to the vast majority of the French and are therefore central to my story. By examining both manuscript and published sermons, we can observe directly what the clergy were teaching about death and the afterlife. Hell was a dominant theme in preaching early in the century, but by its close a more reassuring message was being delivered to Catholics about their likely fate. Although Hell remained a threat, it was one increasingly restricted to those who placed themselves outside the Church. This shift in preaching was accompanied by changes in the way that the clergy dealt with the dying and mediated between the living and the dead. More often than not, priests were still asked to administer sacraments to the dying and to pray over the dead at funerals. But the controversial political situation of the Church that tore at France throughout the century made such occasions subject at times to ideological exploitation, as both the clergy and their opponents struggled to win over the dying and their families. The Church's role in mediating between the living and the dead also generated controversy, because the money earned for masses and indulgences was both an important financial supplement for the clergy and a sensitive issue that made them vulnerable to anticlerical attack.

It was unavoidable that the Catholic cult of the dead be drawn into the full range of problems that the Church at large faced, but clerical teaching and practice should not be seen exclusively as political instruments serving an institutional agenda. Catholicism in general and death in particular were politicized in part because the clergy and many Catholics believed that only involvement in public policy could ensure the preservation of a decent moral code and the salvation of souls in eternity. From the Catholic perspective, political stakes in the nineteenth century extended beyond earthly existence to the next world. This mood may be surprising to anyone familiar with the religious indifference that is widespread in late-twentieth-century France, but it strikes more resonant chords if we think about recent American history. The Catholic clergy in the U.S. who use the threat of Hell to try to discipline American politicians who disagree with Church doctrine on abortion are invoking the afterlife in ways that the French clergy of the nineteenth century would understand.[9]

Anticlericals who appealed for support among the increasing number of enfranchised men in France could profit from the resentment against the Church and the clergy, but they also needed to provide doctrines that could replace the Catholic afterlife and define new and consoling relationships between the living and the dead. Although alternative afterlives had been developed by intellectuals during the seventeenth and eighteenth centuries, they became available to a general audience only when associated with the political and social ideologies that became increasingly powerful after the French Revolution. Liberals such as Victor Cousin and Charles Renouvier and socialists such as Charles Fourier and Pierre Leroux took great pains to integrate doctrines of personal immortality with their visions of human nature and social progress. Even the positivist tradition of Auguste Comte, which rejected personal survival after death, addressed the issue of immortality and imagined ways to think and talk about the dead that would allow for their survival in the collective memory of future generations. All the alternative afterlives that were part of the new ideologies were seen to be a crucial support for the moral code because, like the orthodox Catholics they opposed, liberals, socialists, and positivists understood morality as being intimately linked to attitudes about the dead.

Alternative afterlives were linked to ideological development, but the example of French spiritism shows that they were not mere appendages of narrowly conceived political programs. Although French spiritism owed much to the speculation of early socialists, by the 1850s it had become an independent movement—a rival church whose doctrine and ritual centered on the possibility of communication between the living and the dead. As was true of similar movements in England and the United States, French spiritists believed that the methods of contemporary science could be used to demonstrate the existence of an immortal soul whose nature and fate were defined in ways strikingly different from Catholic orthodoxy. Led by Allan Kardec and Camille Flammarion, the most popular science writer of the second half of the century, spiritism described a universe in which reincarnated human souls continued their progress on other planets into an indefinite future. The séances and literature of the movement, including the famous sessions at Victor Hugo's house on the Isle of Jersey, suggest that deeply personal motives were fundamental to the appeal of spiritism. Hugo rejected the Catholic afterlife, but he could not accept the extinction of self at death and eternal separation from loved ones. Hugo and others like him (including the emperor Napoleon III and his wife) were comforted by mediums who brought the spirits of the dead back into their homes where they talked again with their families.

In a final section I explore the new institutional and material culture of death, focusing on the establishment of state-controlled cemeteries and a commercial funeral industry. During the French Revolution, the Catholic cult of the dead came under direct attack by militants who saw it as a superstitious fraud designed to frighten the laity and maintain clerical power. Although revolutionaries sought to create a new State-centered cult of the dead, by the late 1790s most of the French were appalled by the deritualization and disrespect that surrounded the death of ordinary citizens. In reforms that began under the Directory, which were put into clearer form in the Napoleonic decree of 23 prairial, year XII (1804), new structures were created to ensure decent funerals and burials for everyone.

The proposed arrangements under Napoleonic law required the cooperation of the central administration, local government, and the Church. In the political and social climate of the nineteenth century, harmonizing these various interests proved extremely difficult. By examining the frequently contentious negotiations that accompanied the administration of cemeteries and funerals, we can see concretely how the spiritual and moral issues raised by death were inextricably bound up with the political and social environment. The cultural authority of the Church depended to a large extent on its ability to control the symbols and rituals that most people used to give death its meaning. At the same time the economic health of the Church, whose property was seized during the revolution, was in part dependent on income generated by the reformed cult of the dead. The law acknowledged the Church's cultural and economic involvement with the dead, but it also circumscribed ecclesiastical rights by allowing both local and national government substantial powers of regulation. This ambiguous division of authority was intended to protect citizens from a clergy that many feared was capable of exploiting their authority in the cult of the dead for the sake of political and economic profit.

The tension and conflicts between Church and State over the administration of cemeteries and funerals were generally initiated by families that insisted that their dead be celebrated and remembered with services, decorations, and monuments. During the nineteenth century, the pomp and ceremony that had been restricted to a narrow elite in the old regime and eliminated during the revolution were made available to an expanding middle class. Not everyone, however, could afford to pay for a funeral and a tomb, and those who could were not always happy with the restrictions that both the clergy and public officials introduced into the cult of the dead. For most of the century space in the communal cemetery was allocated on the basis of religious affiliation and social class, an arrangement that could lead to bitter disputes as people came to view their graves as final statements about their religious beliefs and social position. The resentment of Protestants and unbelievers who had been segregated in shamed corners of the cemetery led a Republican majority in 1881 to pass a law declaring cemeteries to be religiously neutral. This act contributed to the pacification of cemeteries, to their removal from the profane world of conflict and commerce, a process also reflected in the displacement of cemeteries out of urban centers that occurred throughout the century. The visit to the cemetery, so important a French family ritual, required a setting that was separate, quiet, and harmonious—traits that visitors can verify as present in contemporary France. A substantial physical and political effort was required to create such a space, which was an ideal in the nineteenth century before it became a reality in the twentieth.

Funerals, like cemeteries, provided a terrain where Church, State, and family had to negotiate carefully in order to protect what they considered to be crucial moral and economic interests. The provision of funerals was complicated, too, by the inclusion of an additional element: the capitalist entrepreneur eager to provide a service and make a profit. Businessmen moved quickly to provide funeral decorations (*pompes funèbres*) and services in Paris during the late 1790s, but the restoration of Catholicism following the Concordat of 1801 created a competing structure, as parish councils (*fabriques*) claimed the right to sell candles, decorations, and transportation for funerals. The Napoleonic reform of 1804 attempted to reconcile these interests, but the complex relationship that it envisioned among parish councils, funeral entrepreneurs, and city governments was difficult to administer. Bureaucratic bickering in Paris was intense in the early part of the century largely because of the rapidly growing demand for elaborate funerals.

The expanding funeral market created more than administrative problems; the commercialization of death pulled mourning families into a social world where money and class were carefully observed. Complaints about aggressive salesmanship that compromised the respect for the dead and their families began early in the century, aggravating the already strained relationships among Church, State, and the new profession of undertakers. All the parties involved claimed that they were interested in keeping death out of the marketplace. Complaints continued, however, and the funeral profession expanded throughout the century. Pompes Funèbres Générales, the enterprise that dominates the contemporary funeral market, was founded in Paris in 1848 and spread to other cities anxious to provide funerals that were both dignified and fashionable. Politicians debated the status of the funeral industry throughout the Third Republic but had difficulty reaching a consensus that could reconcile freedom of conscience, freedom of commerce, and respect for the dead. The law finally passed in 1904 completed the reworking of the Napoleonic legislation of 1804 undertaken by the Republicans. City governments were given the right to establish their own funeral service or to grant a single entrepreneur monopoly rights over the trade. Complaints that the law unfairly limits competition and consumer choice, while driving up prices, are still common and echo some of the arguments made during the nineteenth century. Governments of both right and left, anxious to keep the play of the market at a respectful distance from the dead, have nonetheless resisted further changes. The 1904 reform of pompes funèbres continues to regulate the funeral trade and to establish the enduring influence of the nineteenth-century cult of the dead.

The evidence for this study has been drawn from a wide range of sources. As every English-speaking historian of France knows, writing about the country as a whole is a risky enterprise because cities and regions have their own historians eager to explain the ways in which their distinctive cultures break from any pattern that generalists might wish to establish. I have dealt with this problem by combining research in the department of Maine-et-Loire with work in Paris. Particularly in the chapters on cemeteries and pompes funèbres, I have tried to compare developments in the capital with those in the provincial city of Angers and its surrounding countryside. Although studies concentrating on other regions would certainly yield interesting results, Maine-et-Loire offers several advantages for the historian of death in France. François Lebrun's monumental work on death and the cult of the dead during the *ancien régime* included the territory now part of Maine-et-Loire and thus provides a useful background for this study.[10] As Lebrun and others have demonstrated, the region is culturally diverse; the eastern half lies in the Paris basin, whereas the west borders on the Vendée and Brittany. The area around Cholet in the southwest has long been identified with the counterrevolutionary movement of the Vendée, and the people there remained highly devout throughout the nineteenth century. In the east around Saumur, the revolution was well received, and the clergy generally noted lower levels of religious practice. Angers itself falls into a middle range of cities that grew steadily throughout the century but never reached the preeminence of Lyons, Marseille, Toulouse, or Bordeaux. In addition to combining typicality and diversity, Angers possesses well-organized archives with rich materials on the cult of the dead. I have tried to balance the regional bias of my study by referring both to Paris and to other regions on the basis of research done in the National Archives, the Departmental Archives of the Seine, and in secondary literature. In addition to research in local and national archives I have used legislative records, pamphlets and devotional literature, philosophical essays, imaginative literature, and images from both popular art and the salons. I can imagine having made other choices and followed other leads, but I hope that what follows will provide an introduction to the cult of the dead as it was practiced in the nineteenth century.

I close with a brief epilogue on Gustave Courbet's *Burial at Ornans*. This painting has generated numerous interpretations and much controversy; and the tensions latent in it still puzzle and attract viewers.

I believe that a consideration of some of the concrete problems that the French faced in dealing with death and the dead provides a useful context for appreciating Courbet's achievement. Looking once more at the *Burial at Ornans* will also remind us of how difficult it is to decipher the meaning that the French attributed to death, for the cult they created to surround it was as contested and equivocal as is his masterpiece. It is by probing their struggles and doubts that we can see how the French defined new meanings for their lives and deaths in an age of social change and shifting values.

PART ONE

Mortality and Mortal Knowledge

Chapter One

PROGRESS AND ANXIETY IN
FRENCH DEMOGRAPHY

IN 1855 ACHILLE GUILLARD, a French educator and engineer, invented the term *démographie* to describe the "mathematical knowledge of populations, their general movements, their physical, civil, intellectual, and moral condition."[1] Guillard was not the first person to interest himself in this field; during the eighteenth century a number of Frenchmen made important contributions to the quantitative study of population.[2] But it was only during the nineteenth century that accurate national statistics about birth, marriage, and death began to be collected and that demography established itself as a distinct intellectual discipline. Throughout the nineteenth and twentieth centuries, France was a leader in demographic research; it is not coincidental that the term used to describe the scientific study of population was taken from the work of a French scholar and that demography is, as Pierre Chaunu has written, the last science "to write and speak French."[3]

The study of demography, and particularly of human mortality, provides a crucial background for the cult of the dead that emerged in the nineteenth century. In acknowledging the importance of demography, however, I do not mean to imply a reductionist account in which cultural changes arise exclusively or even primarily from shifting patterns of mortality. Demography is interesting in part because it throws objective light on the emotionally charged subject of death. The questions and conclusions of Guillard and his colleagues, along with the invention of a term to describe a new and specialized discipline, also suggest that in the middle of the nineteenth century changes were occurring in the perception as well as the experience of death.

Demographic research placed death in a rationalistic and quantitative framework that reflected the professional concerns of civil servants and medical professionals who used mortality rates as an index to measure social problems and public health. Their work reveals anxieties about the deadly consequences of urbanization, poverty, crowded housing, changed working conditions, and new family patterns. These concerns were not restricted to a small professional elite. Growing numbers of literate French men and women were eager to learn about the changing patterns of mortality; about how often death struck; which places, professions, and age groups were most at risk; and how these changed over time. Demographic data trained people to think in terms of averages and encouraged them, as well, to adopt an abstract and secular perspective on the self and mortality. We will see in later chapters that folk traditions, ecclesiastical practices, state institutions, and private enterprise provided an increasingly wide range of choices through which families and communities could express their sense of loss and their desire to remember the dead. Although these cultural forms evolved from past practices and contemporary quarrels, perhaps some of the attention focused on the dead was an attempt to preserve a sense of the individual, who needed to be distinguished from the anonymity of demographic statistics.

The following section briefly summarizes the general trends in mortality that prevailed in the nineteenth century. For most of this chapter, however, I will focus on demography as a cultural form that people used to approach and understand death.[4] In the nineteenth century, demography provided not only data but also a new discourse for interpreting mortality.

THE DECLINE OF MORTALITY

Mortality in France during the ancien régime followed the grim patterns of the rest of Europe. The principal features as summarized recently by Michael Flinn were "dramatic short-run fluctuations, low expectation of life, high infant and child mortality, and a high endemic and epidemic incidence of disease."[5] Sometime during the eighteenth century, for reasons that are not yet clear, a decline in mortality began.[6] Survival rates as shown in table 1.1, based on the number of people per thousand still alive according to age group, show that starting around 1750 increasing numbers of people were reaching adulthood (see table 1.1). These figures apply to the countryside; the evidence from urban areas is less clear. Despite all the qualifications that might be introduced, however, John McManners's judgment that "death was being defeated" in the eighteenth century seems a fair one.[7]

Mortality rates continued to decline gradually throughout the nineteenth century. From an average of 29.8 deaths per thousand for the period 1801 to 1805, the rate dropped to 21.6 during the last five years of the nineteenth century. In the period just before World War I, the mortality rate dropped and stayed below 20.[8] Despite the clear

TABLE 1.1
Survival Rates per Thousand Births, Eighteenth-Century France

| | Number of Survivors at Age: | | | |
	1	5	10	15
Before 1750	729	569	516	502
1740–1790	780	632	574	542
1780–1820	806	691	652	636

Source: Flinn, European Demographic System, 94.

progress indicated by these figures, demographers now tend to emphasize the relatively slow pace of change for most of the century. About ten years were added to life expectancy during the nineteenth century, which went from thirty-five to forty-five for males, and from thirty-eight to forty-eight for females. But this performance was no better than that of the eighteenth century, which also added ten years to the life expectancy of the average Frenchperson. By comparison, the twentieth century shows much more dramatic progress. The mortality rate dropped from 21.6 per thousand in 1900 to 12.5 in 1950, and during the same period life expectancy increased from forty-five to sixty-two for men and from forty-eight to sixty-eight for women. This amounts to an increase in the first fifty years of the twentieth century virtually equivalent to that of the previous two hundred years.[9]

From a contemporary perspective it is easy to understand André Armengaud's judgment that the demographic balance sheet for the nineteenth century was far from brilliant.[10] Those who studied population trends in the nineteenth century were also frequently ambivalent about their findings. The overall decline in mortality confirmed by recent research was already evident in the early part of the century, but despite this good news demographers anxiously observed countertrends as well. Studies of mortality focused on the growth of cities and the expansion of industry, on infant mortality, and on the spread of cholera and tuberculosis—all of which were observed to be major threats to health, and to life, and which seemed to be growing more severe. The research that analyzed these problems tells us much about the incidence of death in the nineteenth century but is equally valuable because it illuminates the mortal fear provoked by social change. The beliefs and rituals that people turned to for consolation, which will take up most of my attention in the following chapters, assumed their meaning in part as responses to an experience of death in a world whose dangers were known with ever-greater precision.

The Mortal Dangers of an Urban Society

During the first half of the nineteenth century, demographers were preoccupied by the mortality rates in urban areas. J. P. Graffenauer suggested that the level of anxiety accompanying urban growth equaled that during the plague.[11] The evidence from Paris analyzed by the influential investigator Louis-René Villermé revealed shockingly high mortality rates, especially in the poorer neighborhoods, where they reached 41.7 per thousand.[12] As Louis Chevalier has demonstrated, the work of early demographers reinforced the fears provoked by the novels of Balzac, Hugo, and Eugène Sue—Paris was threatened by violence and disease carried by the laboring and dangerous classes.[13]

In this golden age of statistics, readers sought in figures, including mortality rates, a way of grasping the changes in their society. Even *Le Magasin pittoresque*, a middle-class journal normally devoted to edifying images and texts, published population tables and charts that would allow readers "to calculate the life expectancy in France according to age (see fig. 1)."[14] But despite some of their gloomy findings, demographers frequently made a special point of indicating that mortality rates for all classes had declined over the past several centuries. In his study of Parisian mortality, Villermé concluded with a consoling message that progress had occurred for all social classes by comparison with the fourteenth century. This long-term decline in mortality led him to an encomium to modern civilization that seems at odds with the grim evidence that makes up most of his essay: "The development of civilization, which has purified the air, and reduced the ignorance and misery of the people, has resulted in the considerable decline in their mortality."[15] According to the Belgian statistician Adolphe Quetelet, whose influential essay *Sur l'homme* summarized a vast amount of demographic research from all the states of Europe, "it appears clearly established that in countries where civilisation makes the greatest progress, we may also observe the greatest diminution of mortality." Quetelet's statement exemplifies the indecisive judgments of the early nineteenth century, in that he follows this assertion with a series of twists and turns that reveal his confusion. Quetelet pulls back from his optimistic view about civilization to note the inaccuracy of many mortality statistics but nonetheless reaffirms that progress has occurred in major cities. Quetelet's conclusion is perfectly equivocal: "I repeat that I am far from giving my belief to the prosperous state which these figures seem to point out. However, we cannot but be inclined to admit that deaths have diminished with the development of civilisation and affluence."[16]

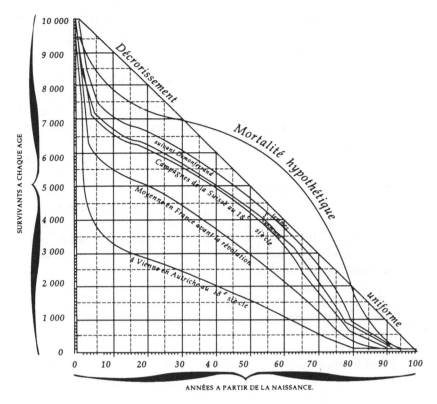

1. *The Law of Mortality.* Demographic studies appealed to a general audience in the nineteenth century. This graph, showing variations in mortality over space and time, appeared in "Lois de la population et de la mortalité," *Le Magasin pittoresque* 15 (1847): 149–152.

Quetelet, like Villermé, was both appalled by the high mortality among the poor revealed by contemporary research and conscious that in the past conditions had been even worse. A positive judgment about the present would seem insensitive, but a negative one would be ahistorical. The liberal principles shared by Villermé and Quetelet led them to argue that individual effort rather than state intervention was the key to progress, but their research pulled them in the opposite direction. The ambivalence of these early demographers was commented on by socialists such as Eugène Buret, who noted in 1840 that "M. Villermé . . . drifts indecisively between optimism and those ideas that have inspired our own work," by which he meant a commitment to dramatic social reforms as the way to correct the problems of inequality.[17] Villermé's capacity to resist such a program testifies to

the strength of his conviction that modern society was progressing
despite the obvious misery that resulted from the growth of cities and
the beginnings of industrialization.

French concern with urban mortality continued in the second half
of the nineteenth century, but at this point the evidence of the dangers of city living began to be challenged more aggressively. In 1869
officials of the Second Empire, proud of Georges-Eugène Haussmann's rebuilding of Paris, claimed that mortality in the capital was
no longer higher than in the countryside.[18] By the 1870s, the article
"Mortalité" published in the *Grand Dictionnaire* of Larousse argued
that it was difficult to determine whether or not mortality was higher
in urban areas: "Although the air is purer in the countryside, and
agricultural labor more favorable to health, the superior quality of
food and the greater availability of medical help when ill reestablish
an equilibrium to the advantage of cities."[19] In an article published in
1893 that reviewed the debate of the previous twenty-five years Gustave Lagneau argued that Paris remained relatively dangerous, but
his work acknowledged that measures of public hygiene had provided the opposition with evidence of progress in urban health.[20]

Although cities themselves may have appeared less deadly in the
later part of the century, a number of changes associated with urban
and economic development continued to trouble demographers.
Influenced by the work of Villermé early in the century, investigators
began measuring social health through a study of mortality rates. Accidental deaths and suicides were among the indexes used, for example, by Alfred Legoyt, director of the Statistique Générale de France
during the Second Empire, to judge the consequences of modern industrial civilization.[21]

In an essay on accidental deaths Legoyt shows that these rose from
fifteen per one thousand inhabitants in the period 1827–1830 to
twenty-eight for the period 1836–1860. In his analysis Legoyt showed
that whereas "natural" sudden deaths and drownings were declining, accidental deaths due to industrial accidents, commercial
transportation, and construction were increasing. Legoyt's purpose,
stated in his introduction, was not only to measure the changes that
were occurring but also to suggest areas where reforms could be
introduced: "If the frequency of accidental deaths is the result of a
particular situation, this situation can be modified by the combined
efforts of individuals and governments." Legoyt's list of potential
reforms includes regulating industrial and mining establishments, requiring cities to take measures to prevent drownings, and inspecting
both new and aging housing to ensure its solidity. The urban and
industrial environment that had preoccupied demographers in the

first half of the century was still seen as a mortal hazard, but with Legoyt the key to the problem is no longer the misery of the laboring classes but the unwillingness of private employers and the state to take effective action.[22]

Official statistics on suicide, like those on accidental deaths, began to be collected in 1826, and as with accidents suicides were understood to be the result of social changes introduced by the modern world. As Lisa Lieberman has written, "Depending upon the perspective of the observer, suicide was explained as a consequence of industrialization and the growth of cities, of poverty and the exploitation of the working class, of decadent art and sacrilegious thought, of the erosion of the family or the rise of an overly ambitious class of citizens, the bourgeoisie."[23] Interest in suicide seems to have intensified in the second half of the century, when it became a leading index for observing and judging a broad range of social problems.[24]

The work of Legoyt, who contributed both an essay in his collected studies and a full-length monograph to the debate, typifies the combination of sociological and moral analysis that prevailed in discussions of suicide. Legoyt began by characterizing suicides as "déclassés" and "misérables," but his analysis went beyond this simple correlation of poverty and suicide. He noted that workers and members of the liberal professions were more likely to take their own lives than peasants, whose lives were "calmer, more regular, less vulnerable to accidents, and more influenced by religious sentiments." Legoyt proposed that the elimination of hierarchy, the increased emphasis on the individual, progress in public education, and the frequency of political and financial crises all help explain why the suicide rate was increasing more rapidly than the growth in population. Legoyt's argument can be placed within the context of the general fear of social dissolution in the nineteenth century—a position that links him to Emile Durkheim, who also used suicide rates as an indication of social malaise.[25]

Ten years before the publication of his classic study of suicide, Durkheim had already begun to explore the links between demographic trends and social health. In "Suicide and the Birth Rate: A Study of Moral Statistics," published in the *Revue philosophique* of 1888, Durkheim argued that the lower birth rate that was a preoccupation during this period and the increase in suicides both resulted from the decay of "domestic sentiments" and the "cold wind of egoism" that accompanied the urbanization of modern France.[26] In *Suicide: A Study in Sociology*, which first appeared in 1897, Durkheim extended his argument in a brilliant analysis that has become one of the seminal works of modern social science. Durkheim believed that the suicide rate increased as a result of social disintegration, which resulted from the loosening of the bonds of religion, family, and polity observed in France and Europe. This is not the place to submit Durkheim's analysis to extensive scrutiny, and at any rate there is no shortage of critical responses to his work.[27] For my purposes, Durkheim's significance resides in the clarity and power with which he expressed an idea that was characteristic of nineteenth-century French demography—that statistical studies of mortality were both an instrument of social analysis and a measure of current anxieties. The fault lines that Durkheim followed in his study of suicide will appear repeatedly in my account, for changes in religious and family feeling and in the role of the state helped determine how people responded to the dead. But whereas Durkheim used suicide to indicate the dissolution of social ties, the cult of the dead can show how people worked to construct new rituals and new meanings that reflected their experiences in an increasingly urban society.

INFANT MORTALITY AND DEPOPULATION

Starting in the 1850s another set of concerns began to preoccupy demographers and affect the public perception of mortality. Although mortality rates as a whole were falling, the growth of French population nevertheless slowed, as fertility also declined. Influenced by Malthus, the reaction of many economists to this development was at first positive. A decline in fertility among the poorer classes showed that they were making more prudent judgments; smaller families would lead to greater affluence and therefore to lower mortality as well.[28] But occasional expressions of concern about the problem of depopulation became more frequent in the 1850s, and a major public debate began in the 1860s following the Seven Weeks' War. The loss to Prussia in 1870–1871 contributed to a climate in which depopulation became a central issue of French social policy. Political concern about the nation's ability to compete with its neighbors led to a series of reforms designed to encourage population growth during the Third Republic. Demographers were instrumental in setting the agenda for this discussion, which included extensive consideration of the problem of infant mortality.[29]

The fact that infants and young children were more at risk than others was not, of course, a discovery of the second half of the nineteenth century. Villermé's famous essay of 1830 included tables showing rates of age-specific mortality, and eighteenth-century demographers had already demonstrated that the possibility of death was highest for the very young and the very old.[30] Quetelet argued that children were at great risk until the age of five, when the "chances of life are the greatest, whatever be the sex or place of abode."[31] The explanations of infant and child mortality offered by Villermé, Quetelet, and their colleagues emphasized the difference between cities and countryside, rich and poor; sensitivity to infant mortality was thus closely related to the concerns that were so apparent during the first half of the century.[32]

Among the major sources of high infant and child mortality identified by demographers during the first half of the century were the prevalence of wet nursing and the high percentage of abandoned children who were cared for in hospices or placed with state-subsidized wet nurses. Government officials were conscious of the problems, and there were some modest attempts at establishing greater control over the practice of wet nursing, including the reorganization of the Paris bureau charged with placing children. But in 1869 the practice was still common; of the 54,937 Parisian babies born that year 22,529 were sent to wet nurses by their parents, and another 2,756 abandoned children were being nursed at state expense. Figures kept by the Paris bureau show that mortality rates remained high for these children into the 1870s. The percentage of those who died ranged from 22 percent in 1841 to 45 percent in 1873. It is likely that figures for those children placed privately rather than through the Paris bureau were even higher.[33] The mortality of children abandoned in hospices, where they stayed for just a few days before being sent to their nurses, was even more severe. Rachel Fuchs's study of the Hospice des Enfants Assistés in Paris shows a mortality rate consistently over 20 percent for the period 1815–1845. Considering that the children were generally there for only three days, it is easy to understand her judgment that this figure is "spectacularly high."[34]

The consistently high rate of infant mortality, especially when compared with the progress of other age groups, led to a number of reforms during the Third Republic. The control of wet nursing, established through the Roussel law of 1874, the reform of hospices that also began in the 1870s, the creation of a network of dispensaries and medical advice in the 1880s, the availability of sterilized milk in the last decade of the century, and the introduction of subsidies for needy mothers at the time of their delivery all helped produce a decline in infant mortality that became apparent around the turn of the century (see table 1.2).[35] The demographers who studied infant mortality concentrated on the social consequences of slow population growth, which weakened France in its competition with neighboring states. Historians who take a broader view of this issue have sug-

TABLE 1.2
Infant Mortality—France

Deaths per 100 Live Births	
1890–94	17.0
1895–99	16.2
1900–04	14.4
1905–09	13.1
1910–14	11.9

Source: B. R. Mitchell, *European Historical Statistics*, abridged ed. (New York: Columbia University Press, 1978), 41–42.

gested that concern about the deaths of infants and young children reflected their increased importance in the emotional life of families, an argument supported by the evidence of the photographs and sculptures of dead children presented by Philippe Ariès.[36] But it is important to note that the attention paid to the deaths of children can be seen by the middle of the century, before the steep decline in infant mortality at the end of the century. Although demographic data can be understood as a useful context for the study of changes in the cult of the dead, culture can also become a context that informs demographic changes.

DISEASE, DEATH, AND MEDICALIZATION

By the end of the nineteenth century demographers were able to present to the government and the public increasingly detailed and sophisticated analyses of mortality rates, which were frequently accompanied by policy recommendations designed to reduce the incidence of death. Unsurprisingly, demographic studies were a principal instrument for studying the incidence and diffusion of deadly disease and of the remedies to prevent it. During the Napoleonic Empire officials used statistical studies to demonstrate that the technique of inoculation with the cowpox germ discovered by William Jenner in the 1790s could protect humans from smallpox. A report from the department of Oise in 1813 revealed that the mortality of those under twelve had declined by 25 percent after the introduction of the vaccine.[37] William McNeill's argument that "the extraordinary population growth that set the nineteenth century apart from all its predecessors in Europe's history was in substantial part a consequence of the effective containment of this long-standing scourge of civilized human communities" may be exaggerated; but his mood reflects the hopes of nineteenth-century doctors and officials that they could fight successfully at least one important source of mortality that especially threatened children.[38]

The introduction of smallpox vaccine was accompanied by clear evidence of its ability to lower mortality rates. In the cases of cholera and tuberculosis, statistical studies were less encouraging. The doctors and demographers who dealt with these diseases were able to trace their impact with increasing precision, but for most of the century they were unable to offer any certain help to those government officials and citizens who sought guidance from them.

The cholera epidemic of 1832 had a profound impact on French society. Government officials, medical experts, and ordinary citizens were shocked by the extent of the mortality and by the horror of the symptoms; diarrhea, vomiting, and fever produced dehydration, so that a victim "shrank into a wizened caricature of his former self within a few hours, while ruptured capillaries discolored the skin, turning it black and blue."[39] In Paris the epidemic of 1832 aggravated social and political tensions. The middle classes feared the poor as a source of infection, while rumors spread among the laboring classes that the wealthy were poisoning them to reduce their numbers. Five men suspected of being poisoners were killed by angry crowds in April, and other riots in April and June were also in part a response to anxieties generated by the epidemic.[40]

The government responded to the crisis by creating special local commissions charged with ministering to the sick.[41] But the proposed remedies, including the traditional purgatives, were of no value, and the medical profession suffered a blow to its prestige as a result of its helplessness. Some people believed that they were being exploited as experimental subjects by callous doctors, an attitude clearly displayed in the character of Dr. Griffon in the popular serial of Eugène Sue, *Les Mystères de Paris*. Hospitals were especially feared, and rumors spread that at the Hôtel Dieu in central Paris doctors were testing remedies for their wealthy clients on the poor.[42]

Cholera was disturbing in part because it ran counter to the hope that catastrophic epidemics had disappeared from Europe following the last occurrence of the plague, which struck Marseille in 1720–1721.[43] The success of smallpox vaccination may also have encouraged doctors and their patients about the capacity of modern medicine to master disease. Of course, infectious diseases remained a chronic problem, but the malaria, dysentery, and pneumonia that continued to ravage France through the eighteenth and nineteenth centuries never provoked the panic inspired by cholera, which returned in 1834–1835, 1849, 1854–1855, with smaller outbreaks in 1865, 1873, and 1884. In part this fear was due to the novelty of the symptoms, and in part because cholera was more widespread and murderous than these other diseases. In Paris the epidemic was responsible for over 18,000 deaths between March 26 and October 1, 1832, and for an increase in mortality from 25,996 in 1831 to 44,463 in 1832. For France as a whole from 1815 until 1914 only the crisis of 1870–1871 produced a mortality rate that surpassed those of the cholera years of 1832, 1834, 1849, and 1854.[44] Cholera was frightening both because of its symptoms and because of the relative helplessness of the medical establishment in dealing with the disease. The care taken to track its path made cholera the first epidemic to have been studied with modern statistical techniques, but these were far from reassuring and may in fact have added another dimension to the anxieties of those who faced the disease.

Following the epidemic of 1854–1855, cholera began to lose its force; outbreaks in 1865, 1873, and 1885 had much less of an impact on mortality than the previous visitations. Robert Koch's discovery of the bacillus responsible for cholera in 1883 was not immediately accepted by all scientists, but it was nevertheless an important development in bacteriology and suggested the enhanced capacity of medicine to understand diseases formerly regarded as mysterious. The fading threat of cholera, however, was no cause for celebration for the doctors and demographers concerned with diseases. During the last two decades of the nineteenth century, new data on the specific causes of death led to the concentration of attention and anxiety on tuberculosis.

The key figure in the growing consciousness of tuberculosis was Jacques Bertillon, the son-in-law of Achille Guillard and the grandson of Dr. Louis Alphonse Bertillon, leaders in the demographic movement in France. After taking control of the Paris bureau of statistics in 1883, Jacques Bertillon oversaw the collection and publication of data on the specific causes of diseases. Pulmonary tuberculosis was clearly the leading cause of death in Paris, followed by diarrhea (which primarily affected young children), pneumonia, and heart disease (see table 1.3). Studies of individual cities and data collected in national studies confirmed Bertillon's finding that tuberculosis was the most serious threat to life in French cities during the last two decades of the century.[45]

The realization of the dangers posed by tuberculosis was accompanied by the isolation of the bacillus that caused it by Robert Koch in 1883. Koch's discovery confirmed the hypothesis defended by the French doctor J. A. Villemin since the 1860s that tuberculosis was a contagious disease passed between individuals, not the result of some obscure miasma in the atmosphere.[46] This combination of dem-

TABLE 1.3
Mortality in Paris (1882–1886)

Cause of Death	Average Number of Deaths per Year	Percentage of Deaths per Year
Pulmonary tuberculosis	10,542	18.6
Diarrhea	4,729	8.3
Pneumonia	3,926	6.9
Heart disease	2,950	5.2

Source: Emile Levasseur, Population française, 2: 115–117.

ographic and medical knowledge evoked the kind of fear and controversy that characterizes our more recent experience with the AIDS
virus. In a debate sponsored by the Academy of Medicine in 1889,
Germaine Sée argued that the contagionist doctrine was violating the
solidarity of the French family.

> People now fear the presence of a victim of tuberculosis in a family, in
> their own family. We see today parents who no longer dare kiss their
> sick child, who are afraid to stay in his room, who split the family by
> separating him from the other children, who demand a total isolation for
> the unhappy patient whose breath is poisonous. He is forced to live
> alone, abandoned, terrified, feared by others, for months and years . . .
> thanks to the theoretical exaggerations of hygienists.[47]

Sée's position amounted to a call for secrecy in the treatment of
tuberculosis, a form of surrender that did not accord with the desire
to do open battle with the disease. The fact that proportionately more
French were dying from tuberculosis than Germans was an added
incentive to take some action. Beginning in the 1880s, organizations
designed to spread information and provide treatment for the sick
began to proliferate. Special commissions named by the French
Chamber published reports to keep politicians and the public informed about the progress of the effort to treat the disease.

All this activity recalls the anxieties evoked by previous discussions
of mortality. In the 1890s doctors and demographers again were arguing that city life, and the depravity of the workers who lived there,
were responsible for the spread of disease, echoing the position of the
first half of the century that had receded in the intervening decades.[48]
The debate about tuberculosis included references to demographic
competition with Germany, the same problem that informed public
concern with infant mortality. As with cholera, greater knowledge
about the incidence and cause of the disease was of little consolation

given the absence of specific remedies and the threat it posed to human life.

Although the medical profession responded with hesitancy to the threat of tuberculosis, its prominence in shaping the terms of the discussion confirms what a number of historians have written about the growing prestige of doctors during the century.[49] Doctors formed their own professional organization in 1858, staffed the growing numbers of hospitals, and influenced politicians, who sought their advice and conceded them increasing control over the definition and treatment of sickness. The introduction of antiseptic surgical techniques and improved diagnostic methods also eased some of the worst fears of patients.[50] The medicalization of sickness and death that has been so pronounced in the twentieth century had its roots in the increasing power of doctors that began in the nineteenth century. But the claims of the medical profession regarding the sick were not accepted without question; the poor still resisted paying fees that remained high, and the fear of hospitals remained in place at the end of the century.[51] Evidence from Angers suggests that over one-fifth of those who died in urban areas did so in hospitals, which were a last resort for the poor who had no place else to go.[52] Alongside traditional suspicions, however, was an increasing reliance on medical expertise that was sanctioned by both the State and by science. The government regarded doctors as essential collaborators whose knowledge could help in the creation of social order. Doctors also profited from the prestige of science, the achievements of which were becoming more and more visible in the buildings and machines displayed at expositions and used in work and daily life. Medicine and demography were related in the careers of individuals such as Villermé and Jacques Bertillon. The two disciplines were related as well in their view of death as a problem for scientific experts, whose detached and rationalistic inquiry would guide the medical responses of individuals and the social policies of the State.

The Profession of Demography

We have seen that in the nineteenth century France profited from the work of a number of pioneers in the new discipline of demography. The studies of Villermé on Paris and the industrial towns of the north, the term itself, coined by Guillard, and the work of Legoyt and of the Bertillon family suggest the development of a cadre of professionals proud of their ability to acquire and analyze data.[53] A brief review of the development of their discipline shows that their attempt to create a rationalistic framework for viewing the movements of population met at times with bureaucratic and ideological resistance, a story that resembles in some ways the development of the medical profession.[54] The success of the demographers represented a victory for those who valued a quantitative and statistical understanding of mortality, a frame of reference that eventually was to become normative for public and health officials and for public opinion as well.

The first reliable national census was not taken until 1836, but well before then social investigators such as Villermé had the advantage of working with an excellent series of vital statistics collected and published by the department of the Seine beginning in 1821—data that went far beyond a simple recording of births, marriages, and deaths. Under the leadership of the prefect Chabrol de Volvic, the statistical office of the department collected evidence on "stillborn children, accidental and violent deaths, intentional or unintentional suicides, deaths from some of the lung diseases, inmates of old people's homes and general hospitals, with particulars of age and occupation"—in short, on a range of facts that Louis Chevalier justifiably labels "astonishing."[55] On a national level an important breakthrough occurred in 1833, when Alexandre Moreau de Jonnès (1778–1870) organized the Statistique Générale de France.[56] Although troubled at times by bureaucratic infighting, for the rest of the century the Statistique Générale provided the data and analysis that allowed demographers to perceive with considerable accuracy the mortal threats to the French population.[57]

Demographers throughout the century worked either for or in close conjunction with state agencies, and their work was intended to assist the government in planning its social and financial policies. The marquis Bausset-Roquefort stated the point clearly in his essay of 1862 on the movement of French population. Knowledge about population change "allows the state to foresee how much food is needed for subsistence, it is essential for the division of public funds, and measures the resources and strength of the nation."[58] Demographers also acknowledged an obligation to the growing insurance industry, which was assisted by the law of 1852 encouraging the formation of mutual-aid societies. In order to assess fairly the charges imposed on their members, these institutions required precise information on the probability of sickness and death for people at various ages. The construction of such tables was a preoccupation of demographers throughout the century.[59]

These professional tasks did not free demographers from the general social concerns about modern society, its cities, industries, and diseases that they shared with the general public. But they did encourage them to develop a self-consciousness about their work, which they defended from criticism and budget cutbacks, and to establish international standards for the collection and publication of basic data. In France the Société française de statistique universelle was founded in 1829, the same year that saw the first issue of *Annales d'hygiène publique et de médecine légale*. This early organization did not have the same success as the review, but in 1860 the director of the Statistique générale de France, Alfred Legoyt, founded the more powerful Société de statistique de Paris, with its own journal. These developments in France had parallels elsewhere, and starting in the 1850s the various national organizations began to hold a series of international conferences designed to encourage standard methods and categories for the collection of data. By 1878, the demographers had outgrown the statistical movement; the first international congress of demography was held that year in conjunction with the International Exposition at Paris. Organized by Jacques Bertillon and Emile Levasseur, the congress drew official delegates from the major states and was followed by additional meetings through the end of the century. There was also an official publication that first came out in 1882.[60]

The demographers resemble other professionals in their growing sense of a need for specialized organizations and national and international standards.[61] Some of them occasionally adopted a defensive, even belligerent, tone as they sought to demonstrate the significance of their work in the face of what they perceived as administrative shortsightedness and willful ignorance. There was, in fact, serious opposition to the statisticians and demographers, who were suspected by the right of harboring socialist inclinations. Louis Veuillot's Catholic daily, *L'Univers*, attacked demographic research being carried out in the newly created Ministry of Agriculture and Commerce in 1852: "The learned have exhausted themselves trying to discover the average life expectancy in different periods. But there is no average life: every creature is given an existence that is absolutely determined. For the rest, the calculations on which this figure is based have never appeared certain."[62] Political opposition from conservatives was not the only problem. Demographers also had to face bureaucratic criticism from officials who were concerned with holding down costs. In the introduction to his two volumes of essays on statistics Alfred Legoyt began with a story about an unnamed neighbor of France in which a budget-conscious official questioned the need for further statistical studies because so much work had already been done. The director of the Office of Statistics responded indignantly:

Well, Sir, do you think . . . that the population has remained stationary, that its mortality and fertility have not varied, that its productive forces are today exactly the same as ten or twenty years ago; that, in a word, by a kind of enchantment things have come to a complete halt? For the honor of the Council of State, Sir, I would not want such a thought to be expressed outside of this office.

The administrator, unrepentant and annoyed, responded sharply, according to Legoyt, "It's completely natural, Sir, that you would try to justify the existence of your service; as for me, I retain my opinion, and will not hesitate to defend it before the Council." This exchange imagined by Legoyt may have been based on his experience in the Office of Statistics, which did not survive his dismissal in 1870.[63] In the happier scenario imagined by Legoyt in the 1860s, an energetic and sympathetic minister reversed a decision to cut the budget of the Office of Statistics. The dialogue suggests both the sensitivity of those involved in demographic research and the struggle they faced in defending their bureaucratic position. By 1885, however, the government belatedly acknowledged the merits of Legoyt's argument and founded the Conseil supérieure de statistique.

Demographers were conscious of their civic and professional responsibilities, but their work involved more than the accumulation of data for governments and colleagues; it was also an expression of their view of society, which they saw as both harmonious and progressive, a position derived from the philosophical heritage of the Enlightenment and later from the positivism that became fashionable in the second half of the century (see chapter 4). Even in the politically and socially turbulent climate of the first half of the century, Villermé and Quetelet believed that the long-term decline in mortality demonstrated the value of the contemporary social system. To them, the most effective solution to the high mortality that struck the poorer classes was hard work and morality, which would produce the prosperity that could lead to longer lives. But even these committed liberals were willing to promote state action to improve public health and eliminate the worst abuses of child labor.[64]

There are some indications that the demographers' liberal belief in progress was at times linked to another idea inherited from the Enlightenment. Guillard's work of 1855 made crucial technical advances, notably in his use of formal symbols, but the spirit of his essay is also informed by natural theology. Borrowing from the influential German demographer of the eighteenth century, Johann Peter Süssmilch, Guillard argued that demographic regularities were part of God's plan for mankind. Perhaps the clearest expression of this view comes when he explains why there are more male than female births:

> The universality of the preponderance of male births demonstrates a law which everywhere tends to restore and conserve the sex most exposed to premature death, whether it be the result of exhausting labor and excessive passion, or due to the organism itself. What is the mysterious force which takes such vigilant care to repair the faults of men and to produce an equality so conducive to moral order? For us, we believe that a general effect must have a general cause . . . a calculated result an intelligent source. This is why each discovery of a new law shows us once more that a superior intelligence exists that man must glorify.[65]

Most nineteenth-century demographers did not attach themselves so explicitly to the tradition of natural theology. Guillard is less exceptional, however, when he claims that the relative quality of a society could be assessed by its mortality; death was "the measure of life."[66] Alfred Legoyt adopted the same position, and he stated it in a characteristically straightforward manner: "The degree of a people's well-being is measured in its mortality rate. This proposition is self-evident. Well-being is, in turn, the truest measure of the degree of civilization."[67] Legoyt found evidence for progress in declining mortality and an increase in the average life span, and he was especially impressed that such changes took place despite the threats to public health posed by industrialization and urbanization. He offered a number of explanations for this improvement: "vaccination, better child care, a rapid development in public wealth, vast improvement in public and private hygiene, more effective organization of public assistance, especially hospital services, and incontestable progress in the art of healing."[68] Legoyt's emphasis on public assistance suggests an important shift in the attitude of demographers during the second half of the century, when they became increasingly willing to contemplate state regulation and intervention to reduce mortality.[69]

Despite their consciousness of overall progress, demographers were not consistently positive in their evaluation of population trends. Guillard is typical in his assertion that the human situation remained precarious, that the progress he and others discovered was still contested.[70] Mortality was declining, but infant mortality stayed high throughout most of the century, accidental deaths and suicides were increasing, new diseases appeared and older ones grew more deadly. Depending on which statistical series they looked at, demographers could be either optimistic or pessimistic. Their research, for all its value, did not lead to the formation of a clear attitude about the state of mortality in the modern world.

Official interest in demography is easy to explain, because demographic data was clearly a useful planning tool. It is much harder to assess the nature and quality of public concern. According to John McManners, the educated stratum's interest in mortality statistics began in the eighteenth century and is "one of the most revolutionary and neglected aspects of the thought of the Enlightenment." But he also points out that, despite the evidence available to them, the French remained unaware "of the lifting of the shadow of death from the human mind."[71] Mortality rates continued to decline in the nineteenth century, but what distinguishes this period most sharply from the preceding century was the certain knowledge that progress was occurring. Despite this realization, however, demographers still seemed to be preoccupied with the shadow of death. There is no direct evidence about how the public interpreted figures that they read in the newspapers and journals, but it seems plausible to assume that ordinary readers were at least as troubled as the demographers whose accounts they read. One reason for this continued anxiety may be inherent in the nature of mortality data: the same figures that showed an increase in the life span of the average person, a concept popularized by Quetelet, also established a clear point at which death could be expected. When the demographer Levasseur wondered why, at the end of the century, people continued to regard the past as somehow superior to the present despite the statistical evidence, his answer was psychological: "Man is never happy with his fate; he never has been and never will be."[72] McManners puts the point nicely when he asks "who can say that any information about death is really consoling?"[73]

The overall decline of mortality familiar to demographers and their public in the nineteenth century was not necessarily comforting, for attention was generally focused on specific problems. As a result of their work, demographers were able to trace the consequences of social changes in ways that reinforced public anxieties. Cities were growing larger and more deadly, industrial accidents and suicides were increasing, children were being abandoned to die with wet nurses, diseases associated with poverty and the working classes were spreading.

Contemporary reaction to the AIDS epidemic offers a useful analogy; for in this case, as in the nineteenth century, attention is focused on the progress of a particular cause of death rather than on the overall mortality rate. The public demands information on AIDS, and demographers respond with statistics that allow governments and individuals to assess the threat and to plan their responses.[74] The availability of quantitative data about death may not always be reassuring, but it has become part of the contemporary appreciation of mortality—a form of consciousness inherited from the nineteenth century that we all share.

PART TWO

Folk, Orthodox, and Alternative Cultures

Chapter Two

FOLK RELIGION: TALES OF THE DEAD

ALTHOUGH French cities grew in the nineteenth century, the shift from a rural to an urban society was nonetheless a gradual process. Only one-quarter of France's population lived in settlements of 2,000 or more in 1851, and peasants still made up 45 percent of the population in 1900. Those who moved to cities to work as domestics and laborers frequently retained ties to the countryside, establishing links for further emigration and for the transmission of folk beliefs to an urban environment.[1] The folklorist Eugène Polain, from a bourgeois family in Liège, describes how in the 1860s and 1870s nurses from the countryside would make him and his cousins behave by promising to tell them the tales that they had heard from their mothers and grandmothers. Polain's interest in these stories led him to a career as a folklorist, a discipline that developed rapidly between 1870 and World War I.[2]

The sayings, stories, and rituals collected and published by French ethnographers are the most direct evidence that we have of peasant beliefs and practices. Of course, much of folklore deals with the agricultural cycle, the weather, work, family and social relations—issues that do not always directly raise the problem of death. But omens of death, rituals to perform after it struck, and ghost stories describing relations between the living and the dead make up a substantial portion of the folklore of the nineteenth century. Although this evidence can tell us much about how rural folk responded to death and the dead, it is important to keep in mind that the study of folklore, like demography, arose in a specific historical context. The growth of interest in folklore at the conclusion of the nineteenth century suggests a curiosity about the countryside and its values just as they were being threatened by urbanization and the integration of rural France into a more homogeneous nation. During this same period French city dwellers were attracted to landscapes of the countryside that presented it as "a symbol of peaceful reunions, the setting for tradition. . . . In the collective memory . . . the painted landscape called on a distant familial past."[3] The appeal of folklore, and particularly of beliefs and practices surrounding death, derived in part from a similar desire to engage with a culture in which value and meaning were thought to be not only uncontested but also sanctioned by family and community traditions.

The appeal of the folklore of death and the problems inherent in using it as a source are both apparent in *The Legend of Death* (*La Légende de la mort*), Anatole Le Braz's important collection of Breton tales that first appeared in 1893. Le Braz, the son of a Breton school-teacher, had a successful career as both a writer and professor of liter-ature, which he taught at the University of Rennes from 1901 until 1924. During his career he wrote novels, stories, and poetry as well as literary criticism, but his most enduring work has been *La Légende de la mort*. This collection of Breton stories went through five editions between 1893 and 1928, and it has been reprinted in both complete and abridged versions in the 1980s.[4] Le Braz always claimed that his account was faithful to the tales told to him by the peasants and sail-ors whom he met during his many excursions along the coast and in the countryside. The Bretons shared these stories with one another, and with Le Braz, at *veillées*, neighborhood evening gatherings of dancing, storytelling, and card games. Even a committed admirer, however, suggested that Le Braz's literary tastes affected his presen-tation of Breton stories.[5]

Le Braz's introduction to his collection suggests other problems in evaluating his tales, for he shows himself to be both drawn to and repelled by the stories he records. On the one hand, Le Braz sees the legends of the Breton sailors and peasants as revealing a pre-Chris-tian religion that the Church has been forced to accept; he seems pleased to report this failure on the part of institutional religion, and his favorable references to Ernest Renan, the Breton scholar who con-verted from Catholicism to positivism, associate him with a tradition of religious skepticism. Le Braz's stories, however, are filled with anecdotes about the clergy—whose importance in Breton belief is confirmed by other ethnographers as well. The complex relationship between folk religious traditions and orthodox Catholicism is one that Le Braz failed to address clearly, and it will have to be dealt with be-fore we can make use of this material.

Le Braz's argument that Breton folklore represents a culture that remained independent of Catholicism anticipates the position of sev-eral contemporary historians who propose that the institutional Church has struggled since the Middle Ages against popular religious traditions. According to Jean Delumeau, the best known of these his-torians, the Counter-Reformation of the sixteenth and seventeenth centuries marked the victory of institutional religion and the suppres-sion of popular beliefs.[6] This model of warring cultures has been amended by scholars such as Peter Burke, who proposes a more com-plex view in which the different cultural strata are seen both as exer-cising mutual influence on each other and as engaged in relations that are not exclusively hostile.[7] The evidence of French folklore, most of it collected in the nineteenth century, generally supports the latter position. There are, as we will see, references to the clergy and the Church in many of the tales, which "attest to the ability of the folk culture to reinterpret elements of Catholicism and to integrate symbols of spiritual power from the institutional church into the folk framework of meaning."[8] Although Catholicism is frequently present, there are also numerous folk narratives that make little or no reference to Christian belief in their handling of death. As Le Braz and his ethnographic colleagues discovered, lay men and women told stories about death and the dead in their own houses—outside the direct influence of the clergy—well into the twentieth century.

In this chapter I will deal primarily with evidence drawn from ethnographic investigations which yield a rich variety of proverbs, rituals, legends, and tales concerning death. The material here is distinguished by its source in lay rather than clerical traditions, which will be dealt with in the following chapter. The oral traditions preserved by French men and women provided them with alternatives to orthodox religion, but these were not necessarily opposed to Christianity and perhaps could be better seen as establishing a cultural line that sometimes parallels, sometimes intersects, and sometimes diverges from clerical orthodoxy.

Le Braz believed that the Breton legends demonstrated their independence from clerical influence; they also revealed the poetry and energy of folk belief. Le Braz's appreciation of the stories and storytellers is evident in a long passage that describes in moving detail the evenings at his home in Port Blanc, where neighbors gathered so that he could transcribe their words.

> You can't live a long time in Brittany without being struck by the purity, uniqueness, and delicacy of the popular soul. . . . And no less remarkable is the unconscious and completely spontaneous art with which this uncultured people translates its emotions and dreams. Just as they are born poets, they are born storytellers. They have an instinctive sense of composition, and an innate gift of the picturesque, and of color. This explains the form and the tone, somewhat literary, of these legends. They are so many small tragedies that the storyteller has often lived himself, that touch him, in any case, in the core of his being, to which he imparts the resonance and, if I dare say it, the vibrancy (frisson) of his personality.

The aesthetic appeal of the tales was strengthened by Le Braz's affection for the storytellers, several of whom became friends, though without, it seems, forgetting the social distance that separated them.[9]

At the end of his introduction, however, Le Braz's mood changes dramatically as he reports the death of his brother-in-law and collaborator, Léon Marillier, who had written the preface to the first edition of *La Légende de la mort*. Following a shipwreck that left him stranded and clinging for his life to a reef off the Breton coast, Marillier called for help to the shore but was rescued only the following morning. He died a few weeks later, and Le Braz was convinced that had help come sooner he would have lived. When Le Braz asked the villagers why they had delayed, the wife of a fisherman responded: "Oh! We certainly heard his calls: they tore through the night! But we thought it was the souls of the Hell of Plougrescant who were yelling." Le Braz's closing paragraph following this admission amounts to a vigorous condemnation of the folk beliefs that he had earlier praised so extravagantly.

> But they have an irrational fear of death, a wild fear, capable of abolishing everything in them, even the most elementary sentiment of humanity. God keep me from seeing this as criminal! It's not their fault if they haven't yet repudiated the ancient heritage of a race on which the yoke of primitive superstition weighs so heavily. . . . May the benefits of modern education free their children from these ghosts from another time! May the *Légende de la mort* soon be nothing for the Bretons than a memory, embalmed by them in the pages of this book, as in a shroud![10]

As far as Le Braz was concerned, Breton legends were marvelous poetry, but he was scandalized that anyone would act on the basis of such "primitive superstitions," which have value only if they are "embalmed" in books.

The ethnographers who collected proverbs and stories from French peasants did not, in general, share their beliefs. They went in search of the picturesque, of exotic and mysterious tales that could please and frighten them. And they were drawn also by the apparent integration of life and death in small communities, symbolized by the survival of cemeteries in the center of many villages.[11] Even the work of a scientifically oriented researcher such as Paul Sébillot can be seen as part of a project designed to provide relief from an increasingly urban and technological society—a society engaged in an effort to hide the presence of death.[12] The fascination with folklore, just when peasants were turning into Frenchmen, suggests that ethnographic concerns were related to the social changes of the era. Le Braz and his colleagues were influenced by a nostalgia for the folk, a frame of mind that may have shaped their perceptions. But Le Braz's final volley reminds us that sympathy and nostalgia could be combined with a sense of superiority and antagonism.

DEATH FORESEEN

Proverbial wisdom in France dealt mostly with the conduct of one's life, but sayings collected in the nineteenth century give us an initial view of peasants as resigned and even fatalistic in the face of death. "When your time has come, nothing's to be done" ("*Quand l'heure est là, rien n'y peut rien*") was a comment made in the Mauges, in northeast Anjou. This attitude annoyed physicians who, if called at all, frequently arrived too late be of any to help.[13] Those who sought a quick end to their suffering would have no more success than those who tried to prolong their lives beyond their allotted time; according to one saying, again from Anjou, "Death desired, death prolonged" ("*Mort désirée, mort prolongée*").[14] Another aspect of fatalism stressed not so much death's inevitability as its egalitarianism, a point that we will see elaborated in other areas of folk culture. According to a couplet from Anjou:

> A little faster, a little slower
> We all end up in the same place.
> *(Un peu plus tard, un peu plus vite.*
> *Nous venons tous au même gîte.)*[15]

These sayings are not very consoling, although one proverb does express a rather grim satisfaction in the fact that "you can only die once (*on n'a jamais qu'un mort à mourir*)."[16] Other proverbs derived from Scripture offered a more hopeful perspective by focusing not so much on death as on the heavenly rewards that might follow:

> The poor in spirit are happy,
> They're sure of being rewarded in heaven.
> *(Les pauvres d'esprit sont heureux,*
> *Ils sont sûrs d'être ravis en cieux.)*[17]

Less-cheerful possibilities were also expressed in rhythm.

> Such is the punishment of the sinner;
> Whoever forgets God while alive,
> Will be forgotten by Him when he dies.
> *(De telle peine est le pêcheur puni;*
> *Qui en son vivant met Dieu en oubli,*
> *Quand il meurt ne se souvient de lui.)*

One final proverb, however, suggests that even with this cultural form French peasants could express a variety of attitudes. For in addition to fatalism and simple religious messages, peasant sayings sometimes conveyed a belief that the good things of life could defend you from death:

> Bread, butter, and good cheese,
> Are the best shield against death.
> *(Pain et beurre et bon fromage*
> *Contre la mort est la vraie targe.)*[18]

The attitudes conveyed by proverbs were complemented by knowledge about death available from the interpretation of omens. When a dog howled at night, or a bird struck against your window, it was a sign that someone close to you, a relative or a neighbor, was about to die. Falling stars could also be a presage of death, an omen based on the belief that each person's soul was tied to a star. Some omens were related to religious rites. In Morbihan a person who fasted on Christmas Eve from daybreak until that moment in the evening when he could count nine stars saw Death at Midnight Mass touch those whom he would take during the following year.[19] In Anjou and the Vosges, when the church clock rang the hour just as the host was being elevated, it was a sign that someone in the parish would die during the week; and a tinkling heard after the tolling of the death knell was understood to be a call addressed to someone who would die soon.[20]

A number of death omens were particularly associated with marriage rituals. If during the ceremony the candle held by either the bride or groom went out, whoever had been holding it would die first—the same fate that would strike the one who first climbed into bed on the wedding night. Martine Segalen plausibly interprets these omens as a way for folk culture to emphasize the life-long commitment expected of a couple. But like the previous signs, they also reveal a desire to foresee death. Such curiosity makes sense when we recall that high mortality rates brought many marriages to a premature end; in the middle of the century, 17 percent of married couples never celebrated their tenth anniversary.[21]

Ethnographers from the last century have left us numerous examples of omens, but their collections generally do not let us see how these were used by people in concrete circumstances. Ellen Badone's research in contemporary Brittany demonstrates that omens, what the Bretons refer to as *intersignes*, are still familiar, especially among the older people. Her study is especially valuable because it suggests how omens are employed, not so much as predictions, but as after-the-fact interpretations of deaths that have already taken place. For the Bretons, omens are part of a worldview that excludes the possibility of random events. The howl of a dog or the screech of an owl might ordinarily pass unnoticed. But if someone is in danger of dying, or if someone dies soon after such an event, it is interpreted as "proof for the existence of fate, or destiny, a supernatural guiding force that controls the course of individual lives."[22]

This sense of destiny, a fatalism that assumes the predetermination of the major events of one's life, is not in Badone's view a gloomy and defeatist perspective that saps the energy to live; for the same people who believe in omens take action to protect themselves from accidents and illness. But when a death does occur, omens are recalled, and they provide the bereaved with "a meaningful context in terms of which the death of a loved one can be explained." Especially in the case of sudden deaths and the deaths of the young, through intersignes "one can to some extent reconcile their apparent lack of meaning with the desire for an ordered, meaningful vision of reality."[23]

Omens of death can also be found in more elaborate folk narratives, such as the legend of the fisherman's three sons whose fate he knows through three magic roses that fade when the children die, then flower again when they are resurrected.[24] But legends and folktales do more than confirm the use of omens. As a number of scholars have argued, they are an invaluable source for enriching our knowledge about past beliefs and attitudes. There is, however, some controversy about how such tales should be interpreted. Bruno Bettelheim's emphasis on the psychoanalytic function of tales has provoked responses from both Eugen Weber and Robert Darnton that emphasize their historicity.[25] In Weber's view, the tales reveal harsh social conditions rather than psychic conflicts. Darnton, influenced by anthropology, sees them as an index of national cultures, and he interprets the French tales as revealing a shrewd and amoral attitude focused on worldly matters, which contrasts with the supernaturalism of the Germans and the comic quality of the Italians. Despite this controversy, it is not at all clear that any single perspective exhausts the meaning of these tales, in so many of which death is a central concern. Valuable insights can certainly be gained from psychoanalysis, anthropology, and other hermeneutic vocabularies, but we should not be afraid to listen and learn directly from these tales—to interpret them on the basis of common concerns about death that continue to link us to the storytellers of the nineteenth century.

The fact that death is a pervasive element in the folk narratives of France is undoubtedly a reflection of the harsh social conditions that prevailed. As both Bettelheim and Darnton have pointed out, however, death is not always viewed fatalistically in the stories. The murderous designs of Bluebeard, who plans to kill his latest wife as he did the previous seven, are foiled by the heroine's delay in dressing, which allows her brothers to arrive in the nick of time and save her.[26] The apprentice blacksmith hired as a domestic by three giants learns that all the previous servants have been murdered, but he manages to kill his masters and then their mother. If we use a psychoanalytic framework, the characters threatening death in these tales might be seen as representing parental figures; a social realist would see them as husbands and bosses, reflecting the distribution of power in marriage and class relations. Both of these positions can be plausibly argued, but a more general point is also being made in these tales: death is a monstrous threat in the face of which we are apparently helpless, but by mastering our fears and using our wits we can save ourselves.

In some legends death is not just a threat posed by a cruel husband, master, or monster, who for all his power could be challenged and killed by a hero or heroine. Death is personified in a number of stories, and his appearance provides us direct insight into peasant attitudes toward mortality. In Brittany, where such tales were especially numerous and popular, Death assumed the name of the Ankou, an emaciated figure the wheels of whose cart could be heard squeaking at night as he made his rounds. Stories were told of nighttime encounters with the Ankou by men returning home late, and a glimpse of him frequently was followed by the death of the unlucky traveler.[27] These legends recall the figure of Death as presented in the *danses macabres* that were still being printed in France through the eighteenth century, which emphasize the inevitable and egalitarian nature of death. A song heard by Le Braz at Port-Blanc in 1891, "The Ballad of the Ankou," is a brief recapitulation of these older texts in which Death declares himself master of everyone—young and old, rich and poor, noble and commoner, priest and laymen, all of whom are subject to his power:

> If I wanted to listen to people, to accept a fee from them, even if it were only a half-penny from each, I would be drowning in wealth! But I wouldn't take a pin, and I wouldn't give a break to any Christian, not even to Jesus, or the Virgin. . . . I wouldn't spare a pope, a cardinal, or a king, not a one of them. Not a king, not a queen, no princes, no princesses. I wouldn't spare an archbishop, a bishop, or a priest. Neither nobles, gentlemen, nor bourgeois, neither artisans nor merchants, and not workers either.[28]

Although Breton folklore is noted for its particular emphasis on death, a number of ethnographers beginning with Anatole Le Braz have argued that its stories and funeral practices bear a close relationship to those of other regions. According to Le Roy Ladurie, "Brittany is not . . . separated by the so-called Celtic Iron Curtain from the rest of French culture, whether of north or south." The tale of Godfather Death exemplifies the broad diffusion of a number of tales, "which spread in similar forms throughout the French hexagon, with Brittany and Languedoc in the forefront."[29] In this tale, as in several others, Death is triumphant only after having experienced a number of humiliating defeats. The tale of Godfather Death illustrates how Death could be tricked by a clever man, and the variations collected reveal the flexibility of stories, which could be adapted according to the preferences of the teller and his audience.[30]

The tale of Godfather Death always begins with a poor man in search of a godfather for his child. In a Breton version he rejects both God, who "leaves the workers miserable and allows the lazy to be rich," and St. Peter, "because he refuses Paradise to the poor, guilty of a trifle, and lets the rich in." Death is accepted as worthy because "he is just, striking the rich as well as the poor, the king as well as the common man."[31] According to one interesting variation collected in Narbonne around 1880, Christ is the godfather, and Death the godmother, whose gift is two-hundred-years of life for all members of the family.[32] In virtually all these tales Death advises the godson to become a physician and, to help him in his career, declares that when he (or she) appears at the head of the bed, it is a sign that the patient will get well. With this knowledge the doctor could prescribe anything, even pure water, and take credit for the cure. But if Death appears at the foot of the bed, the patient would certainly die. In many examples the physician uses this knowledge to cheat Death by turning the bed around in order to save a princess, whom he then marries. In the Narbonne version the doctor, upset by the fact that he will live so much longer than his wife, tricks Death into entering a bottle and frees her only when she promises his wife two-hundred-years as well.

Despite these initial successes, Death eventually claims the doctor, who is frequently warned of his fate during a visit to his godfather's château. There he sees a room full of candles and is told: "Every creature has his candle to which his life is attached. There's a long one, of a child who was just born. The one which is just about to go out is an old man's, who's about to die." In a Breton version the man sees his own candle, which has only three days left to burn, and asks for another, longer one. But Death claims that the longer one belongs to the physician's son and that he could not honor such a request: "If I acted as you wish, I wouldn't be the just godfather you have sought." Resigned to his fate the doctor returns home, puts his affairs in order, and dies. In Dauphiné the tale concludes with the fatalistic observation that recalls peasant proverbs: "The doctor had to die. Although he was rich, although he was the godson of Death, that didn't do him any good." (*"Le médecin dut mourir. Bien qu'il eut de grandes richesses, et bien qu'il fut le filleul de la mort, cela ne lui servit à rien."*)[33]

In a more lighthearted vein, the generous blacksmith of another popular tale uses his wits to trick Death into allowing him some additional years. Although he has "no more religion than a dog," the blacksmith is notoriously hospitable to all who pass by. This open-handedness is costly, however, and after exhausting his funds the blacksmith sells his soul to the devil for money, some of which he spends on Jesus and St. Peter, who are passing through.[34] Given three wishes by his heavenly visitors, the blacksmith, instead of requesting Paradise, asks that anyone who sits on his bench, leans against his grate or touches his pear tree be stuck there for as long as he, the blacksmith, wishes. After seven years, the devil returns to collect his debt but is tricked into sitting on the bench, from which he is freed only after allowing the blacksmith seven more years. The same pattern repeats itself with the grate and the pear tree, from which the devil is released only after tearing up the contract. Finally the blacksmith dies and presents himself to St. Peter at the gates of Paradise. St. Peter, annoyed because of the man's apparently trivial initial requests, refuses him entry, but so does the devil, and thus the blacksmith is finally allowed into Heaven.

Like the doctor in Godfather Death, the blacksmith cheats death for a time, but eventually he must surrender to his fate. In this tale, however, the opponent is the devil rather than Death, and the focus is no longer only on the end of life but on the afterlife as well. Those who heard this tale were presented with a text that denied clerical control (in the person of St. Peter) over the afterlife. Robert Darnton is correct in emphasizing that this tale values cleverness; it also establishes, however, a moral standard of generosity that is contrasted with the rules of institutional religion. It is not only his tricks but also his charity that eventually earn the blacksmith his way into Heaven.

A variation of this tale collected in Artois in 1885 suggests that Death could be regarded as a friend as well as a foe.[35] In this case a charitable and pious woman is granted her wish to have anyone who climbs her plum tree remain there as long as she wishes. When she is nearly eighty, Death comes for her, but he is tricked into the tree, where he remains for six months. During the six months of his captivity, no one can die. "The infirm, the wounded, the sick suffered horribly and called for Death. But he didn't come. The unhappiest were the doctors; they couldn't make even the most debilitated creature die." Eventually the woman agreed to free Death, on the condition that he not come back until she calls three times. Death then descends and renews his work "striking down the living as in the past, to the great relief of some, to the great despair of others." In the end the heroine becomes so old and sick that she calls Death of her own free will, then takes the place that her good works have won for her in Paradise. In this tale Death is not only an enemy to be tricked but also someone to be welcomed for the relief he brings. The Artois version reveals no horror of Death and is, in fact, one of the most serene treatments of the topic to be found in French folklore. By adding (or deleting) details to the basic structure of the tale, in which Death is tricked into prolonging life, storytellers could emphasize religious and social injustice, the humor and nonchalance of the hero, the heavenly reward that awaits the charitable, or a positive interpretation of death as a relief for the sick and the aged.

Beyond the many variations of both Godfather Death and the Generous Blacksmith there is a fundamental tension in these tales between the urge to cheat Death and the recognition of mortality. This polarity is perhaps most clearly evident in the tale of the man who went in search of a country where he would not die. In the version collected in Perche in 1896 the hero is Pierre, an ambitious young commoner who succeeds in a military career and is named the chief minister of the king.[36] When a courtier insults him for his low birth, he has the offender dragged away to jail. Before he leaves, however, the aristocrat tells Pierre that for all his power, he too must die. These words strike home with the hero, who goes in quest of country where no one dies. During his travels, he comes to a place where no one has died since the creation of the world and spends three-hundred-years there. Eventually a giant bird appears and carries away a grain of sand; Pierre learns that this creature comes every thousand years and that when the land has been consumed by him, the country will be destroyed. The inhabitants are not concerned, for "they were all so old that life was a burden to them and they weren't afraid to die." But Pierre refuses to accept this fate and continues his search. He comes to an island where no one dies and stays there for six-hundred-years, until one day a monstrous fish appears who, when he has drunk all the water from the sea, will bring about the end of the world. Pierre again flees but finds no country as favored as the two he had abandoned. Discouraged and regretful about his decision to leave the island, he sits down and sadly contemplates his rapidly approaching death. Without thinking, he frees a fly from a spider's web, and the fly, transformed into a fairy asks what he would like as a reward. When told of Pierre's desire never to die, she responds that such a wish is impossible to grant in this world and takes him to a star where no one ever dies. There Pierre lives for centuries but, according to the tale, "You can become bored with anything, even with being too happy." Pierre wishes to see his village again, and the fairy gives him a magic horse that can take him back to earth—but she warns him not to dismount. Returning home, Pierre fails to recognize his village, which has been transformed into a great city where people no longer understand his language. Chased out of town as a madman, Pierre passes a cart caught in the mud and is asked by the driver to descend from his horse and help. At first Pierre refuses, but he finally gives in to the repeated demands and steps down. Immediately the driver turns into Death and declares his intention to seize Pierre. As Death prepares to take him, Pierre asks for an explanation of the slippers that he sees in the cart. "They're all the slippers I wore out searching for you," answers Death as he cuts Pierre down with his scythe.

Perhaps the first comment to make about this tale is its lack of any reference to Christianity and to the orthodox view of death and the afterlife. Pierre is not interested in gaining eternal life after death but in avoiding death in the first place. This desire places him within a tradition of stories that have their origins in the ancient Middle East, including the *Epic of Gilgamesh*. The tension in this tale is between the inevitability of death and the desire for immortality. Pierre's quest leads him to countries where life is long but not eternal, because the natural forces that erode the earth and dry the seas continue to operate. Pierre rejects the proposition, noted in previous tales, that death can be welcomed as a release from the trials of life. He finds immortality only when magically transported to a star, but eventually he feels himself pulled back to human society, to his native village. In some versions of this tale the hero chooses to leave the star in the hope of seeing again a beloved parent. This acknowledgment of social ties leads to the final confrontation with Death, and the conclusion of the tale suggests that Pierre, by choosing to descend from his magic horse, has accepted the fate imposed on him—and on all humans.

In the story of the country where no one dies, as in Godfather Death and the Generous Blacksmith, Death pursues someone; is resisted successfully for a time, but eventually snares his prey. All these tales express and resolve perennial anxieties about death, thereby fulfilling the function that Claude Levi-Strauss assigns to myths, which are charged with "the resolution of unwelcome contradictions."[37] Those who told these tales in the nineteenth century, however, were able to recast them in terms familiar to men and women of their time. In its most general form, the story of the country where no one dies simultaneously affirms the desire for immortality and the inevitability of death. Immortality is associated with a solitary journey, a rejection of nature and society that is ultimately unsatisfying; death is paired with the forces of nature and social bonds that we choose to affirm even if it means surrendering eternal life—and this contrast is presented in a context that recalls conditions in nineteenth-century France. The hero is a commoner who has managed by means of his personal ability to achieve success in a military and political career, a detail that recalls the social aspirations derived from the French experience of the revolution and the Empire. The fear of death is evoked by an exchange in which an aristocrat reminds a newly empowered commoner of his mortal fate, a telling reversal of the older theme of the danse macabre in which the lower orders were consoled by the fact that death struck the rich and powerful as well as the poor. Finally, the hero's return to earth, where his city has grown and his language is no longer understood, recalls the urbanization of France and the growing strength of the French language at the expense of local dialects that occurred during the century. Social and geographic mobility and the resulting tensions were themes common in the novels of Balzac, Stendahl, Flaubert, and Zola. Storytellers working with oral traditions also integrated these subjects into their work and, by so doing, related their tales of death to the lives of their audience, which included urban readers of the folklorists as well as peasants gathered at *veillées*.

THE EXPERIENCE OF DEATH

Proverbs, omens, and stories could help people express some of their feelings about death, but on a practical level French folk culture was also important in guiding behavior when someone died. The rites surrounding deathbeds have a different quality than the narratives in which death is approached as a potential threat to the living individual. Death understood as a threat to the self provoked a combination of resignation and resistance. Once it occurred, however, avoidance in the form of contemplations of terrestrial immortality had to give way before the brutal fact of the corpse. In contemporary France, as in America, this problem is generally dealt with by professional undertakers, and in chapters 6 and 7 I will trace the development of commercial funerals in nineteenth-century France. Despite the growing importance of professional funeral services in cities, however, in the smaller towns and villages it was relatives and neighbors who were called upon to ensure that the dead were treated with the combination of respect and fear that characterized traditional attitudes.[38]

Throughout the nineteenth century in rural France, the vast majority of deaths occurred in the home. Elderly residents of Anjou, interviewed in 1981, indicated that the hospital became an alternative only
in the 1940s, when old prejudices against it as a place for the poor
began to disappear.[39] We should not assume, however, that this pref-
erence for the home as the place of last repose meant that death was
always a peaceful and harmonious experience. The anxiety felt by
families as they watched the death agony of their loved ones, which
could be prolonged, led to a number of practices designed to provide
information about the fate of the sick. In several regions it was believed that if a piece of cloth floated when placed in certain fountains,
the person would be cured; whereas if it sank, death was certain.[40]
A variety of rites were designed to ease the suffering of the sick
by bringing on death. In Burgundy, Poitou, and Lorraine, villagers
believed that removing feathers from the pillow allowed the soul
to depart more easily. Elsewhere the same goal could be achieved
by placing the bed parallel with the beams of the house, removing a
tile from the roof, lighting a candle in church, or making a pilgrimage
to a shrine whose saint specialized in relieving the suffering of the
moribund.[41]

All these rites suggest a belief that death is the departure of a soul
from the body, an idea also expressed in some of the religious rituals
that were general throughout France. Sprinkling the sick person with
holy water, lighting a candle in his or her room, and having the priest
administer the Last Sacraments were practices designed to help the
dying person successfully pass on to the next stage of his or her existence. The rituals and beliefs of the institutional Church, which were
crucial in shaping nineteenth-century French attitudes, will be dealt
with in the following chapter. The folk religious traditions that will be
treated here were integrated with those sanctioned by the clergy, but
they remained under the control of the laity. Together folk religion
and Catholicism constituted a rite of passage that both allowed the
deceased to be incorporated into the world of the dead and the survivors to reintegrate themselves into the community of the living.[42]

Immediately after death occurred, a number of actions were taken
to indicate the marginal state of the deceased and of those left behind. All clocks in the house were stopped, and all normal activity on
the part of the immediate family was suspended. Other rites were
designed to assist the soul of the deceased, which was believed to
linger in the house and the neighborhood following its departure
from the body. All mirrors and polished surfaces were turned to the
wall or covered, because it was feared that the soul might see its
reflection and refuse to leave. Containers of water or milk had to be

emptied, either because the soul might drown itself as it stopped to drink or because the liquid was thought to be polluted by the sins washed away as it departed. As Ruth Richardson has pointed out, these customs have a "Janus-like ability to be understood *either* as a friendly gesture of protection and help to the soul on its journey, *or* as an expression of dread—revealing a desire to hasten it thither, and prevent as far as possible its remigration."[43] However we interpret particular actions, these rites were in general designed to ensure that the soul "not be prevented from pursuing its normal destiny."[44]

The prohibition against normal activity by the family meant that friends and neighbors were expected to take over the necessary tasks involving the disposal of the deceased. Neighbors knew of the death because the family would close the shutters of the house and send a message to the church, where the death knell would be rung. The tolling of the bells was especially important for notifying people throughout the area that someone had died; the sex and age could be established by listening to the pattern rung by the sacristan.[45]

Although the male clergy were charged with conducting the official services that would assure salvation, women generally assumed the major responsibility for attending to the needs of the body. Either a nun or an experienced lay woman would wash and clothe the corpse in a shroud or, especially toward the end of the century, in his or her best clothes—a practice that seems to have begun with the wealthier classes, and with men. Mademoiselle Neau of Doué-la-Fontaine in Anjou, who practiced as a burial expert (*ensevelisseuse*) in the early twentieth century, described placing the dead in their shrouds "as if they were babies," a comparison that has also struck some contemporary ethnographers. In the Nièvre it was not uncommon for the same woman to be both the midwife (*accoucheuse*) and the ensevelisseuse. On both occasions women specialists watched over a crucial passage in the life of the individual and the family, affirming their entry into a new stage of existence and a new relationship with each other. The washing of the dead, in an age when bathing was still uncommon, parallels the cleaning of the newborn and recalls the ritual of baptism, which also marked the individual for a new state of being.[46]

After the body had been washed and clothed, it was displayed on the bed, and neighbors would pass by for a final visit and farewell. In the course of the century it became increasingly common to place rosaries, crucifixes, and other pious objects in the hands of the deceased. A table next to the bed held a burning candle and a pitcher of holy water, which the guests would sprinkle on the dead with a branch of laurel or a palm preserved from Palm Sunday. During the night the body would be watched over by family and friends, a veillée that many recall as not being an especially sad occasion. Prayers were said, especially the rosary, but anecdotes about the dead, gossip, and jokes were also common. Indeed, in some places—in the Moselle valley, for example—the night has been described as one of "exuberant joy."[47] In Britanny, however, the talk and laughter would stop when the *diseur de grâces* appeared, a layman who would lead the prayers and sometimes surrender himself to violent emotions. Pierre-Jakez Hélias recalls one scene in which a diseur "violently reproached the Lord for the death of a gentle young girl because she hadn't deserved such a fate—after which he threw himself down on his knees, beat his breast, asked for forgiveness, and wept over what he had done."[48] The family offered a drink, usually hot coffee, to those who came to the veillée, although in some places prayers and stories were interspersed with helpings of mulled wine.

The veillée served an important social function in that it renewed the solidarity of relatives and neighbors in the face of their loss. In addition, as Van Gennep has noted, the burning candle, holy water, and prayers also suggest the survival of ideas about the dangers of the first night after death for both the deceased and his family. It was believed that the soul of the dead had not yet definitively left the house, and its presence was both a threat to the living and a sign that the ultimate fate of the deceased had not yet been determined. The holy water, blessed candle, and prayers can thus be interpreted as both protecting the living and helping the dead.[49] This same mixture of hope and fear continued to shape relations between living and dead in the period following the funeral as well.

The dead usually remained at home for two to three days, while invitations to the funeral were extended to relatives and friends who did not live in the immediate neighborhood. Friends might sometimes volunteer for the job of walking (or, at the end of the century, bicycling) to outlying areas and announcing the death and the funeral, but in many places specialists were also available for this work. While the invitations to the funeral were being distributed, the carpenter constructed the coffin. Although some of the poor were simply placed in the ground in their shrouds, for those who died at home coffins were already standard early in the century. Familiar objects were commonly placed in the coffin with the body. With the advance of literacy missals became popular, and the rosaries and crucifixes held by the dead during the visits of neighbors were also frequently sealed in the coffin. In some regions a coin was placed in the hand, either to pay St. Peter for the passage to heaven or, as one mother said as she gave a final sou to her daughter, "To let her have some fun in Paradise." Women would sometimes be buried with their jewels, men with a pipe or a bottle of wine, and children with their toys.[50]

The practice of burying the dead with objects that they might find useful or pleasurable in an afterlife is, of course, an ancient one. Household objects have been found in Egyptian tombs from 4500 B.C.[51] But in nineteenth-century France, and perhaps in ancient Egypt as well, this custom does not necessarily imply a belief that the objects would actually be employed by the dead; their presence in the coffin and the grave can rather be seen in part as designed to present a final, comfortable impression to the living observers of the corpse. A more literal-minded interpretation, in which the objects were understood to be comforting to the dead as well as the living, suggests a view in which the corpse was still somehow identified with a surviving self. Were we able to pose some questions to the participants about this (and other practices), their meaning might be clarified—although contemporary anthropologists have found that, when asked, people will sometimes give divergent and even contradictory interpretations of the same ritual. We can speculate about the meaning they bore, but the people involved did not generally translate the folk rituals that they practiced into doctrine. The reassurance of ritual was based on its ability to guide behavior and channel emotions in a difficult transitional period. The association of the corpse with a familiar object, whatever else it meant, was also a way to domesticate the dead body, which threatened to become an object of fear.

Three days after a death a funeral procession would gather to lead the body to the church for a service, prior to the passage to the cemetery. In many towns in Normandy and in the south and southwest the procession was organized by confraternities of laymen. Originally created to ensure prayers and a dignified service for members, during the nineteenth century confraternities began assuming responsibility for burying all the dead of their parish. The *charités* in the north, with their black stoles, and the *pénitents* in the south, with their hooded robes, played a quasi ecclesiastical role in carrying the body to the church—a role that sometimes led to severe conflicts with the clergy over the control of the funeral service.[52]

In most places, however, the procession (*convoi*) was made up of the relatives and friends dressed in mourning: dark suits and dresses were the usual garb for the nearest relatives and at least a veil or a black cape for the others. During the last part of the period, gray or white could be substituted for black and the veil pulled back for women. Black ribbons would also be worn as arm bands by the men, gifts from the family to the mourners. For parents and spouses, mourning could last as long as two years.

If the deceased had lived in town, the priest would go to the house to lead the procession. Otherwise, the coffin would be carried or pulled by cart to the outskirts of the town, where the clergy would meet it. The bearers were generally four men who were either friends or relatives, but not members, of the immediate family. The coffin was followed by the closest male relatives, then by the other male mourners, and finally by the female relatives and friends. In a number of regions small wooden crosses distributed by the family to the mourners were placed at crossroads, where the procession would stop for a rest and a prayer for the deceased—a practice derived from the belief that the souls of the dead were drawn to these central spots. Frequently, the mourners also carried lighted candles, a practice that could become a source of conflict when the parish council charged with supplying the candles quarreled with the family about quality and price.[53]

The clergy, after leading the procession into the church, conducted a series of ecclesiastical rituals that will be discussed in chapter 3. Even within the church, however, the laity still had a role to play: families sometimes distributed blessed bread to mourners and offered a gift to the priest, after which they would embrace the coffin, sometimes with tears and sighs. During the century this demonstration at the coffin was generally replaced by the sprinkling of holy water, an example of growing emotional restraint and ecclesiastical control.[54]

The church service was followed by a procession to the cemetery led by the clergy, with the men and women divided as in the convoi from the home to the church. Unlike contemporary funerals, during which the coffin remains above ground until after the mourners have left, in the nineteenth century it was placed immediately in the grave. Observers noted that the tears and lamentations that accompanied this moment became rarer during the century, just as they did during the veillée and the church service. Courbet's famous painting of the *Enterrement à Ornans* provides us with a view of a procession in the countryside of Burgundy as it gathers around the open tomb, the women on the right side, several of them weeping behind their handkerchiefs, the men in the center of the painting more restrained. Following some final prayers, the priest would throw a piece of earth on the coffin, and then the mourners, starting with the family, would pass by and sprinkle it with holy water one last time. The family would then gather at the gates of the cemetery to thank all those who had come.[55]

A traditional meal followed the funeral service, for which the family invited to their house some or all of those who had attended. Wealthy families would sometimes distribute bread to the poor as well. Typically the meal would begin somberly, but by its end people would be talking cheerfully. Emile Joulain, a peasant from Mazé in Anjou, recalls conversations at funeral *repas* from early in the twentieth century at which the dead would be recalled in affectionate terms: "The dead, yes we spoke of them. We said 'Well, he really liked to drink his little cup, but not too much,' and 'He was a guy who would never hurt anyone.' "

The day after the funeral the bedclothes, sheets, and other personal linens of the dead would be washed carefully and the straw from his mattress burned, though this last practice became less common in the second half of the century. In the Nièvre it was believed that if any stains remained on the bedclothes after the washing, someone else in the family would die during the year. Fear of contagion was not the only motive for these rituals, however; in some places people said that the dead could not rest peacefully in their tombs unless the washing was done.

It is true that the ritual treatment of the corpse prescribed by folk traditions guided families and friends through the painful separation of death, but the descriptions collected by Van Gennep and others reveal more than custom-bound peasants endlessly recycling ancient funeral practices. Although the ethnographic evidence is not always precise, there are clear indications of changes in funeral customs—for example, the increasing restraint with which grief was expressed and the placing of the corpse in clothes instead of a shroud. Other examples of change were also apparent by the close of the nineteenth century. The lay ensevelisseurs, who were not always thought to proceed in a "tasteful and dignified manner," were replaced by nuns from religious orders.[56] In some towns influenced by the commercial practices of nearby cities, printed announcements replaced the personal invitations to funerals, and hearses rented from the urban funeral establishments (*pompes funèbres*) instead of pallbearers carried the body to the church. The decoration of tombs with elaborate floral arrangements is another practice that spread from the cities to the countryside, starting in the later part of the nineteenth century. Evidence from contemporary Anjou suggests that in recent years the church bells no longer announce a death, the veillée has disappeared, and the wearing of mourning clothes has been generally abandoned. Ellen Badone's research on contemporary Brittany shows how traditional funeral practices have been eroded by changing social conditions, particularly the prevalence of solitary as opposed to shared work.[57]

But even as customary practices disappear, they are recalled, frequently with nostalgia and regret, as typical of times and places where communal solidarity eased the burdens imposed by death. In

La Lanterne des morts, a television film shown on a national network (TF 3) in November 1984, the director François Fehr focused on the death of an old woman in a mountain community in the Massif Central to present the folk customs that presumably still surround death in isolated regions of France. The mirrors are covered, the clocks are stopped, a lantern is placed in the window, and friends and family gather for a veillée, where ghost stories are exchanged in the presence of a young *curé* (priest), who is polite but skeptical. Two elderly women believe that the fall of a weathervane, which lands pointing up, is a sign from their friend that she has been saved. In the final scene a young boy, lost in a blizzard, is guided to safety by the lantern in the window where the veillée is held.

La Lanterne des morts does not make an explicit argument against the contemporary abandonment of traditional rites, nor does it adopt a supernaturalist perspective. The women who see the weathervane as an omen are treated gently, but they nevertheless emerge as comical figures; there is no suggestion that the ghost of the dead woman did guide the boy to safety, though some pious viewers might choose to believe this. The tone of the film is ambiguous, as expressed in the attitudes of several of the characters who are unsure about how to interpret the rituals. When the granddaughter of the deceased asks her mother whether she believes that the laurel decorating the room of the deceased (*chambre mortuaire*) will actually keep the devil away, the mother shrugs and responds that "it does no harm." In some ways the attitude of the film recalls Le Braz's sympathy for the practices of the Bretons; viewers are expected to recognize and respond to the customs of a France that is disappearing but that should nonetheless be preserved, at least in memory. The director Fehr shows none of the hostility that Le Braz felt toward his subjects, perhaps because the participants themselves are so uncertain about the meaning of their actions. Folk customs surrounding the corpse have faded since the nineteenth century, but they are still part of the collective memory of the French. In Le Braz's work there is already a sense that in looking at the Bretons he is looking into the past, and the vitality of folk belief at the time gave to his work an edge of passionate concern. In contemporary France, the attitude is more a sympathetic nostalgia for practices that are difficult to take seriously.

The ethnographic descriptions of peasant funerals seem to portray what Philippe Ariès has called "the tame death." Following Ariès, Ellen Badone sees this as a death that "was accepted with resignation as a natural, familiar occurrence and accompanied by collective rituals that emphasized the permanence of the social group over the loss of an individual life."[58] Perhaps because death was integrated into the everyday world of the living, it sometimes appeared to urban observers that peasants took a cynical or calculating attitude toward the dead. Maupassant's story "The Old Man" ("Le Vieux") first published in 1884, describes a couple in Normandy concerned that the death of the wife's father will disturb the harvest. In order to avoid this misfortune, the husband invites the guests to the funeral while the old man is still in his death agony. By the day announced for the funeral the old man has still not died, but the guests nonetheless enjoy the traditional meal of apple turnovers and cider. One of them remarks that "it's too bad the old man isn't here; he loved these when he was alive," to which another responds, "He's not going to eat any more now, everyone has a turn"—a comment that cheers the guests and leads to a more lively party. When her father finally dies toward the end of the meal and the guests leave, the wife expresses her regret in the following terms: "Now I'll have to make four dozen more turnovers for the funeral! If only he had died last night!"[59]

Maupassant's story betrays the attitude of an urban cynic. Emile Guillaumin, who lived and worked on the land throughout his life, takes a similar view in his novel *The Life of a Simple Man* (*La Vie d'un simple*). Following the death of his grandmother, Guillaumin's protagonist describes not only the standard rituals but also what he characterizes as the "calm selfishness" of his grandfather who says, "I really needed a day like this" (in order to repair a plow). Guillaumin's character is surprised by the grief of his mother and sisters, whom he accuses of insincerity because of their previous fears that the grandmother would live on. To the reader, this last accusation seems unfair, for it is not difficult to reconcile a concern that the agony of an old and sick person not be prolonged with a subsequent regret over her death.[60] Maupassant and Guillaumin remind us that a spirit of calculation may sometimes have accompanied the rituals of death among French peasants, but their lack of sympathy for traditional rites and their religious skepticism color their accounts, just as the more romantic ethnography may exaggerate the respect and solidarity displayed in folk traditions.

A final narrative common throughout France reveals that humor was also part of the repertoire of attitudes that surrounded death and the dead. According to the version told in the Mauges of Anjou, some friends of a shoemaker who claimed to have no fear of the dead wanted to play a trick on him. One of them pretended to die, and the others arranged that the shoemaker would come to the veillée, at which he arrived with his tools and his work. When the supposed corpse began groaning and speaking like a ghost, the shoemaker knocked him on the head with a hammer, saying "when you're dead, you don't talk."[61] The story of the shoemaker, known as "Jean-sans-peur" ("Fearless Jean") in most regions, turns on the expectation that even someone who claims to be unafraid might react with terror when confronted by a ghost. Jean's fearlessness is significant and merits a story because it is exceptional as well as amusing.

THE LIVING AND THE DEAD

The story "Jean-sans-peur" deals not only with the fears that people might have when faced with a corpse but also with those provoked by the return of the soul of the dead. Beliefs and practices having to do with the relations of the dead with the living form a third category of evidence about peasant attitudes toward death. These are not, of course, completely distinct from the rituals surrounding death, for as we have just seen, the treatment of the corpse was intended to ensure the soul a safe passage to an afterlife. But the concern of the living for the dead, and communication between the two worlds, continued after the funeral. Beliefs about an afterlife, however, were more directly influenced by Christianity than were those concerned with the threat of death and the treatment of the corpse. Narratives in which the dead communicate with the living are filled with references to the fate of the soul that reflect Christian ideas about the afterlife as well as the importance of the clergy, masses, and prayers for the attainment of salvation. Christian elements and themes are not presented as doctrine, however, and are mixed with folkloric motifs that have little to do with clerical orthodoxy. As will be seen in the following chapter, the Catholic Church commanded extensive resources that allowed it to communicate its doctrines about salvation and an afterlife to the French, and we should not underestimate the power of this vision to shape popular concepts and attitudes. But folklore and popular tales show that Christian orthodoxy did not have exclusive control over the next world.

Folk beliefs about the dead were derived from a conviction that "for a certain period after their death, the dead continue to lead a life that resembles our own. They return to the places that they frequented when alive, sometimes to harm the living."[62] The dead wandered along the roads in the neighborhood and went back to their houses, but they were especially likely to inhabit the local cemetery and were sensitive to any insult that they might suffer from the living.

The dead were known to visit the living especially at night. Women were advised not to sweep after sunset so as to avoid brushing out of doors the dead who had returned home. In Brittany the tripod in the fireplace had to be carefully folded and hung; otherwise the dead,

seeking the warmth of the hearth, might sit on it and burn themselves. These visits, however, were not dangerous, because the dead
who came home were seeking hospitality and companionship and
were not interested in harming the living.[63]

More frightening was the possibility of meeting up with the dead
out of doors. In one of their manifestations, as a nocturnal horde
wandering through the forest or the sky, the dead of nineteenth-
century France resemble the souls observed by the witches (*benandanti*) of northern Italy in the sixteenth and seventeenth centuries, as
described by Carlo Ginzburg. During the pre-Christian era these
wandering dead were seen as "objects of terror, . . . unrelenting ma-
leficent entities without the possibility of any sort of expiation." The
influence of Christianity led to a new perception of the dead, who
"were no longer a dark and terrible presence passing like a whirlwind
through village streets: they had been introduced into the framework
of the Christian afterlife and had assumed the traditional function of
instructing and admonishing the living."[64] Certain gifted individuals
claimed the power to communicate with the dead and to inform their
surviving relatives of their fate.

In nineteenth-century France stories about the wandering horde of
the dead were still common in most places, but noises heard at night
were now interpreted more precisely. The sound of night winds was
believed to be lords and their hounds condemned to pursue game
until judgment day, in expiation for their obsession with the hunt
while alive. Frequently their preoccupation had led them to violate
ecclesiastical regulations and to behave cruelly toward the peasants,
whose fields they destroyed. In Gascony, for example, King Arthur
was said to have been at Easter Mass when he heard his pack chasing
a wild boar. As he left the church a wind carried him, his dogs, and
horses away. In the area around Retz the hunt in the sky (*chasse aéri-
enne*) was led by a King David who had pursued his game during the
high mass on Sunday and ignored peasant complaints about the dam-
age done to their fields.[65]

The identification of the wandering dead with a lord who is punished for neglecting his religious and social obligations reveals a nar-
rowing of the tradition reconstructed by Ginzburg, in which the
horde was more vague and inclusive. The use of mythical names also
suggests that by the nineteenth century the horde was presented as
a fable to condemn injustice but was not meant to be taken literally.
In some places the noises heard at night were identified with those
children who had died before having been baptized, with the souls of
those in Purgatory who were seeking prayers for their salvation, or
with the damned of Hell—a belief that we saw was embraced by the

villagers of Brittany to explain why they didn't save Léon Marillier following his accident.[66] These beliefs accord with those described by Ginzburg and demonstrate the survival of a combination of pre-Christian and Christian ideas about the afterlife into the nineteenth century.

Lay specialists capable of seeing the dead and communicating their knowledge of the departed to anxious relatives also continued to operate in the nineteenth and twentieth centuries, especially in Languedoc. These seers (*armiers*), who carried messages from the dead to the living, did not claim to be part of a confraternity of benandanti, and they were much more likely to report requests from the dead for masses.[67] The clergy may even have encouraged this channel of communication between this world and the next. Agricol Perdiguier recalls from early in the nineteenth century that priests sometimes paid men to dress as ghosts in order to frighten people into having masses said for the dead, a ruse that is still recalled in contemporary Brittany.[68]

The story of the apparitions at Lourdes, which culminated in the formation of the most important national shrine in France, reveals the importance and power of belief in communication between the living and the dead through the medium of gifted laity. Bernadette Soubirous, the visionary at Lourdes, did not claim after the first apparitions that she was in touch with the Blessed Virgin Mary, and many people thought that she was seeing Elisa Latapie, a young girl admired by the community for her piety and charity. Elisa had recently died in the most edifying of circumstances, assuring her family that she was content with her fate and promising that she would see them soon. A great many in this community of around five thousand were excited by the apparitions in part because they offered the gratifying possibility of gaining certain knowledge about Elisa's state in the afterlife. Eventually, of course, the apparition was identified as Mary, but the initial response to Bernadette's stories about the young woman she saw in the grotto reveals the state of mind of the people in a small town in the Pyrenees where it was easy to believe that a young girl with no religious training was able to communicate directly with the dead.[69] In chapter 4 we will observe the development of spiritism, a movement in which lay men and women presented themselves as mediators between the living and the dead. Although a number of religious and intellectual traditions contributed to spiritism, folk traditions definitely form a part of the background that allowed a religious alternative to official Catholicism to emerge.

As has already been mentioned, the dead visited the house where they had lived and wandered at night, but they were especially likely to manifest themselves in cemeteries. The dead demanded respect for their mortal remains, and they became angry and vengeful if their corpses were disturbed. This view reflects a sense of the self as being intrinsically related to the body, even as it decomposed in the grave. We will meet this idea of the corporeal self again in discussing Catholic beliefs and some of the alternatives to it articulated by nineteenth-century thinkers. In folk traditions, the obligation to respect the bodies of the dead was expressed in popular tales in which skeletons or revivified corpses rose from their graves to defend themselves.[70]

In the tale "The Vengeance of the Dead" ("La Vengeance de la mort") a young man crossing through a cemetery accidentally bumps into a skull, which he angrily kicks away. After realizing what he's done, the man laughingly invites the dead man to dine at his house, an invitation that he is surprised to see accepted the next day when a skeleton appears at his door. After a dinner, during which the skeleton eats nothing, the dead man issues a return invitation for dinner at the cemetery the next day. In most versions the young man accepts the invitation, dines at the cemetery, and dies either immediately or a short time later. But in versions popular in Gascogne, Lorraine, and Brittany he seeks the advice of a priest who counsels him not to eat anything at the meal and therefore saves his life. In the version from Gascogne, the skeleton concludes by acknowledging the value of the clerical advice and asks that the curé say a hundred masses for the dead.[71]

The role of the clergy is less evident in the story "The Glutton" ("La Goulou"), in which a gluttonous young girl insists that her parents bring her some fresh meat from the fair. By the time they try to make their purchase, however, the butchers are closed, and they improvise by stopping by the cemetery and cutting the leg off a corpse buried that morning. The next day the dead man returns, legless, and carries off the glutton to the cemetery, where he eats her.[72]

Failure to respect the bodies of the dead could have deadly consequences, an idea that also underlays some of the rituals for dealing with the corpse just after death. Even though the dead threatened the living when not treated properly, they could also help them out of gratitude for their consideration. In the story "Jean de Calais" ("Jean of Calais"), as told in Gascogne, the hero, sent off by his father to make his fortune, is shocked when he sees a corpse abandoned by the shore.[73] He pays to have the body buried with respect and to have some masses said for the soul of the departed. Jean later saves and marries the daughter of a princess, but he is then thrown off a ship by a jealous villain. The soul of the person whose body he buried, in the form of giant white bird, saves him from drowning and leads him to a desert island where he supplies him with food for seven years. When the villain is about to marry Jean's wife, the bird agrees to carry the hero home in exchange for a promise that Jean will give him half of what he values most in the world. Jean returns home in time to prevent the marriage, and the bird then asks that he cut his son in half to satisfy their agreement. Just as he is about to do so, the bird stops him: "Jean de Calais, stop. . . . I return to you what you promised to me. Keep your child whole. Jean de Calais, you helped me. I've paid you back. We're even. *Adieu*, I return to Paradise."

A number of versions of the first two of these tales, "La Vengeance de la mort" and "La Goulue," assume that the dead are still present in their graves and make no reference to a distinction between body and soul, or to salvation as preached in orthodox Christianity. The dead demand respect for their physical remains and return to life to punish those guilty of violating their rest, but their status in the after-life remains vague. More elements of Christianity can be discerned in "Jean de Calais," in which the hero has masses said for the dead as well as burying him. The dead man, rather than reanimating a corpse, assumes the form of a bird, suggesting not only a distinction between body and soul but also the difficulty of imagining a disem-bodied self. The bird, furthermore, refers explicitly to Paradise, indi-cating a belief in otherworldly salvation. Nevertheless, this story also emphasizes the obligation to treat the dead with respect and implies that their tranquillity depends on proper burial of the corpse.[74]

The ambiguous boundary between folk religious traditions and Christian belief is evident in the uncertain status of the dead, who are sometimes seeking tranquillity in the grave, sometimes salvation in an afterlife, and sometimes both. When salvation is emphasized, the identity with the body in the cemetery becomes a temporary stage—a form of purgatorial existence that will precede the elevation to Para-dise. This tension is expressed in ghost stories in which the dead call for the carrying out of promises that had been made for masses and pilgrimages on which salvation depends. In a version of "The Clever Hunter" ("Le Chasseur Adroit") told in Nièvre the tale begins with the dead father of a family appearing as "something white" to his two eldest sons, who run away in fear.[75] Only the youngest son stays to question the ghost, who reminds the boy of his mother's promise to make a pilgrimage to Jerusalem before he died. The mother, re-minded of her pledge, undertakes the journey—an adventure that leads eventually to her husband's salvation and the youngest boy's marriage to a princess. In a story collected in Picardie in 1883, the forgotten pilgrimage becomes the central element as a dead daughter comes back to remind her father of a promised trip to the shrine of

Notre-Dame-de-Brebières. After the father carries her to the shrine, where they hear a mass said by a ghost-priest, the daughter asks that she be returned to her grave: "Carry me to the cemetery, to my tomb. You will no longer see me, because I'm going to heaven. But never forget, in the future, to do all that you promise. A vow which is not fulfilled keeps you from Paradise."[76]

Elsewhere in Europe the pilgrimage in "Le Chasseur Adroit," which has no integral relation to the tale that follows, disappears; the presence of this motif in France, made central in the story from Picardie, demonstrates the penetration of Christian ideas into narratives concerned with the regulation of relations between the living and the dead. This syncretism is expressed more particularly in the tale of a priest who dies before saying masses for which he has received honorariums and cannot rest until he fulfills his obligation, sometimes with the help of the living. In "The Three Low Masses" ("Les Trois Messes basses"), Alphonse Daudet turned this tale into a story for his popular collection *Letters from My Mill* (*Lettres de mon moulin*).[77] In both its folkloric and literary versions the story stresses the importance of fulfilling earthly obligations, which bind us even beyond the grave. In other tales as well a punishment fitted to the crime is carried out not in some otherworldly prison ruled by demons but in this world, where the transgression occurred. Peasants suspected of moving boundary markers in order to expand their property, for example, were said to be forced after death to carry these stones from place to place, asking "Where should I put it?" They would be freed from this penitence only when some living person responded, "Put it back where you got it."[78] As André Varagnac has proposed, the dead in this genre of tale are still tied to family and village; the act of reconciliation focuses on the importance of earthly relations, with the dead understood to be an integral part of the community, rather than citizens of another world.[79] Unfinished tasks must be completed and crimes compensated for before the dead can rest easily. The idea of a heavenly reward appears in some of these stories, but even in the tale of the unsaid masses references to an afterworld tend to be vague; salvation may be the ultimate goal, but the immediate concern is harmony between the living and the dead, who are still present in the community.

These tales, and the others recounted in this chapter, were told by rural folk to one another, and we know of them because they were collected and published by ethnographers who worked along the boundary that divided peasants from Frenchmen. Folk narratives, with their emphasis on harmony and reciprocity in relations between the living and the dead, may have resonated with the folklorists and their urban audience because they feared that such values were being eroded in the modern world. We will see in the following chapters how Catholics and anticlericals fought to define and control a cult of the dead, which became increasingly politicized and commercialized in the nineteenth century. In this context the tame death presented by the folklorists was an alternative model that, to judge by the work of Philippe Ariès, has continuing appeal in the modern world.

But the tame death of rural folk was not as free from tension and anxiety as Ariès and some ethnographers have suggested. It is true that people in the countryside were more familiar with death than were their urban counterparts, who came increasingly to rely on medical and funeral professionals to deal with the dead. Even in rural France, however, politics and commerce sometimes intruded into the rituals of death, as we will see in the following chapters. Furthermore, it was not only the integration of the countryside into a capitalist and democratic culture that threatened the tame death of the peasant. The tales and rituals surrounding death can be seen as part of a harmonious folk culture, but if they succeeded in taming death it was through a confrontation with some of its most frightening aspects that are present in both rural and urban settings. The doomed struggle against mortality, the meaning of the corpse, and a longing to complete a life's tasks were among the problems that people addressed through their folk culture. Although the cult of the dead that emerged in nineteenth-century France did not mirror peasant beliefs and practices, urban dwellers continued to look to rural traditions for both inspiration and consolation. This fascination was in part based on a nostalgic reconstruction of a tame death in a harmonious countryside, but remembering folk beliefs also provided the French with tools for understanding and consolation that had proven their utility over many generations. Folk practices began disappearing in the nineteenth century, and only vestiges of them remain in some isolated corners of France today. Nevertheless, the recollection of the folklore of death has made it a part of the collective memory, and of the French way of death.

Chapter Three

CATHOLICISM AND THE CULT OF THE DEAD

THE DOMINANT SYMBOL of the crucifix places the death of Jesus at the center of Christianity. In the nineteenth century the cross remained a ubiquitous presence in the rituals of death, and it continued to serve as a symbol of grief and hope. A cross stood at the bedside of the dying and was frequently held by them as they received the Last Sacraments. The parish crucifix carried by an altar boy was at the head of the funeral procession from the home to the church and then to the cemetery. A large cross decorated the shroud covering the coffin, and crosses marked the vast majority of graves. Of course, the cross was evident in more than just funeral ritual. A crucifix was raised over the main altar in every church, and in the nineteenth century, as currents of ultramontane piety spread from Italy, the "stations of the cross" frequently decorated the walls of churches as well. The performance of this ritual, which could be worth a plenary indulgence, took people step by step through the story of the passion and death of Jesus. The missionaries who sought to reestablish Catholicism following the revolutionary era frequently concluded their program of preaching with the planting of a monumental cross in the cemetery or some other prominent location. Private as well as public devotion to the crucified Christ was common, as is clear from the many images of the scene available from the publishers of colportage literature early in the century (illus. 2). The mass-produced holy cards from the second half of the century show a softer, sweeter Jesus, who appears to suffer less than the one presented by the publisher Pellerin (see illus. 7).[1] However presented the death of Jesus was clearly a common sight for the French.

The cross could bear a political as well as a religious message, as was understood by both the missionaries of the Restoration and the opposition. After the fall of Charles X in 1830, mission crosses were attacked throughout the country as a demonstration against the alliance of throne and altar that they had previously announced and sanctioned.[2] The sentiments of these iconoclasts can be glimpsed in the case of a M. Bourreau, a veteran of the revolutionary wars who had retired to the village of Moulierne (Maine-et-Loire). A week after a mission cross had been planted in January 1824, a drunken Bourreau created a local scandal by standing before the cross and shouting at it: "Pig of a Good God. Come down from up there! So I have to

2. *The Hours of the Passion*. The text surrounding this image, which was distributed by the publisher Pellerin in the early nineteenth century, describes in detail the passion and death of Christ. The prayer at the bottom concludes: "O my divine Redeemer, when will you draw me to you? In waiting for this happy moment I will say from time to time the act of acceptance of death which will end my troubles in saying an eternal farewell to all that would separate me from you. Amen" (Photo: Bibliothèque Nationale).

pray to you! You have an ugly black moustache. Scoundrel of a God with pierced hands and feet. Pig, it's all the same to me. I don't give a damn about you. If I had my rifle I'd make you come down from up there."[3] We can safely assume that Bourreau was a political opponent of the Bourbon regime, but this alone would not seem to explain the angry "prayer" he addressed to Christ. We have no precise information about what Bourreau believed, but his performance suggests a complicated as well as a hostile relationship with the crucified Christ. Bourreau presented himself as someone who doubted the resurrection, but he shouted his challenge at the crucifix as if he expected to be heard, and the reference to the pierced hands and feet was a common motif in the prayers said by believers. Perhaps the prayerlike address was merely a show designed to shock those who observed him and to demonstrate his political and religious fearlessness. Perhaps in his drunken state Bourreau was not sure of what he was saying, a claim that he made unsuccessfully at his trial, where he was sentenced to six months in jail. However we interpret this scene, Bourreau's behavior suggests the powerful impact that the cross could have even on those who actively opposed its presence.

The cross bore political meaning in the nineteenth century, but Bourreau's demand that Christ come down suggests that even a drunken republican was sensitive to its religious significance as a symbol of immortal life as well as death. The power of the cross as an enduring symbol flows from the multiple meanings that it can bear and the capacity of these to reflect the changing sentiments of clergy and laity. These variations have been played on a theme established at the foundation of Christianity and common to the beliefs of most Europeans at least since the Middle Ages. The cross recalls not only the death of Jesus but our own mortality as well, and it links the idea of death with the certainty of an afterlife and the resurrection of the body. It is worth remembering that not everyone in Europe was a Christian; despite attempts to convert and exclude them, substantial numbers of Jews continued to worship within this alternative tradition. For the vast majority, however, even for the illiterate, Christianity provided the basis for a worldview in which death was not the end, and in which an afterlife and a resurrected body were unchallenged assumptions.

This central Christian message has been expressed in different ways. Jacques Le Goff has recently called attention to the cultural significance of such shifts. According to Le Goff,

> Ideas about the other world are among the more prominent features of any religion or society. . . . Such mental structures are the framework within which society lives and thinks. . . . [T]o change the geography of

the other world and hence of the universe, to alter time in the afterlife and hence the link between earthly, historical time and eschatological time, between the time of existence and the time of anticipation—to do these things was to bring about a crucial intellectual revolution. It was, literally, to change life itself.[4]

Through the work of Le Goff and others we are now beginning to perceive changes in the map of the afterworld, a new field of research that promises to enlarge our understanding of religious belief and its connections with attitudes toward the self and its destiny that are at the heart of human culture.

Historians have discussed the birth of Purgatory and the decline of Hell, and the landscape of Heaven has recently been described in a survey that covers two thousand years of history.[5] These and other works show how the three-tier model of Heaven-Purgatory-Hell constructed during the Middle Ages was challenged by the Reformation, then subjected to a broad rationalist critique during the Enlightenment. In France, however, the success of the Counter-Reformation limited the impact of the Reformers' critique of Purgatory, and the skepticism of the Enlightenment reached only a literate elite. The abbé Jean Meslier provides a good illustration of the restricted audience for the concept of alternative afterlives in the eighteenth century. This curé of Etrépigny in Champagne believed that after death "I shall be nothing." But he never shared his atheism with his parishioners, so as not to deny them the consolation of hope in an afterworld better than this one.[6]

The sustained influence of Christianity in the nineteenth century has already been seen in some of the folk traditions concerning death. But it was through the Catholic church and its clergy that Christianity most directly and powerfully shaped belief and practice. Michel Vovelle is right to argue that during the nineteenth century orthodox Catholicism lost its "hegemonic position, its quasi-monopoly" over images of the afterlife.[7] Nevertheless, Catholicism continued to provide a model of the afterlife that was familiar to virtually all French men and women. In the next chapters we will see that intellectuals, politicians, and administrators created alternatives to church doctrine and ritual that had a substantial impact on the cult of the dead formed in the nineteenth century. But these changes were controversial, and in the end the cult that emerged was forced to concede a great deal to the institutional church. Any understanding of how the French felt about death and the afterlife must include a consideration of Catholic teaching and practice, because these provided a frame of reference that dissidents as well as believers shared.

The messages of Catholicism were expressed in a number of ways, including theological reflection designed for a clerical audience. Important theological changes were introduced in the nineteenth century, most notably the spread of the moral philosophy associated with the eighteenth-century Italian bishop Alphonsus Liguori.[8] For the laity such discussion was filtered through the parish clergy, and my principal concern in this chapter will be the communications that linked priests and people together. Clerical ideas about death were passed to ordinary Christians in a number of different contexts, and the discourses that resulted were not perfectly consistent with one another. Not only did the different situations in which the laity confronted the clergy require shifts in the messages exchanged; the social and political context within which these meetings took place also affected the beliefs and practices that Catholics embraced in dealing with death.

There were three particular occasions when the clergy explicitly addressed their parishioners about death. First, in sermons they explained formal Catholic doctrine, including the nature of man, his corruptible body and immortal soul, death, resurrection, and eternal reward or punishment. Second, at the deathbed and the funeral that followed, the clergy ministered to the dying and their families—a crucial pastoral act during which consoling the bereaved generally took precedence over teaching them. Third, the clergy were intermediaries between the living and the dead, and the masses that they said and the devotions that they administered provided for mutual assistance between this world and the next. All these relationships changed considerably during the nineteenth century, as clergy and laity adjusted to the altered social and political circumstances. By the end of the century, Catholicism no longer played as dominant a role in the cult of the dead as it had in the eighteenth century and in the years just after the revolution. This erosion of Catholicism's cultural authority was not an automatic process, however, and the clergy and their supporters fought back vigorously. Clerical teaching and behavior concerning death, and the laity's responses to these, form a significant and frequently contentious part of the history of the relationship between Catholicism and French society.

THE PREACHING AND TEACHING OF DEATH

The Sunday sermon in nineteenth-century France was not, as it was in colonial New England, "the central ritual of social order and control." Harry Stout's description calls attention, however, to the importance of this genre of communication in which officially recognized ministers regularly took advantage of a privileged public forum to supply "all the key terms necessary to understand existence in this world and the next."[9] In France the spread of cafés and clubs provided alternative networks which compromised the clerical monopoly on public spoken expression. During the first half of the century the broader distribution of books and newspapers also permitted the public articulation of criticisms directed at Catholic orthodoxy.[10] We should take care, however, not to compress what was a gradual process or to exaggerate the rapidity with which it occurred. The situation described by Philippe Boutry for the department of Ain could easily be applied to much of rural France in the early decades of the nineteenth century: "In the village the curé is a person who is *listened to*: attending Sunday Mass is . . . a rule of conduct for the vast majority of inhabitants, who assemble there regularly, and for everyone of importance in the commune: mayor, councillors, teacher, small and great notables, and their families. . . . The sermon is, in this century, a *serious* act."[11] Sunday sermons were not the only occasions on which the clergy spoke publicly to parishioners. Catechism classes and periodic missions were also important vehicles for the teaching of Catholic orthodoxy, and the display of images and the singing of hymns were used to reinforce the spoken word. But the Sunday sermon, because of its regularity and seriousness, deserves special attention.

There is another more practical reason for beginning a discussion of clerical teaching with Sunday sermons. The preservation of a number of manuscript sermons from the diocese of Angers from the first half of the century allows us an unusually direct apprehension of clerical discourse. In the details of their language they describe a vision of death and the afterlife with roots in the Counter-Reformation and beyond.[12] At the same time, however, they bear witness to a certain resistance to this traditional vision on the part of their audience—an attitude that helped shape a new discourse and a new relationship between clergy and people as they faced death.

The largest collection, which consists of eighty-eight sermons, comes from the village of Bourg, just outside of Angers. These texts were most likely preached by René-Marie Dutertre and Jean-Jacques-Pierre Dutertre, an uncle and nephew who ministered to this parish from 1785 until 1850. Another forty-five sermons were found in the Loire valley town of St. Germain-des-Près, and their dates indicate that they were preached by Joseph Laroche, curé from 1805 to 1835. Finally, seventy-four sermons found at St. Michel-et-Chanveaux, in the generally pious western half of the diocese, include no dates, but their appearance indicates that they were composed in the first half of the nineteenth century, when Joseph Thoré was curé.[13] These were all small rural communes; Bourg had a population of 409 in 1845, but the parish served a population of around 1,200 when the eight other hamlets of the commune are counted. In 1831 Saint-Michel-et-Chanveaux had a population of 666 and Saint-Germain-des-Près, 1,496.[14] Neither the episcopal nor departmental archives yield anything to suggest that these villages or their curés were exceptional, although it is perhaps worth noting that the curés of Bourg and Saint-Germain-des-Près, like most of their colleagues in the region, refused the oath of loyalty to the State following the Civil Constitution of the clergy.[15] Perhaps these priests were unusual in terms of the diligence with which they transcribed their sermons, but we have no reason to believe that the sermons themselves differed in content from those preached by their colleagues. Once these preachers had done the work of recording their sermons, they were tempted to reuse them on more than one occasion. Such was clearly the case with Laroche, for thirty-three of his forty-five sermons carry a careful list of the years in which they were preached, and thirty of them were delivered at least four times between 1805 and 1835.[16] These sermons in general follow the pattern that François Lebrun observed in his analysis of those preached by Yves-Michel Marchais in the late eighteenth century. A brief phrase from Scripture, generally from the day's Gospel or Epistle, is followed by an exordium in which the preacher announces his goal. After the development in the body of the sermon, frequently in two parts, the preacher concluded with a brief peroration in which he exhorted his listeners to profit from his words and seek eternal salvation.[17]

These three substantial collections resemble one another in their themes and development. In analyzing similar evidence from Périgord, Ralph Gibson has emphasized the tension that exists in Christian preaching between "the vision of a God of justice and even vengeance, and that of a God of mercy."[18] During the first half of the nineteenth century it was the God of justice who was most evident in the sermons of Anjou. Each of the collections includes sermons on charity, of which there are fourteen altogether. But twenty-three of the sermons deal with sin and penitence, and another sixteen with death and judgment. There are five sermons entitled "On Hell" but only one called "On Heaven." In the period following the revolution and its assault on Catholicism, the clergy resorted to the strategy of fear that had developed during the Counter-Reformation and that was still considered the most efficacious means of saving souls. During the Restoration (1815–1830) the mission movement in which visiting preachers sought to convert parishes by emphasizing death, judgment, heaven, and hell became notorious for the fearsome vision of God that it carried to the French.[19] Parish clergy may have felt more need to balance this message with sermons on love, but like the missionaries they were inclined to preach about an angry rather than a loving God.[20]

Catholics who attended these sermons were provided with concepts that were intended to shape their perceptions of death, judgment, and the afterlife. The interpretations of these events offered in the sermons were contested by the laity in the nineteenth century and countered by the clergy's own behavior in other contexts. Nonetheless, these preachers have left us an invaluable source, because their sermons allow us to hear along with the people in the pews what the Catholicism that the vast majority of French men and women still identified as their religion was telling them about their ultimate destiny. Anyone who has ever read *Portrait of the Artist as a Young Man* will be familiar with the kind of preaching that French Catholics heard in the early nineteenth century. Like Father Arnall, as described by James Joyce, Angevin clergy saw it as their responsibility to remind their listeners forcefully of their mortality, a fact that was likely to be neglected because of a preoccupation with daily and material concerns.[21] The Epistle to the Hebrews (9: 27) offered them a useful text in this regard: "It is appointed for men to die once, and after that comes judgment."[22] The development of this text in the nineteenth century not only recalls to the modern reader James Joyce; it also looks back to the tradition of Père Brydaine, the eighteenth-century preacher whose evocations of death and judgment continued to be printed and used by clergy through the nineteenth century.[23]

All three sets of sermons include similar descriptions of the death-bed, a theme developed by means of a contrast between the death of the just man and the death of the sinner. How the clergy actually dealt with the dying (*agonisants*) will be treated in the next section; for now I want to reconstruct the experience of death as it was idealized in these sermons. The essential theme that all three preachers used in describing the deathbed was the contrast between the bad death of the sinner and the good death of the just man. The bad death was filled with regret for the past, pain and confusion in the present, and a terrible anxiety about the future. In facing the past, all the forgotten sins come to mind at once, a point that Jean-Jacques Dutertre explicitly directed at the young men in his congregation:

> Now, my brothers, especially you young men, you close your eyes in order not to see the hatefulness of your sins, you refuse to listen to the loud murmurings of the good people who are witnesses to your misconduct. You give yourselves over to pleasure, to dissipation, you make

noise in order to deafen yourselves, to spare yourselves the shame that would result from recalling your sins. Wait, my young brother, because the moment of your death will soon arrive. . . . Then your eyes will open and all at once you'll see to the very bottom of your heart everything there that is most criminal, most foul in all your life. . . . O my brothers, how frightened you will be in the sight of so many sins.[24]

In Dutertre's view, young men were more at risk of a bad death than were young women, a point reflecting the higher levels of religious observance among women that were characteristic of the nineteenth century.[25] Dutertre calls on his listeners to imagine their terror as death approaches, but he holds out little hope for a last-minute conversion. Distracted by pain and saddened by the impending loss of all his worldly relations and possessions, the dying sinner would have difficulty acting on such fear. At the last moment the sinner is utterly alone, "heaven and earth forsake him, a general abandonment doesn't allow him to see any help, any support. The world collapses under his feet, all of nature deserts him and leaves him in a moment alone with God. At the same instant his strength abandons him, his reason is lost, he is no longer himself, he is dying, a confused noise arises and resounds everywhere. He dies, he is dead."[26]

Abandonment, exhaustion, and terror awaited the sinner on his deathbed. The just man might also experience some fear, for as Abbé Laroche acknowledged, "Death is something frightful for human nature which resists it with all its strength . . . so that even the most just would like, as St. Paul says, to be vested with their glorious immortality without having to be deprived of their mortal body."[27] But the just man masters his fears by reflecting on his virtuous life—his attachment to the Church and its sacraments, his practice of charity and the other virtues, and his habits of self-denial allow him to face death with equanimity.

The just man dies without regret and the farewell that he bids to everything which he leaves behind is not at all bitter. . . . He leaves a world that is perverse, unjust, perfidious, to which his heart is not at all attached, a world which was already nothing for him, a world whose pernicious maxims, illusions, and scandals he detested.[28]

For the just man death was experienced as a liberation from the pain of the world. In a passage that recalls the attitude already met with in some of the folktales, Laroche listed the advantages of death: "No more afflictions, no more sicknesses, no more sadness, no more tears." In commenting on popular devotional literature published as part of the "bibliothèque bleue," the inexpensive literature peddled throughout France, Robert Favre has proposed that a scornful rejection of this world was more characteristic of Catholic orthodoxy than was fear about death and judgment.[29] The sermons of Anjou include both sentiments in plentiful quantities. The just man able to die at peace with himself was one who had already dismissed the world as ephemeral and corrupt, an attitude that preachers urged on all those who wished to avoid the fearful death of the sinner.

For both the sinner and the just man, of course, the principal source of anxiety and hope was reflecting on what followed death. First, there was the fate of the body to consider. In the tradition of the Counter-Reformation Joseph Laroche lingered over his description of the corpse, a horrible object that drove visitors away.[30] Exposed on the deathbed, the corpse displayed a

> head lowered and stuck to the chest, the hair still moist with the sweat of death, the skin pale, livid, the face disfigured, the jaws sunk to reveal the bones, the mouth hideously gaping, the tongue motionless and folded in on itself, the eyes blank, under eyelids which no longer move, the lips pulled back, everything about this body is horrifying. . . . People abandon it, everyone flees. But the wife, child, relatives, friends, servants, all those who have loved most tenderly this person hurry to shed some tears, heave some sighs, and have the body taken away from the house.

Laroche went on to describe the corruption of the body in the grave, then reviewed with his parishioners what would happen to their physical remains.

> It is there [in the grave] that we are going to be the witnesses, the sad spectators of the profound humiliation, the implacable destruction of the human body which is so often our idol in the here-below. . . . The body whose absence we weep over is hardly in the earth when it engenders an enormous quantity of worms and other insects. Some attack the eyes, others tear at the face. Some roll themselves in its mouth and breast, its chest starts to gape open, and is completely filled with them, its entrails swarm with them, everywhere worms gnaw and devour it.

Laroche continues in this vein for several lines, until the body has dissolved and has become nothing more than "a dunghill, a cesspool, a pile of rottenness and corruption."

One of the central paradoxes of Christianity that dates from its early history is the combination of scorn for the body and the doctrine of the resurrection of the dead. Jean-Jacques Dutertre insisted that for the just man the thought of physical corruption "was not at all troubling, since the body will know a glorious resurrection. The just man knows that the corruption that waits for him in the grave will become the germ of the immortality with which he will be dressed." The suggestion here is that the physical remains of the dead, regardless of the extent of their decomposition, will serve as the basis for a reconstituted body. At least since the late Middle Ages theologians had puzzled over the relationship of the physical body to the immortal self, and one strain of thought as well as a great deal of devotional practice embraced, as did Dutertre, the doctrine of material continuity. This conviction that the remains of the dead, regardless of their state, would be the basis for the resurrected and immortal self endured in the popular consciousness of English men and women through the nineteenth century. In France, as well, a respect for the physical remains of the dead was based in part on this expectation.[31] The resurrection of the body worked against the hostility to flesh and blood. This doctrine could also be turned in favor of a pastoral strategy of fear, however, for the revived body was liable to torture in Hell as well as reward in Heaven.

Finally, it was the anticipation of eternal punishment or reward that shaped the dying person's attitude toward death. By the nineteenth century, the clergy generally assumed that an immediate personal judgment would follow the death of an individual and that a second judgment would occur at the end of the world, at the moment when the dead were raised.[32] Perhaps the most remarkable element in the preaching of the judgment of the dead is the slight attention paid to Purgatory—the place where those Christians who died in a state of grace, but without having completely atoned for their sins, would suffer until their redemption. In all three collections there is only one sermon on indulgences in which Purgatory is the central theme, but even here the concern was as much to criticize abuses as it was to offer consolation.[33] We will see later that during the nineteenth century the Church expanded the role of Purgatory as an element in devotional life, but in their weekly preaching the clergy apparently felt that reflecting too much on the reassurances of Purgatory would impede conversion. In other contexts Purgatory would emerge as central, even dominant, but not in the Sunday sermon.

In their preaching on death, the clergy generally concluded their sermons with the soul appearing before a God whose attributes at this moment were listed by Dutertre: "great, holy, inflexible, just, all-powerful, sovereign judge of all nature."[34] The majesty of the judge placed the soul in the position of a frightened defendant in a court of law, "uncertain, lost, confused, trembling before its eternal destiny." Even in his description of the particular judgment that followed death Dutertre limited the possibilities to eternal reward or punishment, Heaven or Hell: "God crowns him in the end, or condemns him forever. Heaven or earth will open. . . . Such are the consequences of the frightening moment of death." But it was in their preaching on the last judgment that the clergy developed this contrast in the stark-est fashion. Taking off from Matthew 25:46 ("And they will go away into eternal punishment, but the righteous into eternal life.") and from a passage in the Nicene Creed ("He will come again in glory to judge the living and the dead"), all three preachers used details drawn from the Apocalypse to describe the end of the world. The sun would be eclipsed, the moon would turn the color of blood, the stars would fall from Heaven, while fire, war, and desolation reigned. Fol-lowing the terror of this scene, Christ would come again, the dead would rise from their graves, and the angels would divide them into the saved and the damned. Only such a public display of God's power and justice could compensate for the humiliation that Christ and his followers had been forced to endure during their lifetimes.

Once this final judgment has been delivered, the damned will be punished with eternal hellfire and the saved rewarded with Paradise. In interpreting Hell for their parishioners the preachers followed the patterns established since the Counter-Reformation: a fire that burns but does not consume, hideous demons, instruments of torture, a darkness that still allows you to perceive your suffering and that of the other damned, shrieks of pain and anguish, and the unbearable knowledge that all this was to endure forever. One passage selected at random from the sermons on Hell can give the flavor of this preaching. Jean-Jacques Dutertre, preaching at Bourg during the Lenten season in 1840, insisted repeatedly and at length on the reality of the fires of Hell:

> It is thus true, my brothers, that there is in Hell a fire that devours the condemned without ever destroying them. Come, Christians, come and descend in spirit to Hell and see what it is for the damned, and it is for them a house of fire, their bed is a bed of fire, their food is fire, the air they breathe is fire, see the condemned in the flames. They are not only in the fire, says Jesus Christ, they are buried in it, immersed in it, en-tombed in it. . . . In Hell the condemned is penetrated and salted with fire; this fire insinuates itself into the entrails, it circulates in all the veins, it reaches and devours even the marrow of the bones. The un-happy sinner is plunged in a lake of fire, fire above him, fire below him, fire outside and fire within, the blood boils in his veins. . . .

We can leave Dutertre here, for as Ralph Gibson commented in dealing with similar materials, "the passage is long and the genre known."[35] By the late eighteenth century preachers had begun to in-clude references to the loss of God's company as causing the greatest suffering in the damned, and preachers generally made this their ini-tial argument. But Laroche acknowledged that it was difficult to ex-plain this point to sinners, who would grasp it only after they had been condemned. Hellfire, on the other hand, could be interpreted much more easily by graphic references to the analogous pains of earthly fire. Theologians and clergy might hold that the loss of God was the worst of all penalties, but this was too abstract a concept to merit emphasis when teaching the people in the pews.

Sunday preaching generally followed a cycle—one that allowed parishioners to know that the last judgment, for example, would be the chosen subject for the first or second Sunday in Advent. Beyond this yearly rhythm were the periodic missions that were common throughout the nineteenth century, during which specially trained preachers from outside the parish would attempt to renew its spiritual fervor. Death and salvation were even more emphasized in mission sermons, and some preachers at these revivals kept alive techniques from the baroque period. As late as 1841 Jean-Marie de Lamennais used a coffinful of skulls, which he addressed one by one from the foot of the cemetery cross to evoke the fear of death and Hell.[36] Demographic catastrophes such as the cholera epidemic of 1832 also provided exceptional occasions for the clergy to preach on death and salvation—an ecclesiastical response that Albert Camus was still familiar with in the middle of the twentieth century, which he describes with passion and detail in *The Plague*.[37] During missions and epidemics people were more likely to attend church services and listen to sermons, and public officials sometimes expressed concern that the fears evoked at such meetings endangered public tranquillity.[38] These special occasions, when the laity were believed to be particularly receptive, provided an opportunity for the clergy to confirm the truths that were more easily ignored in the normal circumstances of the Sunday sermon.

Preaching was not the only method of communicating Catholic doctrine on death and the afterlife. Catechisms from this period repeated the same messages in calling on Christians to reflect constantly about their salvation—*pensez-y bien* (think about it carefully) was the message drilled into children.[39] Because catechism answers were designed for memorization, they tended to reduce the more elaborate rhetoric of the preachers to simple formulas. The catechism prepared for the diocese of Angers, for example, included this brief exchange:

Q. What is Hell?
A. It is the place where the evil are deprived of the sight of God and burned eternally.[40]

Hymns were also used as pastoral tools and, like catechisms, had the advantage of requiring a more active participation in the transmission of basic truths. Through much of the nineteenth century the hymns

of the seventeenth-century missionary Grignon de Montfort remained popular, and their singing was described by one nineteenth-
century preacher as "electrifying" the audience. Frequently sung to
the melodies of familiar songs, hymns responded to the taste for collective singing, and even the men commonly joined in loudly during
the refrains.[41] The choruses of one of Montfort's frequently reprinted
hymns repeated the themes of the preacher in simple couplets, while
the verse made the fundamental point over and over again.

> To death, to death,
> Sinner, this time will come;
> To death, to death,
> Everything will end.
>
> We have to die, we have to die;
> From this world we have to go;
> The just sentence is heard,
> It must be carried out.
> To death, to death . . .
>
> Come, worldly ones, see the coffin,
> Come to shame your pride;
> There, what you most esteemed
> Is finally reduced to nothing
> To death, to death . . .[42]

Images provide one final inheritance from the Counter-Reformation that complemented messages of sermons, catechisms, and
songs. Through the first half of the century Pellerin and other publishers continued to distribute inexpensive prints such as *The Mirror
of the Sinner* (*Le Miroir du pécheur*), which displayed in graphic terms
the death of the just and of the sinner (see illus. 3).[43] The dying man
in these images faces his supernatural enemies and friends alone; not
even a priest is near to provide assistance as the book of his life is
read as the basis for his future. Curiously, the text from the print repeats the standard contrast between Heaven and Hell, but the image
whose text describes the happy soul in Paradise in fact depicts both
Purgatory and Heaven. This confusion about the afterlife might
reflect some of the inconsistencies in pastoral practice that will
emerge in this chapter, or it might simply have been sloppy editing.
But there is no confusion about Hell, where the image of the man
being roasted on a grill and tortured by demons repeats themes
found in contemporary sermons as well as similar literature from the
ancien régime.[44]

From a variety of convergent sources we can form a clear idea of
church teaching on death and the afterlife. It is much more difficult to

3. *The Mirror of the Sinner*. This print, distributed by Pellerin throughout the nineteenth century, contrasts the death of a man in mortal sin, and his punishment in the flames of Hell, with the death of a man in a state of grace (Photo: Bibliothèque Nationale).

determine how the laity responded to the clerical evocations of the deathbed, judgment, Heaven, and Hell. There is enough evidence, however, to suggest a certain resistance to the harsh truths about salvation. Joseph Laroche chose to preach on death on the feast day of the parish patron, and his opening and closing comments suggest why he made such an apparently odd choice for a festive occasion. At the outset Laroche advised the young men who planned to celebrate with "horrible disorders" to think about sin and salvation, but he went on to note that "the scorn that many of you have directed at the word of God takes away almost all my hope, but no matter, your pastor will fulfill his duty."[45] In preaching on Hell Laroche referred to those sinners who "sought to reassure themselves . . . by saying that they renounce without difficulty the happiness of the saints, and content themselves with having in another life neither punishment nor reward."[46] According to Jean-Jacques Dutertre the young men of Bourg made jokes about the eternal torments of Hell and laughed at the credulity of the simple people who believed in them, an attitude of doubt that he claimed disappeared on the deathbed.[47] It appears from these comments that the kind of religious skepticism that was evident within intellectual circles in the seventeenth and eighteenth centuries had reached rural parishes in Anjou by the nineteenth century. It also seems that men rather than women gave public voice to disbelief; perhaps some women also rejected the Catholic afterlife, but in the villages of Anjou the expression of such ideas was the domain of the men, and particularly the young men.

Sermons such as the ones I have examined were also subjected to ridicule by artists such as Lavrate, whose grotesque image of a sermon on mortal sin shows a curé addressing an audience primarily made up of woman (see illus. 4). The preacher, searching for a metaphor to illuminate the horror of mortal sin, compares it with the behind of his beadle, and he concludes: "Oh my very dear brothers, mortal sin is as ugly, as abominable as [the behind of the beadle]. May this picture be always before your eyes and prevent you from roasting eternally in the flames of Hell."[48] Those in attendance at the sermon are represented as having the kind of bestial physical characteristics familiar to anyone who has looked at Daumier parodies, and the artist seems to have intended parishioners and preacher to appear both credulous and hypocritical. Lavrate's print shows a preacher addressing his parishioners on the terrible consequences of mortal sin—a common-enough occurrence—but the artist was appealing to and reinforcing the disbelief, scorn, and hostility that such scenes were capable of eliciting in the first half of the nineteenth century.

4. *A Sermon on Mortal Sin*. In this print by Lavrate from the 1840s the artist parodies the hellfire preaching of the clergy by having the curé compare the horrors of mortal sin to the rearend of his beadle (Photo: Bibliothèque Nationale).

It is impossible to know how many people were genuinely frightened by the deathbed scenes and hellfire of Catholic preaching or
how many were consoled by thoughts of Heaven. Nor can we say
with any certainty how many were doubters, or at least inclined to
doubt. The preachers themselves express some anxiety about the extent to which their message was taken seriously, and public chal-
lenges employing ridicule were now possible. Among intellectuals
Hell was a doctrine that had been criticized at least since the seventeenth century, at first in manuscript treatises and then in published
critiques in which authors showed themselves troubled by a concept
that associated a loving God with the cruelest tortures inflicted eternally.[49] The spread of such doubt continued in the nineteenth century
and constitutes an important fact in the history of attitudes toward
death and the afterlife. The shift in preaching that can be discerned in
the second half of the century may in part have been a response by
the clergy to the unpopularity of Hell, although we will see that other
reasons were also significant. As unpalatable as Hell was, however,
it remained a force in the consciousness of Christians and among
those who doubted as well. Hell might have provoked increasing disbelief, but the certainty of death central to Catholic preaching and
teaching led inevitably to questions about the afterlife. Both doubters
and believers were given frequent and firm warnings about the certainty of death and their eternal destiny. Thus whatever position
someone adopted was bound to have been made within a context in
which death, judgment, Hell, and Heaven as described within the
orthodox tradition would have to be pondered as an option to be
faced, even if rejected.

If we shift our focus from the Angevin countryside in the 1830s and
1840s to the cathedral of Notre Dame in Paris in the same decade, an
immense difference in the words spoken from the pulpit is immediately apparent. At Paris the lectures (*conférences*) of Henri Lacordaire
and Gustave de Ravignan were drawing huge crowds and favorable
attention. Lacordaire's sermons, in fact, are generally associated with
a revival of Catholicism among the Parisian bourgeoisie. But the program of preaching followed by these two men bears little resemblance
to the one followed by their more humble rural colleagues. The nature of man and of the church, human obligations toward God and
man, the role of Christianity in the moral history of mankind, and the
sacraments are among the topics considered; the deathbed, the last
judgment, Heaven, and Hell are virtually absent.[50] Perhaps it is unfair
to compare Lacordaire's and Ravignan's sermons with rural preaching, because the Notre Dame conférences were intended to be show-
pieces where the Church reestablished its intellectual legitimacy. Still,

it is noteworthy that in pursuing this goal stylish preachers were careful to avoid reference to themes that might prove frightful and offensive. Hellfire and brimstone were apparently not considered an effective means of winning back the urban elite.

The milder message that was heard in Paris in the 1830s seems gradually to have spread to the rest of France. Sermons preached in the cathedral of Angers in the 1860s, for example, avoid the terrifying subjects that we observed in the countryside. When Abbé Deschamps included a description of a deathbed scene in a sermon of 1862, he began by describing the fear of the Christian but then quickly moved to the services of the priest, whose words "consoled and fortified this soul. . . . show him the beauties of heaven, and the infinite merits of the Redeemer which compensate for our sins"[51] Père Rochard, who was principal of the college at Beaufort in the diocese of Angers from 1859 to 1863, wrote a series of instructions designed for young men that he entitled "The Lovable Yoke of the Lord." Rochard played on the fear of Hell, but he followed this with an appeal to the sinner to have confidence in God and to avoid despair:

> This excessive pain, this preoccupation with oneself, this unreasonable remorse and lack of confidence can lead you to discouragement and be the occasion for new sins. I forbid it. Accustom yourself to look on God as a father, as a tender father, the best of fathers. It is this touching name that he gave himself and that he taught us to use when we pray to him: Our Father who art in Heaven. It is not the terror of a slave that we must feel with regard to him, but the sorrow of a son.[52]

No manuscript sermons from the Angevin countryside have survived from the second half of the century, but those from Périgord studied by Ralph Gibson indicate that the "earlier Catholic obsession with hellfire and damnation was decisively weakened."[53] The notes of Jean Pialoux, who served a number of rural parishes in the region between 1847 and 1887, suggest that he did not preach on Hell; and other collections from the Third Republic confirm this impression of a softening of the clerical message as well.[54] By the early twentieth century, it was possible for Abbé Ferdinand Batut to associate death exclusively with the joys of Heaven: "Death! It is the hour of reward for the faithful soul! Death! It is Heaven, Heaven with all its joys! Heaven with its infinite happiness!"[55]

The decline of Hell as a topic of preaching should not be exaggerated. Collections of sermons used by the clergy to assist them in their preaching continued to include models that dealt in a traditional manner with death, judgment, and the afterlife well into the Third Republic. In published devotional works as well the emphasis on fear

continued to play a prominent role at least until the 1850s.[56] However, in sermons the space devoted to these themes had significantly
declined in comparison with the manuscript collections earlier in the
century, and some topics have disappeared entirely. The fearful
death of the sinner and the small number of those saved were no
longer given special attention, and even Hell disappears from some
collections as a topic worthy of independent treatment. In *The Friend
of the Parish Clergy* (*L'Ami du clergé paroissial*), a journal that began appearing in 1889, which provided sermons for virtually every occasion,
attention has shifted away from a contemplation of one's own death
to a consideration of the services that the living can render the dead.
The comprehensive index covering the 1901 sermons lists one reference to Hell, in a sermon on confession, and thirteen to Heaven, including one asserting that Heaven is easier to obtain than the goods
of this world.[57]

There are a number of explanations available for the shift away
from the preaching of Hell that occurred in the second half of the
nineteenth century. The spread of the moral philosophy of Alphonsus de Liguori was undoubtedly an important factor. One consequence of the battles between Jansenists and Jesuits during the
seventeenth and eighteenth centuries was the victory of a rigorist morality, because most clergy, even those opposed to the Jansenists,
were unwilling to be accused of laxity. The debate in the ancien
régime revolved around confessional practice, with the Jansenists
accusing the Jesuits of trying to win souls by means of moderate pen-
ances and quick absolution.[58] The severe morality that the Jansenists
were able to introduce into clerical training shaped preaching, as
well, and contributed to the pastoral strategy of fear that was inherited by the church in the early nineteenth century. Liguori's moral
philosophy, which counseled a more generous attitude toward peni-
tents so as to keep them from despair, was introduced in France
in the 1820s and spread rapidly following the publication of Abbé
Thomas Gousset's *Justification de la théologie morale du B. Alphonse-
Marie de Ligorio* in 1832.[59] Preaching as well as confessional practice
was shaped by the Liguori's ideas, which by 1844 had reached Jean-
Jacques Dutertre in the Angevin countryside. In his sermon on the
death of a just man Dutertre cited Liguori's interpretation of the fear
of damnation as a favor granted by God; in experiencing this sentiment the dying were allowed to extirpate their least faults.

Dutertre's paradoxical turn from fear to confidence suggests a
larger shift in the teaching of Catholic doctrine inspired by the philosophy of Liguori. The single most famous curé of the nineteenth century, Jean Vianney of Ars, began his preaching career as an "intransi-

gent rigorist," evolved to a more indulgent posture, and by the end of his life was known as a priest of charity and sensibility—a change associated with the influence of Liguori, mediated by a sympathetic bishop and a young vicar.[60] In a conversation with the British minister Thomas Allies in 1848, Père Ravignan reflected the emerging mood when he criticized clerical rigor as an unfortunate leftover from Jansenism and concluded that "we may hope that a great number come within the terms of salvation."[61]

The availability of Liguori's ideas helped shape milder pastoral tactics. But why were the clergy interested in these new ideas in the first place? Any answer to this large and complex question must be rooted in the relationships that tied together priests and people. We know that these were troubled by the harsh rhetoric of the clergy and, as other scholars have pointed out, by clerical attempts to suppress dancing and drinking and to control sexual practices by prohibiting contraception. All this contributed to the alienation of parishioners and to the generally declining levels of religious practice that characterized many areas of France in the last century. At the same time, the improvement in the standard of living, which Eugen Weber sees as becoming especially notable in the closing decades of the century, may have made it more difficult to continue emphasizing the misery and pain of this world. In commenting on changes that occurred in Brittany during the twentieth century, Yves Lambert puts the question bluntly: "The increase in the means of realizing earthly happiness, has it replaced all concern with an extra-mundane salvation?"[62] Lambert's question oversimplifies the problem of declining concern about the afterlife. Even in contemporary Britanny, for example, an improved standard of living in this world has not eliminated a concern for the next.[63] Nonetheless, the comforts brought by economic development and modern technology that were already evident a century ago both changed the context of pastoral care in fundamental ways and contributed to the erosion of a pastoral strategy based on the misery in this world and anxiety about the next. As one of Lambert's informants put it in commenting on contemporary preaching: "They've had to mix some water in with their wine, for otherwise they'd have no one."

One social change, however, may have had an even more direct impact on the attitudes of the laity and on their unwillingness to accept the old preaching. The image conveyed by orthodox teaching in the early nineteenth century shows us a sinner alone before God, thus continuing the emphasis on individual salvation that was characteristic of the ancien régime. The family does appear in some sermons from Anjou but generally at the deathbed, where they are part of the worldly life that the agonisant must leave behind with regret. In the only Angevin sermon exclusively on Heaven Abbé Thoré establishes the sight of God as the principal source of happiness, and the family is mentioned only to create an analogy for heavenly bliss:

> What pleasure, my brothers, for a tender father coming back from a long trip, who sees his dear children run to him, throw themselves on his neck, and kiss him with fervor! What joy to see again his dear and virtuous wife! A weak representation, however, of the pleasure that a faithful soul experiences in the sight of his God. . . . Yes, I have you, my soul's love; nothing can deprive me any longer of your presence, O my only Love![64]

In this curious passage Thoré calls on the deep affections that tie together parents and children, husbands and wives, only to suggest their insignificance when seen from a heavenly perspective. Hymns on the "happiness of heaven" confirm this impression of a theocentric paradise in which other social ties lose their significance.[65] Bossuet had encouraged people not to grieve for the dead but to "strive to render ourselves worthy to rejoin them," and the eighteenth-century theologian Abbé Nicolas-Sylvestre Bergier argued that individual affections endured beyond the grave. But these ideas were not central themes in Catholic teaching before the middle of the nineteenth century.[66] A growing intensity of family feeling, however, was evident throughout Europe in the eighteenth century and contributed to the formulation of a more anthropocentric Heaven, as displayed in the visions of Emmanuel Swedenborg and the illustrations of William Blake.[67] The popular prints that described the "Ages of Life" reflect this change as well, because by the end of the century the last judgment, which had formerly occupied the center of their spatial field, was giving way to Paradise.[68] By the 1860s the French Jesuit François-René Blot was able to console readers with a work entitled *In Heaven We Know Our Own*, which by 1902 had gone through thirty-eight editions.[69] In 1901 a long sermon in *L'Ami du clergé paroissial* concluded by affirming that

> our friendships in the here-below have only been sketches, we will complete them in the next world in light and love. Children, we will see with respect and pride the extension of our ancestors back to the beginning; fathers, we will know all those that we have known during life. We will possess all our friends, we will love them. We will enjoy their society without fear, without reserve, since we will be certain to have them forever. . . .[70]

This affirmation of universal salvation may not have been theologically orthodox, but by the end of the century the clergy were willing

5. *Another Angel in Heaven*. Holy card distributed by Bouasse-Lebel, mid-nineteenth century (Photo: Bibliothèque Nationale)

to make such concessions to family sensibilities. One sermon from earlier in the century, preached in Bourg in 1840, also describes a family reunion, but it takes place in Hell, where a son calls out

> barbarous father. . . . it is you who has driven me to these flames by your examples; I saw you live without frequenting the sacred tribunals of penitence, without seating yourself at the holy table. . . . Barbarous father, look at your son in the middle of these flames. Worthless mother, says this condemned daughter, it is you who has thrown me into this abyss. . . . Well, cruel one, do you recognize your daughter devoured by the fires of eternity?[71]

In this vision of Hell, parental suffering is magnified by having to observe the agony of their children. In the course of the nineteenth century such images became too painful to contemplate, and dead children were instead described as angels whose prayers in Heaven would redeem their entire family (see illus. 5). In responding to the new sensibility the clergy embraced an ideal of the solidarity of families whose love would endure in eternal and heavenly bliss.

DEATHBEDS, FUNERALS, AND THE CHURCH

In the image of the good death as described in Catholic preaching, the priest was a reassuring presence whose prayers and exhortations consoled the dying person about his fate in the next world. Although they resisted some of the harsher aspects of Catholic teaching, most of the French accepted this description of a good death and were persuaded of the value of the Last Sacraments and a religious funeral. Religious practice varied widely from region to region, and in a number of areas regular attendance at Sunday mass and the reception of Easter communion declined dramatically during the century. But even in areas such as the Beauce in the diocese of Orléans, where only 14 percent of the population made their Easter duty in 1868, 76 percent received the Last Sacraments.[72] In working-class neighborhoods in Paris and Lyon there was an exceptionally high level of alienation from orthodox Catholicism, but even in these areas the numbers of people willing to accept a civil burial rarely rose above one-third of the population.[73]

The fear of a sudden death, as described in popular literature, offers another indication of the continued attachment to Church ritual. The pamphlet *The Doctor of the Poor* (*Le Médecin des pauvres*) published at Rouen in 1851 consists mostly of prayers designed to heal the sick of specific afflictions, but it also includes a prayer to the Virgin Mary introduced with the comment that whoever carries it with devotion will be assured of confessing any mortal sin before his or her death.[74] The fear of dying suddenly and without the assistance of the clergy shows up as well in official correspondence in which villagers pleaded for the continued presence of a priest as the only way to assure the administration of the spiritual assistance (*secours spirituel*) required for the dying, the Last Sacraments of the Church. In 1809 the municipal council of Béhuard, an island in the Loire, wrote to the prefect that the frequent flooding of the river isolated it for much of the year and that assigning it to another parish and removing the priest in residence (*desservant*) would mean he would no longer be able to "minister to the sick in their last hour."[75] Such a concern was not restricted to the pious countryside: the parishioners of St. Léonard, in Angers, asked to retain their priest because "there are frequent accidents in the stone quarries that result in death or serious injuries to the workers; it is then that these unfortunate men have special need of the spiritual aid of our religion and of the assistance of a priest who resides there."[76] Death, along with baptism, first communion, and marriage, was one of the *rites de passage* that most people still expected the Church to administer, a situation that remains true in the late twentieth century.

The attachment of the majority to Catholic funerary ritual was not, however, an unproblematic issue for either clergy or the laity. For the clergy, their assistance at the deathbeds and funerals of people who had spent most of their lives outside of the Church created pastoral problems that could be painful and divisive. For the laity the trauma of death might be eased by the consoling presence of the priest, but they were sensitive about the power implicit in this role and objected strenuously when they believed it was abused. The resentment of spiritual blackmail, which some clergy were believed to practice, contributed to the disaffection of a minority who advocated a dechristianized death ritual. By the end of the century increasing numbers of the French chose to die without the assistance of the Catholic clergy, and the Church was understandably concerned about such evidence of decline.[77] But from the point of view of the dissidents, ecclesiastical control over this crucial rite of passage remained a problem that had to be addressed with both aggressive propaganda and legislative intervention.

From literature directed at the clergy we can form a precise idea of how the Church defined the obligations of priests in the face of death. Disputes concerning the performance of these rituals were eventually responsible for diminished Catholic control over death. But the religious and political significance of these conflicts can be understood only if we see them against the background of the standard ritual practices. The clergy's responsibilities began at the bedside of the sick, because visiting them was, according to the diocesan manual from Angers, "one of the most essential parts of their solicitude, since the faithful never have a greater need of their ministry."[78] In the case of grave illnesses, priests were to encourage the sick to receive the Last Sacraments, which consisted of the confession of their sins, the reception of the viaticum (a form of communion for the sick and dying), and extreme unction. It was assumed by the clergy that they might meet with some resistance, for the sick and their families generally believed that receiving the Last Sacraments was an irrevocable sign of death.[79] In making their pleas the clergy were to remind the sick of the dangers of waiting too long, because the viaticum could not be administered to someone who was unconscious or wracked by coughing fits or nausea. Extreme unction could be and frequently was administered to people after they had lost consciousness, but the power of the sacrament to cleanse the soul and free the dying person from some of the punishment that would follow judgment depended on the level of contrition, and thus on the level of consciousness. Waiting too long could add to one's time in Purgatory, or so the clergy claimed.[80]

The gravity with which families viewed the reception of the Last Sacraments suggests that calling the priest represented their acknowledgement that death was likely, and perhaps inevitable.[81] The entry of the priest into the home and the administering of the sacraments provided a ritual setting that prepared both the dying person and the family for the death that was now viewed as imminent. One of the goals of the Counter-Reformation that had been effectively realized by the nineteenth century was an enhanced consciousness of the special status of the priest, whose life revolved around the rectory and the church.[82] For most people the presence of the priest in their home would be regarded as an exceptional event. Catholic ritual was generally concentrated at the church, where Baptisms, First Communions, and Marriages all took place, as well as the Sunday masses and the exceptional services held on feast days or civic holidays. The Last Sacraments represented a rare incursion of the sacred into domestic space, and the entry of a priest, robed, bearing the eucharist and sacred oils, and uttering Latin prayers can be assumed to have created a ritual atmosphere in the home that was unique.

The administration of the sacraments was controlled by carefully constructed regulations, and although punctilious clergymen raised questions about their details, in most cases it seems likely that the rituals followed the pattern established in manuals. After robing himself with a surplice and a purple stole at the church, the priest carried the holy oils and the eucharist to the home of the sick person. In villages this act might be accompanied by the ringing of the bells to warn the parishioners and call on their prayers. The *Rituel* of 1828 for Angers called for all those pious Christians who were available and for members of the Confraternity of the Holy Sacrament, if it existed, to accompany the priest. During the cholera epidemic of 1832 one observer in Angers heard a small bell sound and saw from his window the curé of the parish of Notre Dame carrying the viaticum followed by a hundred people.[83] Homais, the anticlerical pharmacist in Flaubert's *Madame Bovary*, "compared priests to ravens attracted by the odor of death," but he felt obligated to accompany the curé to Emma Bovary's deathbed, which Flaubert describes as following the pattern presented in the clerical manuals.[84] This public dimension of the Last Sacraments, typical of the ancien régime, grew less common in the nineteenth century, especially in Paris. By the end of the century clerical literature made few references to those accompanying the priest, suggesting that the standard of family privacy during the administering of the Last Sacraments was now general.[85]

At the house of the dying person a table was to be prepared, covered with a white cloth and furnished with a candle, holy water, several pieces of cloth for the anointing, and some white bread or clean cloth with which the priest could dry his hands. After sprinkling holy water on all those in attendance, the priest would offer the sick person a crucifix to hold and ask if he or she had anything to confess. Absolution would be followed by a brief exhortation and the reception of the viaticum, then by the administering of extreme unction.[86] This sacrament began with an exhortation in which the dying person was called on to have hope and confidence in God's mercy as he looked forward to eternal life. There then followed several prayers in Latin, including the Confiteor, the granting of a plenary indulgence, and then the actual anointing, during which the priest made the sign of the cross with the holy oil on the eyes, ears, nostrils, hands, and feet. Then came the Kyrie Eleison, the familiar prayer for mercy said at every mass, and a final brief exhortation in French (see illus. 6). All these gestures and prayers carried great significance, for as Philippe Boutry has claimed, "Extreme unction . . . was the ultimate path to salvation. . . . It knitted together the community of the living and the dead in the hope for salvation and the belief in eternal life."[87]

Directions for clerical behavior at the funeral were equally explicit. The priest was charged with the *lévée du corps*, the procession of the body from the home to the church, led by the cross, the altar boys, and the clergy, and followed by the coffin, the family, and friends. In

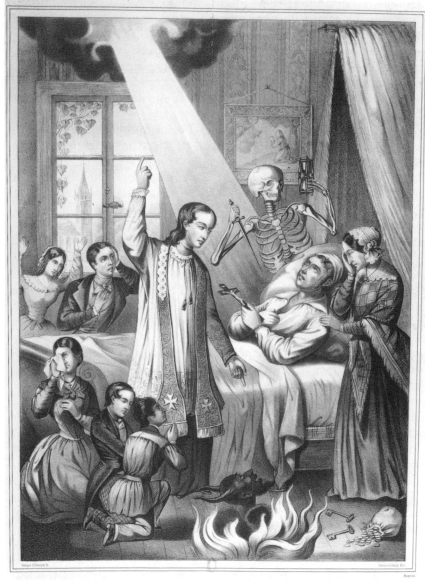

6. *The Dying Man Prepares to Meet God*. In this image produced at Metz in the early nineteenth century, the family surrounds the dying man, but the priest is given a central role. While Death prepares to strike his blow, the devil peers up from below. The grief of the family contrasts with the calmness of the priest, who points toward Heaven, while the man looks up in confidence (Photo: Bibliothèque Nationale).

cities the practice of receiving the body at the church door became increasingly common, but in the countryside priests were still arguing about the right to the fees charged for the lévée late in the century.[88] At the church a mass was recommended, a service that would be more or less solemn depending on the luxury of the decorations and the numbers of candles and clergy. The elaboration of a complex scale of services based on the family's ability and willingness to pay accompanied the development of the funeral industry, and will be given more consideration later in this chapter and in my treatment of pompes funèbres. The purchasing of religious honors was a source of resentment among some laity, but despite such feelings the clergy remained central figures in rituals that separated the living from the dead. Following the mass the procession re-formed, and the priest led the body to the cemetery, where he said a final prayer, sprinkled the coffin with holy water one last time, and threw the ritual handful of dirt into the grave.[89]

This bald summary does not convey, of course, anything of the actual impact of the services, which would vary depending on the setting, which could be a cathedral or a village church, on the character of the dead, his or her wealth and religious commitment, on the choices made by the family, and on the quality of the clerical performance. On the one hand, letters from priests published in L'Ami du clergé suggest an attentiveness to the details of the ritual; on the other hand, we know from literary sources that some assistants at funerals behaved with indifference, noticing one another and talking of mundane matters.[90] We have little direct evidence, however, about the reactions of the family and friends, although we will see that many fought bitterly any attempt to refuse their dead the normal religious honors. The impact of funeral services could be especially pronounced in the midst of a crisis, such as the cholera epidemic of 1832. The tutor, a M. Adville, complained to the mayor of Angers in that year that the clergy were using funeral processions and the administration of the Last Sacraments to create fear, and he proposed that the city move to prohibit them: "For burials, can't you restrict the singing to the interior of the church, and during the epidemic stop all the chanting in the streets and at the doors of the dead? What deadly effects these lugubrious songs have when they reach the ears of a sick person already anxious about his fate."[91]

Adville's desire to limit the public ceremonial surrounding death anticipates the attitudes that Ariès has argued are characteristic of the twentieth century. Adville's letter also presents a vivid picture of the clergy leading crowds of mourners to cemeteries in rituals that used songs, candles, and the sounding of the church bells. It is difficult to avoid the conclusion that the prayers, hymns, and general atmosphere of the funeral service had a deep impact on the participants. The *Miserere*, the *De profundis*, and the *Deis irae* are expressions of grief and anxiety that must have frequently touched responsive chords, especially when sung. These feelings, however, were balanced by the hopeful message of salvation that the priest had brought to the deathbed, which was the central theme of the chant that accompanied the body as it left the church: "May the angels take thee into paradise; may the martyrs come to welcome thee on the way, and lead thee into the holy city, Jerusalem. May the choir of angels welcome thee, and with Lazarus who once was poor may thou have everlasting rest."[92]

These words suggest that Catholic ritual provided reassurance to families about the fate of their dead in an afterlife, a message that may have been all the more crucial given the threats that we have seen the clergy wield in other contexts. When a dying person showed both resignation and hope on the deathbed, and when the funeral was conducted with pomp and solemnity, the impact of this ritualized death on both family and community could be enormous. This effect is evident in the case of Elisa Latapie, a teenage girl whose edifying death captured the attention of the town of Lourdes in 1858. According to Curé Peyramale, Mlle Latapie prepared for her death for a period of three months; just before her death she made her father promise to fulfill his religious obligations each year, had herself dressed in the white robes of the Daughters of Mary (an elite club of pious girls of which she was president), announced "I belong to Jesus," and then died. As the daughter of the director of the local post office, Mlle Latapie was able to leave 1,500 francs to finish work on the prison chapel. Peyramale reported to his bishop that the whole town had assisted at her funeral, and that in the eyes of everyone, she was a saint. In the fervent mood that followed Elisa's death another girl, Bernadette Soubirous, began having visions of a young woman in a grotto just outside of town, and many people initially believed that she was seeing Elisa Latapie, who had come back to ask for prayers, or perhaps to console her family with the news that she had been saved. The apparitions at Lourdes, which established the most important popular shrine in the Christian world, owe a great deal to the atmosphere created by the Catholic rituals of death.[93]

The death and funeral of Elisa Latapie provide a textbook illustration of the good death as described by clerical manuals, but it would be naive to restrict ourselves to such evidence in interpreting Catholicism's role as mediator between life and death. Few deaths were as edifying as Latapie's; in fact, most were uncontroversial affairs.

Nonetheless, throughout the century there were many deaths that provoked controversy which drew in clergy, families, villages, local and national government, and political organizations. Some of these attracted so much national attention that government ministries were concerned about the threats that they posed to the public order. Through these conflicts we can begin to see more clearly the complex feelings that people had when faced with the priest who was the crucial intermediary between the world of the living and the dead.

In sermons the clergy drew a sharp contrast between the good and the bad death. By the eighteenth century, however, this distinction was no longer based on a deathbed conversion from a life of sin; preachers and theologians insisted that only in exceptional cases could a person who had lived a disreputable life be saved.[94] Jean-Jacques Dutertre, in preaching "On the Death of Sinners" in 1841 carried this point to an extreme in his distinction between a "beautiful" and a "good" death. According to Dutertre, even someone who had apparently repented of his past life, received the sacraments, kissed the crucifix, returned property that he had acquired unjustly, and left an endowment for the poor could not be assured of salvation. Dutertre acknowledged that he would not challenge those who praised such a "beautiful" death out of a desire to console them. Were he to admit to the family that he "trembled over the salvation" of someone who died in such circumstances, he would "change their days of feasting into days of mourning, their songs of joy into cries of lamentation." Despite this pastoral timidity Dutertre claimed that "death is the faithful echo of life"—a phrase popular with all the preachers. In his conclusion he stopped short of placing deathbed converts clearly in Hell but insisted that only those whose entire lives were just could face death without fear. Dutertre's criticism of a "beautiful" death was designed to counter what he believed to be excessive reliance on deathbed conversion, a reliance that he himself tolerated and even encouraged through his desire to console the aggrieved. To judge by this sermon, the clergy at times experienced ambivalent feelings about the administering of the Last Sacraments—feelings that had to be repressed out of respect for the family and friends, and perhaps also because to admit them would be to deny the sacramental efficacy that was the basis for clerical authority.

According to his own testimony Dutertre's criticism of a "beautiful" death did not reflect his behavior at the deathbed; his sermon seems even more ironic when we place it in the context of militant Catholic pride about the return of the sinner on his deathbed or the scaffold. John McManners has shown how the Church sought to take advantage of the conversion of skeptics and libertines in the eighteenth century as a sign of the truth of its doctrines and the power of its rituals.[95] Following the attacks of the revolution and in the face of the anticlericalism that grew throughout the nineteenth century, the clergy continued to publicize whenever possible how their enemies were forced in the end to acknowledge defeat, confess their sins, and die within the Church. Deathbed conversions were family drama, but they were also fuel for the political/ideological quarrels of the Church.

During the 1820s and the 1830s the Church took special interest in reporting deathbed conversions of priests who had abjured their ministry during the revolution. The nephew of Jean-Claude Benaben, an Oratorian priest who became a Jacobin during the revolution, has left a particularly detailed account of the return of his uncle to the Church just before his death. Following an active political career during the revolution, Benaben became a professor of mathematics at the lycée of Angers. After falling ill in 1835, at the age of eighty-nine, Benaben turned not only violent in his attacks against Christianity but also bitter toward his family. To a niece he complained, "I'm dying, and you give me no word of consolation. . . . you're going to let me die without saying anything to me." Finally, his sister called for a priest, and when the family visited him the following day they found him transformed. Benaben had managed to leave his bed for his office, where he sat in his armchair properly dressed. Upon seeing his family he arose and approached them with a smile saying "My nieces, I am very happy, I've confessed my sins, the priest is going to come back and give me absolution by the powers he has received from the holy church, our mother."[96] This account was no doubt embellished by the family in the retelling, and we can imagine the pious satisfaction as the return of the renegade uncle was recounted at family occasions long after his death. The fact that such scenes became part of family traditions should not lead us to lose sight completely of the situation in which Benaben found himself in 1835. Born in 1744, ordained in 1774, he was already in his forties at the time of the revolution. Looking back on his life in 1835, and forward to death, surrounded by a pious but discrete family, Benaben decided to die with the help of a priest. Perhaps he did so in part to please his family, but it does not seem to be stretching the facts too far to say that he may also have done so to save his soul.

Benaben's story is not at all exceptional; L'Ami de la religion includes similar accounts during the years of the Restoration and the July Monarchy. Abbé Dupanloup's administration of the Last Sacraments to the dying Talleyrand is a more prominent example of the pattern, and one that gave the young priest a boost in his career.[97] Clergymen were not the only ones whom the Church sought to save on their deathbeds. The devotion of Our Lady of Victory, which became one of the most numerous and significant cults in the nineteenth century, was founded by the Parisian curé Desgenettes in 1836 as a means of converting sinners; Desgenettes and the original members of the confraternity he founded became convinced of the divine origins of their work when Etienne Joly, an eighty-year-old minister from the last government of Louis XVI, was converted on his deathbed following their prayers.[98] The enormous *Dictionnaire des conversions* published as part of Jacques-Paul Migne's *Nouvelle Encyclopédie théologique* in 1852 reported similar tales, with special attention paid to the conversions of Protestants and materialists. As with Abbé Benaben many of these stories focused on the family context, which the editor C. F. Chevé used to illustrate the adage "The faithless husband is sanctified by the faithful wife."[99] The availability of such tales was useful for a Church affected by memories of the revolution and what was felt to be a mounting tide of disbelief. Stories of deathbed conversions were thus a useful vehicle through which the clergy could demonstrate their ultimate triumph. The exploitation of these stories, however, and the pressure that the clergy placed on the dying, did not work exclusively to their advantage. The account of Benaben's happy reconciliation and the similar tales in Chevé's collection need to be balanced by recalling some of the tenser scenes in which the clerical presence at the deathbed seemed more intrusive than consoling.

The gradual exclusion of all but family members from the death chamber that began in the eighteenth century was accompanied by the construction of an ideal death characterized by affectionate farewells to loved ones, an image captured and reinforced by the death of Julie in Rousseau's much-read *The New Héloise* (*La nouvelle Héloïse*). The Protestant Julie sees a minister, but she is not at all preoccupied with her salvation. She proposes that the time remaining to her would be better spent devoted to her family than to God: "I have to concern myself with them; soon I'll be concerned only with Him."[100] Catholics might still feel the need for the Last Sacraments, and Romantic literature such as Chateaubriand's *Atala*, Lamartine's *Jocelyn*, and Balzac's *The Country Parson* provided them with touching death scenes in which family sentiment was not compromised by the presence of a Catholic priest. Nonetheless, the tightening of family control over the deathbed could lead to tension and on several important occasions to outright disputes.

Death within the bosom of the family was a middle-class ideal. For the urban poor, though, it was still common to die alone in the hospital, which remained a charitable as well as a medical institution throughout the nineteenth century. The role of the clergy and of the growing numbers of nursing sisters was contested in hospitals, where doctors increasingly asserted their rights over the sick and dying.[101] At the Hospital of St. John in Angers, where over one-quarter of the deaths in the city took place for most of the nineteenth century, the medical staff objected in 1848 to the procession of the Eucharist that was traditionally held on the Fête-Dieu, the Feast of the Blessed Sacrament. The noisy preparations, the flowers and incense in the rooms, the disruption of the hospital schedule, all this it was felt compromised the health of the patients. The administration of the department sided with the doctors, and despite the objection of the bishop the procession was limited to the corridors.[102] The conflict between religion and medicine in Angers was relatively mild, however, compared to the dispute that arose in 1878 in Paris, when an anticlerical municipal council began the process of secularizing hospitals. The nuns who staffed hospitals were accused both of pressuring the unbelieving sick into seeing a priest and of general ignorance about modern medical techniques; Catholics responded that militant anticlericals were depriving the dying of the religious consolation that they sought in the face of death. The Paris city council dealt with the controversy by replacing sisters with secular nurses, removing religious symbols, most notably the crucifix, and protecting the sick from active proselytization.[103]

Although the clergy actively opposed the secularization of Paris hospitals, they nevertheless acknowledged the increasing power of the medical profession over sickness and death that was manifest in the second half of the century. In *Moral Theology and the Medical Sciences*, the standard work on the relationship between moral theology and medicine, Père Pierre Debreyne, who was a medical doctor as well as a Trappist priest, assumed that a doctor as well as a priest would be assisting the dying. The later editions of this work, which was intended for the clergy, were amended by Dr. Pierre Ferrand, who acknowledged that although canon law required the doctor to inform the sick that they were in danger of death, this was no longer practical "in the current state of our society and manners."[104] Doctors concerned themselves with the physical health of their patients, and within this domain they were judged to have absolute authority: "The doctor is most often the best judge of what course to take in the presence of a dying person."[105] In Ferrand's view the doctor assumes a quasi-ministerial role in his relations with the family, for whom "the presence of a devoted man who, at once calm and sympathetic, will be able to impose by his authority and prestige respect for the last glimmers of existence."[106] The professionalization of medicine that occurred in the nineteenth century created a corps of specialists to whom the family could turn for physical and moral relief when one of their members was threatened with death. Antimedical sentiment remained, but the growing prestige of doctors may have made it easier for some families to resist the claims of the clergy to preside at the deathbed.

Families were uneasy about the clergy in part because they feared that they might use their spiritual leverage over the dying to extract promises of financial gifts. The importance of such legacies in the seventeenth and eighteenth centuries, when wills frequently included generous bequests to the Church, has been studied by Michel Vovelle, Pierre Chaunu, and others.[107] Philippe Ariès has associated the decline in such bequests with the rise in family feeling, as a result of which the dying left it to the discretion of their heirs to do what was necessary to ensure their salvation. This may be true, but motives of self-interest also worked against such gifts, as is indicated in the Civil Code, which protected heirs by explicitly prohibiting a confessor from inheriting from a penitent.[108] In the nineteenth century bequests to the Church could be made only with State approval, and after the July Revolution a royal decree of 14 January 1831 required that inheritors be informed of any such grants so that they might exercise their right to appeal the will.[109]

Legislation restricting the rights of the Church was the result of family concern about a venal clergy exploiting the fears of the dying, a point confirmed by numerous complaints about priestly behavior. The parishioners of Douce in Maine-et-Loire, for example, wrote to the prefect that their abbé Martin had been heard to say at the deathbed of a woman parishioner "Give, give, you owe nothing to your children."[110] In 1844 Le National reported that a M. Deligmère, from a village in Oise, complained after a half-hour visit of the local curé: "My God, how that man has tormented me; I have children, after all, and I'm not a millionaire."[111] In Le Mans during the late 1840s the Benedictines (led by the famous liturgical reformer Prosper Guéranger) were criticized for fighting a court battle to gain a legacy from a Louise-Henriette.[112] Georges Bordillon, member of the general council of Maine-et-Loire and prefect of the department during the Second Republic, complained frequently of clerical spoliation and asserted that priests used their powers over the elderly and the sick to recover lands seized from the Church during the revolution.[113] Toward the end of the century concern about the amount of money being transferred to the Church continued to be a topic of concern and contributed to the anticlerical legislation passed during the Third Republic.[114]

Suspicions and accusations of venal motives created tension at the deathbed, but conflicts over the priestly role also arose from complicated issues involving belief and belonging. These disputes recall controversies that arose at the deathbeds of Jansenists in the eighteenth century, which Dale Van Kley has interpreted as prominent events in both the religious and political history of the ancien régime.[115] In the nineteenth century as well deathbeds provided a dramatic setting in which the Church used its claims to control salvation as a way to bend the will of the dying. At this point, however, the struggle was not between Jansenist and Catholic but between anticlerical skeptic and the Church.

Early in the century the clergy were frequently accused of denying the Last Sacraments to people on their deathbeds. In doing so, the priest was not only excluding the dying from the parish community but also positioning himself to refuse religious services at the church and burial in consecrated ground; we will see that at each of these stages those refused the rituals reacted with anger and sometimes with violence. By the end of the century popular discontent with clerically controlled ritual led to greater independence from the Church, and instead of denying access to the sacraments the clergy found themselves prevented from reaching the dying. Throughout the century, however, the presence or absence of the priest at the deathbed could be a delicate and troublesome matter for those with an ambiguous relationship to the Church.

The pattern for the first half of the century is typified in the case of a M. Parent, a revolutionary official who had retired to the village of Barace in Maine-et-Loire. When Parent died in 1820 the curé claimed that he had refused the Last Sacraments. The family, on the other hand, argued that it was the priest who had refused to come, telling Parent's servant that "your master won't pray for me, and I'm not going to pray for him."[116] Such disputes were common in the first half of the nineteenth century, and in one case a national scandal erupted over a clerical refusal. In December 1838 the bishop of Clermont-Ferrand demanded that the dying Comte de Montlosier sign a retraction of ideas he had published that were contrary to Church teachings. Montlosier had been one of the leading opponents of Vatican intervention and Jesuit influence in the French Church during the 1820s and 1830s. A priest heard Montlosier's confession, but his refusal to sign a retraction led the bishop to deny him the viaticum, extreme unction, and a church service after his death. Montlosier's body was brought directly from his house to a country property where he was buried. These events provoked a debate in the local and national press, as liberals and anticlericals attacked the intolerance of the bishop. The issue was debated in the Chamber of Peers, where Victor Cousin criticized the Church's refusal. The minister of religion sided with the liberals and supported the complaint brought by the family before the Conseil d'Etat, which condemned the bishop's action in January 1839.[117]

Even if Montlosier had agreed to retract his writings, controversy would have resulted from the pressure exerted on him to repudiate his life's work. From the Church's point of view, of course, such an abjuration was a price worth paying because it would lead to eternal salvation. But critics resented such pressure as a violation of the rights of the individual conscience and the spirit of family harmony. For them what was at stake was personal and family integrity, not salvation. Jules Michelet has left us an illustration of this sentiment in his private journal, where he described his despair over the alienation of his companion, Mme Dumesnil, who on her deathbed began to confide increasingly in the fashionable preacher Abbé Coeur rather than in him. "In such crises the soul becomes distant from those who love it without effectively helping it. She seeks life from strangers, from foreigners. That, for me, is an unexpected form of death, to feel her confidence and affection dying. It is as if I myself were dying."[118] Michelet's experience with the clergy found public expression a few years later when he wrote *Du prêtre, de la femme, de la famille* (*About Priests, Women, and the Family*), perhaps the most influential anticlerical tract of the nineteenth century.[119] Clerical intrusion into death could be challenged as a violation of family solidarity, a supremely important value that the anticlericals used as part of their campaign against the Church.

In the second half of the nineteenth century death outside of the sacramental system continued to provoke extensive public discussion, but during this period skeptics were increasingly able to plan their deaths so as to protect themselves from clerical efforts to convert them. By the late 1860s societies of freethinkers and masonic organizations were available to support those anticlericals who wished to exclude the clergy from their deathbeds.[120] M. Douaire, a property owner from Broc, exemplified this spirit of independence when in 1870 he raised the following sign over his mantelpiece.

> I, the undersigned, Douaire, property-owner of Broc, forbid any Catholic priest from entering my house when I am sick, even if I ask for one, because such a request could only be a result of delirium.[121]

Douaire's attempt to guarantee a deathbed free from clerical interference is echoed in elaborate detail by Jean Barois, the protagonist in Roger Martin du Gard's novel *Jean Barois*. As a young, militant freethinker, Barois was appalled to find himself uttering a "Hail Mary" as he faced death in a cab accident. While recovering he wrote a will in which he asserted his commitment to materialism and insisted on the meaninglessness of any future conversion. Barois clearly expressed the sentiments of anticlericals concerned about their deathbed behavior:

> I know nothing more harrowing than to see an old man, whose whole life has been devoted to the furtherance of some noble idea, go back in his declining years on the principles that inspired his life's work and play traitor to his past. When I reflect that conceivably this may be my fate, and my life's work end with a betrayal of this nature, and when I picture the use to which those whose lies and malpractices I have combated with so much ardor will not fail to put this final, miserable lapse of mine, my whole being is up in arms, and I protest in advance, with all the energy of the man I now am, the *living* man I shall have been, against the groundless repudiations—even, perhaps the prayers *in extremis!*—of the dotard that I may then have become.[122]

Despite these efforts, Barois did convert near the end of his life, and his wife and her priestly adviser burned his will so as to ensure him a Catholic burial. The case of the positivist Emile Littré, pressured by his family to convert on his deathbed, suggests that such last-minute returns to the faith occurred in the real as well as the fictional world. But anticlericals were also able to applaud those such as Victor Hugo and his family, who turned aside the archbishop of Paris Cardinal Joseph Guibert, who had offered to see the poet on his deathbed.[123] Hugo's death and burial were part of the anticlerical movement that resulted in increasing numbers of civil burials in the late nineteenth century, a trend that I will explore later in this chapter when examining the clerical role at funerals.[124] But if we stay at the bedsides of the dying we will see that conflicts continued to occur there well into the twentieth century, as is clear in the 1951 controversy over the meaning of André Gide's dying words: "The struggle between reason and unreason continues." Some Catholics argued that this statement had metaphysical significance and claimed Gide as a convert, an interpretation vigorously opposed by Roger Martin du Gard. As François Mauriac noted in reacting to this affair, "The same war of religion has been pursued from one deathbed to another."[125] In the case of Gide, however, there was no question of seeing a priest or receiving the sacraments; in the mid-twentieth century Catholics were still eager to draw in prominent unbelievers at their last moments, but the kind of direct pressure exerted in the nineteenth century was no longer common. In the nineteenth century, however, Littré and Barois did convert, exemplifying the pressure that even militants from that period felt to conform to the traditional deathbed rituals of Catholicism.

Deathbeds could become tense theaters where Catholics and anti-clericals faced each other while demanding a final act of commitment from the dying. Such conflicts could become even more hostile when they involved the right to a Catholic funeral following death. After all, conflicts at the deathbed were not intrinsically public events, though they could become so when Catholics and anticlericals chose to use them for ideological ammunition. Funerals, however, were clearly in the public eye. The procession to the church, the sounding of the bells (the *glas*) which announced the death to the parish and called on those who heard to pray for the soul of the departed, and the service at the church and at the cemetery—all these rituals offered an important source of consolation to the survivors. To refuse these honors was to suggest that prayers in this case were useless and that the soul had been judged and presumably condemned. Of course, the absence of ritual could also simultaneously be a source of shame for the surviving family members, forced to bury their dead without the bells, prayers, and processions that would mark their place in the community.

In the nineteenth century the role of the clergy in funerary ritual was complicated by an ambiguous division of responsibility toward the dead as defined by ecclesiastical regulations and the Napoleonic decree of 23 prairial, year XII (1804). Church law prohibited the clergy from providing religious services for certain categories of people, including heretics, duelists, actors and actresses, and other public sinners. Those who died in an apparent state of mortal sin, such as drunkards, or those who lived as man and wife without the benefit of marriage were also to be excluded.[126] The responsibility of the State toward the dead was detailed in article 19 of the law of 23 prairial, which specified that in cases where ministers refused a funeral service the mayor was to have the body "carried, presented, deposed, and buried."[127] This wording was to cause trouble throughout the century, because it gave the laity a powerful weapon in their attempt to secure religious services for the dead.

During the first half of the nineteenth century conflicts were generally the result of requests made by what we now call "lapsed" Catholics for a funeral service and burial in consecrated ground. A clerical refusal of a Catholic service also meant burial in unconsecrated ground, but until the Second Empire family resistance to such decisions concentrated on the church rather than the cemetery. Mayors charged with policing the cult of the dead and ensuring that funerals and burials were conducted with dignity sometimes used this authority to break into churches, lead a service, then proceed to burial in consecrated ground. The family of Michel Mignon, for example, objected when the abbé Briffaut of Varennes (Maine-et-Loire) refused to provide a Catholic service for him after he was found drowned in a gully following a night spent drinking with friends. The mayor broke into the locked church and led the village in prayers for the dead man, then proceeded to bury him in consecrated ground, against the explicit request of the abbé.[128]

The story of Michel Mignon was not exceptional; Maurice Agulhon has acknowledged the importance of such conflicts in the formation of political attitudes in the Var during the Restoration and July Monarchy.[129] Clerical refusals and civil burials threatened public order and led the ministers of the interior and of religion to distribute throughout the century a series of regulations designed to clarify civil and ecclesiastical responsibilities and prevent further trouble. In general the government urged bishops and prefects to encourage a tolerant attitude in the clergy with regard to religious services for the dead, but for most of the century they also discouraged municipal authorities from directly challenging clerical authority by forcing their way into churches when there had been a refusal.[130]

Some of the most dramatic instances of funeral conflict, such as Mignon's, suggest that communities had to fight for religious services against a clergy that jealously defended its canonical authority. But there is, for the first half of the century, evidence that qualifies this impression of an intolerant clergy willing to violate family feelings and communal solidarity. Although no firm statistics are available, in many cases suicides were given ecclesiastical burial. Even during the ancien régime, diocesan ritual allowed for the ecclesiastical burial of those who took their own lives due to madness, and very few deaths were officially judged to be suicides.[131] In the nineteenth century doctors were frequently willing to provide medical certificates testifying to the *aliénation mentale* of the deceased, which allowed the clergy to provide a religious service.[132] Furthermore, on some occasions it was the community rather than the curé that acted to prevent the burial of suicides in consecrated ground.[133] The importance of a community's attitude can be seen clearly in a long and detailed letter written in 1842 by the abbé Duret, curé of Champtoceaux, to the bishop of Angers, in which he reports on two recent deaths in his parish.[134] Abbé Duret began his letter late at night, just after having assisted at the death of a barrel maker who had lost consciousness after an afternoon drinking contest with a friend. The description of the man and the circumstances of his death show the curé to have been troubled and undecided about whether or not to provide an ecclesiastical service: "This man, formerly a Christian, and even a member of the choir, had a reputation for drunkenness and swearing for twelve years, and there are even some who talk of sodomy. For a long time I have seen him only rarely in the church." By the time Abbé Duret was called to administer the Last Sacraments, the barrel maker appeared to be already dead. The physician present, however, believed that a slight pulse remained, and the curé therefore administered absolution, but not extreme unction.

Abbé Duret was especially troubled because this latest death recalled another recent tragedy in his parish, which he also recounted to the bishop. A woman suffering from a form of leprosy, but who also attended mass each Sunday and made her Easter Duty, had recently committed suicide. When told of the death the curé had tried to talk the relatives into saying that the deceased had acted without the use of her reason. But they persisted in believing her sane, and the woman was thus denied an ecclesiastical service and burial in consecrated ground. There were no complaints about the curé's refusal; in this case the community had not only accepted but encouraged a decision to refuse a Catholic burial. As he concluded his letter Abbé Duret continued to hesitate about the case of the barrel maker, whose situation he compared to that of the suicide. The next morning, just before sending the letter, he added a note commenting on the public mood: "Opinion of this morning: a terrible misfortune, the judgment of God." In these circumstances, the curé was inclined not to provide a religious burial.

The curé of Champtoceaux's letter shows him to have been sensitive and concerned about the spiritual state of his parishioners, as well as anxious to grant them a Catholic burial if at all possible. The letter also reveals a clergyman highly conscious of public opinion, against which he measured his own judgment. Abbé Duret agonized over the decision to refuse someone burial, which created a conflict between his generous pastoral instincts and clerical regulations. But his decisions to deny services and a place in the cemetery were reinforced and, in one case, initiated by the community. Conflicts over refusal of burial sometimes reveal tension between priests and parishioners, and in such cases it is difficult not to cast the priest in the role of villain. But the evidence from Champtoceaux suggests another way of looking at the issue. Communities as well as the clergy habitually judged the dead and on some occasions acted to exclude those considered unworthy. Refusals of religious rites and of burial in consecrated ground were not just penalties used by the clergy to impose Catholicism on their parishes; they were also sanctions that communities could use to enforce standards that condemned suicide and drunkenness. From the point of view of the Church and of some communities, those who had abandoned their social responsibilties did not deserve a place in the cemetery amidst their families and neighbors.

Clerical refusals in the first half of the century forced families to bury their dead in a civil ceremony, and in both Paris and the provinces these *enterrements civils* could be occasions for subversive political statements directed at the Restoration and the July Monarchy. When the famous actor Talma died in 1826, for example, his civil burial was an important event that contributed to the growing self-consciousness and sense of power within the the liberal opposition.[135] But Talma's funeral breaks from the pattern of civil burials based on clerical refusals, because in this case it was the dying actor who insisted on a civil ceremony. Starting in the 1860s the active choice of civil burial became more common, as anticlericals and freethinkers began to define an appropriate ritual for death and burial outside of the sacramental system of the Catholic church. This wave of civil burials was supported by the same masonic and freethinking groups that sought to strengthen the will of the dying; by the 1870s networks of *solidaires* were sufficiently well organized to mount impressive funerals for their members both in major cities such as Paris and Lyon and in the smaller towns of the countryside.

The funeral of Gustave Bernard, a tanner from Gennes who died in 1874, illustrates the kinds of services that were available outside the Church in the last third of the century. For Besnard's funeral freemasons and tanners from throughout the area arrived on trains from Saumur, Angers, and Tours. The local curé struggled to limit the size of the demonstration by having the mayor schedule the funeral at an early hour, before the trains could reach Gennes. But the family would not be rushed, and most of Besnard's friends had arrived by the time his convoi left his house for the procession to the cemetery. The convoi was led by the masons from Saumur, all wearing small red flowers, *immortelles*, pinned to their coats. Some of those family members who opposed the civil ceremony followed the procession, but at a distance. At the graveside a speech referring to "the human personality, conscience, and the future life" was delivered, after which the mourners surrounded the grave, clasped hands, whispered a masonic password to one another, and placed their flowers on the coffin.[136]

By the end of the century more than 20 percent of those who died in Paris chose civil services, and these included some of the most impressive funerals of the 1880s, such as those of Léon Gambetta and Victor Hugo.[137] Two million people came to see Hugo's body lying in state in May 1885, and an enormous crowd viewed the procession to the Pantheon, where he was buried. The state funerals of Hugo and others can be interpreted as an attempt to sanction civil burial as a dignified alternative to Catholic ritual—and as a climactic event in a century-long conflict over funeral rites. Early in the century civil burials had sometimes been imposed on an unwilling population, and the resistance was manifested by families and village communities that resented attempts to deny someone the normal religious honors. During the second half of the century, however, and particularly in the Third Republic, demonstrations at civil burials were organized and attended by outsiders, with the local community observing rather than participating. In the course of the century civil burials had lost some of their shameful aspect, and support for those who were buried without the clergy had shifted from groups motivated by communal solidarity to those inspired by ideological fervor.[138]

Although the majority remained loyal to Catholic ritual, the clergy were understandably concerned and defensive about the success of the civil burial movement, and their behavior reflected this new attitude. Scandalous incidents were still being reported in the anticlerical press at the end of the century, but already in the 1880s the clergy were more likely to bury people who died in ambiguous circumstances in order to avoid presenting freethinkers with another occasion to demonstrate the intolerance of the Church.[139] The willingness of some Protestant ministers to step in and provide services in the face of priestly refusals may also have made the clergy more willing to give the dying and their families the benefit of the doubt.[140] The shift in clerical practice parallels the more moderate tone of preaching observed earlier, and in both cases priests seem to have become more concerned to extend the boundaries of the Church.

The gentler treatment of those who were willing to define themselves as Catholic accompanied a harsh rhetoric and exclusionary policy directed against the anticlericals, who were castigated as demonic and hateful. These men and women were now willing to do without the Last Sacraments and a Catholic funeral, but by using provisions of the law of 23 prairial concerning *pompes funèbres* and cemeteries, the clergy also attempted to deny them the access to rituals and public space that had come to be regarded as normal and decent for both Catholics and non-Catholics. This effort to exclude anticlericals led to a long period of anxious debate and the passage of three major reforms by the anticlerical republican regime. In 1881 cemeteries were declared religiously neutral, and the clergy lost the right to control the placement of graves in the burial ground. In 1887 safeguards were introduced to guarantee individuals the right to a civil burial; and in 1904 the Church monopoly on pompes funèbres was replaced by communal control of the funeral industry. Church-State conflict has long been recognized as a major issue in the politics of the early Third Republic, but attention has generally focused on the issues of education, divorce, and family policy. Without discounting the importance of these questions, Avner Ben-Amos has recently concluded that "the most important battles with the Church were fought at the time on the front of death ceremonial."[141] The laws on cemeteries and pompes funèbres will be considerd in later chapters, where we will see how central and local governments, private entrepeneurs, and families struggled to define a new relationship with the Church. For now I want to focus on the law that most directly involved redefining the role of the clergy at the deathbed and the funeral—the law concerning the liberty of funerals, which passed in 1887.

The initial proposal of Chevandier in 1880 followed a decade of bitter argument about government policy toward those who chose death and burial outside of the sacramental system. Two notorious cases had concentrated national attention on the issue.[142] In June 1873, just after the fall of Thiers and the coming to power of the conservative government of Moral Order, the newly appointed prefect Joseph Ducros issued decrees restricting civil burials in Lyon to early-morning hours, forcing mourners to follow a restricted route to the cemetery, limiting the procession to three hundred, and prohibiting speeches at the cemetery. Battles in the press followed, and government policy was questioned in the National Assembly by the radical republican Le Royer. The Assembly failed to uphold the complaint, however, as the moderate republicans sided with Catholics in supporting Ducros. Other cities adopted similar restrictions on civil burials, giving anticlericals an issue that became a chronic grievance.

The right to choose a civil burial was raised at the same time over the burial of the republican deputy Fortuné Brousse. Deputies had the right to a military escort at their funeral, but when the cavalry detachment assigned this task reached Brousse's house in June 1873 they withdrew (as did a delegation from the Assembly) when they realized that he was to receive a civil burial. In defending this action before the Assembly, the minister of war Général du Barail argued that civil ceremonies undermined belief in an afterlife, and that without the conviction of immortality he could not ask soldiers to sacrifice their lives. Three years later the same issue was debated again, when military honors were refused the musician Félicien David, a member of the Legion of Honor. According to the minister of interior Emile de Marcère, "the belief in the immortality of the soul and religious faith are the basis of the soldier's moral power."[143] The center-left government of Jules Dufaure was deeply embarrassed by the issue and tried to seize the initiative by proposing a law that would deny a military escort to all members of the Legion. Following a negative vote in the Chamber, the Dufaure government resigned, and as Avner Ben-Amos has remarked, "The first in a long series of ministerial crises in the Third Republic took place because of the religious policy of the government concerning matters of death."[144]

The behavior of the government during the 1870s set the stage for the debates and reforms of the 1880s. Republicans won quick passage in 1881 of their proposal to neutralize cemeteries, and the republican Chevandier's proposal of 1880 insisting on the rights of freethinkers to military honors was generally associated with the principles used to support this measure—it would defend liberty of conscience and equality before the law in the face of an authoritarian and intolerant Church. However, in debates in the Chamber and later in the Senate Chevandier's proposal on the liberty of funerals was criticized, and not just by militants such as Msgr Charles-Emile Freppel, the bishop of Angers, who led the Catholic opposition to the bill.[145] Chevandier's law not only guaranteed state honors to those who chose a civil burial, it also allowed mayors to see that a will requesting a civil burial would be carried out, even against the wishes of the family.

In the years that followed, the republicans had great difficulty gaining majority support for a law that would in certain circumstances take the decision about a funeral away from the family. In the report on the law submitted in 1882, for example, the commission charged with considering it raised the possibility of a young man writing a will asking for a civil burial and then becoming a father of a family and raising his children as Catholics. At his death he might have no intention of causing trouble for his wife and children and expect to be buried according to their wishes. In such a situation, however, the law would intervene. "No, the law will say; you made a declaration 30, 40, or 50 years ago, according to which you wanted to be buried without the ceremony of a cult; this declaration must be carried out, under pain of prison for the wife, and for the mayor of the commune." The commission upheld Chevandier's proposal that military honors be granted even in the case of a civil burial, but it called on the Chamber to reject any attempt to intervene in family decisions about the nature of the final service in order "to safeguard the natural and sacred rights of the family."[146] In the debates that followed Catholics and anticlericals engaged in heated exchanges in which they accused each other of trying to steal corpses, and both sides were able to cite cases to support their claims.[147] The problem was in fact a real one, and decisions about whether to bury someone with a Catholic or a civil service caused consternation in familes throughout the period.[148] The

difficulty of balancing individual and family rights delayed passage of
legislation until 1887, when a law on the liberty of funerals finally
cleared both the Chamber and the Senate. In its final version the law
gave justices of the peace rather than mayors the power to decide
whether or not a deathbed conversion to Catholicism had occurred—
a concession that acknowledged the danger of political bias in such
cases but that failed to satisfy Freppel and the other defenders of the
right of families to choose a Catholic service.[149]

The law of 1887 clarified the right of the individual to control his or
her own funeral, but the strained political and religious atmosphere
of the end of the century continued to manifest itself in arguments
over other aspects of death rituals. City councils, for example, in
some cases prohibited funeral processions, and following complaints
from the clergy their actions were generally upheld by the conseil
d'état.[150] Arguments over the monopoly rights of parish councils to
provide candles, decorations, and hearses for funerals lasted until
1904 and served to keep death on the political agenda throughout the
period. Compared to the situation that they faced during the Restoration, the clergy at the end of the century had reason to be concerned
that their ritual responsibilities in the face of death were being seriously eroded. And given the cultural signficance of such rituals, they
were also right to see this loss as a blow to their general authority. In
the debates of the 1870s, and again in the 1880s, civil burials were
interpreted by Catholics as public expressions of atheism and the denial of the doctrine of the immortal soul. As such they were seen
to undermine the basis for morality, for only a conviction that right
and wrong would ultimately be punished in an afterlife could guarantee moral standards. In the particular case of the army, the government of Moral Order claimed that only the assurance that their
sacrifice would be compensated in the next world could convince
soldiers to risk their lives. Debates over civil burials demonstrate how
deeply the Catholic image of the afterlife was implicit in the social
and moral order, and why republicans felt compelled to attack the
Church's control over death rituals. By challenging clerical control
over deathbeds and funerals the republicans hoped to create a cultural space in which people would act with independence and fearlessness, traits they believed were inhibited by the Catholic culture of
death. I will explore this effort to create alternatives to the Catholic
culture of death in the following chapters. But as important as these
alternatives were in creating choices that had not previously existed,
most men and women still found it impossible to die without the
Catholic rituals—a familiar setting that provided reassurance and
consolation as they faced a separation that might otherwise have
been unbearably fearful.

MASSES, INDULGENCES, AND SALVATION

The clerical presence at deathbeds and funerals established Catholic priests as crucial intermediaries who guided the living into the world of the dead. The Church's responsibility, however, did not cease with the final blessing in the cemetery, for the clergy had a continuing obligation to maintain contacts between the living and the dead. The curé of Ars provides a dramatic illustration of this role, because his saintliness and visionary gifts frequently led pilgrims to consult him about the fate of dead family members and friends.[151] Jean Vianney was not unique in his ability to see into the other world. Abbé Théodore Ratisbonne, the Jewish convert who became a prominent leader among the French clergy, told visitors of a vision he had had a few days after having administered the Last Sacraments to a young woman of Strasbourg: "I was in my room about noon, looking out on the garden. Suddenly I saw her within two steps of me, the same exactly as when living, but with a great brightness all around her. She made a motion to me of inexpressible sweetness and happiness, as if thanking me for a great service, and disappeared."[152] Ratisbonne told the woman's husband and friends of this vision, and we can imagine their happiness at hearing this news from the other world. This vision confirmed on the one hand the efficacy of the Last Sacraments, the "great service" that had won the apparition salvation. On the other hand, it also established the priest as possessing privileged information about the afterworld, which he could pass on to the living. The clergy did not monopolize the privilege of seeing the dead, however. Lay visionaries operating within folk traditions and mediums influenced by techniques fashionable in the United States and England also communicated with spirits. In the following chapter we will see how proponents of French spiritism in the 1850s and 1860s believed that their séances would provide the foundation for a new religion based on a revised understanding of the afterworld and its relationship with earthly existence. In folktales and Catholic devotional literature, however, ghostly apparitions frequently asked for masses to be said for their souls, thus confirming the importance of the clergy as intercessors and of the mass as a principle means of assisting the dead.

The practice of remembering the dead at mass is deeply rooted in the history of the Middle Ages, and we know that during the baroque period studied by Vovelle and Chaunu hundreds and even thousands of masses were requested in wills as a means of ensuring the salvation of the soul.[153] Criticism of the *casuel*, fees charged by the clergy for administering the sacraments and saying masses, was endemic in this earlier period, as is clear from one of La Fontaine's fables, "Le Curé et le Mort." This poem, in which a coffin being carried to a cemetery is dropped and kills the accompanying priest, was based on an actual incident that occurred in 1672. In re-creating the event, La Fontaine imagines the priest being killed in the midst of contemplating his earnings from the prayers, candles, and other charges—money he will use to buy wine for himself and petticoats for his niece and chambermaid.[154] The list of grievances (*cahier de doléance*) from Joussé, a village now in the department of Vienne, shows a similar resentment still prevalent in 1789; the authors of this document claimed that "right after the burial people often saw vicars pulling the father, the son, the widow or the widower by the corner of their clothes to ask them for their burial fees (*droit de sépulture*)."[155] The clergy were undoubtedly eager to collect their money, but the journal of Denis Boutroue, a curé in the Beauce, reveals another aspect of the issue; in the 1780s Boutroue kept careful accounts of all his income and possessions, including a detailed listing of all the masses requested of him. The journal tells us nothing directly about Boutroue's relationship with his parish, but the crosses that were entered after each request for a mass had been satisfied suggest that he was conscientious about fulfilling priestly obligations. Perhaps this explains why he was able to return to his parish of Ormeville after the revolution and remain there peacefully until his death in 1819.[156]

The decline in bequests for masses that can be traced to the late eighteenth century is a significant development in the history of religious practice, but it should not veil the fact that masses remained the most typical means through which the living helped the dead. The mass was, according to the clergy, "the most glorious of all the acts of Christianity, and the one most useful for the salvation of men."[157] The point was made graphically on a holy card that appeared in several different versions during the nineteenth century. At the top left a priest is shown at the moment of consecration, while at the lower right an angel is shown pulling someone from the flames of Purgatory (see fig. 7). The caption states the matter in simple terms: "Pray today for your suffering brothers; tomorrow they will pray for you in heaven."

Money earned for funerals and commemorative masses constituted the greater part of the casuel and remained an important source of income throughout the nineteenth century. For the diocese of Orléans Christianne Marcilharcy found that from fifty to eighty masses were requested in the smaller parishes, whereas the curé of a larger city might have as many as six hundred—figures that are generally confirmed in Yves Hilaire's study of the diocese of Arras and my own work in Angers.[158] In Angers the casuel remained a lively issue for clergy and laity throughout the nineteenth century, and clerical correspondence on this problem reveals a great deal about the use of masses in the cult of the dead as well as the implications of this practice for clerical finances.

Although the financial situation of parish clergy in the nineteenth century varied from region to region, and even from parish to parish, Yves Hilaire's judgment that their lives were "relatively comfortable" seems a fair one. The level of comfort frequently depended, however, on how much beyond the basic state salary the clergy could collect from the local community. Throughout France curés in large towns made a base salary of either 1,200 or 1,500 francs in the 1840s, while desservants in smaller communities earned 800 francs. In Maine-et-Loire the bishop estimated that in towns of five thousand or more the casuel produced an average supplement of 660 francs, while in smaller towns the figure was 413 francs. We will see that these averages distort the picture, because the clergy in the western half of the diocese of Angers generally earned more than their colleagues in the east. Nevertheless, the bishop's numbers make it clear that the casuel provided a margin of comfort of great interest to the clergy of Maine-et-Loire.[159]

In 1843 Bishop Montault of Angers asked his clergy to comment on a new price list for religious services that he was circulating to them before releasing it to the public. In long and detailed responses, the clergy reviewed the implications of this change for themselves and their parishioners. Their letters attest to the vitality of the practice of saying masses for the dead in exchange for an honorarium. In many parishes a special collection on Sunday allowed the priest to say one mass for all the dead of the parish, an act that suggests a sense of collective responsibility for the dead. But, for the most part, requests came from individuals desiring masses intended for their own dead. Clerical attention focused primarily on the increase in the charge for a simple sung mass (messe chantée simple) from one franc to one franc fifty centimes. The clergy from the eastern half of the diocese, the arrondissements of Saumur and Baugé, complained vigorously that such a change amounted to a decrease rather than an increase because they had been accustomed to charging two francs for such masses, an amount that the new price list allowed only for solemn sung masses (messe chantée solennelle).[160] The lack of a clear distinction between these masses prior to Montault's proposal had allowed the clergy to charge the higher rate, and according to the desservant of Ambillou-Château, publication of the new tarif would therefore cost many of the clergy from his area more than one hundred francs a year. For the clergy in the eastern part of the diocese the problem of lowering prices was aggravated because of the decreasing number of requests, with many people now asking only for masses on the day of the funeral, a week later (*la messe du huitaine*), and at an anniversary service one year later (*la messe du bout de l'an*).[161]

The clergy from the western arrondissements of Beaupréau and Segré were in a much different situation because their parishioners were more devout and more inclined to request masses for their dead. In the arrondissement of Beaupréau, an area associated with the counterrevolutionary uprising of the Vendée, families still frequently requested a *trentaine*, a group of thirty masses. The greater demand for masses in the west led to a much higher income from the casuel and allowed the clergy of this area to support holding prices steady or even lowering them. René Grange, the curé from Noellet, expressed the point clearly when he wrote the bishop that "it is to God's glory that the honoraria for masses and services be kept as low as possible; especially in our parishes, where there is still faith, but little fortune. Because I conceive of nothing more painful and dishonoring than for a curé to hear himself reproached by his parishioners for being too selfish and for earning more in a few hours than they can earn in fifteen days."[162] From the point of view of the clergy in the eastern part of the diocese, however, colleagues such as René Grange could afford to be generous because they profited not only from a large number of masses but also from contributions in kind and cash from the local communities. The clergy from the eastern canton of Vihiers defended their plea for higher prices and also expressed their resentment toward the privileged west:

> We know that we are priests only to save souls for Jesus Christ, and not to amass perishable wealth; but we cannot forget that the priest must live from the altar and that if we sow among Christians spiritual goods we have the right to collect from them temporal goods that are necessary for our subsistance. Those clergy from the arrondissements of Segré and Beaupréau ask for reduced prices because most of them have sung masses every day of the week, salary supplements, contributions in kind, and land attached to their rectories. But in the arrondissements of Saumur, Baugé, and even Angers, a good number of priests have hardly fifty masses, no supplement, no contributions, no land.[163]

Other issues involving masses also divided the clergy of Anjou; in order to create demand some curés from the east had taken to announcing low masses for the following week from the pulpit on Sunday, a right that had formerly been accorded only to those who paid for a high mass. This innovation led parishioners in neighboring villages where the curé kept to the traditional practice to resent a discrepency that made them pay more for an announcement.[164]

The debate over the tarif of 1843 shows the clergy reacting not only to its effect on their income but also to its impact on their relationships with the laity. In the 1850s an agricultural laborer in the area earned about one franc fifty centimes a day, whereas artisans made between between one franc fifty and two francs fifty centimes.[165] Surrendering a day's wages or more for a mass was a hardship and one that made the laity highly sensitive to any changes in the prices of religious services. "Murmuring" (*murmure*) is the word that the clergy frequently used to describe the hostile reaction. In fact, popular dissatisfaction with the charges for services was great enough to encourage proposals for abolishing them and replacing lost revenue with an increase in the state salary. When a clerical writer suggested this on the first page of *L'Univers* in 1857, however, the editor pointed out the danger of breaking all such direct financial ties between priests and people. Once abolished the casuel could never be restored, and should the State ever withdraw its support, the clergy would then be left with no income. As a result of this concern and the State's unwillingness to raise clerical salaries, the clergy continued to rely in part on income from masses, and people continued to murmur whenever they sensed that they were being exploited.[166]

In addition to mass fees, the prices for a broad range of services sometimes strained relations between clergy and people.[167] How much should each receive for solemn services to which several priests were invited? How much could a curé charge for a levée that required him to travel a great distance from the rectory in order to lead the body back to the church? (As one priest from Anjou remarked, if the price were too low his parishioners would have him constantly in the mud, seeking the bodies of his parishioners.) How much for a Psalm from the office of the dead, but without a mass? How much for candles, and how much of the profit from them should be shared with the parish council? And finally, what was the obligation of the clergy with regard to masses paid for at an older and lower rate? On this last question the bishop was usually generous in permitting a reduction, which allowed the priest to say fewer masses at the newer, higher rate.[168]

All these issues could provoke trouble with parishioners and lead to angry accusations on the part of the laity that they were being overcharged. In 1863 a M. Gelineau complained that the 53 francs charged by Curé Turlain of St. Melanie for the funeral of his daughter did not comply with the diocesan rate, and the bishop ended up agreeing with him. Gelineau continued to complain, however, when the curé announced that he was accepting a lower fee only to be agreeable, and that he had the right to the original amount.[169] Prudent clergymen were slow to raise prices, even if the increase was sanctioned by the diocesan tarif because as one of them wrote in 1882, "I don't want to run into serious difficulties with my parishioners, who are used to paying the old price."[170]

Clerical concern about fees for masses and other services continued in the second half of the century. Prices for masses increased only modestly, and toward the end of the century the declining revenues from the casuel had become a serious problem.[171] In 1889 the bishop of Angers noted that requests for the *service du huitaine* and the *service anniversaire* had diminished, and that people were generally replacing these elaborate masses and offices with simple sung masses.[172] Even more troublesome was the tendency to invest money in pompes funèbres rather than in religious services, and a national campaign was undertaken in the 1880s to encourage people to have masses said rather than purchasing porcelain wreaths. But this effort failed quickly, and the Church could do nothing more than tolerate the demand for funeral decorations and monumental tombs that increased steadily throughout the century.

Despite this shift, however, pious Catholics remained firmly committed to religious services as well as to the newer customs of the nineteenth century. The letters exchanged by the Montbourg family between 1892 and 1902 show this family from the *petite noblesse* as attentive to the smallest details involving religious services for their dead. Emilie de Montbourg decides on a solemn anniversary service for her son Charles, but not in Normandy, where it would entail the additional cost of printed announcements (*faire-part*). Her brother Charles advises Emilie to economize with four rather than six or eight priests at the funeral of her daughter Eleanore, which costs a total of 183 francs.[173] Mary McCarthy reacted harshly to the spirit of calculation in these exchanges, which show how "piety and avarice combine in these morose natures."[174] The Montbourgs are certainly an unsympathetic family; they maneuver with very few scruples to preserve their family reputation, compromised by Emilie's daughter Marthe, whose pregnancy leads them to hide her and than marry her off to a man who is both brutal and unfaithful. But their letters show the same kind of conviction regarding the efficacy of Catholic rituals as displayed by the scandal-free La Ferronays family earlier in the century.[175] When her grandson dies Emilie writes that "the decrees of heaven are mysterious and our affliction very great, but in the midst of our sadness there remains the certainty that the little one is eternally happy."[176] When Marthe dies, although divorced and in disgrace, the family is consoled by the fact that she confessed and received extreme unction, and the masses said for her reassure her companion and servant that she will see her again in heaven.[177]

Masses for the dead, however, were not said only to ensure salvation. They were acts that recalled the dead to mind in a prayerful and solemn setting, ritual moments that preserved continuity and loyalty across generations and beyond the grave. In Balzac's story "La Messe de l'athée" Doctor Desplein is a thoroughgoing materialist who mocks the mass as "a farce . . . a papal invention which does not go back farther than the sixth century." But over a period of years he is observed by his student assisting regularly at an anniversary mass for the dead and, when finally confonted with this, tells the story of his youth. As a poor medical student he had been saved by the friendship of a poor water carrier, a devout Auvergnat who died fearful of his fate in the next world. Despite his atheism, Desplein founded a mass for his friend at Saint-Sulpice, which he attended four times a year.

> I go there in his name, and recite for him the appointed prayers. With the good faith of the doubter I say: "Lord, if there is a sphere where you place after their death those who were perfect, don't forget good Bourgeat. And if there is something for him to suffer, give me his sufferings so that he may sooner enter what is called paradise!" That, dear fellow, is all that a man of my opinions can allow himself. God must be a kind old fellow and he won't blame me. I swear to you that I would give my entire fortune if Bourgeat's belief could penetrate my mind.[178]

Balzac wrote his story in 1836, and we have seen anticlericals from the latter part of the century take a much more hostile view of Catholicism. To stay for a moment within the world of fiction, Jean Barois clearly would have disapproved of Despleins's concession to his friend. But even at the end of the century skeptics were sometimes willing to attend a Catholic service to express their sense of loss, as happened in 1897 when many prominent republicans assisted at a mass in memory of a group of young women who had died in a fire at a charity ball. On this occasion, however, they were greeted by a harsh sermon by the Dominican preacher Père Ollivier who blamed the catastrophe on the sins of the age, an accusation that many present took personally. The hostile publicity that followed this service was based on a sense that a mass for the dead was an occasion for mourning and consolation, not for the scoring of points in the current religious and political debates.[179] National politics as well as family, village, and economic concerns could intrude into the relationship that the clergy were supposed to maintain between the living and the dead.

Masses were not the only ritual Catholicism offered to the living so that they might assist the dead. By saying special prayers, joining confraternities, going on pilgrimages, wearing medals or scapulars, or doing these in certain combinations, which might include assistance at mass, the laity could gain indulgences, grants from the Church that would allow them to reduce their time in Purgatory, or relieve the suffering of the dead. A number of writers noted the increasing popularity of indulgences, which proliferated in the nineteenth century even while requests for masses declined.[180] The clergy who encouraged and profited from this growth were frequently members of religious orders and leaders of specialised devotions that linked believers by means of printed literature. Although the parish clergy did not complain openly of this competition, and sometimes found ways to collaborate with the new cults, the purgatorial devotions nonetheless contributed to the creation of national constituencies of believers, a situation that presages the effectiveness of television evangelists in America.

Indulgences are linked directly with Purgatory, and both have been among the most controversial doctrines of Catholicism since the Reformation. Indulgences are based on the theory that the Church administers an infinite store of grace earned by Christ, Mary, and the saints and that this can be applied to the suffering souls in Purgatory. Purgatory is the site where all those who die without having completely atoned for their sins must suffer until they have been sufficiently purified to enter Heaven. In the sixteenth century abuses attached to these doctrines were common; the famous couplet associated with the Dominican preacher John Tetzel typifies what made reformers such as Luther so angry:

> As soon as the coin in the coffer rings
> The soul from Purgatory springs.[181]

An attempt to control such abuses began with Council of Trent and continued into the seventeenth century with Clement IX's establishment of the Sacred Congregation of Indulgences and Relics in 1669, which was charged with issuing decrees that would confirm or establish indulgences.[182] Despite this effort the circulation of false indulgences that made excessive claims continued throughout the eighteenth century, as is detailed in Jean-Baptiste Thiers's catalogue of superstitions.[183] Efforts to regulate the practice continued in the nineteenth century; in 1818 the Sacred Congregation sanctioned the publication of the *Raccolta*, a semioffical list of indulgences that served as the basis for French works on this subject throughout the nineteenth century.[184] The effort to control indulgences did not mean, however, that the Sacred Congregation was parsimonious in granting them. The decrees issued by the Sacred Congregation in the nineteenth century suggest an increasing willingess to tap the Church's treasury of grace; eighty-six decrees were issued between 1850 and 1884, compared to thirty-eight for the first half of the century. As Père Lépicier claimed proudly, "There has never been, in previous periods, a comparable prodigality."[185]

The vast range of prayers and practices that merited indulgences defies comprehensive treatment, but some of the elements and a few prominent examples can provide a basis for making some judgments about the consequences of such devotions for the cult of the dead. There was, first of all, a fundamental distinction made between plenary and partial indulgences. Plenary indulgences allowed a suffering soul to be received immediately into Heaven, whereas partial indulgences remitted only some of the temporal punishment due to sin and specified the amount in days, months, or years. What all this actually meant, however, was not as clear as a simple statement of the doctrine might imply. In fact, theologians acknowledged that no one could ever be certain that the full value of the indulgence had been gained. Complete remission depended on the degree of contrition, which only God could know. The value of indulgences applied to souls in Purgatory was doubly uncertain, for theologians acknowledged that the Church Militant on earth could not technically claim any rights over the Church Suffering in Purgatory, where the pope had no jurisdiction. Nonetheless, it was generally believed in the nineteenth century that offering up good works, including the prayers and practices that merited indulgences, was pleasing to God, who would generously apply them to the souls in question. The extent of his mercy, however, would depend on the act in question, on the state of the soul in Purgatory, and on God's inscrutable will.[186]

Theologians might raise questions about the face value of indulgences applied both to oneself and to the souls in Purgatory. The intent was not to discourage the practice, however, but to make clear the need to continue praying. As the author of one pious manual argued, "Even when we've tried to obtain for the poor souls several plenary indulgences, we should still continue to pray, because *we never know to what point these indulgences will have been applied*."[187] By the end of the century Abbé Lépicier was willing to criticize those who emphasized the difficulty of obtaining the full value of an indulgence, an effort that he felt was alienating Catholics from the practice. In fact, although the doctrine of limited applicability was commonly referred to in theological treatises, it was by no means a central

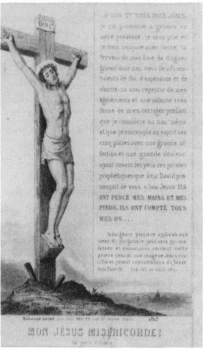

7. *Left: My Jesus Mercy.* The image of the crucifix and the accompanying prayer to the sweet and gentle Jesus was one of the most popular of the holy cards distributed by the publisher Bouasse-Lebel in the second half of the nineteenth century. Saying the prayer while contemplating the image carried a three-hundred-day indulgence. *Right: Pray Today for Your Suffering Brothers.* This image from Bouasse-Lebel illustrates the power of the clergy, whose celebration of masses could liberate souls from Purgatory (Photo: Bibliothèque Nationale).

element in the devotional tracts used to spread the word about indulgences. These generally avoided such technical questions in favor of simple descriptions of the prayers and practices required and a listing of the benefits that would result.

The holy cards that were ubiquitous in the nineteenth century were among the most popular means of spreading information about indulgences and the afterworld. Images produced by Parisian publishers such as Bouasse-Lebel became increasingly popular in the second half of the century, when they gradually displaced the older colportage literature of Epinal. Holy cards were used as rewards for schoolchildren, as mementos of baptisms and marriages, as bookmarks,

8. 9. *Images Mortuaires*. Holy cards were frequently distributed as funeral souvenirs. On the back of the images were printed the names of the deceased, the day of their death, and a number of short prayers (Photo: Bibliothèque Nationale).

and as domestic decorations.[188] They were also used as souvenirs to mark and remember the deaths of family members and friends, a practice that became especially common after 1870 (see illus. 8 and 9).[189] These *images mortuaires* could be designed around a number of themes. Images of Mary were popular, a choice that suggests the wide appeal of the grieving mother as well as Mary's power to ensure a good death and salvation. In the second half of the century one of the most popular images portrayed the crucified Christ and the prayer "O Good and Gentle Jesus" ("*Oh bon et très doux Jésus*"). The prayer affirmed the repentance of the sinner as he contemplated the five wounds and reflected on the suffering of Jesus. At the bottom of the card or on the reverse side the devotee learned that reciting the prayer before an image of the crucifix—after having confessed, communicated, and prayed for the intention of the pope—would earn a plenary indulgence applicable to the souls in Purgatory (see illus. 7).[190] Angels carrying souls to Heaven were another popular and reassuring motif, especially for the parents of children who had died young (see illus. 5). In addition to reinforcing belief in the Catholic afterworld, holy cards registered important shifts in religious sensibility when compared with the cruder colportage images of the early part of the century. In the same period when preaching began to emphasize the possibility of salvation over the fear of Hell, cards provided lessons and prayers that could guarantee a heavenly reward.

Confraternities, which had been an important source of indulgences since the seventeenth century, continued to operate in the nineteenth century, and those associated with the scapular of Our Lady of Mount Carmel and the rosary were especially popular. The devotional literature suggests, however, that increasingly these were merely paper organizations with no real collective life and that their major function was to gain indulgences for individual members. Scapulars and rosaries had to be blessed by priests delegated with the appropriate authority, and these and similar blessings were a cause of much technical correspondence in the clerical journals. Once obtained, however, a blessed scapular or rosary was the source of a large number of indulgences, few of which required any collective prayer. As a result of decisions made by the Sacred Congregation of Indulgences in 1838 and 1868, it was no longer necessary to be inscribed on a register of the Confraternity of the Scapular in order to be eligible for the indulgences.[191]

Older devotions like the Scapular and the Rosary competed with newer ones, all of which used indulgences to draw followers. Our Lady of Lourdes, the most important of the several Marian cults created in the nineteenth century, offered a full range of benefits, including plenary indulgences on the day of joining the Confraternity of the Immaculate Conception, the day of death, and on several Marian feast days. In order to receive these blessings, devotees had to wear the medal of Lourdes, the scapular of the Immaculate Conception, say one decade of the rosary a day, and kiss the earth in a spirit of humility once each week—an act that recalled Bernadette Soubirous's behavior during one of the founding apparitions of 1858.[192]

The huge numbers of indulgences available and the competition for devotees by proponents of particular cults led to marketing practices that were vulnerable to anticlerical attacks. In the last quarter of the nineteenth century the critic Paul Parfait had no trouble finding writings such as Abbé Cloquet's *The Easiest Indulgences* or the anonymous work whose title suggested that readers would learn *The Way to Go Right to Heaven*.[193] Parfait was particularly troubled by the claims of Pére Gay, the editor of the periodical *L'Echo du Purgatoire* and the author of a number of popular works. Gay was fond of using financial metaphors in arguing his case; he claimed that an indulgence gained for a suffering soul in Purgatory would be returned at a rate of one hundred to one, much superior to the 5 percent that drew earthly investors.[194] This argument, based on the expectation that saved souls would intercede for their benefactors once they reached Heaven, shifted the focus of devotional life back to the living individual. Thus, a supposedly selfless act turned out to be a prudent investment.

Gay's language suggests that indulgences were part of a spiritual economy in which consumers carefully pondered their decisions, a kind of behavior with which parish clergy involved in the market for masses were also familiar. Manuals offering a wide variety of prayers and practices that merited indulgences proliferated in the same period when department stores were issuing mail-order catalogues, and in both cases consumers were given the opportunity to browse at their leisure, to compare offerings, and choose according to their taste and resources. Other metaphors derived from contemporary culture were also popular with devotional writers. Abbé Lépicier explained the increasing ease with which indulgences could be obtained—a development that would seem unfair from the perspective of previous generations—as comparable to the practice of spoiling younger children: "In order to free themselves from their penalties, our older brothers had to engage in long fasts, tears, and prayers; we can, however, by simple ejaculatory prayers, pay all our debts and thus escape the torments of Purgatory. The Church acts towards us as a good mother who has renounced for the most part her former severity."[195]

Critics inside as well as outside of the Church opposed the aggressive marketing of indulgences and the competition that drove down their spiritual cost and inflated the returns on prayers. But defenders remained numerous and vocal well into the twentieth century. They claimed that indulgences made people appreciate the redemptive graces earned by Christ and the saints and the power of the Church to distribute them. Furthermore, indulgences created a bond between the living and the dead that worked to the advantage of both. In the twentieth century, however, and especially since the Second Vatican Council of the 1960s, indulgences have lost both institutional support and popular appeal. A great deal of theological language now concerns itself with liberation rather than salvation, a shift that has been in part due to Catholic sensitivity about the practices of the last century. In the nineteenth century as in the fifteenth, the growth in the market for indulgences allowed critics to argue that the system had become bloated and corrupt. But whereas the clergy of the sixteenth century sought to preserve the system by correcting abuses, those of the twentieth seem content to let it linger on at the margins of the Church. The clergy of the nineteenth century who made elaborate claims about the indulgences that they promoted are in part responsible for the current discredited state of the doctrine. Given the importance of Purgatory within the history of Catholicism, their behavior also deserves a place in any description of the broad process of the alienation of Europeans from the Church. It may be worth the effort, however, to recall that even in the age of its decadence the doctrine of indulgences offered many people consolation and hope about the afterlife. The innumerable stories in devotional literature of the dead coming back to thank the living for the help that they had given are sentimental and banal, as are the nineteenth-century altarpieces dedicated to the souls in Purgatory, as described and depreciated by Michel Vovelle.[196] Readers of these stories, however, and those who knelt before the altars, wore the scapulars and medals and thumbed a holy card while saying a prayer were able to convince themselves that they were engaged in saving the souls of family members, friends, or even strangers who would help them in turn gain eternal life. The collapse of this edifice may not be regrettable, but it is part of an important shift in the history of religion and the history of consciousness.

Chapter Four

ALTERNATIVE AFTERLIVES IN THE
NINETEENTH CENTURY

DURING the nineteenth century in France Catholicism was forced to compete with a number of different visions of the afterlife. These alternatives were proposed by philosophers and social theorists who looked back to the eighteenth century and beyond for their inspiration, and despite the innovations that they introduced their debt to the past is generally clear. But unlike in the previous century, criticism and discussion about the afterlife was not limited to an intellectual elite.[1] In the nineteenth century alternative afterlives were part of a public debate that took place in newspapers and journals and on the floor of the French Chamber, as well as in philosophical treatises.

The public and politicized context within which discussions about the afterlife occurred had its origins in the French Revolution. During the 1790s revolutionaries attempted to create a new and purified religion distinct from Christianity. The revolutionaries were divided internally, however, with some drawing inspiration from deism while others tried to introduce practices based on atheism. This last debate reached a climactic moment at the conclusion of the Terror in July 1794. Near the end of his last speech, a day before his arrest and execution, Robespierre made an impassioned plea for the doctrine of an immortal soul.

> The good and the bad, tyrants and the friends of liberty, all disappear from the earth, but they do not suffer the same fate. Frenchmen, do not allow your enemies to debase your souls and to weaken your virtue by this deadly doctrine! No, Chaumette, no Fouché, death is not an eternal sleep! Citizens, erase from your tombs this impious saying, which throws a funeral pall over nature and is an insult to death; carve there instead this saying: *Death is the beginning of immortality.*[2]

Robespierre's affirmation of immortality was not the conclusion of a calmly reasoned theological argument; it was shouted from a podium before divided revolutionaries in order to win their support. Robespierre's appeal was in part a political tactic, for he clearly intended it to undermine his critics who were identified with controversial religious policies inspired by atheism. Joseph Fouché, while on a mission from the Convention at Nevers, had issued a decree on funerals that required local cemeteries to place at their entrances placards announcing "Death is an eternal sleep." This decree influenced revolutionaries elsewhere, including the Parisian Anaxagoras Chaumette, who introduced similar reforms in the capital.[3] Robespierre believed such practices were unpopular, and his comments on immortality were designed to mobilize political support.

This context, in which politics and theology become intertwined and in which the creation of a virtuous citizenry is linked to ideas about death and the afterlife, forms a background for the development of the three general alternatives to Catholicism that emerged during the nineteenth century. Spiritualism, positivism, and spiritism were not systematic schools of thought; but these terms were used by thinkers to identify and distinguish themselves, and they provide categories that allow us to observe and compare the general contours of alternative afterlives.[4] Studying these can lead to a new and deepened understanding of the anticlerical agenda, which included religious and moral questions that were inextricably tied to debates about the status of the institutional church and its relationship to civil society. This rethinking of human destiny also contributed to the reshaping of the material culture of death that occurred in the nineteenth century, which will be dealt with in the final chapters of this book.

The politicization of the afterlife should not lead us to conclude that those involved in these debates were insincere or that the new afterworlds were significant only as a projection of this-worldly interests. We have no reason to doubt Robespierre's commitment to the immortality of the soul. In fact, there may even be an echo in his words to suggest that he was consoled by this belief as he confronted a personally dangerous situation. Alternative afterlives gave individuals faced with their own deaths and the deaths of those they loved a new framework for mourning and remembering. In some ways those who proposed alternatives resemble orthodox theologians; like Catholic thinkers, the innovators labored to connect mortal existence with a transcendent realm and to see these connections as crucial for defining moral standards and providing human life with meaning. By posing a public challenge to the received tradition, alternative afterlives changed the ways in which French men and women thought not only about the next world but also about the basis for morality, the nature of the self, and human destiny.

SPIRITUALISM

Nineteenth-century spiritualists derived two of their fundamental principles from eighteenth-century deism; both traditions affirmed the existence of God and of an afterlife where good would be rewarded and evil punished. For deists such as Voltaire these postulates were accompanied by a skepticism in the face of particular religious systems whose elaborate theologies were irrational and whose priestly classes were corrupt. We have seen how Robespierre appealed to the doctrines of deism in 1794. His execution, however, did not mean the triumph of official atheism. On the contrary, the revolutionary cult of Theophilanthropy supported by the Directory followed Robespierre and the deists in its insistence on the existence of God and the immortality of the soul.[5] During the nineteenth century the radicalism of the Terror was associated with the atheism of individuals such as Chaumette and Fouché, a connection that inclined those who identified with liberalism to align themselves with deism.[6]

Victor Cousin (1792–1867) was a crucial thinker in the formulation of liberal ideology during the Restoration, when the Catholic Bourbons returned to rule France (1814–1830). Cousin is also identified with spiritualism, a philosophy influenced by Scottish epistemology and German idealism as well as by French deism. Although he has not earned the lasting respect of philosophers, for the educated young men who came of age around 1820 Cousin has been described as a "guru" who offered a synthesis that would "provide the answer to the question of not only what to believe but also how to live."[7] An analysis of Cousin's ideas about the afterlife does not lead to conclusions that challenge this judgment, but it does direct attention to the substance of his religious thought and to the links between his religious beliefs and political ideology. Whatever we conclude about the validity of his ideas, the position advanced by Cousin exerted enormous influence throughout the nineteenth century. During the July Monarchy (1830–1848) Cousin served on the Royal Council of Public Instruction, as minister of education, and director of the Ecole Normale Supérieure, positions that resulted in the acceptance of spiritualism as the semiofficial philosophy of the regime. Through the appointments that he made and his personal prestige Cousin's influence extended beyond the July Monarchy. Many liberals throughout the century thought of spiritualism as the philosophical basis of their ideology.[8]

Like the deists of the eighteenth century, the spiritualists' defense of immortality was tied to their theodicy. For Cousin, good and evil were universal moral principles that necessarily implied reward and punishment: "A principle which is attached to the very idea of good tells us that every moral agent merits a reward when he acts well, and a punishment when he does evil. This principle is universal and necessary, it is absolute."[9] Cousin claimed that in most cases the "law of merit and demerit" would produce appropriate rewards and punishments in this world, but he acknowledged that this result was not accomplished "with mathematical rigor."[10] To conclude that the universe was thus unjust was impossible, because "the creator of the world is just and good." Following the deists, Cousin reasoned that the only possible way to preserve a conviction in the goodness of the universe was to postulate an afterlife.

Such a conviction was important to Cousin in part because it upheld the principles of morality that he believed must be taught to the common man as the basis of social order. This last point, however, cannot be found in Cousin's long and polished essay of the 1850s but in *Philosophie populaire*, a pamphlet produced at the height of the revolutionary crisis of 1848. In this short work, Cousin betrays his anxiety about the moral consequences of socialist doctrines. Socialists talked of God, according to Cousin, but for them this term was only a rhetorical device through which they expressed a materialistic and atheistic mysticism. Cousin was especially disturbed by the socialist doctrine of immortality: "Their immortality is a series of reincarnations without conscience and without memory, through which man has the advantage of being in turn water, earth, plant, animal, and the rest. Beyond this immortality he can also claim that of glory, which is a very great resource and a highly effective consolation for the shepherd and the artisan."[11] Cousin continues his ironic critique of socialism, which includes among its "great discoveries" that "the only goal of life is pleasure, resignation is a fraud, virtue a hypocrisy, God an invention of the rich for the exploitation of the poor." This caricature of socialist religious beliefs (which will be examined later in this chapter) is contrasted with the "natural and human" doctrines of true philosophy, the first principle of which is that "man is not entirely a creature of his senses; he has a soul which is in him distinct from the body and from all other nature." This soul, a gift from God, "feels itself made for immortality, and claims it in all its voices and its most intimate sentiments."[12] Immortality, with its consoling promises of rewards to the virtuous poor, was a doctrine derived from the common sense available to all men, even the simplest, but that nevertheless had to be taught to them as well, to counter the evil effects of socialist teaching.

Cousin was not alone in his anxiety about the consequences of atheism in 1848; politicians as well as philosophers were convinced of the close connection between an afterlife and social order. At a meeting of the general council of the department of Maine-et-Loire in 1848, one member proposed that the council vote a proposition condemning the doctrine that "man, his rights, duties, his future, his hopes, are limited and circumscribed by the present life. . . . In excluding God, his laws, and a future life, this doctrine deprives human laws of a complement, a necessary sanction, renders them powerless and, in a time of revolutions, leaves society defenseless in the face of the excesses of anarchy."[13] The council, although it expressed sympathy for the principles advocated in the motion, decided that a formal vote on such a measure was inappropriate. Nevertheless, this debate among political representatives to a departmental council recalls the speech of Robespierre in 1794 and suggests that the afterlife remained a highly politicized issue through the first half of the century.

Reason, justice, and morality required Cousin to defend an afterlife, a stand that solved the moral and philosophcial problem of evil and (in 1848) the social problem of disorder. Cousin, however, was also attracted to the introspective method that he found in Rousseau, and from this source he developed a psychological argument that was ambiguously related to the defense of immortality flowing from his concern with theodicy. When Cousin looked inward he found a principle of self-consciousness, a *moi* whose identity, continuity, and aspirations were supremely valued. The annihilation of this self at death was unthinkable for Cousin, who conceived of it as an immaterial and immortal soul—and, thus, a crucial element in the spiritualist conception of human nature.[14]

In 1848 Cousin linked his moral and psychological theory to a defense of immortality. At other times, however, he established distinctions that counter the facile associations made in his essay of that year. In several passages from the more fully developed statement of his philosophy, Cousin argued that morality could not be based on the promises and threats of rewards and punishments in an afterlife. He rejected the utilitarianism of a morality based on such rational calculations of self-interest, because from this perspective actions would not be good or evil in themselves but would derive their moral quality only secondarily, on the basis of the rewards and punishments that they would entail. He insisted that although "merit and demerit" required reward and punishment, these should nonetheless be carefully distinguished, because to do otherwise would be to "confuse cause and effect, principle and consequence. Even if reward and punishment did not occur, merit and demerit would remain. Punishment and reward satisfy merit and demerit, but do not constitute them. Suppress all reward and punishment and you will not suppress merit and demerit; on the contrary, suppress merit and demerit and there would no longer be true reward and punishment."[15] Cousin believed that too close an association of immortality and morality led to a coercive ethical system; moral obligation should flow instead from a conscience informed by reason and introspection. As we have already seen, however, for Cousin the introspective method yields not only moral principles but also a perception of an immortal self that looked forward to reward and punishment after death.

Cousin was inconsistent in his attempt to establish immortality by means of psychological self-examination and to free the doctrine from the calculation of rewards and punishments in the afterlife. But his complicated juggling with these concepts yields a tension that was symptomatic of spiritualist reflection on the afterlife. Immortality was closely associated with a commitment to the universal principles of reason, justice, and morality. To Cousin and the spiritualists it was irrational and unjust, and therefore impossible, that God would permit evil to go unpunished and good unrewarded. This philosophical commitment to immortality fitted well with the liberals' concern for social order because it provided them with a basis for counseling patience and resignation to those who suffered in this world. This argument linking morality and immortality was common both to deists and to Christian theologians, but Cousin's emphasis on the subjective perception of an immortal self is much less orthodox. The link that Cousin attempted to make between the immortal self and traditional moral values is weak because there is nothing in his analysis that explicitly and necessarily relates the subjective conviction of an immaterial soul to the objective values that he upholds. The concern that drives the psychological argument for immortality is not morality, but annihilation. Cousin's defense of immortality thus reflects not only traditional philosophical and moral issues but also a preoccupation and anxiety about the self that relates his doctrine of the soul to the concerns of Romanticism.[16]

Cousin's philosophy was not accepted uncritically, and many philosophers during the 1850s and 1860s believed that he had made too many concessions to Catholicism.[17] Nonetheless, spiritualist principles provided a starting point for some of the most influential philosophers of the second half of the nineteenth century. Cousin's student Jules Simon (1814–1896) was professor of philosophy at the Sorbonne, and like his mentor he combined his career in education with a lifelong commitment to public service. He was a member of the Liberal opposition in the French Chamber during the 1860s and served as minister of education and religion (1871–1873) and president of the Council of Ministers (1876–1877) during the Third Republic.[18] Simon was raised in a pious Catholic milieu, and his break from family tradition was lengthy and painful. But guided by Cousin, and shaped by the philosophical environment of the 1830s and 1840s, Simon eventually embraced spiritualism, which he defended against both Catholics and positivists throughout the second half of the century. In *Natural Religion* (*La Religion naturelle*), which went through nineteen editions between 1856 and 1912, Simon repeated many of Cousin's arguments, affirming his belief in God and an immortal soul.[19]

Charles Renouvier (1815–1903) was not directly connected with Cousin, and during his stay at the Ecole Polytechnique in the 1830s he came under the influence of his mathematics tutor Auguste Comte. Renouvier was also familiar with the Saint-Simonian social-ists and contributed articles to Pierre Leroux's *New Encyclopedia* (*Ency-clopédie nouvelle*). But Renouvier's education in Paris during the 1830s and 1840s inevitably brought him into contact with spiritualist ideas, which are reflected in his work on the afterlife.[20] Like Cousin, Re-nouvier was impressed with Kant's *Critique of Practical Reason*, the ar-guments of which he elaborated on and amended in his defense of immortality. The contrast between the moral conscience, with its goals of harmony and self-fulfillment, and the disappointing reality of human achievement during a single lifetime led Renouvier to pos-tulate an immortal soul. The terms of his argument were more cau-tious than those of Cousin; he introduced his position by claiming that he offered nothing more than "motives for belief." But the belief that he came to was also seen as sufficient for yielding certitude. De-spite his criticisms of those who engaged in metaphysical specula-tion, the results of Renouvier's philosophy as it pertains to an afterlife were close to those of Cousin.[21]

Simon and Renouvier are the most prominent representatives of the spiritualist position after Cousin, but they were by no means iso-lated figures—a point easily demonstrated by recalling Simon's politi-cal career. In their public activity these men combined spiritualism with a commitment to republicanism, a political position that distin-guished them from the much more cautious Cousin. Both Simon and Renouvier, for example, wrote for the journal *Freedom of Thought* (*Li-berté de penser*), founded in 1847 to oppose the political stagnation of the July Monarchy and to defend their philosophical and moral prin-ciples.[22] During the July Monarchy spiritualism also influenced French Freemasonry, for as the Church acted to force Catholics out of the organization the members who remained cast their ideas in terms that increasingly resembled the philosophy of Cousin and Simon. Ar-ticle 1 of the Constitution of the Masonic Order of France which was approved in 1849 opened, for example, with the assertion that "Free-masonry, an essentially philanthropic, philosophical, and progres-sive institution, is founded on the principles of the existence of God and the immortality of the soul."[23] During the Second Empire spiritu-alist ideas were defended in newspapers, pamphlets, and public lectures by individuals such as Léon Richer, Etienne Vacherot, and

Patrice Larroque; and the Alliance religieuse universelle provided them with an organizational base.[24]

Spiritualism was deeply entwined with liberal and republican ideology, where it functioned as the philosophical justification for a moral code that no longer relied on revealed religion and the authority of the Catholic clergy. The rationalist defense of the afterlife proposed by spiritualists, however, was not based only on a political agenda that required them to find an alternative to the Catholic moral system. Spiritualist belief in an afterlife could also provide a measure of personal consolation for religious skeptics. In a moving letter to Mme Sofia Swetchine written in 1857, Alexis de Tocqueville revealed his most deeply felt religious convictions, which can be taken as a concise statement of spiritualist belief:

> I firmly believe in another life, since God who is sovereignly just has given us such an idea; in this other life, I believe in the remuneration of good and evil, since God has permitted us to distinguish between them and the freedom to choose; but beyond these clear notions everything that is beyond the limits of this world appears to me clouded in a darkness that frightens me.[25]

De Tocqueville's letter suggests a combination of earnestness and anxiety that may not be typical; Cousin's affirmations, for example, are generally more self-confident, although this tone may be the result of their appearance in published essays. But de Tocqueville's statement, because it is part of his personal correspondence, is perhaps a more telling witness to the quality of spiritualist belief.[26]

POSITIVISM

Cousin's attack on socialist ideas of the afterlife in 1848 suggests that spiritualism faced competition from doctrines other than those of orthodox Catholicism. Spiritualists, like Catholics, frequently used the term "materialist" to describe those who rejected the idea of an immortal soul and an afterlife. From the point of view of Catholics, such a doctrine undermined any possibility of a moral order; for without the reassurance of compensation and the threat of punishment people would have no reason for restraining their behavior, and anarchy would result. Although spiritualists were more ambiguous about the relationship between immortality and morality, in the end they sided with the Catholics in acknowledging their connection as philosophically necessary and socially useful. There were, however, a number of philosophers and social theorists during the nineteenth century who opposed this position and denied the existence of both God and the soul. Like the spiritualists, these thinkers could trace their roots to the Enlightenment, especially to La Mettrie, Holbach, Diderot, and Condorcet.[27] During the revolution the influence of this tradition could be seen both in the cult of Reason and in the radical dechristianization of Fouché. The nineteenth-century heirs to this position, however, did not generally choose to adopt either materialism or atheism as an identifying label, perhaps because many people associated these concepts with the advocacy of violent revolution.[28] No single term or category was used consistently through the century to include all those who rejected personal immortality. Positivism, however, the philosophical system founded by Auguste Comte (1798–1857), was the most important representative of this position and was used broadly to characterize those who rejected supernatural and metaphysical speculation about the afterlife; this is the sense in which I employ the concept.

Comte began his philosophical career as the secretary of Claude Henri Saint-Simon (1760–1825), a seminal thinker whose ideas about social organization, progress, and morality fed into utopian socialism as well as positivism in the first half of the nineteenth century. Saint-Simon was a materialist, but unlike many of the radical *philosophes* of the Enlightenment, he combined his rejection of God and an afterlife with a respect for Christianity, interpreted on the basis of his own heterodox principles. One of the fundamental criticisms that Saint-Simon directed at institutional Christianity was its concentration on happiness in the next world, and he insisted that Christ and all true Christians were committed instead to earthly felicity. Writing in 1817 he claimed that "the hope of paradise and the fear of hell are no longer able to serve as the basis for the conduct of men. . . . Morality can now have no other motives than those of palpable, certain, and present interests."[29] Saint-Simon also resented Catholic orthodoxy because of its focus on individual rather than collective salvation. For him, the creation of an earthly paradise in which the condition of the poor and the oppressed would be ameliorated constituted the goal of human history—a goal that would be realized when mankind had succeeded in passing through stages dominated by theological and metaphysical abstractions.[30] Saint-Simon's reorientation of salvation from a vertical to a horizontal plane, his emphasis on social rather than individual happiness, and his conviction that this felicity would be achieved in historical time as a result of human effort were all ideas that reoccur in more elaborate and systematic form in the positivism of Auguste Comte.

The study of positivism is complicated by the two stages of Comte's career.[31] In a first period, during which time he published the *Positive*

Philosophy (*Cours de philosophie positive*) (1830–1842), Comte elaborated a historical scheme that incorporated all human knowledge. In this work he claimed to have discovered a law of progress which he summarized briefly: "The law is this: that each of our leading conceptions, each branch of our knowledge, passes successively through three different theoretical conditions: the Theological, or fictitious; the Metaphysical, or abstract; and the Scientific, or positive."[32] Comte's philosophy of history provided followers with both an empirical and a normative basis for opposing Christianity and the moral system associated with it that relied on an afterlife. For positivists such as Emile Littré it was Comte's early philosophy that constituted his permanent achievement. In fact, many of his adherents regarded Comte's later years as an aberration.

Comte's career was altered in 1844 by his acquaintance with Clotilde de Vaux, the wife of a public official whose gambling debts had forced him to flee France. Comte's love for Mme de Vaux inspired him to reformulate positivism as a religion in which the affections would play as prominent a role as reason. In one of the annual Confessions that he dedicated to her after her death Comte recalled the founding moment of positivist religion at their meeting of 16 May 1845, when he pronounced the crucial sentence: "We can't always think, but we can always love." ("*On ne peut pas toujours penser, mais on peut toujours aimer.*")[33]

It was the death of Mme de Vaux in April 1846 that inspired the elaboration of a new cult in which the memory of the dead was a central element. The new Religion of Humanity, with its calendar commemorating the great men of the past and its elaborate prayers and rituals, never attracted an important following. This later stage of positivism is nonetheless a significant and characteristic development which can be related to beliefs and cultic practices concerning the dead that were widely accepted in the second half of the nineteenth century.

The philosophical doctrines associated with the first half of Comte's career initially went unnoticed; but after Emile Littré discovered and began publicizing positivism in 1844 Comte's system extended its influence, and by the 1870s it had become a powerful force in the intellectual and ideological life of France.[34] Positivism appealed to liberals and republicans who were searching for a philosophical basis for their opposition to monarchy and Catholicism. From Comte they learned of the inevitable triumph of the scientific method, which would provide the basis for social organization and a moral code superior to those constructed during the theological and metaphysical stages of human history. Although Comte had generous comments to make about Catholicism, he unequivocally asserted that the historical mission of the Church was now completed. According to positivism, supernatural explanations and sanctions were appropriate for an earlier age but not for the nineteenth century.

Comte was not the only thinker to reject the afterlife and express the need for a new basis of morality. In the 1840s Pierre-Joseph Proudhon, influenced by his reading of Comte but also of Ludwig Feuerbach and the Young Hegelians, came to a similar position—one that Steven Vincent has characterised as antitheistic rather than atheistic. Proudhon, like Comte, accepted the need for retaining religious language, because "our monuments, our traditions, our laws, our ideas, our languages, and our sciences, all are infected by this indelible superstition outside of which we can neither speak nor act, and without which we do not even think."[35] But for Proudhon, again as with Comte, the term "God" only made sense if it was understood to represent all of humanity; moral obligations had to be based on responsibilities toward mankind rather than toward God. Among other socialists Louis-Auguste Blanqui was unequivocally atheistic, whereas Etienne Cabet was more inclined to retain religious language, especially in his later years. Like Proudhon, Blanqui and Cabet refused to make any connection between personal immortality and the moral code. When Cousin criticized socialists for denying immortality, it is likely that he had Blanqui and Cabet in mind.[36]

During the 1850s and 1860s, the critique of a morality sanctioned by either a Catholic or a spiritualist afterlife was clearly articulated in the press and through organizations that represented the positivist position. Hippolyte Taine's hostile review of Simon's *La Religion naturelle* drew clear boundaries between spiritualism and positivism, which remained in place through the end of the century.[37] During the Second Empire many Freemasons grew more sympathetic to the idea of an "independent morality." In 1877, after intense debate, the General Assembly of the Grand Orient voted to suppress references to the Grand Architect of the Universe and the immortal soul, an indication of the growing ascendancy of positivism over spiritualism which was increasingly apparent in the first decades of the Third Republic.[38] The powerful lobby for education reform, Jean Macé's League for Education, was another institution that lent support to the idea of a secular education freed from references to an afterlife, a position that it defended from its origins in 1866 into the early twentieth century.[39]

As a result of the positivist campaign, the rejection of theism and personal immortality as the basis for a moral system had a major impact on the debates about educational reform that took place in the second half of the nineteenth century. We have already seen how the

issue of civil burials brought the issue of the afterlife to the floor of the
National Assembly in 1873, when the minister of war General du Barail claimed that the doctrine of immortality was essential for maintaining a disciplined military. As the French state moved toward universal primary schooling, politicians were forced to consider what
children should be taught about God, good and evil, and human destiny. Catholics, of course, had very clear ideas about these questions
and argued that moral training could not occur without religious instruction that included references to God and an afterlife. On this
point they received at times the support of spiritualists, but positivists argued that the sanction of an afterlife was neither effective nor
necessary.

Jules Ferry, the minister of education who led the battle for educational reform in the 1880s, identified himself explicitly with Comte
in making his profession of faith at his initiation into the Masons in
1875. The Catholic doctrine of the afterlife, according to Ferry, was in
ruins. Although its preaching of resignation and otherworldly compensation had been well adapted to the authoritarian and militaristic
Middle Ages, such ideas were unpersuasive in the egalitarian nineteenth century. A new morality in tune with the age was needed, and
it would be one that appealed to mankind's innate altruism rather
than to the selfishness that was encouraged by the Catholic emphasis
on individual salvation. Following Comte and Littré, Ferry insisted
that the generous impulses that would provide the basis for a new
morality could be established with scientific rigor. A year after his
acceptance into the Masons, Ferry addressed his brothers again. This
time he summed up his position as one in which the fear of death
would be overcome not by an afterlife but by the consciousness that
one had participated in the work of human progress: "I believe it is of
the essence [of Freemasonry], that it is one of its virtues, to free man
from the fear of death, because against this ancient terror, this servi-
tude so difficult to reject, you oppose the fortifying and consoling
sentiment of the continuity and perfectibility of the human species."[40]

Paul Bert, another leading republican politician identified with positivism and with the need for educational reform, also took issue with
the moral code that relied on an afterlife. In a polemical speech to the
Union of French youth in 1880 Bert set up a sharp contrast between
an afterlife and progress as contending principles underlying moral
education:

> Religious education disdains this earth; it claims to see there only a val-
> ley of tears, only a testing place where the primary concern is to render
> yourself worthy of Heaven; it scorns, apparently, all the grandeur of the

world and concludes, in order to prove its renunciation of the things of the earth, by considering marriage as an inferior state! The education of the public school, on the contrary, upholds the student, encourages him, shows him progress, teaches him to devote himself to everything that is great, to everything that can work for the development of man, and it makes of the family both the first of his duties and the first of his joys.[41]

Progress, science, solidarity, the family—Ferry and Bert pushed all these levers in order to establish confidence in their moral doctrine. Following the republican victory of 1876 and their consolidation of power over the next few years, the way was opened for them to translate their positivist principles into educational policy. Legislation proposed by Ferry in 1881 called for "moral and civic instruction," language that eventually appeared in the final version of the law in 1882. But for over a year this clause provoked controversy and debate, a fact that revealed how troubled many politicians were about the abandonment of a morality sanctioned by the doctrine of immortality.[42]

Both Catholics and spiritualists refused to accept the positivist-inspired disjunction between morality and religion and its doctrines of God and the immortal soul. When the law on primary education reached the Senate after passage in the Chamber, Jules Simon proposed an amendment that would require primary-school teachers to instruct their pupils in "their duties toward God and the fatherland." Simon's famous speech to the Senate on 2 July concluded with an impassioned appeal to retain the afterlife as an essential element in the education of French youth: "I believe that religious morality, traditional morality, with providential reward and punishment . . . is necessary to the elementary education of our youth."[43] Simon was successful, but the victory of the afterlife was temporary; for an adroit Ferry, aided by the results of the elections of August 1881, pushed through the original and secular version of his law in 1882, despite a final attempt by Simon to keep God in the public school. Ferry's victory was won in part because he adopted an equivocal policy that reassured many republicans who were dubious about the proposed language. He reminded everyone that most teachers were in fact spiritualists and that the instructions drafted by the National Council of Education would respect the religious beliefs of both teachers and students. Although a few of the manuals used by teachers were condemned by the Church, most of the early texts embraced spiritualist principles. Some have argued that Ferry's accommodation to spiritualism was a clever ploy, and that by the end of the 1880s a harder-

edged scientism was making its presence felt in the classroom.[44] Even
if this judgment is accurate, however, the need to adopt such a position reflects the uncertainty among republicans about the advisability
of freeing morality from religion.

Hesitancy about rejecting the afterlife is clearly evident in one of
the most famous positivist texts from the period, Ernest Renan's *The
Future of Science* (*L'Avenir de la science*). Written in 1848, but not published until 1892, this essay affirms positivist moral doctrine but at
times conveys a palpable uneasiness that suggests a combination of
social fear and religious nostalgia in contemplating the end of the
afterworld:

> We have destroyed Paradise and Hell. Whether we've done well or
> badly in this, I do not know. But what is certain is that the thing is done.
> We can't recreate Paradise, nor relight the fires of Hell. We have to stay
> the course, and make a Paradise here-below for everyone.[45]

Renan was unconvinced that any but an elite were capable of attain-
ing the level of culture that would allow them to participate in the
religion of science and humanism that he preached. The government
nonetheless had the obligation to take on the task of education and
enlightenment, and to do so without recourse to the convenient and
attractive doctrine of immortality:

> God keep me from saying that the belief in immortality is not in a sense
> necessary and sacred. But I maintain that when a skeptic preaches this
> doctrine to a poor man without believing it, in order to keep him quiet,
> this must be called a fraud. . . . We cannot deny that too much preoccu-
> pation with the future life would in many ways be damaging to the well-
> being of humanity. . . . Appealing incessantly to the future life silences
> the spirit of reform, lessens the zeal for the rational organization of hu-
> manity.[46]

Commentators have frequently noted the tension in Renan's attitude toward religion, which combined a sensitivity to religious concepts (derived from a pious Breton upbringing) with a commitment to
science and progress.[47] Despite the regret he felt for the "necessary
and sacred" doctrine of immortality, however, Renan accepted the
implications of his rejection of the supernatural, which included
abandoning it as a moral sanction. Renan's internal debate on this
point replicated the public discussion that led to the adoption for the
elementary schools of a secular morality based exclusively on obligations in this world.

The debate on education reform suggests that even at its most
influential moments positivism did not go unchallenged; in the early

twentieth century Henri-Louis Bergson was just one of several philosophers to criticize the hegemonic claims of science and the scientific method.[48] Positivism nonetheless continued to exert a powerful
appeal and to shape personal views and public policy during the first
decade of the twentieth century. Georges Clemenceau has left a monumental testament to the persuasive force of its all-encompassing vision of progress; his *In the Evening of my Thought* explored at length
the physical world, geological and historical evolution, and the problem of death and the hereafter, all within a positivist framework that
generates an attitude somewhere between optimism and stoicism.[49]
However, perhaps positivism's most enduring effect has been the
reshaping of moral education, an achievement that Fernand Buisson
proudly proclaimed before the French Chamber in 1910: "Here is the
originality of France. It is the only country which has attempted to
establish morality apart from religion and metaphysics."[50]

Emile Durkheim's lectures on the science of education delivered at
the Sorbonne in 1902–1903 sum up the claims made by positivists as
they had developed over the previous half century. Durkheim proceeded with absolute confidence in his ability to determine and link
the elements of morality (discipline, the attachment to social groups,
and self-determination) on the basis of a rationalistic and scientific
investigation. He sets his work in a broad historical framework and
sees the secular education introduced in 1882 as "latent and half realized before then."[51] Much remained to be done, however, because in
France an absence of intermediate social groups between the family
and the state had stifled the sense of collective identity and aspiration. The school was an ideal institution for remedying this
deficiency; it "possesses everything it needs to awaken in the child
the feeling of solidarity."[52] This sense of identity, however, would
have to focus on the group that was emerging as the primary moral
agent in the late nineteenth century—the nation. Durkheim was careful to place the nation within a universal context, and he insisted that
the nation not be "conceived as an unscrupulously self-centered
being, solely preoccupied with expansion and self-aggrandizement to
the detriment of similar entities."[53] Nevertheless, Durkheim's analysis reminds us that the rejection of traditional religious sanctions as
the basis for morality occurred in the context of an intensely national-
istic period of French history.[54] Positivists were fond of pointing out
the dismaying social consequences of Catholic and spiritualist doctrine, which emphasized human weakness and resignation. Despite
vigorous opposition, their criticisms ultimately persuaded a majority
and, as I observed in the conclusion of the previous chapter, even
many Catholics have now abandoned the understanding of God and

the afterlife that underlay the moral code a century ago. The history of the twentieth century, however, casts an ironic shadow over the aspirations of the positivists, who were so convinced that they had inaugurated an era in which reason and science would yield a superior morality.

Durkheim's evocation of the nation as the primary object of moral aspiration amended Comte's more general appeal for a religion of humanity, conceived of as a Great Being, a single moral entity encompassing all who have ever lived and ever will live. Whether it was the Great Being, the nation, the family, or some combination that included references to all these, positivists insisted that moral instruction must refer to these human and social concepts in cultivating the spirit of generosity and self-sacrifice. Although positivists combined their criticism of the traditional afterlife with an appeal to such impulses, preaching them as vague abstractions was understood to be an ineffective technique. Positivism required a cultic dimension, and it found this in recalling the dead, who were to serve as example and inspiration. The leading positivists rejected the particularities of the religion of humanity, in which Comte set himself up as a high priest. Nevertheless ritual commemorations of the dead similar to those that he advocated became an integral part of the positivist educational program.

The idea of recalling the virtues of the dead in order to inspire the living was not invented by the positivists. The Christian saints were traditionally invoked in this way, but their cult was not just based on subjective memory; the saints were believed to exist in Heaven, where they could intervene with God on behalf of the devotee. During the eighteenth century a new understanding of the dead arose among some of the philosophes and their readers which placed an exclusive emphasis on the subjective memory. During the revolution and the Empire the cult of the virtuous dead, manifested in statues and funerals, was part of the program of civil education that these new regimes employed to legitimize their authority and mobilize public support.[55] Comte's Religion of Humanity elaborated and systematized this earlier tradition. In his view, the dead could be understood as governing the living because after they have passed into the Great Being of Humanity, their influence continues through the "subjective immortality" that they have attained.[56]

Comte, in his Religion of Humanity, imagined a sacrament that he called "incorporation," which would celebrate the absorption of individuals into the Great Being seven years after their deaths. Following a solemn procession from the cemetery the remains of the dead would be placed in a tomb decorated by a bust or a statue in the sacred wood surrounding the temple of Humanity.[57] Comte's ritual parallels in its general form practices developed in the eighteenth and nineteenth centuries that were designed to honor the great men of the past. The Pantheon, although it was returned to the Church on several occasions, was designated as the site for honoring the great men of the past and was turned into a republican shrine following the death of Hugo in 1885.[58] Comte's ceremony also recalls the famous return of Napoleon's ashes to France in 1840.[59] Not only in Paris, but throughout France statues dedicated to the great men of the past and funerals to celebrate the heroes and martyrs of the present were employed throughout the nineteenth century. These manifestations reached their apogee during the Third Republic, when they were integrated into the positivist program of moral education proposed by the republican reformers.[60]

The positivist cult of the dead and the concept of "subjective immortality" seem at first to be very far from the doctrine of the survival of an individually conscious self shared by Catholics and spiritualists. These differences, however, may veil some common features that link positivists with the general mood that prevailed in the nineteenth century. The dead recalled in statues and ceremonies were intended to inspire the living, but this effect required that the dead be psychologically present, available to subjective experience. The royal funerals of the fifteenth and sixteenth centuries described by Ralph Giesey offer a parallel; the effigy used in these ceremonies was designed to ease the transition to a new reign during the awkward interregnum that preceded the coronation of the successor. The ceremonial use of the statue of the dead king prolonged his reign, but eventually he was buried, and power was vested in his heir. In the nineteenth century effigies of the dead were raised in public places, immortalized in the public conscience which would act according to their lives and principles.[61]

The public cult called for by Comte was complemented by a private cult that he practiced, which worked to maintain affectionate relations between the living and the dead who had shared their lives with each other. In his devotion to the dead as displayed in the private cult, as in his descriptions of the public cult, Comte reflected the general mood in which even those who denied an immortal soul felt obligated to keep the dead alive. Comte's personal cult revolved around Clotilde de Vaux. Comte made weekly visits to her tomb and on his return would stop for a half hour of prayer at the church of St. Paul, where they had assisted at the baptism of her nephew. At home Comte prayed daily to Clotilde, where her chair and a medallion that she had woven from her hair called her to mind. Every year following her death he addressed long and intimate letters to his "noble and tender wife," his "annual confessions" in which he reviewed the events of his life, recalled their happy days together, and pledged his eternal fidelity.[62]

Comte distinguished between "subjective" and "objective" immortality, but the form of direct address used in his prayers and letters to Clotilde de Vaux works against this distinction. He denied in theory the "objective" survival of his beloved, but his cult did not restrict itself to simple recollection. He called on Clotilde to help him with his difficulties, to console him, and to continue assisting him in his moral development—an obligation that wives generally were charged with in the Religion of Humanity. For Comte, "subjective immortality" involved the active involvement of the dead with the living in a manner that resembled the Catholic cult of the saints, a parallel that gains strength when we recall his tendency to refer to Clotilde de Vaux as his "guardian angel." Although Comte attempted to concentrate the relationship between the living and the dead in the subjective consciousness of the living partner, his words and practices nonetheless grant the dead a status in which they seem to escape from the subjectivity in which he intended to enclose them.

Comte had few followers in has last years, and the details he introduced into both the private and public cult—along with his utter conviction that the Religion of Humanity was destined to convert the world—suggest a certain mental imbalance. Comte's cultivation of psychological intimacy between the living and the dead, even while he denied personal and "objective" immortality, was not unique. We will find similar sentiments expressed in the cult of the dead as it was practiced in French cemeteries. Comte's habit of addressing the dead as if they still possessed their own subjective independence was also practiced by positivists who rejected the Religion of Humanity. In the dedication of his *Life of Jesus*, Ernest Renan called on his dead sister in the following terms:

> Dost thou recall, from the bosom of God where thou reposest, those long days at Ghazir, in which, alone with thee, I wrote these pages, inspired by the places we had visited together? . . . In the midst of these sweet meditations, the Angel of Death struck us both with his wing: the sleep of fever seized us at the same time, and I awoke alone! Thou sleepest now in the land of Adonis, near the holy Byblus and the sacred stream where the women of the ancient mysteries came to mingle their tears. Reveal to me, O good genius, to me whom thou lovest, those truths which conquer death, deprive it of terror, and make it almost beloved.[63]

Renan, like Comte, found himself addressing words to a departed loved one in a manner that belied his overt rejection of the traditional understanding of personal immortality. This complicated psychological state suggests an uneasiness about death and the afterlife among those who had rejected orthodox Christianity and spiritualism. Individuals such as Comte and Renan were religious skeptics, compelled by their ideas to reject "objective" immortality as a superstitious leftover from the Middle Ages. The growing confidence in science and progress, represented in the appeal of positivism during the second half of the century, coincided with an increased emphasis on the affectionate relations among family members. Catholics and spiritualists could accommodate these changes because their belief in immortality allowed them to imagine family reunions in a heaven. Positivists were equally affected by romantic notions of family life, but reason and science apparently denied them the consolation of such eternal solidarity. The cult of the dead that they practiced offered them solace by allowing them to imagine the dead as present, but the boundary between such positivist recollections and the more traditional devotions is in practice not always easy to discover. The doctrines and rituals of spiritists can be seen in part as an attempt to resolve the tension within positivism that resulted from the simultaneous attachment to family, which fed a desire for eternal togetherness, and science, which denied the existence of an immortal soul that could make it possible.

SPIRITISM

Spiritism never achieved the intellectual legitimacy accorded Cousin, Comte, and their followers, but it was nonetheless a significant alternative to Catholicism, and to spiritualism and positivism as well. Unlike spiritualism and positivism, spiritism offered believers both a clear outline of the next world and rituals that allowed them to explore it. The development of French spiritism paralleled the spiritualist movements in America and Great Britain, which have been described by R. Laurence Moore and Janet Oppenheim [64] In France, as in England and America, spiritism offered a way "to synthesize modern scientific knowledge and time-honored religious traditions concerning God, man and the universe."[65] French, English, and American spiritists read one another's journals, attended international congresses, and were members of the same associations.[66] Perhaps the best example of such contacts is the French philosopher Henri Bergson, who gave the presidential address to the English Society for Psychical Research in 1913, a speech in which he defended the immortality of the soul on the basis of apparitions of the dead.[67] French spiritism, although it confirms much of what Oppenheim and Moore have argued in their work, also differs from the English and

American movements in ways that can help illuminate the religious landscape of France.

A comprehensive history of French spiritism would take us back well before the nineteenth century, to the occult ideas of the late eighteenth century, to the belief in spirit possession that spread from the mountains of southern France in the late seventeenth century, to the magical practices and neoplatonism of the Renaissance, and beyond.[68] Spiritists made broad claims about their own genealogy and sought to legitimize themselves by claiming Pythagoras, Plato, and Jesus as precursors. But the immediate origins of the movement are located in three speculative traditions that flourished during the first half of the nineteenth century.

Socialism, Swedenborgianism, and mesmerism were not discrete and coherent schools of thought.[69] Perhaps the best way to grasp the tendency of these elements to overlap is by recalling some of the enthusiasms taken up and abandoned in turn by Charles Baudelaire. Jules Fleury recalls him in the 1840s as being devoted to Swedenborg one day and to the Polish mystic Hoene-Wroński the next.[70] Attracted to the work of Edgar Allan Poe, Baudelaire's first translation of the American's works, "Révélation magnétique," described an experiment in which a hypnotist "magnetized" a dying man whose soul was unnaturally retained for weeks in the body. This story first appeared in the socialist paper *Liberté de penser* in 1848.[71] Baudelaire's dabbling in mysticism, science, and politics reveals a religious skeptic searching for new beliefs that would satisfy his doubt. His were typical concerns of the age; for many writers, social and religious speculation necessarily involved consideration of the afterlife.[72]

The afterlives imagined by socialists have not played a prominent role in current interpretations of this movement. As we have seen, socialists such as Proudhon and Blanqui rejected the possibility that individuals somehow survived after death. Historians have generally emphasized the traditions of corporate solidarity, political radicalism, and the expanding influence of market capitalism as the keys to an understanding of early socialism, and all these are of undoubted importance.[73] Recently, however, Edward Berenson has pointed to a religious dimension to socialism that previous historians had neglected.[74] For Berenson, however, the Christianity of Louis Blanc, Pierre Leroux, and others is essentially a medium for the expression of political and social ideals, and it seems fair to say that he is interested in religion primarily because of its political consequences.

The career of Alphonse Esquiros, a typical representative of social-democratic ideology in the 1840s, suggests that these previous accounts have missed some fascinating aspects of socialism that need to be integrated into our understanding of the movement and of the connections between religious belief and political ideology. Berenson tells us that Esquiros was critical of the domination of capital and a vigorous defender of the right to work. As editor of the most important *démoc-soc* paper outside of Paris, he was responsible for the spread of radical ideas into the countryside around Marseille. In addition to his career as politician and journalist, however, Esquiros was a novelist, a historian, a playwright, and a theologian. In his literary work he displayed an interest in metempsychosis, an idea that he explores more fully in a pamphlet published both in Marseille and Paris during the Second Republic, *The Afterlife from the Socialist Point of View (De la vie future au point de vue socialiste)*.[75] In this essay, Esquiros argues that a future life is "a truth of natural history" that can be established by reason and observation. Death is another birth, following which our lives will continue, first on this planet, and then perhaps on others. Our future lives will not be exclusively spiritual, for we will retain a body composed of a subtle matter with which we will experience all our earthly sensations, as well as some new ones that are not specified. The idea of the continued life of the body is essential for Esquiros, who asserts that "I don't believe in the immortality of the soul; I believe in the immortality of man."[76] Esquiros explicitly links the future life to his political ideals: "Belief in philosophic immortality is the most secure boundary from which one can defend against the invasion of brutal strength. Let the persecutors attack their victims; time will seize them by the throat and strangle them. . . . The doctrine of the immortality of the soul is a revolutionary doctrine, a democratic doctrine."[77] As far as Esquiros was concerned, working for the social-democratic republic was possible only because he was convinced that all those who participated in the struggle would someday personally enjoy the fruits of their labor. The certainty of a future life was necessary to his ideology as a shield against despair in a battle that was difficult and that had cost many socialists their lives in the revolution of 1848.

Charles Fourier shared this perspective, but he was even more daring in his speculation about the afterlife. Jonathan Beecher, in his recent biography of Fourier, argues that his cosmological system was neither a joke nor an aberration, as previous scholars had claimed.[78] Fourier himself saw his doctrine of immortality as "one of the pivots of the harmonian system: it would be a scrawny runt without the solution of this problem."[79] Fourier begins his argument by reflecting on the desire for immortality that can be observed as a general characteristic of humanity. It can be seen, for example, in a veiled manner in the regrets of old people who wish that they could start their lives over again—albeit possessed the second time of all the wisdom of their experience. In Fourier's system such a desire is a clue to human destiny, for God would not have allowed for such an Attraction unless it were to be in some way fulfilled.[80] Starting from this desire, Fourier postulated that we would return to life armed with our experience, in a series of reincarnations that will last for eighty thousand years. Half of these lives (810 of the total of 1,620) would be on earth, the other in a vague extramundane state comparable to sleep.

Although Saint-Simon rejected the immortality of the soul, his followers, led by Barthélemy-Prosper Enfantin, played with ideas about reincarnation similar to those of Fourier.[81] Jean Reynaud and Pierre Leroux, Saint-Simonians who later became influential in the socialist movement, retained an interest in the existence of the afterlife and wrote major works in which they addressed this issue. In 1836 and 1837 Reynaud published in the *Encyclopédie nouvelle* a series of articles in which he defended the idea of extraterrestial life and the transmigration of souls, which were reincarnated on other planets. Reynaud's argument drew the attention of Jules Michelet, and when collected and published separately during the 1850s these essays also had a profound influence on Camille Flammarion, who became the most popular science writer of the second half of the nineteenth century.[82] As was the case with writers who advocated similar ideas in the 1850s and 1860s, Reynaud claimed his system was compatible with the most recent discoveries of science, including biological evolution and astronomy, His argument was able to persuade many in an age when professional science had not yet established clear boundaries that would distinguish it from mesmerism and similar systems of thought that were competing for scientific legitimacy. Reynaud's ideas were no impediment to an active political career; during the Second Republic he served as a deputy in the Constituent Assembly, as under secretary of state for education, and as a councilor of state.

Pierre Leroux has recently drawn attention as a socialist whose influence was undervalued by previous historians.[83] As is true of Fourier and Reynaud, the afterlife plays a central role in Leroux's ideology. In his two-volume work, *De l'humanité*, which first appeared in 1840, Leroux emphasizes the relationship between individual perfection in an afterlife and social progress.[84] Leroux's version of the afterlife is rooted exclusively in earthly society, for unlike Fourier and Reynaud he does not postulate any "trans-mundane" existences. Our future lives will be lived on earth, and they will be very much like our current existence.[85] Leroux's formulation of the afterlife made him liable to attacks from Catholics and spiritualists on the ground that he was a pantheist. Indeed, some passages in his work do suggest an understanding of immortality as the absorbtion of the self into a larger whole. "You *are*, thus you *will be*. Because, being, you participate in being, that is to say the eternal and infinite being."[86] But Leroux was explicitly critical of the materialist tradition and defended a self, a "*moi*," that endured and took on successive corporal forms in which previous experience was present but not explicitly remembered. Individual lives, although not recalled in detail, were nonetheless incorporated into the self. He compared this process to the experience of sleep, a period when

> our ideas, our sensations, our sentiments from the previous day, are transformed and incarnated in us, become us. . . . Sleep regenerates us, and we leave it more alive and strengthened, but with a certain forgetfulness. In death, which is a greater forgetting, it seems that our life is digested and elaborated in a manner that, while effacing itself in its phenomenal form, is transformed in us, and augments, in passing by this latent state, the potential force of our life. . . . We have been, we no longer remember the forms of this existence; and nevertheless we are, by our virtuality, precisely the result of what we have been, and always the same being, but enlarged.[87]

Socialists such as Fourier, Reynaud, Leroux, and Esquiros all rejected materialism as demoralizing and postulated individual immortality as necessary in a social philosophy that sought the reconciliation of individual and social progress. Not every socialist accepted such an argument; we have seen that Saint-Simon and Proudhon attempted to construct a moral system without reference to future lives. The socialism of these skeptics, and the atheism of Marx and Engels, have contributed to a tendency among contemporary intellectuals to assume a polarity in which conservative political and social ideologies are aligned with a belief in personal immortality, whereas a commitment to social change is associated with denial of an afterlife. Socialist reflection on personal immortality during the nineteenth century, however, testifies to the powerful appeal that this doctrine still exercised even among some of those radically critical of the social and ecclesiastical systems.

Although socialists sometimes made general references to mesmerist experiments, the afterlives that they described were essentially speculative derivations from their philosophical principles. During the first half of the nineteenth century, similar claims about the afterlife were made on the basis of testimony from travelers to the next world. Direct access to the next world was an integral part of the Swedenborgian and mesmerist movements that flourished in the Romantic era and prepared the way for the séances that were the central ritual of the spiritist movement of the 1850s.

The writings of the Swedish mystic Swedenborg were first translated into French in the 1780s as part of the mystical current of the late Enlightenment. Swedenborg's doctrines influenced the Cercle social, an association of mystic revolutionaries that included a number of writers and politicians prominent during the early years of the revolution.[88] There was a second wave of interest in the 1820s, when Swedenborg's *Apocalypse réveillée* appeared in France.[89] During the 1840s and 1850s multivolume editions of Swedenborg's writings were edited and published by J. F. E. Le Boys des Guays.[90] Swedenborg's teachings were based in part on visits he claimed to have made to the heavens, which he described in extensive detail. According to Swedenborg, three days after death humans revived in a world of spirits that was neither Heaven nor Hell. There they were provided with a spiritual body "which appeared to be material, but was not."[91] From this transitory state the soul would rise or fall through a series of heavens and hells based on personal inclination and the charity that one had displayed while on earth. Swedenborg claimed to have communicated personally with the dead: "I have spoken with all those that I knew in their life of the body, with some for hours, with others for weeks, months, years."[92] Swedenborg's visions of afterlives in which individuals retained spiritual bodies, engaged in social relations, and continued to develop their personalities and moral qualities became essential elements in spiritist doctrine of the 1850s. Unsurprisingly, Swedenborg himself became a popular spirit in the séances of the 1850s.

The German physician Franz Anton Mesmer went to France in 1778 and began to conduct healing services based on his ability to control the magnetic fluid that he believed flowed in and around all bodies. By the end of the 1780s, some occultist circles in France had already began to combine Mesmer's practices with the ideas of Swedenborg and to use the fluid as a means of communicating with the spirit world.[93] Mesmerism was a perfect complement to Swedenborgianism because it provided a ritual allowing devotees to repeat Swedenborg's own experience and to communicate directly with the spirit world. This mixture of science and mysticism survived the revolution and flowed into the Romantic era, where it formed the basis for the work of mesmerists such as Alphonse Cahagnet, who gradually became convinced of the metaphsyical implications of his work.

Despite its failure to win recognition from the Academy of Science in 1784 and the Academy of Medicine in 1837, mesmerism remained an active movement in France throughout the first half of the nineteenth century.[94] For the ordinary Parisian, mesmerists along with fortune-tellers provided advice about medical problems and personal relationships that was sometimes attributed to spirits. The fortune-teller Mlle Le Normand, for example, who gained fame through her connection with Josephine de Beauharnais, claimed to have visited Heaven, where she talked with spirits who passed along political advice and social gossip.[95] Contact with the spirit world was a common claim among consultants such as Mlle Le Normand and shows up as well in the literature of Hugo and Balzac, who were powerfully influenced by Swedenborg.[96] The skepticism of the scientific community toward such beliefs and practices did little to check their appeal, which was based on a potent combination of desires. The occult satisfied both a popular market that demanded help with immediate problems and a literary audience that sought evidence of and contact with a transcendent world of spirits.

Alphonse Cahagnet, a mesmerist active in the 1840s and 1850s, was a transitional figure whose work links the diffuse ideas and practices of the Romantic era to the spiritist movement of the 1850s. Cahagnet began his career as a hypnotist-healer whose "somnambules" gave medical advice to clients. He was familiar as well with the occult tradition and its defense of the spirit world, as presented in the works of Saint-Martin and Swedenborg. In the late 1840s his somnambules began to report meetings with angels, then with the dead, and to carry messages back and forth between this world and the next. By 1848 spirit communications had become more important in his work than healings and formed the basis of his first book, *Mysteries of the Future Life Unveiled* (*Arcanes de la vie future dévoilés*). Cahagnet claimed that mesmerists had become too preoccupied with physical phenomena and hesitated to report on the evidence of spiritual forces and their implications. The interviews with his somnambules that were transcribed and published in *Arcanes* established a new program for mesmerist research

> This work will offer you the proof of a world better than ours, where you will exist after having left your body in the here-below, and where an infinitely good God will reward you a hundredfold for the evils that it was useful for you to suffer in this world of pain. I am going to prove that your relatives, your friends wait for you impatiently, that you can, while in this world, enter into communication with them, speak with them, and obtain information that you will judge necessary; in order to do this, it is not necessary to deny the existence of the soul, or abandon all good will and justice in order to obtain the desired proofs; by somnambulism you will have as much proof as you will desire.[97]

For Cahagnet, mesmerist contact with the spirit world provided a theodicy, guaranteed family solidarity beyond the grave, and ensured the truth of its claims by an appeal to empirical evidence and scientific method. The clear statement of this potent mixture of religious and family sensibilities, legitimized by science, make Cahagnet a key figure in the early history of French spiritism—a fact already accepted by Emma Hardinge Britten, an English devotee who published a comprehensive history of the European movement in 1884.[98] According to Britten, however, Cahagnet was a John the Baptist in relation to the personalities who came after him—an analogy that she doesn't complete but that suggests something of the millennial mood attached to spiritism in France and elsewhere.

Spiritism in France became an organized movement in the 1850s in response to the immediate stimulus provided by news of the "turning tables" in the United States and England. If we judge by the journalistic reaction and the anxiety of the clergy, large numbers of French men and women repeated the practices of Americans and Britons by sitting around tables, and invoking spirits that answered by rappings or by taking possession of one of the assistants, who became a medium through which they communicated with this world.[99] The best documented of these séances is the series of invocations that occurred in the home of Victor Hugo, in exile on the island of Jersey, between September 1853 and October 1855.[100] Of course, it would be impossible to claim that these sessions, conducted in the presence of and frequently transcribed by one of the literary giants of the nineteenth century, were completely typical. But the practices of Jersey and the questions considered were not all or even primarily initiated by Hugo. The first experiments were introduced by Delphine de Girardin, the wife of the liberal journalist Emile de Girardin and a prominent figure in Parisian society. Arriving on Jersey in early September, visibly weakened by the cancer that would soon kill her, she described the séance tables of Paris and arranged the circle of participants according to her previous experiences in the capital. Victor Hugo was at first skeptical and only gradually let himself be absorbed into the spirit conversations. Finally, the séances were open to frequent visitors from the Continent, a detail that may help explain why the events on Jersey resemble those that occurred elsewhere.

The initial questions posed to the spirits of Jersey were tests in which the participants asked the table to tell them what they were thinking or what they had written. The results were disappointing, but on the evening of September 11, a breakthrough occurred. In answering a series of questions about the thoughts of the participants a spirit was identified as Léopoldine Hugo, the much-loved daughter who had drowned in a boating accident soon after her marriage in 1846. From this point on Victor Hugo was a regular and active assistant. Over the next few months a number of topics were discussed with the spirits, but by 1854 literature and literary gossip were the dominant subjects, as writers from the past, including Shakespeare and Molière, acknowledged the genius of Hugo and dictated new works.

Political circumstances as well as family sentiment may help explain Hugo's fascination with the turning tables. Exiled from France following the collapse of the Second Republic which he had supported, Hugo and his circle undoubtedly found it consoling to receive assurances from beyond about their ultimate success; even the spirit of Napoleon III, traveling during the Emperor's sleep, paid a call to Jersey to confess his guilt and ask pardon. There was some talk among family members that the séances might be a distraction from the political work to be done, but isolated on Jersey in the face of Napoleon's apparent triumph, Hugo did not have many options.[101]

Fascination with spiritism was clearly in the air in Paris as well; according to psychiatrists of the period such as Jules Baillarger and Alexandre Brierre de Boismont, this taste "was symptomatic of a collective hysteria that had developed out of the failure and frustration of the political dreams of the 1848 Revolution."[102] The experience of the former editors of the socialist newspaper *Démocratie pacifique* tends to confirm this judgment. In 1853 the socialist playwright Eugène Nus and some former collaborators on the paper, which was associated with Fourierist doctrine, came across an article on spirit rappings in an American newspaper. Bored and disillusioned, they immediately began to experiment, and the tables responded with messages that showed the spirit world to be in accord with their socialist convictions.[103] The existence of a spirit world had been affirmed by a number of prominent socialists prior to 1850; in the face of political defeat some disciples began to make regular contact with the next world and were thereby reassured about the ultimate success of their principles.

Family and political concerns provide an important background for understanding the Jersey séances. For Hugo and his friends, however, the experiments were significant because they illuminated the ultimate context within which all personal and social problems could be resolved. The cosmology revealed by the spirits provided Hugo and the other questioners with guidance and reassurance on fundamental religious and metaphysical problems.

Hugo was repelled by the doctrine of eternal punishment, but he was equally anxious that good and evil men not share the same fate.

The afterlife as revealed by the spirits reconciled the need for reward and punishment with the rejection of Hell. On September 13 a spirit confirmed Hugo's belief that there is no Hell, and on September 29 a spirit from Jupiter, in response to a series of leading questions, affirmed that "depending on whether their conduct is good or bad, human beings after their death are on happy or unhappy planets."[104] These ideas were familiar to the Hugo circle from contacts with the socialists and mystics who had considered the problem of evil from a non-Christian perspective during the Romantic decades of the 1830s and 1840s. Pierre Leroux, for example, was a friend who passed through Jersey late in September with whom Hugo had serious discussions about the phenomena.[105] Mme Hugo, addressing the spirits in December 1853, asserted that the key revelations about the immortality of the soul and its extraterrestrial reincarnations on other planets were already established dogma among the Hugo circle. As was typical on Jersey among both humans and spirits, her comment concluded with an adulatory bow in Hugo's direction: "You see, she told the spirit, that insofar as men are concerned, his thought preceded your revelation."[106]

The Jersey séances, and those in France as well, may not have communicated original ideas, but they did offer what was apparently direct empirical evidence of an afterlife. When questioned about publishing the transcripts of the séances, however, the most impressive of all the spirits, L'Ombre de Sépulcre, hesitated and ordered that they be shown only to those who already believed.[107] The Hugo circle accommodated itself willingly to this advice. Some of what transpired on Jersey appeared in a book by Auguste Vacquerie in 1863, and many of the ideas discussed at the séances turn up in Hugo's Les Contemplations, which first appeared in 1856.[108] But Hugo never published a word about the séances—a surprising show of reticence on the part of a writer whose productivity and vanity are as legendary as his genius. One reason for Hugo's hesitancy was the doubt that he periodically experienced about the precise nature of the phenomena. Perhaps, he speculated, there were no spirits, and the sessions only produced thoughts that were circulating among the participants. The fact that some of the poetry dictated by the spirits resembled his own verses clearly gave weight to this position. On a more philosophic plane, Hugo may have been concerned that the revelations would somehow diminish the sublimity and mystery that he valued in his vision of the universe.[109]

Spirits did not reveal themselves exclusively to the left; in 1857 the imperial family had a number of sessions with the famous Scottish medium Daniel Douglas Home. The empress Eugénie was convinced that her dead father had squeezed her hand during one séance, and the emperor was also favorably impressed.[110] The vogue of turning tables widely commented on during the 1850s was broad enough to include the emperor and his most famous opponent. Flaubert's decision to ridicule spiritism as one of the fads adopted by his representatives of bourgeois fatuity, Bouvard and Pécuchet, is further evidence of its cultural impact.[111] By the 1860s public as well as private séances were a familiar part of the Paris social scene—a point that can be illustrated by describing the performances of the Davenport brothers, two American mediums whose spirit show was a widespread topic of conversation in September 1865.

The Davenports' act consisted of letting themselves be tied by ropes inside an armoire, which was then closed.[112] Next, ostensibly while they were bound, spirits were evoked that played guitars, tambourines, and other instruments. The reports in *Le Temps*, the leading liberal journal of the day, were consistently skeptical and explicitly compared the Davenports' tricks to those performed by magicians—including the famous Robert Houdin, who claimed no supernatural assistance. While the Davenports were performing, the magician Robin was providing similar entertainment, at a lower price than the twenty francs charged by the Americans, at the Paris Hippodrome. Robin, in fact, was drawing crowds in part by claiming that he could perform the same feats and therefore refute the claims of the spiritists—a posture that led some Davenport supporters to try to disrupt his act. The first séance of the Davenports was disorderly, with members of the audience leaping onto the stage trying to verify that no fraud was being committed. The show ended in chaos when one skeptic mounted the stage and claimed to show how the brothers were able to escape from their bonds using the folding seat in the armoire. The crowd began shouting, and the French translator and master of ceremonies responded by promising to return the admission fees. The disorder led the police to enter the room and force everyone to leave.

The next evening the Davenports' experiments were repeated, but only before an audience of invited guests, each of whom had paid an admission fee of thirty francs, more than what the average worker would earn in a week. With no journalists present, the performance went smoothly, but *Le Temps* commented ironically that had the problems continued, another session would have been scheduled and the admission fee doubled. Responding to this sarcasm, the Davenports arranged a third performance, to which they invited a number of journalists. This time no problems occurred, and even *Le Temps* admitted its representative was unable to discover the trick. But despite the lack of clear evidence that would provide a natural explanation for the performance, the journalists continued to doubt. One contributor to *Le Temps* asked why the Davenports required the presence of armed guards at their performances, a security measure unnecessary at Houdin's shows. His explanation addressed the central issue in the public controversy over spiritism. The need for protection was the result of the "highly unusual pretension of the Davenport brothers, who don't want to be conjurers, but mediums. The guitars which grate, the tambourines which wander . . . obey supernatural powers."[113] The article concluded by demanding to know why powerful spirits would need the crude material security provided by police and why the authorities should be defending fraud when political and civil liberties were being denied.

The experiments on Jersey have suggested that spiritism offered devotees hope of resolving difficult philosophical and religious questions. The Davenport show and the general attention given spiritism in the press and literature during the 1850s and 1860s reveal public fascination with spirit manifestations. The intellectual and popular appeal of the movement in the second half of the century was based in large part on the work of two French thinkers, Allan Kardec and Camille Flammarion. Kardec and Flammarion were theorists, publicists, and organizers whose work was well known to the general public; and the attention that they paid to the movement won for spiritism, at least for a time, some legitimacy as a discipline on the margins of modern science.

Allan Kardec was born Hippolyte-Léon-Denizard Rivail in Lyon in 1804; the son of a lawyer, he was educated at the Protestant school of Johann Heinrich Pestalozzi in Geneva, where he apparently suffered from religious prejudice because of his Catholicism. Rivail moved to Paris in 1824, and there he ran his own school for almost a decade. When financial troubles forced him to close the school, he worked as a lycée teacher and wrote a number of manuals to prepare students for state examinations.[114] During the 1830s and 1840s Rivail also kept abreast of developments in mesmerism and, starting in 1854, he began attending the séances of a number of Paris mediums; in 1856 Rivail, now known as Allan Kardec—names that he believed he bore in previous existences—published *The Book of Spirits* (*Le Livre des esprits*), a work that became the most important document of the spiritist movement and, in fact, is still in print after dozens of reeditions in the nineteenth and twentieth centuries.[115] In 1858 Kardec founded *The Spiritist Review* (*La Revue spirite*), a journal that he edited until his death in 1869 which was the official publication of his Society of Spiritist Studies (Société des études spirites). Kardec's work as both publicist and organizer resulted in the creation of a network that his followers claimed may have linked as many as six hundred thousand people. This estimate was exaggerated, but if we take into account the enormous success of his many books and the attention he received in the press, it is clear that Kardec was an influential thinker. He is still revered by spiritists, who have made his tomb in Père Lachaise cemetery a shrine the popularity of which rivals that of Edith Piaf (who was also a spiritist).

At his death in 1869 Kardec was eulogized by Camille Flammarion (1842–1925), a scientist and author whose career suggests the powerful appeal of spiritist ideas in the second half of the nineteenth century.[116] As a child Flammarion was at first destined for the priesthood but was forced to leave the minor seminary of Langres following a financial crisis in his family. As an apprentice engraver in Paris Flammarion continued to educate himself, and eventually he won a position at the Paris Observatory. In 1862 he began a publishing career that lasted sixty years and included over seventy books. Flammarion's works were an important factor in the success of the firm established by his brother, which continues to be a force in the world of French publishing.[117]

Flammarion is perhaps best known for his defense of the doctrine of extraterrestriality. Starting with *The Plurality of Worlds* (*La Pluralité des mondes*) in 1862, Flammarion consistently argued for the existence of intelligent life on other planets as well as the sun.[118] As Michael Crowe has recently shown, the concept of extraterrestriality was at the center of nineteenth-century astronomy. As founder and first president of France's *Société astronomique*, an organization that primarily attracted amateurs with an interest in recent scientific discoveries, Flammarion was a key figure in the popularization of astronomy. He also served in the 1860s as editor of the popular magazine, *Magasin pittoresque* and as a writer for the newspaper *Le Siècle*. He presented his ideas through the genres of philosophical dialogues and fiction as well as in popular accounts of science, such as his *Astronomie populaire*.[119]

Kardec and Flammarion were not alone in their work; a number of other authors also gained notoriety by describing afterlives that resembled those evoked by the spiritists.[120] Kardec and Flammarion were the most prominent, however, and it is their work that became the basis for the contemporary spiritist movement.[121] Under their leadership spiritism developed into a public statement of the beliefs already seen at work in the séances on Jersey. Personal immortality, reincarnation on earth, and the transmigration of souls to other planets where they experienced moral progress or decline based upon their inclination and will were the key elements in spiritist cosmology. Kardec and Flammarion chose to emphasize certain features in their system, however, which distinguish their work from the previous loosely formulated Romantic tradition and from British and American spiritualism as well. These distinctions can help illuminate the changing features of French religion in the nineteenth century.

First, the spiritist movement of the 1850s appears to have retreated from the commitment to social progress evident in the first half of the century. The socialists (Esquiros, Fourier, Reynaud, Leroux) who speculated about the afterlife were inspired by a vision in which social progress remained a central concern, and they understood individual progress in the afterlife to be conditioned by the collective experience of the human race. Although Kardec retains a few references to social progress, he places more emphasis on the ways in which spiritist doctrines justify the fate of individuals in this world.[122] In the earlier period, the doctrine of immortality was consoling because it guaranteed that the individual would participate in the future glory for which he had worked. Spiritism in the 1850s looked backward as well as forward and saw earthly existence as expiation for personal imperfection. These later spiritists believed that human lives are not conditioned so much by social circumstances as by individual moral choices made in previous existences. Spiritism was able to gain the loyalty of some socialists, and it seems to have been especially popular among the working class of Lyon. Kardec found most of his recruits, however, among the middle class, a fact that he noted with pride and tried to use as an advertisement for the movement.[123]

Spiritism in the 1850s also took an ambiguous position on the material conditions of the afterlife. During the first half of the century, the afterlife was frequently described as a material as well as spiritual existence; influenced by Swedenborg, thinkers such as Fourier, Esquiros, and Cahagnet proposed that embodied selves would continue to experience physical sensations and even have sexual relations in their future existences. Kardec was also unable to imagine a self that was exclusively spiritual, but his conceptualization of the self involved a more complicated view of embodiment than that of his predecessors.

Kardec proposed that the individual in his earthly life consists of a physical body, a spiritual soul, and a third element that he called the *périsprit*, which was composed of an ethereal matter that mediated between the soul and the body.[124] This entity, an ancestor of the astral body that figures largely in the thought of Shirley MacLaine and her New Age colleagues, resembles the body and allows the self to continue to interact with earthly beings and other spirits. It was the périsprit that spiritists used to explain the ghostly apparitions and physical manifestations of the séances. The périsprit is asexual; in future reincarnations it can assume the body of either male or female, and the choice is an arbitrary one.[125] Furthermore, as the self continues to progress through the universe, it eventually is freed from the need to seek embodiment and survives as a combination of périsprit and soul. In the final stages of development, even the matter of the périsprit disappears, and all that remains is the spiritual soul.[126]

Kardec's formulation of the body-soul relationship suggests that he was torn between a vision in which the essential self resided in a spiritual soul and one that emphasized the importance of material continuity as the basis for personal identity. Caroline Bynum has shown how the concept of material continuity can be traced in philosophical and devotional writings of the Middle Ages, and she concludes that medieval Christianity, for all its "spirituality," retained a sense of self that was rooted in a permanent identity between the person and the physical body.[127] The Catholicism of the Counter-Reformation, and of the nineteenth century, took a harsh view of corporeality, which was seen as a source of temptation, sin, and corruption. But throughout this period the doctrine of the resurrection of the body paradoxically implied a positive view of the body as ultimately and necessarily a part of the self. Following the last judgment, soul and body would find each other and remain together for all eternity. In folk religious traditions as well the self was understood as being intrinsically related to the body, even after death. Spiritualists such as Cousin took a much more ethereal view of the afterlife and of the permanent self than is found in folk traditions or orthodox Christianity; but the writings of Swedenborg, the socialists, and the mesmerists suggest a continuing desire to envision the afterlife as a corporeal as well as spiritual existence. Kardec's formulation of the périsprit reveals a hesitant attitude toward the definition of matter and spirit that reflects these tensions. Like the spiritualists he imagines the possibility of a definitive break between body and soul, but the appeal of a concept of embodiment pulled him in the opposite direction. He believed that in the end a fully spiritual self is possible, but only after centuries of moral and spiritual development. Although Kardec's doctrine may not seem coherent or plausible from a contemporary perspective, it does illuminate a struggle over the conception of self that was being worked out within the systems of religious belief available in the nineteenth century.[128]

Finally, French spiritism is distinctive in its emphasis on the astronomical context of future lives and in its alienation from Christianity. In England psychology, biology, and physics all played a role in the debates surrounding the spiritualist movement, but in France it was the sidereal revolution—the growing realization that the universe included countless stars—that had the greatest impact on speculation about the afterlife.[129] To judge on the basis of Flammarion's experience, this focus may be due in part to the enduring predominance and clarity of the Catholic model of the next world. Although they debated the implications both of extraterrestrial life and spiritualist experiments, on the whole English Christians showed themselves able to accommodate themselves to these positions.[130] In France, however, where Christianity was expressed almost exclusively within the Catholic Church, there was less space available for debate and discussion about these questions. At the age of eighteen, when Flammarion began to ask himself about the location of Heaven, Hell, and Purgatory, the existence of which seemed incompatible with his knowledge of the universe, he found no one within the Church able effectively to address his questions.[131] Previous thinkers, including Fourier and Reynaud, had already speculated that the physical universe could be viewed as the site of future lives. Flammarion adopted this position as a means of reconciling his knowledge of the physical universe and his commitment to immortality, and his scientific expertise provided it with a legitimacy that worked to the advantage of the spiritist movement. In France, however, such a position required him to move away from the Church and from Christianity.[132]

Spiritism did not go uncontested during the Second Empire. Catholics such as the Marquis de Mirville claimed that the spirits were demons, while the newly formed association of French psychiatrists castigated the movement as the product of mental disease, immorality, and antisocial instincts.[133] The spiritists' attempt to claim legitimacy as scientists was challenged by positivists such as Emile Littré, and the movement suffered from public scandal in 1875 as a result of a successful prosecution of Kardec's follower, M. Leymarie. Leymarie was convicted of conspiring with a photographer, Buguet, to defraud the public by producing photographs of spirits standing behind the living relatives who came to their office on the boulevard Montmartre.[134] The professionalization of science and medicine that occurred late in the century, including Dr. Jean-Martin Charcot's research at Salpêtrière, which provided a naturalistic framework for hypnotic phenomena, further constrained spiritism. Even the loyalist Flammarion disavowed an early work supposedly written with the help of Galileo.[135] But Flammarion continued to believe in the possibility of communicating with the spirit world, and he was not alone. Even in the decades when positivism was fashionable the influential scientist Charles Richet, who was later to win a Nobel prize, continued to take spirit manifestations seriously.[136] Spiritism in France, as in England and the United States, never established itself as a fully legitimate science, but it has continued to attract public attention and considerable support. In a survey conducted in 1981, 22 percent of the French interviewed said that they believed in reincarnation.[137] The availability of this idea as a response to death for the contemporary French can be largely attributed to the spiritist movement of the nineteenth century.

How are we to interpret the evidence of spiritism in nineteenth-century France? Traditional lines of analysis are certainly a useful starting point. We can argue, with Oppenheim, Moore, and Ariès that, in an age marked by religious skepticism, the growing prestige of science, and greater affectivity between family members, spiritism provided scientific sanction for reassuring beliefs about the future of the self and the eternal solidarity of the family. A more hostile and functionally oriented analysis might stress the escapism implicit in spiritist practice and doctrine. Oppressed workers, and later a bored middle-class, sought relief and entertainment by imagining a world better than this one. From the perspective of the history of religion, spiritism illustrates the continuing spread of doubt about the afterworld preached by orthodox Christianity, whose God was willing to condemn people to eternal punishment for even momentary and trivial lapses.

Although all these approaches help us understand spiritism, I believe that they should be supplemented by applying some insights drawn from recent work in intellectual history. Influenced by linguistic theory and literary criticism, historians of ideas have questioned our reading of texts that can no longer be seen as yielding univocal and unambiguous meanings or as bearing an uncomplicated relationship to a nonlinguistic reality to which they refer.[138] Spiritist texts, in their attempt to describe a ghost world with the help of scientific language, and thereby solve once and for all profound metaphysical problems concerning the self and its destiny, seem to me especially appropriate for this kind of analysis.

Devotees of spiritism not only read the extensive publications produced by Kardec, Flammarion, and others. They also actively responded to them, and their own experiences became part of the spiritist literature. In his later years Flammarion's published works are increasingly taken up with the reports that he received from correspondents eager to share with him stories about ghosts, haunted houses, second sight, and telepathy.[139] Flammarion's audience was responding to an author who experimented with a number of genres,

including imaginative fiction, as vehicles for expressing his ideas
about death and human destiny. Flammarion was not the only writer
in the spiritist tradition drawn to fiction. Esquiros included a long
ghost story as a preface to his philosophical essay on the future life.[140]
Fourier's early writings, for all their seriousness, were presented as a
parody in which the truthful elements would be protected by a veil of
more absurd inventions that would draw the attention of critics.[141]

With this blurring of genres in mind, I would like to conclude with
the suggestion that spiritist texts can be understood if we associate
them with the *conte fantastique*, a literary form roughly equivalent to
the Victorian ghost story popular throughout the nineteenth century.
Literary critics who have grappled with defining this genre focus on
its combination of psychological realism and supernatural incident.
According to Pierre-Georges Castex, the fantastic is characterized by
"a brutal intrusion of mystery into the framework of real life."[142] For
Tzvetan Todorov the fantastic is "the hesitation experienced by someone who knows only natural laws when he confronts an event apparently supernatural."[143] Todorov's analysis is especially interesting: he
proposes that uncertainty is at the core of the fantastic; as soon as a
character can determine the exact nature of the experience, the story
ceases to be fantastic. Although the conte fantastique has a history of
its own, these general characteristics can be found in stories written
throughout the nineteenth century by authors including Charles
Nodier, Prosper Mérimée, Théophile Gautier, and Guy de Maupassant.[144] Of course, the stories of Poe, as translated by Baudelaire, also
fall within this genre.[145]

The fantastic element in many of these stories includes contact with
the dead, who are met in a dreamlike state. In its classic form, as
represented by Gautier's "La Cafetière," a young man joins a party of
ghosts who descend from their pictures in the bedroom that he occupies at a friend's house. He dances with and falls in love with one of
them, a young woman named Angela, who then disappears as the
morning light comes through the windows. After the young man is
awakened, he passes off his experience as an illusion, then begins to
sketch aimlessly at breakfast. His friend identifies the sketch as his
sister, who died two years previously.[146] The appeal of this conte fantastique rests on its ability to combine the experience of belief and
doubt in contemplating death and the afterlife. But the choice of a
genre that is explicitly imaginative creates a distance between the
reader and this experience; the possibility of an afterlife, and of contact with the dead, is implicitly denied by being expressed in a story
that is invented. Many spiritist texts, especially Kardec's, promise a
more direct experience of the afterworld. Kardec also leaves room for

doubt, however, by noting inconsistencies in the spirit messages and looking to the future for the confirmation that will eliminate the skepticism evoked by his doctrines. Flammarion is even more willing to accept uncertainty, as is suggested in the titles of his works, which refer to the infinite, the unknown, and the mysterious.[147] Hugo's hesitancy to publish the results of the Jersey séances resonates with Flammarion's implicit acknowledgement that, despite their volume and overt self-confidence, his writings were unable to uncover the secrets of the universe.

A similar ambiguity can be observed in the Davenport performances. Critics made a particular point of comparing the tricks of the Davenports with those performed by magicians who claimed no supernatural powers, a position repeated by skeptics in subsequent cases in France and elsewhere. This skeptical posture, and the evidence it employed, can help undermine supernaturalist claims, but it passes over the question of what drew audiences to the performances of both mediums and magicians and assumes that a sharp distinction existed between the two in the minds of audiences. Was this in fact the case? Were those who attended the shows of Robin, and later Houdin, drawn exclusively because they admired the art that these men employed in making guitars strum and tambourines sound without any apparent physical action on their part? We know that in the eighteenth century performers in the fairs of Paris still played on doubts that people had about the explanations for their magical acts.[148] And even if the audience assumed that the performers were using "natural" means, what accounts for their fascination with the pretense that the person in fact responsible for the trick could not be seen to have done anything? The famous relationship between Arthur Conan Doyle and the American magician Houdini (who took his name from the French conjurer Houdin) shows us that someone convinced of the mediumistic powers of a performer can deny even the explicit disavowal of such powers by the performer. I am willing to accept the skeptical argument that natural means were used in the performances of both mediums and magicians, but the appeal of these acts may nonetheless be in part the result of an audience's desire to contemplate, within the context of a performance, the possibility of spiritual reality.

We will never know for sure what went on in the minds of the readers of contes fantastiques and of spiritist literature, nor can we be certain of the attitudes of the audiences that attended public séances and magic shows. But we do know that many French men and women were drawn to these in an age of declining religious practice and public discussion about the fate of the self after death. These texts and performances suggest an odd psychological state, in which artist and audience agree to consider immortality, the afterlife, and relations with the beyond in carefully limited circumstances (in the pages of a book, in a theater, or at the movies) that I take as characteristically modern.

PART THREE

The Material Culture of Death

Chapter Five

FROM CHURCHYARD TO CEMETERY

VISITORS to Paris interested in seeing the most famous sites of the capital generally include Père Lachaise cemetery on their itinerary. Maps are available at shops in the neighborhood for the tourists interested in finding the tombs of Balzac, Michelet, Bizet, and all the other great writers, artists, and musicians who are buried there. Edith Piaf's tomb remains a popular site, and rock cultists have made Jim Morrison's grave into a shrine that draws thousands every year. Political as well as cultural history is commemorated in Père Lachaise; the *mur des Fédérés*, the wall where hundreds of communards were shot and then buried in a mass grave, is the scene each year of memorial services in late May organized by a variety of socialist and labor organizations. Communards who survived the defeat of 1871, as well as prominent socialists and communists from the twentieth century, have chosen this area for their tombs. The victims of Dachau and other concentration camps have their memorials as well, not far from the mur des Fédérés.[1]

Parisians and tourists stroll the tree-lined *allées* of Père Lachaise, looking at the tombs which are now packed closely together, reading the inscriptions, and reflecting on the dead. The visit to the cemetery is, as Philippe Ariès indicated, a crucial ritual for the French, and even though some commentators have expressed concern about declining interest, on the whole they remain remarkably devoted to their dead. The creation of the modern cemetery and the inculcation of a devout atmosphere toward those who lie there are among the most important innovations that occurred in the nineteenth-century cult of the dead. Contemporary visitors might be surprised to learn, however, that the current mood of quiet reflection that characterizes Père Lachaise, and provincial cemeteries as well, was not a natural phenomenon but one that had to be constructed in a frequently troubled physical and emotional environment. The material evidence from cemeteries provides us with direct and moving testimony, but—as valuable as tombs and epitaphs are—it would be misleading to rely exclusively on them to tell us about the sentiments that people of the past had toward their dead. The institutional history of cemeteries, the debates and decisions about where to build them and how to divide their internal space, are a necessary context for interpreting the physical evidence available to visitors to Père Lachaise. When placed in their historical context, cemeteries are a privileged site for examining the cultural values that both divided and linked the French in the nineteenth century.

THE REVOLUTIONARY CRISIS

For reformers of the revolutionary era, the cemeteries inherited from the eighteenth century were unhealthy enclaves of death and disease. Radicals associated them with the superstitions of Christianity and the privileges accorded wealth and rank during the ancien régime, all of which made them offensive to the egalitarian and rationalist sentiments that prevailed in the early 1790s. As we saw in the last chapter, cemeteries figured in the plans of dechristianizers such as Joseph Fouché, who called for a simple burial for all citizens and the removal of religious symbols from cemeteries, which would now announce through a sign placed at their entrances "Death Is an Eternal Sleep."[2] Cemeteries underwent dramatic changes during the revolutionary era, but the reformist ideals of decency and simplicity articulated by Fouché were not always honored. The most famous example of the desecration of the dead occurred at St. Denis, the abbey just outside Paris that housed the remains of the French kings. In August and October of 1793, the royal monuments were destroyed and their remains thrown into a common grave. The corpse of Henri IV was abused for two days by the crowd, and the skull of Saint Louis was brandished by Citizen Pollart, a former Benedictine, in a speech before the Convention.[3] Less dramatic, but perhaps more disturbing, was the condition of cemeteries that served ordinary citizens. Through a decree of 2 November 1789 the government had confiscated ecclesiastical property, and later decisions confirmed that city officials rather than the clergy and parish councils were now in charge of cemeteries.[4] Anaxagoras Chaumette, the prosecutor of Paris during the Terror and like Fouché an advocate of dechristianized cemeteries, called on Paris to use its authority to create burial places that would inspire "tender feelings" and "sweeter, more philanthropic ideas."[5] In 1795, however, two years after Chaumette's appeal, the pamphleteer Gaspard Delamalle described the Parisian cemetery where his mother was buried as a "narrow plot encumbered in the middle by an enormous pile of earth and debris bordered by a path covered with a foot of mud over which a wretched plank had been laid to provide a means of access."[6]

The Thermidorian reaction of 1794 brought with it a wave of criticism of the cemeteries as managed by the previous revolutionary regime. In pamphlets and then in legislation the French called for cemeteries that would meet the hygienic and aesthetic standards that they felt were appropriate for the cult of the dead. About religion, and especially about Christianity, the critics were less certain, but by the turn of the century there was a consensus that the state must tolerate, even if it did not encourage, the expression of Christian sentiments and doctrines in the cemeteries.

The reforms discussed in the late 1790s were not merely a reaction against revolutionary abuses. They were based on debates and proposals about cemeteries that had begun early in the eighteenth century and that continued through the revolutionary period. The criticism of cemeteries during the Enlightenment was based above all on the increasing anxiety that reformers felt about the threat to public health posed by the presence of decaying corpses in the churches and churchyards where the living met and sometimes worked. By the 1740s these concerns began to produce proposals that cemeteries be moved *extra muros*. The typical cemetery until this time had been either next to or near the parish church that it served, but now reformers called for their removal outside the city walls, where the living would be protected from the noxious odors believed to carry disease and death. In 1763 the Parlement of Paris took an active role by ordering an inquest into the condition of Parisian cemeteries. Two years later the Parlement prohibited all burials in churches and called for the removal of parish cemeteries from the city. For the rest of the century reformers reported a number of cases in which the opening of common graves released gases that sickened and sometimes killed those in the vicinity. The king responded with a decree in 1776 that extended the removal of cemeteries to the entire nation. By the 1780s urban landscapes were being reshaped as old cemeteries were closed and new ones opened that satisfied the desire for the separation of the living and the dead.[7]

As all the historians who have described this process have noted, the hygienic arguments used to justify the transferring (*translation*) of cemeteries are not sufficient to explain a decision so rich in cultural significance. The removal of cemeteries reflects not only concerns about public health but also a new understanding of the appropriate relationship between the living and the dead. In competitions sponsored by the Royal Academy and then by the Institut National, artists and architects experimented with a number of designs that suggest this cultural shift. For some the cemetery offered the opportunity to commemorate the dead, whose heroic achievements, it was felt, should be honored with magnificent tombs. Others took a more austere view and proposed geometrically precise plans that would replicate the social hierarchy. By the end of the century a model derived from English landscape architecture was becoming fashionable, and cemetery design began to reflect a new understanding of nature as a regenerative force. Now the appropriate setting for tombs was seen to be an area of trees and serpentine walks, which would provoke recollection and contemplation that would be morally beneficial. These ideas were developed and combined in a number of ways, but they were linked in their rejection of the macabre imagery that had been central to the Christian presentation of death since the Middle Ages. The fascination of the baroque era with skeletons and skulls that would remind people of their mortality and of the need to prepare for the next world was no longer considered appropriate.

Enlightenment reformers sought to remove cemeteries from urban areas and to design them according to fashions that emphasized the contemplation of heroic deeds and natural sublimity rather than the physical remains of the dead. These ideals were shared by leaders of the revolution, who acted to transfer control of cemeteries from churches to communes.[8] The reforms of Fouché and Chaumette in 1793, which resulted in the destruction of Christian monuments as vestiges of "superstition," were balanced by measures to establish a national cult of the dead based on the enshrinement of heroes in the Pantheon.[9] Despite these efforts, by the conclusion of the Terror, there is already substantial evidence that public opinion was appalled by the indifference to the dead observed in the neglect of cemeteries. Delamalle's description of the cemetery where his mother was buried was repeated by many others, including those who could influence legislation. Abbé Jacques-Michel Coupé, a curé from Sermaize who became a member of the Legislative Assembly, the Convention, and the Council of Five Hundred, called in 1796 for cemeteries that would no longer appear "repulsive and desolate. We owe this decency to our friends, to our relatives, to ourselves: it is the resting place of virtuous men."[10] In the same year P. B. F. Bontoux, a magistrate from the Hautes-Alpes and also a member of the Council of Five Hundred, condemned the revolutionary excess that had led Fouché to raise the sign "Death Is an Eternal Sleep" over cemeteries. He associated the lack of respect for the dead displayed by the leaders of the Terror with their murderous tyranny: "They had no more regard for the dead than piety for the living."[11]

Coupé, Bontoux, and their colleagues were disturbed by the condition of cemeteries, and they associated the negligence that they observed with a general moral crisis. Their recommendations reflect some of the debates about the meaning of death that we reviewed in the previous chapter—debates that plagued civil officials throughout the nineteenth century. According to Coupé, death could be seen philosophically as "a necessary end, an unconscious sleep, a light that goes out; the body returns to the elements, matter passes into other combinations and perpetually transforms itself." Understood from "its moral aspect," however, death took on a wholly different meaning; it is "the supreme power which extends its severe hand over society."[12] This moral significance led previous societies to venerate their dead, who were buried with dignity and remembered with the help of monuments.

The legislator faced with these different views could not afford to adopt the materialist perspective, for this would offend the moral sensibilities of the people and put the social order at risk, as happened during the Terror. The role of the legislator was to strike at those institutions that encouraged tyranny but not to "triumph over the invincible power of the imagination, to tear from the heart illusions that are sweet, consoling, and never pernicious." The term "illusion" occurs repeatedly in both Bontoux's and Coupé's discussion of the cult of the dead that they sought to encourage.[13] These legislators were not convinced that the materialist position that regarded death as a morally neutral biological event was false, but prudence and social utility required that they encourage people to take a more hopeful view. In a pamphlet published in 1801 Coupé made the connection linking the cult of the dead, religion, and morality more explicit: "In the end philosophy abandons man to death, and shows him only nothingness; and it is there that popular opinion has placed the consolation of a new life, and this admirable power of morality."[14]

Popular opinion demanded the consolation of "a new life," and the prudent legislator, even if personally skeptical, had to respond in order to protect the moral standards that underlay the social order. The new system of pompes funèbres to be described in chapters 6 and 7 was one element in the new cult of the dead that began to emerge in the 1790s; cemeteries were the other preoccupation. The public-health considerations prominent in the eighteenth century were still present, but Napoleon and his legislators also hoped to create cemeteries that would allow people to express the hopeful illusions that most of them still had about death. The enabling legislation for this task was included in the decree of 23 prairial, year XII (1804).

The decree of 23 prairial confirmed a number of decisions made during the previous half century. Burials in churches were prohibited, and cemeteries were to be established outside of towns. Scientific theory of the time maintained that cemeteries threatened public health because of the emanations of "fixed air" released from the dead.[15] To deal with this problem legislators called for cemeteries to be placed on elevated ground and exposed to the north, so that cleansing winds would carry away the morbid vapors. After an old cemetery had been closed, it was to be untouched for five years. Then it could be rented by the city, but only for gardening; no construction was to be allowed on the site. All these provisions reflected the public-health concerns that had emerged in the eighteenth century, but other articles revealed a concern for encouraging the cult of the dead. The distance from town, for example, could be as little as thirty-five to forty meters; the dead were to be removed, but not so far away as to make regular visits difficult. Unlike some of the earlier proposals, the decree of 23 prairial eliminated the common graves typical of the ancien régime, in which the dead were piled on top of one another. Instead, each individual was to have his own space, one and one-half to two meters down, separated from his neighbor by twenty to thirty centimeters on the sides and thirty to fifty centimeters at the head and feet. Such a provision was crucial for establishing the direct and intimate relationship between the living and the dead, which was now seen as essential for public morality. Finally, families and friends were permitted to decorate the tombs of their dead, a departure from the revolutionary policy that saw funeral monuments as a symbol of human vanity and a violation of the spirit of equality.

The application of the decree of 23 prairial created the setting for the visits to the cemetery that were central rituals in nineteenth-century French family life. Although Philippe Ariès noted the importance of this law, he never explored the administrative and religious struggles that surrounded its implementation. The problems involved in carrying out the law should not be seen, however, as mere background for a study of the cult of the dead. The construction and management of cemeteries constitute an essential element in the material culture of death, and therefore of French culture in general during the nineteenth century.

THE DISPLACEMENT OF THE DEAD

For most of the nineteenth century, officials of the central government insisted on the dangers of the proximity of the living and the dead. Ministers and prefects exerted constant pressure on municipal councils to see that they honored the provisions of the law enforcing this separation. Local officials, however, although they sometimes shared the concerns of the Parisian ministries, were not always able and willing to comply with the law. Changes occurred, and especially in the larger cities of France the removal of cemeteries was substantially achieved by the middle of the century. But this process involved difficult negotiations between the interested parties; what may have seemed clear to the legislators of 1804 was frequently ambiguous to the city councilors, clergy, and citizens confronted with the challenge of removing the dead from their previous resting places. The problem was complicated by continuing urban expansion which caught up with the cemeteries. New burial grounds thought adequate early in the century invariably proved too small, and the spread of cities frequently reincorporated them within city walls. In the countryside the transferring of cemeteries was more openly resisted, a tactic whose success is still evident in the number of churchyards that have managed to survive. By the end of the century, resistance to another round of transferrals had spread to the cities and was reinforced by advances in medical science that challenged the belief in dangerous emanations from cemeteries. Nevertheless, public officials still had to deal with the problem of finding places for the dead and of managing the corpses in the face of serious financial and religious pressures.

By virtue of its size and influence Paris is the city whose cemeteries have drawn the most attention from previous historians. Through the work of Richard Etlin we now have a clear picture of the discussions that led to the creation of new cemeteries in Paris in the first quarter of the nineteenth century. In 1801, even before the decree of 23 prairial, the prefect Nicolas Frochot had called for the closing of the current cemeteries in favor of three new sites outside the walls to the north, east, and south of the city.[16] The most famous of these, Père Lachaise, to the east of the city, was opened in 1804 and within a few years had become a major attraction both for Parisians and foreign visitors. The cemetery of Montparnasse was opened for the southern arrondissements in 1824, and Montmartre in the north was opened in 1825.[17]

Although the citizens of some neighborhoods complained about the distance that they would now have to travel, the displacement of Parisian cemeteries was generally uncontroversial, in part because of the evil reputation acquired by the parish cemeteries during the revolutionary era. Following the decision to close the cemetery of Saints Innocents in 1780, the new cemeteries opened by the city were still within residential areas, and burials continued to occur in a number of parish cemeteries as well. The continued presence of the dead within the city became especially troublesome during the Terror, when citizens complained of the polluting effects of the corpses of those guillotined. The executed added only very few to the total number of those buried. Nevertheless, people who lived near the cemeteries attached to the church of la Madeleine and the parc Monceau feared epidemics—a complaint that Michelet has identified as part of the *"imagination populaire."*[18] The opening of Père Lachaise in 1804, which allowed the government to close a number of cemeteries, was therefore welcomed by Parisians anxious to put behind them memories of crowded graves and the thoughts of the Terror that they evoked.

Elsewhere in France, however, the movement to new cemeteries did not always proceed so smoothly. In a number of cities—including Nantes, Tours, Rouen, Orléans, Marseille, and Angers—the process of reform was more protracted than in Paris, a fact that reveals social pressures opposed to as well as in favor of the displacement of cemeteries. The case of Angers illustrates the ways in which expense and bureaucratic inertia combined with a desire to live in close proximity to the dead to delay implementation of the reform for almost half a century.[19]

In the eighteenth century Angers was served by ten cemeteries within the city walls, most of them bordering churches. Like Paris, the city responded to the decree of 1776 by closing and consolidating cemeteries, which had been reduced to five by the beginning of the nineteenth century.[20] This first stage of translation, however, did not produce burial grounds whose size and distance from the city accorded with the Napoleonic reform of 23 prairial (1804). In the early nineteenth century, complaints about overcrowded and unhealthy cemeteries similar to those heard in Paris were common. City officials in a report of 1808 tried to claim that the cemeteries were outside the city, but three of them were actually within thirty meters of the nearest building; and individuals were living in houses only fifteen meters from the cemetery of St. Laud, a neighborhood incorporated into the city during the revolutionary era.[21]

Despite the cemeteries opened by the city administration in the 1780s, then, the Napoleonic reform of 1804 mandated a second set of translations twenty years later. For the western sector of Angers (commonly referred to as "la Doutre"), on the right bank of the Maine, this additional move was relatively unproblematic. Primarily a working-class neighborhood with a concentration of textile and clothing workers, la Doutre represented one-third of the population of Angers, but one-half of the deaths in the city occurred there.[22] The city had closed the two cemeteries that served the hospital and the parishes of this quarter in the 1780s and replaced them with the single cemetery of Guinefolle, just outside the city walls. By 1808, however, the city engineer reported to the city council that Guinefolle was too close to houses in the outlying neighborhood of Saint-Lazare, that the earth was "hard, rocky, and damp," and that it was surrounded by swampy areas that gave off dangerous vapors.[23] The poor conditions of the site and its proximity to the town made it a scandal for some inhabitants, one of whom complained that children from Saint-Lazare played catch with the bones of the dead.[24] In 1810 the city authorized the purchase of land farther from Saint-Lazare, and the Cemetery of the West was opened in 1813. Enlarged on several occasions, this site remains one of the two principal cemeteries of Angers.

The creation of the Cemetery of the East, which still serves the older and more fashionable neighborhoods on the left bank of the Maine, proved much more difficult. Four cemeteries served this area at the time of the Napoleonic reform of 1804. Complaints about these sites were already common, but the legislation of 23 prairial gave critics an additional reason for insisting on changes. The cemetery of St. Laud was the first to draw the attention of both citizens and officials. Already in 1802 the prefect warned the mayor that the "femme Trouillard's" practice of pasturing her animals in the cemetery showed "lack of respect for the ashes and memory of the dead which cannot be tolerated in a civilized society."[25] Three years later the prefect reported to the mayor that the grave diggers of St. Laud were known to exhume the dead in order to steal and sell the boards of their coffins and their cloth shrouds.[26] This lack of respect for the dead was not the principal concern of the sixteen citizens from the neighborhood who submitted a petition to the prefect in 1805.[27] For them, the issue was one of public health; during the summer the air around the cemetery was so foul that they were unable to open their windows. These petitioners were well informed; they cited both the 1776 decree and the recent law of 23 prairial in calling for the closing of St. Laud, the presence of which threatened the city with an epidemic. After a second petition was sent to the municipal council in 1808, action was finally taken, and the cemetery was closed in 1809.[28]

A few years later, in 1818, similar complaints led to the closing of the cemetery La Madeleine. Eliminating these two sites was no solution to the problem of overcrowding, however, because the city did not move to create a new cemetery. It simply ordered that those formerly buried in St. Laud and La Madeleine now be buried in the cemetery known as le Clon, which already received the dead from a number of other parishes. By the 1820s complaints about the inadequacy of le Clon and the other remaining cemetery, St. Michel, were being received by the mayor, the prefect, and the minister of the interior. In 1823 the curé of the cathedral parish of St. Maurice wrote that grave diggers in le Clon were turning up partially decomposed bodies, and that the earth was releasing *miasmes fétides*.[29] The city responded by shifting one parish from le Clon to the cemetery of the faubourg St. Michel, but this only served to anger those who lived in that neighborhood, some of whom were agitating about the fact that their cemetery was also overcrowded and should be closed.[30]

Throughout the first two decades of the nineteenth century, Angevin city officials attempted to solve the problem of providing a decent burial ground on the left bank by transferring the dead among existing cemeteries. Despite citizens' complaints and the questionable legality of the current cemeteries, they resisted purchasing land for a new cemetery until well into the 1830s. This hesitancy was the result of practical difficulties and cultural prejudices that shaped the cult of the dead during the first third of the century, both in Angers and in other provincial cities.

The most obvious impediment to reform was the expense of purchasing and developing the land needed for a new cemetery. The law of 23 prairial required local administrators to create spacious cemeteries separated from their cities, but there was no provision for financial help for this move. In Angers land on the right bank was relatively inexpensive; it cost the city only 2,202 francs for the original site of the Cemetery of the West. On the left bank to the east, however, prices were almost twice as high, making it much more difficult for the city to find affordable space for burials.[31] In Marseille complaints about overcrowding and respect for the dead had been common since the late eighteenth century; stories circulated about dogs carrying off human bones and (as in Angers) of children playing catch with skulls. But despite a plan in 1794 that called for three new cemeteries, the city continued to use the overburdened parish churchyards until 1819, when the new site of Saint-Charles was opened. According to Régis Bertrand, the "essential obstacle" to reform during this period was the high price demanded by the owners of the prospective cemetery grounds.[32]

Cost was not the only consideration deterring city officials in Angers and elsewhere. Not everyone who lived near the cemetery of St. Michel thought that it was dangerous, and there is some evidence that complaints came from only a minority of the inhabitants. The clergy of the parishes of St. Serge and Notre Dame which used St. Michel responded to a petition of 1823 by arguing that many of their parishioners had several family members buried there and would be "extremely distressed" by the closing of the cemetery.[33] Elsewhere such attachments had already been expressed with vehemence, and sometimes with violence. In Lille and Cambrai riots broke out in 1779 and 1786 when the municipal officers attempted to close parish cemeteries in favor of sites that complied with the royal ordinance of 1776.[34] In country parishes such sentiments became an important argument against the application of the law of 23 prairial. Angevins may have been slower to defend their traditional graves, but by 1829 fifty-eight inhabitants of St. Serge and Notre Dame opposed the closing of St. Michel, claiming that the vast majority of the neighborhood sided with them.[35]

Finally, city officials suspected some of the motives of the plaintiffs who draped themselves in the law of 23 prairial and the defense of public health. Defenders of the status quo pointed out that a M. Danger, one of the organizers of the petition opposing St. Michel, had intentionally built his house next to the cemetery expecting that it would someday be closed and then made available to him as a garden.[36]

Despite the opposition to change, by 1830 city officials were increasingly sensitive to arguments in favor of closing the cemetery. The population of Angers, which had held at about 30,000 for most of the revolutionary era, began to grow in the 1820s—a point noted by petitioners who argued that urban cemeteries hindered new construction.[37] The prefect, acting under instructions from the minister of the interior, periodically raised the issue with the mayor; and although most of these interventions were polite, the repeated call for the city to comply with the law increased the pressure on city officials.[38] Even after agreeing to close the cemetery of St. Michel in 1829, the city continued to move slowly, citing the high cost of land as a reason for its continued procrastination. Only after the cholera epidemic of 1832 did public officials develop the will to create a larger and healthier cemetery.

Cholera struck Angers in May of 1832 and again in December of 1833, taking close to five hundred lives and frightening the survivors by the horror of its symptoms and the rapidity with which it killed.[39] In June of 1832, at the height of the epidemic, the citizens of faubourg St. Michel submitted a final petition reminding the city of the condemnation of their cemetery in 1829. The continued use of the restricted site forced grave diggers to reopen common graves every two to three years, which released "a cadaverous gas, a very subtle poison: of all the emanations which contaminate the air and menace the health of the inhabitants, there is certainly none more dangerous than those which are exhaled by the graves of the dead."[40]

As had been the case since the eighteenth century, the fear of infection was a major consideration in the closing of an urban cemetery. Mayor Auguste Giraud referred to the "noxious miasmas" from the current sites in his favorable report on a proposal for a new cemetery submitted by a commission of the city council in 1834.[41] Fears related to cholera may have been the immediate grounds for the decision to construct a new cemetery; but the reports of the city council in the

1830s also indicate that public sensibilities were offended by the "humiliation into which the cult of the dead has fallen," and the mayor referred to the "sad and painful spectacle of seeing the remains of corpses torn from the earth before it has had time to consume them."[42] Some citizens had been complaining about the unearthing of partially decomposed bodies since the beginning of the century, but it was only in the 1830s that public opinion and official will led to action.

It would be a mistake to draw too sharp a contrast between the hesitancy of the first third of the century and the implementation of reform in the 1830s. The owners of the property where the new cemetery was to be constructed had to be approached and prices negotiated. Public hearings were held at which some of the standard complaints about the proximity of the new site to houses and the loss of access to family graves were voiced.[43] The property had to be landscaped with trees and curving roads: the Cemetery of the East was to be a garden, an up-to-date showplace worthy of a growing provincial capital, modeled on Père Lachaise, which had become famous throughout France by the 1830s. It was over a decade before the land was acquired and developed; the first burial in the Cemetery of the East did not take place until 1848. From that time on, however, it became a center of social and religious life. The most important families chose to be buried there and raised impressive monuments to themselves that still stand, although they are now increasingly in disrepair. The continued growth of the town, and other developments within the cult of the dead, led the city to expand the cemetery on several occasions, but no further *translations* have occurred; the Cemetery of the East that opened in 1848 remains the principal burial ground of Angers.

During the first half of the nineteenth century the displacement of urban cemeteries resulted in a restructuring of the geography of relations between the living and the dead. In the small towns of the French countryside, however, churchyards were much more likely to survive. This contrast was initially encouraged by the government, which wrote into the law of 23 prairial that its provisions were designed only for "cities and towns" ("*villes et bourgs*"). Churchyards were perceived as posing a threat in crowded cities but not in communities of fewer than two thousand. In 1843 this discrepancy was no longer acceptable, and a royal decree extended the law to all communes, "thus eliminating a cause of embarrassment, or at least uncertainty, concerning the application of this measure to communes that are neither *villes* or *bourgs*."[44] From this point on it was technically illegal for any municipality to tolerate the existence of the dead within thirty-five to forty meters of its residents, but village officials, like their urban colleagues, did not act quickly to implement the reform. In fact, in some cases when they tried to move the dead they were prevented by a public attached to their old cemeteries and supported by the local clergy. Some of the murmurings heard in Angers were loudly and forcefully articulated elsewhere. Opposition to new cemeteries was not uniform, however, and many communes did move their cemeteries outside of town during the nineteenth century. But by the second half of the century resistance to *translation* was vigorous, and a new image of the cemetery that allowed it a place within the town had emerged. This image in turn affected the attitudes of city dwellers, including those of Paris, and made them anxious to retain their cemeteries even as cities grew around them.

The attachment to traditional practices can be seen in the early years of the nineteenth century in the continuing attempt by some individuals to be buried inside the parish church, a practice prohibited by the law of 23 prairial. A circular letter from the prefect of Orne to all the mayors of his department in 1804 urged them to enforce the provision of the law of 23 prairial against burial in churches, "a dangerous and abusive custom still common in many places."[45] During the period of the Empire and the Restoration exceptions to the law were apparently frequent, as aristocrats, local notables, and curés sought privileged treatment.[46] If special permission for such a burial was not granted, tense confrontations between the state and the village could occur. When the abbé Regnier, the curé of Pouancé (Maine-et-Loire) was buried in his parish church in 1827, the subprefect called on the gendarmes to transfer the body to the churchyard. In his report the lieutenant who oversaw this operation described how a sullen crowd, almost the entire town, observed the exhumation that took place at midnight. The gendarmes were forced to break into the church, whose lock had been jammed with stones, and the reburial was completed by four in the morning. Throughout the whole process the inhabitants murmured against the exhumation, "but they were held in check by the presence of the gendarmerie."[47]

The establishment of the July Monarchy in 1830 led to a more stringent application of the law excluding the dead from churches. In December of 1831 the minister of religion Montalivet wrote to the prefects to remind them that the decree of 23 prairial forbade all burials in churches. Only bishops and archbishops were exempt from this provision; families with private chapels and curés, who were making increasing numbers of special requests, were explicitly denied access to churches, and violators of this provision were to be prosecuted.[48] Philippe Ariès has observed the erosion of the tradition of burial *ad sanctos*, within the church, starting in the late seventeenth century.[49] During the Restoration (1815–1830), as part of the general reaction against the irreligiosity of the Enlightenment, there seems to have been a brief countertrend, one that indicates the uneven presence of new attitudes about the appropriate distance to be maintained between the living and the dead.

Villagers such as those of Pouancé might look on threateningly as the gendarmes removed the body of their curé from the parish church; they were even more likely to resist the translation of their burial ground, a move that many found both costly and offensive. This is not to say that churchyards were not replaced by cemeteries; as early as 1804 roughly one-third of the communes of Calvados, in Normandy, had already isolated their cemeteries.[50] During the nineteenth century as many as three-fourths of the cemeteries in the department of Ain, in the southeast, were moved to sites outside of towns.[51] But by the 1830s complaints about the construction of new cemeteries were already common. The prefect from the Pyrénées-Orientales wrote the minister of religion in 1832 that despite pressure from the government there was "strong opposition" to the removal of cemeteries, and that "mayors and city councils have withdrawn into a deep silence, and nothing has changed." In 1838 the bishop from Vosges wrote the minister that he found during his pastoral visits "general irritation" about the policy of moving cemeteries.[52] In his study of the five departments of the southern Massif Central, P. M. Jones concluded that "nothing caused more resentment and indignation than attempts to close, move or in any way alter the spatial organization of burial grounds."[53] The famous cemetery displayed in Courbet's painting *Burial at Ornans* was opened in 1848 only after thirty-three years of bitter argument among the citizens of Ornans about the translation.[54]

People resisted the closing of their cemeteries because of their strong attachments to the remains of their ancestors. As the bishop of St. Flour wrote in a confidential letter to the minister of religion in 1822, "These mountain people cleave to the ashes of their fathers; they cleave to the place where they rest."[55] The inhabitants of the villages of Port-Gévrieux and Mas-Durand (Ain) wrote their bishop in 1853 to protest the transfer of their burial ground to a neighboring parish, asking that they be allowed to "continue to fulfill in peace our duties, and to have one day the hope of sleeping next to the bones of our fathers, without experiencing the fear of being moved elsewhere."[56] As P. M. Jones has written, these sentiments of filial loyalty were bound up with a sense of community; cemeteries were emblems of family and local identity that allowed people to observe and recall their continuity through time. Cemeteries were a privileged "memory place" that embodied the deeply felt ties holding together families, neighborhoods, and villages.[57]

We will learn more about the content and nature of these ties when we study the internal arrangements, decorations, and epitaphs that are found in nineteenth-century cemeteries. What is evident at this point is that by the middle of the century such attitudes were clearly influencing debates and decisions about the location of burial grounds. The clergy were quick to perceive and respond to these feelings, and at times they may even have played a crucial role in articulating them and organizing dissent. In the village of Chavaroux (Puy-de-Dôme) the plans for a new cemetery were unopposed (at least according to the local anticlerical paper) until the curé attacked the idea with an appeal that linked filial and religious devotion:

> Inhabitants of Chavaroux, so distinguished by your piety . . . according to the Charter you have the right to be buried where it seems right to you. . . . In forcing you to be buried in the new cemetery, they want you to abandon your religion. You will be constrained by armed force and the gendarmerie. Will you allow them to rebury your fathers with the same wagons used to cart dung?[58]

By the second half of the century even some clergy with a reputation as liberals were arguing that the removal of cemeteries was an impious act. Félix Dupanloup, the bishop of Orléans, feared that anticlericals intended to replace churchyards with public squares. "People will come to dance, he wrote in 1861, where once they prayed for the dead."[59] For the vitriolic Monseigneur Jean-Joseph Gaume, writing in the 1870s, arguments about public health were "merely an excuse." The real motives for moving cemeteries were "to rebuke the Church; to lessen, if not to entirely extinguish, devotion for the dead; to blot out remembrance of their own last end; to break the golden chains that bind together the children of the Church on both sides of the grave."[60]

Despite Gaume's rhetoric, there were still occasions when the clergy acknowledged that public health required the removal of a cemetery. When Monseigneur Bourret, the bishop of Rodez, visited the village of Verrières in 1876 he mentioned in passing that the churchyard might soon have to be moved because of the "humidity" it communicated to the church. This comment provoked a riot in which the crowd left the church, turned the *arcs de triomphe* raised in the bishop's honor into barricades, and pushed a cart against the doors to prevent him from leaving. Bishop Bourret claimed later that he did not know that the mayor and curé had recently agreed to move the cemetery, a decision that had obviously agitated the villagers. Aside from the passion with which people defended their cemetery, this incident also shows the clergy cooperating in a policy of displacement.[61] The advice column in the weekly *The Friend of the Clergy* (*L'Ami du clergé*), in which editors responded to questions from parish priests, was sympathetic to clerical complaints about mayoral pretensions regarding cemeteries but also reminded correspondents of the law that required *translation*, and of their obligation to comply with it.[62]

By the end of the nineteenth century many rural cemeteries had followed the pattern observed earlier in urban areas. Protests and delays for a variety of economic and religious motives were overcome, and cemeteries replaced churchyards. But some churchyards nonetheless remained (and still do) to remind people of an older pattern of intimacy between the living and the dead. The contestation over and survival of churchyards reveal an attitude that challenged the agenda of Enlightenment reformers. As cities and towns continued to grow during the second half of the nineteenth century, a renewed respect for the sanctity of burial places seems to have spread to urban areas as well. Administrators were increasingly faced with cemeteries out of compliance with the law; but rather than repeat the process of transferral many settled for compromises, the results of which are still evident in contemporary France.

This new acceptance of proximity of the living and the dead can be seen clearly in the history of Paris. The population explosion in the capital that began at the turn of the century continued during the Second Empire and the Third Republic; already in the 1850s Père Lachaise, Montmartre, and Montparnasse were filling up, and in 1863 the prefect Baron Haussmann asked the city council to begin searching for a new burial ground.[63] The physical expansion of the city complicated the problem because as neighborhoods spread, houses gradually surrounded cemeteries that were intended to be separated from residential areas. Victor Norbert's painting of Paris, done in 1855 from sketches made during balloon ascensions, clearly shows the cemetery of Montparnasse, which is divided into twelve squares, only half of which were apparently filled at the time. Development of the surrounding neighborhood was well under way, however, and construction of buildings had already begun on the border of the cemetery.[64] When the boundaries of Paris were enlarged in 1859 to accommodate this urban spread the conseil d'état decided that the current cemeteries could still operate, despite the prohibition in the law of 23 prairial.[65] To deal with what they considered a threat to public health, Haussmann and the city council announced in 1867 plans for a new cemetery at Méry-sur-Oise, thirteen miles northwest of Paris.[66] But a public outcry followed this proposal, one that contributed eventually to Haussmann's dismissal. In the 1870s city officials opened new cemeteries near the city at Ivry and Saint-Ouen, but these were understood to provide only a respite, and the old idea of Méry-sur-Oise was also reconsidered.[67] Opposition continued, however, and public statements by both Pierre Laffitte, the leader of the Positivists, and Monsiegneur Guibert, the archbishop of Paris, stressed the importance of retaining urban cemeteries where Parisians could continue to honor their dead.[68]

In Angers and other provincial capitals the growth of the city led to several enlargements of the cemeteries, which were eventually surrounded by residential neighborhoods.[69] The same process occurred in some rural communities, such as Chanzeaux, the village in Anjou studied by Laurence Wylie and his team of research assistants. There the cemetery opened in 1777 was at first a healthy distance from town, but by 1868 sixteen buildings and several wells had been constructed nearby, leading the prefect to order its closing. The mayor and the city council responded with a petition, typically noting the inhabitants' desire to stay close to their "precious ashes" ("cendres précieuses") and the good health of those who lived nearest the cemetery.[70] Visits to other towns in Anjou recall the experience of Chanzeaux. In many cases cemeteries have been moved away from churches, but their location nearby allowed the town to expand and to reabsorb the burial site; even when this did not occur, cemeteries in small towns are still generally only a short walk away. The displacement of cemeteries did not mean the repression of the cult of the dead, although it did provide an opportunity for the reshaping of this cult in the light of attachments and values that emerged in the nineteenth century.

The original impulse, or at least the most consciously articulated motive, for translation was public health, with attention concentrated on the "miasmas" released by cemeteries. Unsurprisingly, the emergence of a more tolerant attitude toward the presence of the dead was accompanied by a revised understanding of the medical consequences of such proximity. According to an 1881 pamphlet written in defense of Parisian cemeteries, "The gases given off by buried matter in the process of decomposition are always free of bacteria."[71] The discovery by Pasteur that microbes and not miasmas were the source of infection was accepted as doctrine by the end of the nineteenth century.[72] Medical concern about cemeteries now concentrated on their effects on water supply; if studies showed that wells were not contaminated by a cemetery located within a town, there would be no reason to move it.[73] For the nineteenth as well as the eighteenth century, however, the medical justifications used in arguments about the disposition of cemeteries must be judged within a cultural context in which the relations between the living and the dead were being redefined.

CLASS, IDENTITY, AND CONCESSIONS

Until this point, my argument suggests that people in both rural and urban France were intensely attached to their cemeteries during the nineteenth century. In the case of the countryside, this attitude may be less a new development than an enduring trait based on long-standing feelings of devotion to the remains of ancestors. For cities, however, more sentiment was invested in cemeteries around 1900 than had been the case a century earlier. Why is it that people felt so attached to their burial sites and to their dead? Clearly the abuses of the revolutionary period were a shock that made both legislators and ordinary citizens anxious to restore an atmosphere of respect and decency. The public-health concerns that led to the initial effort to close and move urban cemeteries in the eighteenth century were never eliminated from discussions, but throughout the nineteenth century the conviction that the dead had to be treated with respect dominated public policy and practice.

The impact of the revolution is only the beginning of an answer to the question of why people invested so much emotion (and money) in their cemeteries. The reform of 23 prairial contained provisions that defined the internal space as well as the location of cemeteries. Although limits were imposed, and sometimes battled over, on the whole nineteenth-century cemeteries gave people an opportunity to express in public their most intensely felt commitments—to class, confession, and family. Gender and age differences also shaped the ways in which people remembered their dead. We have already seen how rural parishioners viewed cemeteries as privileged sites where family and communal loyalties were linked and displayed. During the nineteenth century, these and other social experiences were embodied in the location and decoration of tombs. Cemeteries thus became an important vehicle through which people constructed identities that conveyed the meaning of their lives to themselves and others.[74] But during the nineteenth century the social experiences of people changed, as loyalties to class, religion, and family became more complex. Cemeteries could not fail to become absorbed into the debates about these experiences and were, in fact, on several occasions a point of contention between groups that sought to control the ways in which people identified themselves through their tombs. At times these controversies disturbed the tranquil atmosphere that all agreed was the appropriate setting for the cult of the dead. But these debates also demonstrate the seriousness with which cemeteries were viewed; the arguments that sometimes raged around grave sites and tombs confirm that people viewed them as climactic statements about the meanings that they wished their lives to bear.

Of all the changes involving cemeteries in the nineteenth century none reflects so dramatically new attitudes toward the dead as the right of everyone to be buried in his or her own grave. Philippe Ariès has noted that by the end of the eighteenth century some artisans had begun to mark their graves with crosses, a modest imitation of the aristocratic fashion of raising monuments to the dead. For the majority, however, the common grave in which corpses were piled indiscriminately on top of one another was still a likely fate.[75] By granting everyone the right to "a separate grave" (*"une fosse séparée"*), the law of 23 prairial imposed a certain minimal equality in terms of the burial of the dead.[76]

The Napoleonic reform, however, went well beyond this endorsement of civil equality among the dead. It also conceded to individuals the right to obtain a "concession" in the cemetery, which was defined as "a distinct and separate place where people can establish graves for themselves, their relatives, and heirs, and where they can construct vaults, monuments, or tombs."[77] This distinction between the ordinary grave and the concession was the basis of the development of the funeral monuments that have become such a prominent feature of French cemeteries; for whereas ordinary graves had to be dug up and reused once every five or ten years, the concession provided a more permanent site on which families could build tombs with confidence that they might endure. The privilege of a concession, however, was to be based on a fee to be divided between local charities and the city.[78] The Napoleonic law gave everyone the right to an ordinary grave and allowed individuals with resources to add on to this in exchange for a transfer payment to the poor.

Concessions were first established in Père Lachaise in Paris on the basis of a decree issued by Prefect Frochot in 1805. Frochot distinguished between common graves and concessions, as the law required, but he made a further distinction as well between "temporary" and "perpetual" concessions—a distinction that was to become embedded in subsequent regulations both for Paris and for France as a whole. The innovation of a temporary concession was designed to allow those with moderate resources the chance to renew every few years their exclusive rights to a gravesite; failure to pay would result-in the city's recovery of the land.[79] The possibility of preserving the tomb of a family member beyond the five-year minimum granted to those buried in common graves appealed to the Parisian middle class, and concessions grew in popularity through the first half of the nineteenth century (see table 5.1). Temporary concessions were popular in part because at fifty francs they were relatively inexpensive. A permanent concession of two square meters, the minimum required for an adult who desired a vault of stone or brick, cost Fr 552 in 1838, and a site of six meters Fr 3,184.[80]

The land was not the only expense involved, because graves had to be landscaped and decorated. By the 1820s Parisian cemeteries, and especially Père Lachaise, were being filled by monuments, a development duly recorded in the *Recherches statistiques sur la ville de Paris*. And the desire to raise a monument to the dead was not restricted to those with enough money to purchase a concession; during the period 1821 to 1823 17.5 percent of all those buried in Paris purchased concessions, but monuments were raised on 41 percent of all the graves. Table 5.2 indicates that the vast majority of these were modest stones or crosses, with an average value of less than one hundred francs. The table also demonstrates the attraction of Père Lachaise, where a concentration of imposing tombs harmonized with the landscape design of Alexandre-Théodore Brongniart, leading Richard Etlin to describe the cemetery as reaching "its most glorious moment" by 1825.[81]

Observers were acutely conscious of the fact that dividing cemeteries into concessions mirrored the class structure of contemporary Paris. According to Alphonse Esquiros, in the Parisian cemeteries of 1844

> I find an image of the inequalities of rank and birth which govern society. The degrees of fortune are marked by levels: the people in the common grave; the middle class in temporary concessions; the aristocracy of finance in perpetual concessions. The population of cemeteries thus finds itself divided between the dead who own their grave and those who don't: the proletarians and the taxpayers.[82]

TABLE 5.1
Concessions in Parisian Cemeteries

	Common	Temporary	Perpetual
1821–23	82.2%	13.2%	4.4%
1839–48	77.9%	16.5%	5.6%

Source: Recherches statistiques sur la ville de Paris (Paris, 1826), tables 59, 60, 61; *Recherches statistiques sur la ville de Paris* (Paris, 1860), 316.

From the work of Balzac we learn of the intense interest of Parisians in money and status in the early nineteenth century. Cemeteries provided a particularly clear reflection of this preoccupation and allowed those with money to fix their social identity with enduring and ostentatious monuments. Concessions and tombs were an expression of social ambition, but as Esquiros suggests, they could also become focal points for the experiencing of class resentment.

During the first half of the nineteenth century provincial cities began copying the Paris fashion of dividing up the internal space of their cemeteries, just as they had in relocating them. In Rouen a concession of twenty-five years cost one hundred francs and a permanent grave of two square meters, four hundred francs. In Angers five-year concessions began at ten francs for one square meter, a plot that as a perpetual concession would cost sixty francs. In Rouen, Marseille, and a number of other cities in Provence, the purchase of perpetual concessions was slow in the 1820s and 1830s, but by mid-century increasing numbers of people were raising permanent monuments to commemorate themselves and their families.[83] The numbers of provincials purchasing concessions may never have reached the Parisian level; in Angers about 10 percent of the dead were buried in concessions between 1867 and 1893.[84] Apparently, even these numbers were unexpected, because cities had not included sufficient space in their new cemeteries to accommodate both the concessionaires and the ordinary citizens whose graves were reused every five years. Increasing demand for concessions among members of the middle and artisan classes—what Régis Bertrand and Michel Vovelle

TABLE 5.2
Monuments in Paris Cemeteries, 1821–1823

	None	Small	Medium	Large	Very Large
East (Père Lachaise)	17,108	11,898	508	014	104
North (Montmarte)	3,426	2,650	107	157	
Southwest (Vaugiraud)	9,442	4,390	255		
Totals	29,976 (58.9%)	18,938 (37.2%)	870 (1.7%)	971 (1.9%)	104

Small = value of Fr 100 or less; Medium = value from Fr 100 to 1,000; large = value from Fr 1,000 to 3,500; very large = value from Fr 3,500 to 35,000 francs. *Source: Recherches statistiques sur la ville de Paris* (Paris, 1826), tables 59, 60, 61.

have referred to as the "democratization" of the cemetery—was creating a crisis of space in urban cemeteries.[85]

Local governments responded to the popularity of concessions by reallocating space in cemeteries. Initially concessions were limited to the borders of allées, surrounding the ordinary graves which would fill the space inside; but as demand grew concessions began to penetrate the inner areas, cemeteries expanded in order to have enough room for ordinary graves, and cities reclaimed temporary sites or abandoned concessions more quickly. From Paris the central government attempted to help with a royal edict in 1843 that called on cities to discourage interest in "perpetual" concessions by raising their prices. Cities were also asked to create thirty-year concessions, which would be priced substantially lower than the permanent sites; a third category of ordinary graves would still be provided free to everyone for at least five years.[86]

Despite the effort to discourage perpetual concessions, these continued to increase until late in the century. In 1868 Baron Haussmann was forced to prohibit any additional permanent sites in the cemetery of Montmartre, a move that angered the builders of funerary monuments.[87] In Paris and Angers the shortage of space led city councils to expand existing sites, but in so doing they altered the character of their cemeteries. Areas added to Père Lachaise in the 1850s and the Angevin Cemetery of the East in the 1860s were divided into rectangular quadrants with none of the curving paths of the initial sites. As the city council of Angers viewed the situation, the gardenlike design had become too inefficient because the "curved lines result in a loss of considerable space, since it is necessary to place in these areas rectangular tombs; it is therefore desirable in the new portion to trace the alleys in right angles."[88] By the end of the century the large number of concessions decorated with stone tombs and the addition of rectangular zones resulted in a decidedly urban look that contrasted sharply with the rural atmosphere evoked earlier in the century. As cities expanded to encompass their cemeteries, these responded by mimicking their urban environment.[89]

The creation of concessions, which gave some people proprietary rights in the cemetery, posed serious problems to city administrators. Those who purchased a concession could be aggressive in protecting their rights, and those who could not afford a concession at times expressed resentment toward a system that denied them a permanent grave. Graves and monuments provided a means for people to make climactic statements about their wealth and position in the community, but this assertiveness occurred in a public space that was also designed to ensure a certain measure of equality. The expression of class could be especially telling and troublesome in cemeteries because there social identity was permanently enshrined. The cemetery thus became an institution that had to mediate between both the democratic and egalitarian impulses inherited from the revolution and the class-bound nature of French society as it developed in the nineteenth century.

The original reform in 1804 never clearly defined the proprietary status of a concession. Communes owned their cemeteries, but portions of them were to be given to individuals in exchange for a fee. The question of whether or not such an exchange constituted the purchase of private property was first raised when cities were forced to consider the transferring of their burial sites. If concessions were private property, then the city could not recover them without extraordinary judicial action. The jurisprudence that emerged during the century dealt with this problem by clearly asserting that perpetual concessions did not constitute private property, merely "a right of enjoyment and usage" ("*un droit de jouissance et d'usage*").[90] But families with perpetual concessions sometimes resisted such an interpretation. When Baron Haussmann's plans for redesigning Paris led him to cut through the cemetery of Montmartre and thus disturb a number of monuments built on permanent concessions, families responded with a petition challenging the government's right to violate their family tombs. Although the conseil d'état ruled against them, they carried their case to the Senate. The petition that the families submitted to prohibit any violation of their tombs was defeated by a vote of fifty to thirty-eight, but only after a debate described in *Le Temps* as "exceptionally animated."[91] The government may have established its ultimate rights over concessions, but families that invested in cemeteries understandably retained a sense of ownership toward their graves.

It was not only those with enough money to purchase a concession who developed a proprietary attitude toward their tombs. People buried in ordinary graves provided at no charge could be offended when cities attempted to retake possession of the site. In Angers the city had extended the minimum period for the use of a common grave to ten years, but a shortage of space forced the government to pull back from this position in 1874. When Mme Josephine Malton was informed that her father's tomb of 1869 was to be repossessed just six years later, she wrote a passionate note to the mayor. How was it possible, she demanded, that the right to the "inviolable possession" of a grave could be challenged in a century in which revolutions had established social progress and equality. "A whole life of work and exorbitant taxes . . . shouldn't that pay several times over for this sacred right? Nephews, mothers, children, even men . . . won't they be heartbroken by the spectacle of open graves, the debris of broken monuments and coffins?"[92] This same attitude figured at times in the discourse of politicians. The socialist prefect of Maine-et-Loire complained to the minister of religion in 1848 about the sale of concessions because "privilege and vanity should never cross the threshold of the cemetery. Every man coming into this world should have a respected and permanent place there, so that no family, as poor as it might be, would be deprived of the consolation of conserving inviolably the tomb of those that it has lost."[93] Jacques Fernand took the same position in 1873 in a pamphlet that condemned the common graves of Paris whose crosses and crowns were thrown away when the city had need of the space. "A permanent grave should be given free to the poor! One grave for every coffin!"[94]

Fernand was responding in this last appeal to the Parisian practice (technically illegal) of burying several coffins side by side in the same large grave. Those forced to accept burial in such a grave were denied the right to the precisely individualized space called for in the reform of 1804. Even on the common graves of Père Lachaise the poor sought to indicate either over the coffin or as near to it as possible some sign of personal identity. When Francis Head visited the cemetery in 1851 he found tiny gardens enclosed by an oak rail eighteen inches high. Cypresses and small crosses were planted inside, with the latter bearing the deceased's name, age, and date of death.[95] While some critics called for a permanent grave for each individual, families that could afford concessions in fact buried several members in the same site. In some of the larger family monuments spaces were reserved for individual coffins, but in many cases family members would be buried in the same soil, assuming that at least five years had passed between deaths. Burial practices thus reveal how in death the poor sought individual autonomy and equal treatment with the wealthy. For the middle classes, however, tombs raised on concessions became crucial vehicles for the expression of family solidarity.[96]

In the course of the nineteenth century the law of 23 prairial (1804) succeeded dramatically in encouraging a cult of the dead based on devotion to a carefully defined grave that held the physical remains of a beloved family member or friend. This success led in turn to the resentment of attempts by cities to reuse or otherwise disturb graves—feelings that were intensified by the favored treatment of those who were able to purchase an expensive concession. The debates about concessions reveal the tension generated by the conflict between individual and collective values. In some ways the battles over cemeteries recall the disputes over public forests that took place in the same period; in both cases people with limited resources were defending their right of access to communal property.[97] Cemeteries, however, are a more ambiguous example, because what people were asking for was a more enduring appropriation of a collective resource. Both those who could afford concessions and those who could not sought a permanent space within a communal setting where the dead could be preserved and commemorated. The division of cemeteries into concessions reflects not only class structure and consciousness but also an obsession with individual identity and family solidarity that became focal points of the cult of the dead.

Segregation and Equality in the Cemetery

Social class helped determine the ways in which the dead were distinguished and remembered in cemeteries; but religious affiliation and belief were also crucial, for they influenced the location of graves and the decorative motifs that embellished them. Throughout the nineteenth century non-Catholics accused the clergy of using placement in the cemetery as a means of dishonoring the dead—complaints that assumed that the precise location of the body would be read as a collective judgment on an individual life. Disputes about the location of a grave arose because the initial legislation of 23 prairial (1804) ambiguously defined the authority over cemeteries held by communal and religious authorities. On the one hand, the law confirmed that communes were proprietors of cemeteries and responsible for policing the cult of the dead; but on the other hand, it granted the organized religions substantial authority to bless and administer the burial grounds, thus opening the way for conflicts that affected how grave sites would be chosen.[98] Article 15 of the law of 23 prairial granted each cult the right to its own cemetery; where this was impossible, cities were responsible for separating cemeteries into sections with walls or hedges and providing each religion with its own entrance. Sorting out communal as opposed to ecclesiastical rights over cemeteries would have been difficult even in the absence of Church-State conflict. The suspicious and frequently hostile relations between these institutions made the law even more difficult to apply, especially given the increasingly important investments (both financial and emotional) of French men and women who were turning graves into family shrines.[99]

The legal requirement for separate but equal cemeteries was applied with little controversy in areas where there were sufficient numbers of Protestants and Jews to establish their own congregations. Separate Protestant cemeteries were established at Nîmes, Castres, and Montpellier, for example, and Jews had their own burial grounds at Nîmes and Strasbourg and a separate space in Père Lachaise.[100] For large areas of France, however, this ostensibly equitable policy proved difficult to put into practice. The law assumed, first of all, that everyone would belong to one of the three recognized denominations and would live alongside coreligionists in communities of worship. This idealized view of the religious landscape failed to accommodate those Protestants and Jews who lived isolated or in small enclaves within a predominantly Catholic population. As the minister of religion pointed out in a confidential letter to the bishops in 1845, such a situation raised "delicate questions" that the law did not answer.[101] The minister's proposed solution was that individual graves rather than the entire cemetery be blessed, a policy that had been applied with success in Paris. There is no evidence that this practice was adopted elsewhere, and problems arising from clerical attempts to exclude individuals from consecrated ground occurred throughout the century.

Deciding on where to bury Protestants and Jews could sometimes be troublesome, but at least the law of 23 prairial provided some guidance on how municipal authorities ought to proceed. When problems arose, administrators consistently referred back to the "separate but equal" clause of Article 15 as the way to resolve the conflict. The appropriate location of other categories of the dead, however, was not foreseen at all and led to confusion and anxiety which grew in the second half of the century. The law was silent, for example, on where to bury people who were baptized as Catholics but failed to practice their religion or who had died in circumstances that prohibited Catholic burial. Children who had died without baptism formed another category that proved troublesome in the course of the nineteenth century. French cemeteries generally included unblessed sections for these individuals, but burial there was considered shameful both to the individual and his or her family. Interment in the *"cimetière des pendus"* ("cemetery of the hanged"), the name popularly associated with such areas, was something families struggled to avoid. Clerical refusals to bury suicides, drunks, and stillborn children in consecrated ground provoked increasing public discontent and led families to appeal to the government to intervene on the grounds that their dead were being treated disrespectfully. The history of religious segregation in cemeteries illuminates an important aspect of the anticlerical campaign and shows how anticlerical legislation built on grass-roots support. This issue is perhaps even more interesting, however, because it reveals cultural assumptions about identity and community that were being contested and reformulated during the century.[102]

Conflicts over cemeteries were related to those that divided clergy and laity at the deathbed, which I explored in chapter 3. A clerical refusal of a Catholic funeral also meant burial in unconsecrated ground, but until the 1830s family resistance to such decisions concentrated on the church service. Beginning in the late 1830s, however, the arena of funeral conflicts began to shift from church to cemetery. Initially this resulted from a clerical initiative to divide cemeteries that had previously made no distinctions among the dead. The request was ostensibly designed to create space for unbaptized infants, whom most people still believed should be buried separately. But the mayors who objected to the division emphasized their concern that referring to such children was only a pretext; once an unconsecrated portion was established, the clergy would use it as well for all those who had died without receiving the Last Sacraments. The assertion of clerical authority over "consecrated earth" ("*terre sainte*") was intended to be a minatory pastoral tool that would pressure skeptics and anticlericals into dying with the assistance of the clergy in order to be buried alongside their families.[103]

Clerical assertions of authority over cemeteries during the first half of the century occurred at the same time that many communes were involved in purchasing land and moving their burial grounds to new sites some distance from the parish church. This shift, which highlighted communal responsibilities for cemeteries, helps explain the troubles that arose between the clergy and municipal authorities; mayors increasingly objected to clerical control of property purchased and developed by the commune. As churchyards became communal cemeteries, all citizens, regardless of religious affiliation, could claim their rights to burial with their families. The families of unbaptized children, Protestants, and freethinkers all made claims for the right to be buried in the "communal" cemetery, and their appeals were based on the ambiguities in law and practice that were evident by the 1850s. The right of the clergy to exclude non-Catholics meant that children could be separated from parents, husbands from wives. Families were being divided in death for the sake of religious solidarity, a practice that became increasingly objectionable as families focused more attention on graves as symbols of their identity and continuity.

The clergy looked to the law to preserve their rights to consecrate burial grounds and segregate the dead by religion, regardless of the location of other family members. Despite the opposition of some mayors and local officials, governments during the first half of the century acknowledged clerical rights over the cemetery. If the clergy insisted on burying children who had died without baptism in unconsecrated ground, there was nothing that civil officials could do. But the minister of religion, in stating this policy in 1838, went on to argue that mayors should oppose any effort to bury adults who had died without the Last Sacraments in these corners of the cemetery, because such an attempt would be "an innovation damaging to the true interests of religion and dangerous for public tranquillity."[104] In the second half of the century public tranquillity was disturbed by a number of scandalous incidents that drew national attention. Public opinion seemed less willing to tolerate clerical exclusions, an attitude encouraged by anticlerical politicians who succeeded in 1881 in passing legislation abolishing the separate-but-equal clause of the law governing funerals and cemeteries. The shift in public mood against religious segregation can be traced through the study of conflicts in which families, clergymen, and municipal authorities struggled for control of burial grounds.

The segregation of unbaptized children was already an issue early in the century, but public opinion was not always clearly aligned with those families who desired to bury these infants in consecrated ground. In 1814 a midwife from the village of Pompierre (Vosges) was unable to assure the local priest that the child of a M. Guilgot, an officer of the Legion of Honor, had been alive when she administered conditional baptism. The child was thus buried in unconsecrated ground, despite the objections of the father. In defending his decision the priest of the parish was able to submit a petition from the townspeople supporting the segregation of the unbaptized child.[105] At Arras in 1838 a woman and her child who had died during birth were both placed in the same coffin. The curé, learning of this during the funeral service, had the coffin opened and the mother and child separated, to the anguish of the family and friends.[106] In the second half of the century such behavior became increasingly troublesome, and families began calling on public officials to rein in what they considered to be excessive and intolerant behavior. In 1859, and again in 1863, mayors in the department of Maine-et-Loire ordered the burial of unbaptized children in consecrated ground. Following clerical complaints the mayors were ordered to exhume the bodies and place them in unconsecrated ground. Both mayors apologized for their actions, which they explained as due to ignorance of the law and sympathy for the families. The mayor of Longué, in a letter to the prefect, claimed that other mayors had done the same thing without meeting clerical resistance and added a revealing note about the children in question: "In adopting this measure I have only followed the example of several of my colleagues who, I am assured, will not tolerate exceptional treatment of these little beings who are completely innocent of not having received baptism." This belief in childhood innocence was opposed by Catholic dogma, which asserted that such infants were corrupted by original sin. The insistence on this doctrine, which led to the exhumations, must have been painful for the families in question, and it no doubt contributed to the anticlerical opposition that eventually succeeded in eliminating clerical rights to exclude unbaptized children from consecrated ground.[107]

As families increasingly objected to the segregation of unbaptized children, more extended communities also began resisting the exclusion of their members. When the Protestant Philip Schwarz died in Cholet in September 1858, the curé ordered his grave dug in the unblessed portion of the cemetery reserved for unbaptized infants and suicides; but the mayor instructed that Schwarz be buried alongside his fellow citizens, even though this meant placing him in ground consecrated by the Catholic clergy. A large crowd attended the funeral for Schwarz, who had worked in a restaurant and been well liked within the community. Following Schwarz's burial, the curé complained to the prefect and the minister of religion that Catholic rights had been violated, and the clergy refused to officiate at ceremonies in the desecrated cemetery—a move that agitated the population. The Paris ministry supported the clergy, and as a result the body was exhumed and reburied two weeks after the funeral.[108]

The decision to exhume Schwarz conformed to the letter of the law, but it raised questions of identity and belonging in ways that were painful and symptomatic of changes occurring the nineteenth century. M. Vaurigaud, the president of the Protestant consistory of Nantes, insisted that Schwarz belonged with the other citizens of Cholet in the "communal cemetery," a phrase that he emphasized in his letter to the minister of religion.[109] According to Vaurigaud, the sections ordinarily reserved for non-Catholics were considered shameful, which was not at all the intent of the law. Vaurigaud argued, as did others in similar cases, that separate burial was intrinsically unequal and offensive.[110] As a respected citizen, Schwarz deserved burial in the communal cemetery; his identity as a Protestant was less important than his membership in a civil community of citizens who should be treated equally both in death and in life.

The case of Schwarz was typical of several that occurred beginning in the 1850s in which Protestants claimed a right to burial alongside Catholics in communal burial grounds. Schwarz was refused his place, but in other instances such exclusions were even more troublesome because family solidarity and proprietary rights were added to the argument in favor of integration. In 1856, for example, a Protestant property owner from Quimper, M. Karatsch, purchased a concession in the communal cemetery where his Catholic mother, wife, and daughter were buried. But when Karatsch himself died in 1859 the mayor refused to permit him to join his family, despite the complaint of his son.[111]

This separation of husband and wife, like the separation of parents from children, was increasingly difficult to justify. By the 1860s some bishops were willing to tolerate the burial of family members together, as was the case in La Rochelle, where religious intermarriage was increasing.[112] Monseigneur Bouvier, the bishop of Le Mans and a respected theologian as well, wrote his colleague in Angers that his clergy "closed their eyes" when Protestants were buried in consecrated ground.[113] But for those Catholics who took an aggressive posture and insisted that Protestant identity meant exclusion from the community of the dead, the law and jurisprudence were on their side until the 1870s.

Following the collapse of the Second Empire in 1870, a new and more tolerant interpretation of the law began to emerge in the jurisprudence. A first indication of this shift can be seen in the case of Mlle Tamelier, a Protestant girl from Ville d'Avray (Seine-et-Oise), who was buried in an isolated section of the cemetery of her village in 1870. When her brother objected, she was exhumed; but the local curé refused to permit her into consecrated ground, and her body lay unburied in a toolshed for eighteen days while the family, the mayor, and the curé fought over what to do. The case was widely commented on in the press and finally provoked the intervention of a deputy from the corps législatif, which resulted in the girl's burial in a nearby village where the curé was more tolerant.

The Tamelier case drew attention because it combined a number of features that anticlericals could call on to generate sympathy for their cause: an innocent young girl forced to lie isolated in a shameful corner of the cemetery, a loyal brother defending her honor, and an intransigent priest willing to humiliate her and her family. The Catholic Church was vulnerable to such an attack, which rested on an appeal to family and communal solidarity. During the 1870s when property rights to a concession were added to the argument based on family solidarity the government began conceding the point and making exceptions to the law that segregated those of different religions. When the Protestant M. Lesage of St. Florent (Maine-et-Loire) died in 1874, he was buried in an impressive monument built on a perpetual concession carved out of consecrated ground. Twenty years earlier Karatsch had been denied burial in a similar situation, but now the right to purchase a concession took precedence over Catholic identity and merited Lesage a prominent place in the cemetery. Lesage's tomb rose eighteen feet in the air and was surmounted by a cross; the vault underneath would accommodate six people. Before his death at age ninety he announced his intention to sell some of the remaining places in his vault to other Protestants, a move opposed by the mayor, who insisted he still planned to bury Protestants in the cimetière des pendus (see illus. 10). The cemetery of St. Florent thus became the site where individuals sought to define themselves and their relations to the community. In the case of Lesage, his claim for equal treatment was based on the wealth that distinguished him from most of the others in his town. His tomb, simultaneously a symbol of equality and difference, reveals what sensitive indicators cemeteries and tombs could be of the nuances of social identity.[114]

The tombs of the Prince and Princess Ferdinand d'Orléans in the chapel of the Orléans family at Dreux are a poignant expression of the problem of where husbands and wives of an intermarriage between Protestants and Catholics would be buried. The tomb of the prince, sculpted by Pierre Loison in the 1840s, lies within the royal chapel, but his Protestant wife could not be buried with him. To accommodate her, a separate chapel was built alongside her husband's tomb. The figure of the princess, sculpted by Henri Chapu and first displayed at the salon of 1885, shows her turning toward her husband, with her right arm reaching past the balustrade that separates her chapel from the rest of the church. The principle of separate burial was thus upheld, but at the same time a way was found, in the chapel and the sculpture, to overcome the distance between husband and wife. The tombs, in representing both separation and union, negotiate a difficult relationship between family and religion that troubled the French, especially in the second half of the century.[115]

Cases such as those of Mlle Tamelier and M. Lesage arguing for their rights in the communal cemetery multiplied in the 1870s, and freethinkers as well as Protestants were now insisting on burial alongside families and friends. Even before the Republicans established clear control of the government in 1879, administrative judgments by the conseil d'état had eroded clerical claims; and in 1880 the case of Henri Gasnier made it evident that Article 15 of the law of 23 prairial was a dead letter. M. Gasnier, of Baugé (Maine-et-Loire), refused to receive a priest at his deathbed, leading Monseigneur Charles Freppel, the militant bishop of Angers, to conclude that "whatever religion M. Gasnier belongs to, one thing is certain; by his own choice he has ceased to be a member of the Catholic cult; therefore he cannot legally be buried in the cemetery designated for this cult."[116] Despite this objection, the mayor allowed Gasnier to be buried in the permanent concession that he had purchased in the consecrated portion of the cemetery. The curé and eleven parishioners petitioned for Gasnier's exhumation and removal, a claim that earlier

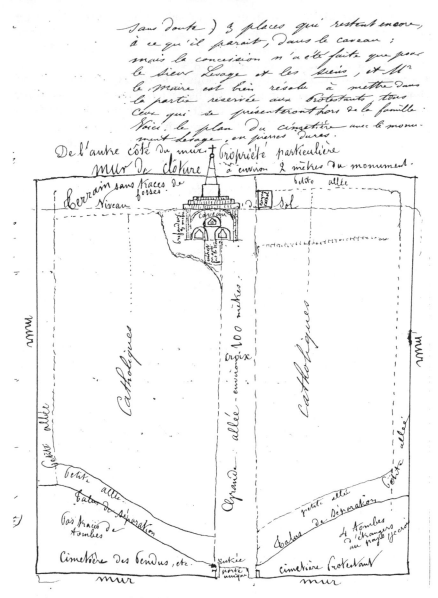

10. The cemetery of St. Florent, Maine-et-Loire. In this letter to Bishop Freppel of Angers, the curé of St. Florent sketches the cemetery of St. Florent, indicating the separate areas for suicides (*cimetière des pendus*) and Protestants and the projected tomb of the Protestant Lesage (Archives d'Evéché, Angers).

in the century would have been honored. Faced with a complaint that was ostensibly legitimate the conseil d'état resorted to a technicality, ruling that the plaintiffs were not qualified to bring the case.[117] By the time this decision was made in 1880, administrative jurisprudence had resulted in the secularization of the cemetery—a change that was formally introduced into law in 1881, when the Republican majority pushed through the abrogation of Article 15.

The results of the debate over Article 15 of the law of 23 prairial were not much in doubt, given the Republican majority that was committed to laicizing French life. But the debates on this law were nonetheless animated, for people on both sides sensed the cultural significance of their actions and struggled to find language that could express their complex feelings about death and burial. Both the advocates of the reform and the Catholic defenders of Article 15 attempted to appropriate the language of liberty in making their cases. Those who supported neutrality argued that segregation violated "freedom of conscience" by forcing individuals and families to publicly state their religion; Catholics responded by saying that "freedom of religion" required that they be allowed to bury their dead together.

Both sides agreed that the burial of the dead should be a free act, although it is characteristic that anticlericals focused on the freedom of the individual, whereas Catholics insisted on the rights of the Catholic community. Even more telling, however, was the shared belief that cemeteries ought to be resting places where the dead could sleep in peace. Philippe Ariès has traced this association of death and sleep to the rituals of the early Church and has argued that it was subsequently replaced among elites by a more animated vision of the afterlife. The debates about the neutralization of cemeteries suggest that the idea had regained considerable power among the political leaders of the Third Republic, and perhaps among their constituents as well. In defending their vision of what a cemetery should be, these men also revealed attitudes toward death and the afterlife that say a great deal about the culture of France in the late nineteenth century.

Both Catholics and the Republican reformers used the metaphor of sleep to describe death and burial, but for Catholics the peace of the dead could be preserved only if they remained undisturbed by the "disorder" and "confusion" that would result from neutralization of the cemetery.[118] Monseigneur Freppel typically went further than any of his colleagues and described the reform as encouraging "promiscuity" in the cemeteries, a remark that provoked angry exclamations from the Republicans, perhaps because of the connection that it implied between cemetery integration and sexual misconduct.[119] An example from the polemical debate that surrounded this controversy illustrates both the depth of feeling and the confusion that it evoked among some Catholics. When Monseigneur Gaume set out to defend segregated cemeteries in the 1870s, he combined an argument based on religious liberty and respect for the dead with an older tradition of vilification. The juxtaposition of these stands is jarring to the contemporary reader, and perhaps the difficulty in reconciling them helps explain the Republican success on this issue. For Gaume, the respect for the body of the dead is intricately linked to the belief in an immortal soul. Skepticism about this doctrine, such as Gaume found in the Republicans who sought access to consecrated ground, would necessarily empty any ritual of its significance. Gaume also believed that the bodies of unbelievers would pollute the cemetery and he did not hesitate to use harsh and abusive language to describe those dead who have rejected Catholic ritual:

> You believe that all men, including yourselves, are nothing but living dirt, soulless creatures, with no higher destiny than to gratify your appetites. You cannot have a conscience, for there is no conscience in a heap of dirt.[120]

This kind of language, which is close to what Freppel used in the Senate, worked against the initial claim that Catholics were defending the respectful treatment of the dead.

Republicans, on the other hand, although they occasionally referred to the Catholic position ironically, never excoriated the Catholic dead in such terms. Also, the services that they provided for their dead were far from the contemptuous handling of "a heap of dirt" that Catholics like Gaume described. Perhaps Catholic apologists were engaged in reading current events as a simple replication of the revolutionary era, when the bodies of the dead were indeed treated with disrespect. But the reformers of the Third Republic took their responsibilities toward the dead much more seriously. Gaume's accusation of disrespect was misplaced, and reformers consistently pointed out that segregation was more clearly dishonorable than the integration that they called for.

In proposing the version of the reform that was eventually to pass, the anticlerical deputies Charles Rameau, Léon Journault, and Albert Joly claimed that the troubles resulting from Catholic attempts to separate the different religions "prolong the quarrels of the living beyond life itself, provoke these strange conflicts over human remains even in the field of common rest. Liberal opinion asks what is the basis of such posthumous scorn, and if the dead have the right to be respected by everyone, then why don't they all have the right to burial in the same earth."[121] Republicans rejected the argument that "separate-but-equal" cemeteries ensured respect for all; according to the drafters of the law, "Whoever occupies a place apart in the cemetery occupies an inferior place; even where there is no difference between these sites, the fact alone of being put some distance away is itself an insult."[122] Finally, the argument rested on a belief that only "fanatics" would seek to separate wives from husbands, children from parents.

From the Catholic point of view, the ideal cemetery would preserve rather than abolish religious distinctions, because to do otherwise would be to disturb the Catholic dead. The Catholic vision looked backward to a time when religious differences were of crucial importance in defining both self and community. The passage of the reform of 1881 suggests that the weight of political and public opinion no longer regarded these differences as important enough to merit permanent recognition in the cemetery. The proponents of the reform believed that the cemetery ought to be a place that enshrined religious and political harmony, civil equality, and family solidarity. According to the Republican newspaper *XIXe Siècle*, the cemetery is the "commune of the dead, where all of those who lived together will come to sleep together, affirming after their death the solidarity which united them during their lives."[123] It does not take a great deal of knowledge about French society during this period to appreciate that these ideals were far from being realized among the living. The cemetery thus took on for Republicans a utopian aspect; it was a projection, a kind of heaven where French men and women all slept peacefully, undisturbed by the quarrels of the living.

The Visit to the Cemetery

The relocation of cemeteries, accompanied by quarrels about costs and location, and the carving up of their internal space to reflect class and religious differences suggest that the reformers' vision of a cemetery as a privileged site where social harmony would be manifest was an ideal to be realized rather than one already attained. But although the disputes attending the creation and management of cemeteries allow us to observe how social experience shaped the cult of the dead, it would be a mistake to see cemeteries exclusively as battlegrounds where groups contended for social esteem. The harmonious cemetery that the Republicans advocated through the reform of 1881 was a potent political symbol because it was a partial reflection of social practices that had developed during the previous decades. The problems that troubled the sleep of the dead were real, but by the end of the century they were also becoming intolerable precisely because they violated the consensus that had formed about the attributes of a cemetery.

The discussions surrounding the displacement and management of cemeteries have already suggested the intense interest that the French took in their burial grounds and confirm the point made first by Philippe Ariès: the visit to the cemetery was one of the most significant rituals of the nineteenth century. In Paris, officials estimated that approximately seventy thousand people visited the various cemeteries each week in the 1860s and 1870s. On November 2, the feast of All Souls' Day, as many as four-hundred-thousand went to pay their respects, a figure that suggests that almost one of every three Parisians went to a cemetery on that single day.[124] Guides to Parisian cemeteries were available as early as 1816, and elsewhere as well sentiment and pride drew people to their burial grounds. In Angers an 1867 appeal for contributions to build a chapel in the Cemetery of the East was based on the observation of frequent visits, which were described as an innovation of the 1850s and 1860s.

> The care that each family takes of these touching monuments has introduced new habits. Formerly the cemetery was opened only for funeral ceremonies, or for the procession on the great day of Toussaint, or finally, on a few rare occasions . . . when the solemn silence, broken only by the songs of the Church, communicated to the soul an impression of respect, close to a vague terror. Today, the gate is always open; pilgrimages are frequent; people go to sit near their well-loved dead, they feel closer to them, they seek to overcome their absence.[125]

The visit to the cemetery was a frequently observed ritual. But what was it that the French saw and felt when they visited their cemeteries? Such a question can never receive anything like a definitive answer, but exploring it is nonetheless a crucial exercise for anyone trying to grasp what the French felt about death and the afterlife. In fact, the attention that the French lavished on their cemeteries and the care that they still give them make it possible for us to form an accurate impression of what they saw when they visited their tombs a century ago. Their feelings at such moments are less accessible, but the physical evidence provides us with clues that, when combined with some texts, can help us understand the emotions that people experienced during their visits to the cemetery. Visiting the cemeteries and contemplating tombs from the nineteenth century may bring us as close as we can come to the experiences of those French who made similar visits a century ago.

For an American, perhaps the most striking characteristic of a French cemetery is its careful enclosure behind solidly constructed walls, some of which reach as high as twenty-five feet. Although some American graveyards are similarly enclosed, most tend to be open or are surrounded only by a metal grille. The passerby sees easily into the cemetery, a perspective unavailable in French towns and villages. Enclosure was one of the requirements imposed on French communes by the law of 23 prairial (1804), but the expense of such construction led many city councils to drag their feet, just as they did on the question of *translation*. Correspondence in which both local citizens and officials of the central government complained about animals wandering through graveyards is common for the first half of the century.[126] By the end of the nineteenth century, however, the process of walling in the dead was virtually complete, and the walls of the French cemeteries were familiar enough to serve as an iconological motif. An artist who wished to evoke the presence of the dead could do so by using a wall as background, behind which only the characteristic cypress trees could be observed (see illus. 11).

The arguments for enclosure repeated commonplaces about cemeteries familiar since the late eighteenth century. Hygienic considerations required them as a break against deadly emanations, and respect for the dead meant that animals must be denied access. Walls were raised because of concerns about health and decency, but they also provided a clearly defined boundary between the space of the living and the dead. As cemeteries were removed from cities, and then surrounded again, such precise delimitation may have made it easier to accommodate the close proximity of the dead. The cemetery of Passy, in the fashionable sixteenth arrondissement of Paris, is surrounded by monumental walls that protect it from the gaze of tourists who come to visit the place de Trocadero and from the Parisians and others who sit in the cafés that face the museums, the Seine, and the Eiffel Tower. Passy is exceptional because it borders on a fashionable square, which perhaps explains why its walls are so high, but the other cemeteries of Paris and those of cities such as Angers are similarly protected. Walls also have been raised around both the surviving churchyards and the newer cemeteries placed on the outskirts of towns and villages. Everywhere in France they create a carefully protected space for the dead.

The enclosure of cemeteries made possible the cultivation of a special atmosphere in which visitors could quietly contemplate the tombs of their families. Churchyards during the ancien régime were frequented by parishioners who might stop by after Sunday mass to visit an ancestral grave, and we have seen how these attachments figured in the debate about the transferral of cemeteries. But the centrally located churchyard had other functions besides providing a setting for the cult of the dead: in Brittany public announcements were made there; cemeteries could also be the sites of markets and meet-

11. *All Souls' Day in the Countryside*. In this print
by Hermann Paul from the late nineteenth century an old man returns from a visit to the cemetery, which is situated on the outside of town and
protected by the walls that were raised around
burial grounds in the nineteenth century (Photo:
Bibliothèque Nationale).

ings where products, property, and conversation were exchanged. It
was precisely this undifferentiated quality that offended reformers in
the eighteenth and nineteenth centuries and led them to propose the
removal and enclosure of cemeteries. During the nineteenth century
a campaign to enforce a quiet mood untroubled by crowds and commerce accompanied the transferral and enclosure of cemeteries.

Communes were charged with the responsibility of ensuring that
no behavior offensive to the cult of the dead be allowed within the
cemetery walls, but the law of 23 prairial left particular regulations to
the discretion of local governments. These were formulated and
posted at the entrances to cemeteries, with details added as new
problems arose.[127] For cities, a concierge housed on cemetery grounds

was made responsible for controlling access and maintaining order. Hours were regulated, and the gates were unlocked only during daylight. Children were especially troublesome, to judge by regulations in both Paris and Angers, where they were prohibited from climbing on the tombs, trees, and walls—in short from treating the cemetery as a playground. It was also necessary to protect the cemetery from certain kinds of adults; in Paris entry was to be denied to "drunks, smokers, peddlers, unaccompanied children, students out for a walk, individuals with dogs or other domestic animals, and anyone not dressed properly." Similar prohibitions were in effect in Angers, where the city officials also noted that "no profane song will be tolerated." Such regulations were apparently intended to control observed as opposed to possible behavior. Soon after the Cemetery of the East was opened in Angers, the police commissioner filed a report with the mayor in which he detailed a long list of violations. On a Monday evening in May of 1849 he observed the following:

> Around seven in the evening there were perhaps three hundred persons who had come to the cemetery for a walk. Among them were many young children who amused themselves playing on the tombs; there were even some women seated on the grass who were nursing their infants. I was especially pained by this spectacle, which took place at the same time as a burial, and I expressed my unhappiness energetically to the concierge, who excused himself by telling me it wasn't his fault.[128]

Citizens initially may have regarded the new cemeteries as parks where they could stroll, smoke, play, and even sing; such behavior makes sense when we recall that these cemeteries were, after all, designed as gardens. The sociability targeted by regulations may have reflected memories of churchyards frequented by city dwellers who only recently had arrived from the countryside. The atmosphere of relaxation and play was also due to the relative scarcity of green and open spaces. In Paris Père Lachaise was opened in 1804, sixty years before the Bois de Boulogne and Bois de Vincennes were created as city parks where people could amuse themselves without disturbing the dead.[129]

In addition to restraining an exuberance felt to be inappropriate, regulations also prohibited businessmen from offering their services to the bereaved families within the cemetery walls. In Paris the municipal decree of 1850 specifically forbade the distribution of business cards to those participating in a procession, at the side of the grave, in the surrounding allées, or at the gates—details suggesting that entrepreneurs anxious to build or maintain funeral monuments were a ubiquitous presence in and around cemeteries. The porters from the pompes funèbres, the grave diggers, and the concierge were also warned not to ask for tips (*gratifications*) after completing their work—a restriction that perhaps requires some interpretation. Certainly the government was seeking to protect families from offensive requests. From the point of view of those who were asking for the tips, however, the atmosphere in the cemetery may have been ideal because the distance that it created between the profane world of commerce and work would make it difficult to reject such requests. Funerals had traditionally been an occasion for the distribution of charity to the poor, a custom that was still observed once in a while in the nineteenth century. Workers who provided services for a middle-class funeral may have profited from the residue of this older obligation, and families may have felt constrained by it as well. However that may be, cemeteries provided funeral workers the chance to ask for a supplement, and the stream of prohibitions that lasted throughout the century demonstrates how difficult it was to abolish this practice.[130]

Finally, the workers who had been employed to construct monuments (or to destroy them, in the case of abandoned concessions) were required to remove the evidence of their labor; the sight of debris that might normally surround such construction could not be permitted in a cemetery. Wagons involved in such work had to be drawn at a slow pace, and in Paris the size of the cart wheels permitted inside the cemetery was controlled to reduce the noise that they might cause.[131] During the ancien régime cemeteries had frequently been thoroughfares and meeting places for villages and neighborhoods, but during the revolution some of them became little more than dumps. In the nineteenth century, local governments established rules designed to create within the cemetery walls a solemn atmosphere that excluded the world of commerce and labor.

The purpose of these regulations was to provide a setting in which people could visit the tombs of family and friends and, in the case of urban cemeteries, of those great men buried there as well. We saw earlier how concessions and funeral monuments became increasingly popular during the century; the survival of many of these has provided historians such as Ariès, Vovelle, and Etlin with crucial evidence about the cult of the dead. Since the nineteenth century, changes have certainly occurred: in urban cemeteries the ordinary concessions marked by small wooden crosses have disappeared, and the gardenlike atmosphere intended for cemeteries such as Père Lachaise has been transformed by the dense construction of stone monuments.[132] These changes were already apparent to observers by the middle of the nineteenth century, by which time long-term and permanent concessions, and their accompanying monuments, had established their popularity. In the countryside large numbers of tombs have also survived from the nineteenth century. Some of these mimic the grandiose statements found in the fashionable cemeteries of large cities, but in the villages and towns of Anjou, for example, a contemporary visitor is more likely to be struck by the large number of more modest graves.

In commenting on the cemeteries of the nineteenth century, historians have generally focused on the impressive monuments raised by affluent members of the bourgeoisie. These can be read as evidence of how sensibilities changed in the course of the century. In Père Lachaise many of the earliest tombs were modeled on Greek and Roman temples, a survival of the eighteenth-century taste for classical motifs. Funeral urns and truncated columns were fashionable, with the latter deemed especially appropriate for young women. In the middle years of the nineteenth century the neo-Gothic chapel became popular, and the main allées of many urban cemeteries are still dominated by these monuments.[133] Placed next to one another, and concentrated along the borders of the allées, these monuments reflected the wealth and self-consciousness of the bourgeoisie. The names of the family members buried on the site were frequently displayed on the interior walls, with the entryway barred by a metal grille. Philippe Ariès has suggested that families were attracted by the idea of burial together as a way of reaffirming ties in an age when they were being increasingly separated by work and marriage. Family tombs testify to the importance that the cult of the dead played as a means of establishing and maintaining a sense of family solidarity—a sentiment that was manifested elsewhere in French culture as well, but perhaps nowhere else with such poignance.[134]

For those without great resources the luxury of an elaborate tomb was impossible. As we have already seen in discussing the question of concessions, however, even those with limited funds frequently insisted on marking their graves, generally with a small wood or metal cross. In Provence, between 80 and 90 percent of all graves were marked with a cross of some form throughout the nineteenth century.[135] Illustrations from the first half of the nineteenth century reveal a clear contrast between these crosses and the tombs of the wealthy, which were more likely to be decorated with urns and carved wreaths.[136] An 1867 description of the Cemetery of the East in Angers clearly distinguished among the several categories of tombs: "For more than twenty years our city has possessed a vast cemetery of an imposing and touching aspect. At the entrance we discover a great number of tombs, sculpted monuments for the rich, more modest tombs for those less favored by fortune, then, the wood cross for the most poor. . . ."[137] This devotion to the cross can still be observed in the latter part of the century, when the poor of Angers purchased secondhand crosses from the city for five francs or less. This commerce in abandoned crosses led to complaints by merchants, who objected to competition from the city. City officials were firm in rejecting the merchants' position, pointing to the "real service the city renders to a rather large number of people who, unable to purchase an expensive new monument, are happy with those made available to them cheaply, and which can be restored by a light sanding done by themselves."[138]

It was not just the poor who were attached to the cross, however; in the middle years of the nineteenth century it became the dominant symbol on a large number of monuments that, in terms of opulence, rank just below the funeral chapel. The aspect of most cemeteries in France suggests a forest of crosses, most of them raised over tombs that date from the middle of the nineteenth century to the 1920s. Earlier in the century crosses had been planted directly in the ground or displayed horizontally on the tombstone, as can be seen on the monument of Curé Dutertre (see illus. 12) from Bourg (Maine-et-Loire), who died in 1835. During the second half of the century the horizontal cross from tombs such as Dutertre's has been raised to a vertical position; or, to state the point in another way, the crosses placed over the poorer graves early in the century have been added to the monuments of the wealthy. The cross on such tombs is frequently mounted on a stele that displays the names of the family dead and in some cases an epitaph as well.[139] In cemeteries in the countryside, these triumphant crosses are placed alongside less-expensive ones, metal crosses that have survived from the same period. These latter ones sometimes display the names of individual family members on metal hearts that are hung from the cross. The transept of the metal crosses provided another site for a decorative motif, often a depiction of the Virgin Mary. The increasing use of representations of Mary at the center of the cross suggests that Marian piety, fueled by the apparitions and new shrines that they engendered, was quickly integrated into the cult of the dead (see illus. 13).[140]

In Père Lachaise and the Cemetery of the East in Angers, the sections that contain tombs from the most recent period create a very different impression from those dating from the nineteenth century. First, there is a greater degree of homogeneity; the contrast between elaborate and more modest tombs has diminished over the past thirty years. Second, the cross, although still present on most monuments, no longer rises from the headstone but instead is either attached to or carved into it.[141]

It is easier to trace the changes in the use of the cross than it is to interpret its significance. As Ariès has noted, even societies that are not apparently religious remain attached to the cross, which has be-

12. Tomb of Curé Dutertre, Bourg (Maine-et-Loire), 1835. (Photo: T. Kselman)

come a symbol of death without necessarily suggesting any specific commitment to Christianity. Nevertheless, the triumphant cross of the middle of the century may reflect a self-conscious insistence on the doctrine of death and resurrection, one from which more recent tombs have clearly retreated. An 1883 epitaph on Henri-Nicholas

13. Metal cross with figure of Virgin at transept, St. Michel-et-Chanveaux
(Maine-et-Loire). (Photo: T. Kselman)

Richon's headstone in Avrillé, which is surmounted by a monumental cross, certainly suggests such a commitment: "I know that my Redeemer lives, and that on the last day I will rise from the earth, and restored to my flesh I will see God my Savior." However, even if we hesitate before such a specific interpretation of the place of the cross in the French cemetery, its reabsorption into the headstone suggests that although it retains its power as a "vaguely recognized symbol of hope and protection," it does so in a diminished form.[142] In those sections that contain only contemporary tombs the cross no longer dominates the horizon of the cemetery, suggesting a similar retreat from the horizon of consciousness about death.

Richon's message was an elaborate one and exceptional in its lengthy evocation of bodily resurrection. Most epitaphs were briefer, in part because the simple crosses that marked the majority of tombs barely had space on them for the name of the deceased, the date of his or her death, and perhaps a brief invocation. These elements were the first to emerge on the epitaph when it appeared between the twelfth and fourteenth century, a development that Ariès relates to the heightened consciousness of individual mortality. Over the centuries this sensibility spread down the social hierarchy, but it was in the nineteenth century that the an individual grave and an epitaph identifying its inhabitant became a right claimed by all.[143]

From the fifteenth to the eighteenth century some epitaphs began to include biographical details and references to family relations that personalized the tombs. These continued to appear on the more elaborate tombs of the nineteenth century, although they were not universal. In the cemetery of Aix-en-Provence biographical epitaphs were popular during the period from 1830 to 1860, when they appeared on 27 percent of the tombs raised on perpetual concessions. This figure fell to 13 percent for 1860 to 1890, and to 6 percent for the period from 1890 to 1920. Unsurprisingly, family virtues were the most frequently cited qualities on these epitaphs, outnumbering civic virtues and socio-professional status, which were mentioned less and less frequently as the century progressed.[144]

The epitaphs that have survived from the nineteenth century have been described as sentimental and banal, a criticism already current in the nineteenth century. Count F. de Gramont complained of their lack of taste and associated them with the ceramic flowers and wreaths placed on the tombs, which "smelled horribly of the factory."[145] Ariès is nonetheless right to argue that "in their naive and garrulous manner, which we tend to find ridiculous and hypocritical, the epitaphs of the nineteenth century express a real and profound feeling, which the historian has no right to deride."[146] The tender

14. Tomb of the Legoy family, listing deceased members from late nineteenth and early twentieth centuries, in Cemetery of the East, Angers. (Photo: T. Kselman)

mothers, virtuous fathers, and docile children recalled in the surviving epitaphs were described in a conventional vocabulary, but this language may nonetheless have been able to call up memories of particular individuals and of their relations with the living.[147] Most writers who have dealt with this material have drawn their examples from major urban cemeteries, but it is perhaps worth noting that similar epitaphs can be found in village cemeteries as well. In Murs, a

15. Family vaults in Cemetery of the East, Angers, from the second half of the nineteeth century. (Photo: T. Kselman)

village in Anjou, the oldest surviving tomb is a horizontal stone,
partly destroyed, with the following inscription:

> Here lies
> Laurette Courtigne born the
> 20th of October 1818, died the first of June
> 1832
> She was a model of piety and filial love
>
> Alas! At the age most tender
> Pain and care could not defend her
> From the blows of a cruel death
> Oh, passerby, pray on her tomb
> Where her parents bemoan their fate[148]

Epitaphs such as this one played a dual role in the history of affections. By evoking memory and recreating a relationship between the
living and the dead they could console the living, but while so doing
they also sustained the grief of loss. An epitaph from a child's tomb
in St. Vincent's Cemetery in Orléans, raised in 1818, provides a telling illustration of the paradoxical feelings of absence and presence
associated with a visit to the cemetery:

> Death has harvested this child in the cradle
> Pitiless and barbarous death
> Ah! in vain your scythe has separated us
> Henri speaks to our hearts, from the depth of his tomb.[149]

Epitaphs were not the only way for parents to assert a continuing
relationship with their children. Ariès has noticed that on sculpted
images children were represented with their eyes open, a sign that
"the deaths of children were the first deaths that could not be tolerated."[150] The tombs of husbands and wives were also intended to provide a place where death and separation would be simultaneously
acknowledged and denied. The increasing importance of the tomb as
a family gathering place helps explain why elaborate epitaphs became
rarer as the nineteenth century progressed.[151] Biographical epitaphs
evoke a particular person and were well suited for the individual
graves called for by the reform of 23 prairial. As concessions became
popular—a development not foreseen by administrators—grave sites
began to collect a number of bodies. The stele that would previously
have been used for an epitaph was now filled with the names of all
those buried in the family tomb (see illus. 14).

Elaborate epitaphs declined in the nineteenth century and have virtually disappeared from the most recent tombs, but the older ele-

ments—the name of the deceased and the invocation to pray for the soul (or souls) of the dead—have remained common. At the Cemetery of St. Jean in Orléans, 51 percent (108 of 210) of the inscriptions recorded between 1808 and 1824 included one of the traditional appeals: "Pray for him" ("*Priez pour lui*"), "Pray for his soul" ("*Priez pour son Ame*"), "Pray to God for the repose of his soul" ("*Priez Dieu pour le repos de son Ame*"), and "Rest in peace" ("*Requiescat in pace*").[152] The first and briefest version of these phrases is the one generally chosen for contemporary tombs, but the request for prayers no longer seems tied to the Catholic belief that the living can help the dead attain salvation by shortening their time in Purgatory.[153] The call for the living to pray for the dead is related instead to the desire to remember. Despite doubts about the Catholic model of the afterlife, this association between praying and remembering has endured and become a central characteristic of the visit to the cemetery.[154]

Contemporaries had no doubts about the importance of these rituals of remembrance, which were observed and commented on by artists, writers, and politicians. The reform of 23 prairial, which created the modern cemetery, was generated by a belief that respect of the living for the dead was a natural sentiment that could not be denied without seriously compromising public morality. For Chateaubriand, in *Génie du christianisme*, tombs were essential to ancient civilizations and to Christianity, and he feared that the proposed *translations* would threaten the relationship between living and dead.[155] Later in the century, writing in a more scholarly vein, Fustel de Coulanges claimed that Greek and Roman civilizations were born of the family's worship of their dead, a cult carried out in part at their tombs, which recall those raised on perpetual concessions in the nineteenth century: "Every family had its tomb, where its dead went to repose, one after another, always together."[156]

Cemeteries were centers for family shrines, places where the living and the dead could be united. The feelings of community and solidarity evoked in the cemeteries could also be extended to the village and the city as a whole, and used to link local sentiments with the French nation. Civic monuments and privileged areas where veterans and victims of World Wars I and II are buried are a constant reminder of the sacrifices that local communities have made for France. In the Cemetery of the East in Angers there are three different sites that suggest how communal cemeteries became places for commemorating tragic and historic events that had marked the collective consciousness. In April 1850, just two years after the cemetery had opened, a metal bridge that spanned the Maine collapsed under the weight of a brigade of soldiers stationed in the city, killing over two hundred of them. This "catastrophe of 1850" drew attention throughout France, as readers of both the local and national press consumed stories of the tragedy and of the heroic acts of those who ministered to the injured and dying. Two days after the accident the bodies of the dead had been pulled from the river, and a massive funeral procession was held to conduct them to the Cemetery of the East. Within a few years a large column was raised in honor of those who had perished.[157] The dead of World Wars I and II are also given a privileged position in the Cemetery of the East. The graves of the soldiers of World War I and of the civilians who died as a result of the fighting during World War II are gathered in separate sites. A cross decorates each of their graves. For the soldiers of World War I the cross is shaped to resemble the hilt of a sword, but no such military reference is made for the civilian graves of World War II.

The public monuments in Angers's Cemetery of the East fall into the category of *Monuments aux Morts* analyzed by Antoine Prost and David Troyansky.[158] According to Troyansky, the first wave of such monuments followed the Franco-Prussian War. After World War I virtually every village in France raised a monument to recall those who had died. The Monuments aux Morts have become central to the civil religion of modern France, shrines were citizens gather on November 11 (armistice day of World War I) for ceremonies and speeches that recall the dead and the reason for their sacrifice. Prost and Troyansky are correct in emphasizing the ways in which these rituals have been used to reinforce republican and nationalist sentiments. The power of these monuments to evoke such sentiments was built, however, on the previous experiences of French men and women who had visited their cemeteries to contemplate family graves. The juxtaposition in Angers's Cemetery of the East of family tombs and public monuments suggests that the civil religion of twentieth-century France owes much to the cultivation of a sentimental attachment to the dead that had developed around family tombs in the nineteenth century.

During the first half of the nineteenth century Romantic literature reflected the intense feelings that were supposed to accompany the visit to the tomb. Already in the late eighteenth century poets such as Aimé Feutry and Philippe Bridel had written verses in the style of the English poets Edward Young and Thomas Gray, both of whom drew inspiration from cemeteries. Although this work anticipated and prepared the way for the sentiments that were to become common in the nineteenth century, the poetry of the eighteenth century retains a macabre element recalling the baroque era. The consolation and moral illumination that would flow from remembered attachments has not yet become central to their experience.[159] Scarcely a generation later, however, Jacques Delille, whose tomb was one of the first important monuments constructed at Père Lachaise, described the cemetery as a place of "peace, love, and mourning" where his wife would come "and shed a tear or two upon my coffin / From each falling drop would roses spring."[160] In his influential poem *Joceyln*, Lamartine has Father Jocelyn describe in detail his feelings at the tomb of his mother, which culminate in a denial of the reality of their separation.

> No! You see, you hear me, you answer me, you love me;
> Our places have changed, our ties are the same.
> Soul who was my mother, oh! speak! speak to me!
> My conversation is in heaven with you.[161]

The visit to the cemetery was more than just a literary device; a number of famous writers from this period were known to visit and draw inspiration from the tombs of their loved ones. We have seen in chapter 4 how Auguste Comte went regularly to the grave of Clotilde de Vaux, and his love and regret for her passing contributed to his creation of the "Religion of Humanity." From Michelet's private journal we learn of his continual visits to Père Lachaise starting in 1815, when his mother was buried there. As early as 1839 Michelet made sure to purchase a perpetual concession for himself and his family in this cemetery, on the site where his monument still remains.[162] Michelet was especially moved by the death of his friend Paul Benoit Ponsot, and his reflections written during a visit to this tomb provide a privileged glimpse of how the dead influenced both memory and morality among the living. On 12 August 1821 Michelet wrote:

> Today I am writing this sitting on my friend's tombstone. May the memory of his rectitude benefit my heart. I notice that I am exactly the same as I was last year, as feeble in my good resolutions, that is, equally corrupt. Oh, my friend, if only you could be with me right now, you who showed me so much compassion for foolishness that you didn't share! My heart is very weak and very ill and doesn't know in whom to confide. Oh, dear friend, what has become of you? I wish that your tomb would speak! Why can't pure spirits communicate with us? How can I convey my anxiety? How often, those days, cowardly, I wished to be completely unprincipled! Each time I experience this cruel state, these words appear to my mind in all their cruelty: "Poinsot is dead."[163]

Victor Hugo, during his exile on Jersey in the 1850s, was frequently inspired by his visits to cemeteries, where he reflected on the paradox of physical corruption and spiritual immortality, which was then being demonstrated at the séances in his dining room.[164] For all these writers the tomb never lost its melancholy character, and in Hugo especially we can hear echos from the tradition in which cemeteries are fearful places. We should recall as well the folktales in which cemeteries were dangerous zones from which the dead threatened the living, stories that still circulated throughout the nineteenth century and influenced Romantics such as Hugo. Following the revolution, however, the emphasis shifted, as cemeteries were seen to be consoling and moralizing institutions. This innovation was superimposed on the older views, and the emotions evoked by cemeteries consequently became more complex.

Perhaps the most straightforward account of the new mood was presented by Jules Simon, who spoke before the Senate in June of 1868 against Haussmann's plans to replace the current Parisian cemeteries with a new site at Méry-sur-Oise. According to Simon, Parisians were drawn by the hundreds of thousands to their burial grounds by "the most pious sentiments which exist in our hearts," a phrase that drew shouts of "C'est vrai!" ("It's true!") and "Très bien!" ("Very good!") from the left. Simon believed that by tampering with this ritual Haussmann was undermining the entire social order, a point on which he claimed that a consensus existed:

> And you, administrators of Paris, like us and like everyone, you experience a profound respect for this sentiment which draws the living to the places where the dead rest, and where they search for memories of the past, the most inspiring and the most fortifying of all memories. . . . Do you believe that the number of Sunday visitors, of the workers who, instead of going to places of pleasure, take with them their wives and children, buy a crown of everlasting flowers (*immortelles*), and pose them on a dear tomb, do you believe in good faith, do you dare to promise yourselves that the number of pious visitors will not be diminished?

According to Simon, the earth where the dead were buried had become sanctified by family visits and was therefore inviolable. "It is earth, yes, without a doubt; but it is the earth which has drunk tears; it is earth, but it is also a memory, a feeling, a past of love and virtue. It is there that the mother has kneeled, it is there she has wept, it is there that the family is reunited after death in the tears around its father!"[165] For Simon, the cemetery was a useful polemical weapon to attack the arbitrary administration of Haussmann, a context that helps explain his unsubtle and nearly hysterical interpretation. On the face of it, Simon's implication that visits to the cemetery were crucial in terms of inculcating morality in the working class and maintaining social peace seems exaggerated; in fact, visits to the graves of martyrs, especially to the the the wall in Père Lachaise where the Communards were executed in 1871, were to become a means of heightening socialist political consciousness.[166] This detail also confirms an aspect of Simon's account, insofar as it shows how social values were reinforced by remembering the dead at their tombs. For Simon, however, family sentiments rather than political and social solidarity were at the center of the visit to the cemetery, and his position throws into sharp relief the image of the cemetery that had become dominant by the second half of the nineteenth century.

Simon referred to visits that working men paid to Parisian cemeteries, but he also described a scene in which a wife weeps at the tomb of her husband. Artists were especially fond of posing women and children at the graves of their husbands and fathers, a choice that can be explained in part by recalling the position occupied by women in the nineteenth century, especially in the middle-class family where they were given special responsibility for establishing and maintaining religious and moral values. The tendency to associate women with events in the natural life-cycle also may have encouraged artists to place them at the grave. Esbrard's 1830 print, Les Regrets, places a woman and her young boy at the modest tomb of her husband; the caption refers to the "faithful friendship" that leads her to pray that she join him in Heaven (see illus. 16). These images reinforced conventional ideas about the role of women, and they may also have consoled husbands and wives that sentiments that they feared would not survive death did indeed endure. The living wife and child, in visiting the tomb of the dead husband, re-create the nuclear unit and reassure the viewers about the permanence of marital fidelity.[167] Such concerns were related to a demographic pattern in which almost 10 percent of all French women were widows, whereas fewer than 5 percent of French men were widowers.[168]

Toward the end of the nineteenth century, however, some images that appeared in the popular illustrated newspapers of the era suggest a different perspective. During the 1890s the illustrated weekly Le Soleil de Dimanche used the occasion of All Souls' Day to show young women paying their respects to the dead; but in these images the moralizing and familial element has been effaced, and instead the artists emphasize sensuality and coquettery. On the cover of the issue of 5 November 1899, no children are present, and the tomb is not identified as that of a husband (see illus. 17). The woman swoons on the cross with an expression that could easily be interpreted as one of sexual arousal.[169] When we look again at the Esbrard engraving after reflecting on this later image, certain features become more

16. *Les Regrets*. Print by Esbrard, 1830. French artists frequently depicted women mourning at the graves of their men (Photo: Bibliothèque Nationale).

prominent. The curved left leg of the mourning wife is displayed with great care, and I am tempted to find something provocative in the way in which the woman holds the child between her legs while she gazes upward. Such an interpretation is admittedly speculative, but it gains strength when we recall the extensive documentation found

17. *All Saints' Day*. Cover illustration from *L'Illustré Soleil du Dimanche*, 5 November 1899 (Photo: Bibliothèque Nationale).

by Philippe Ariès, Mario Praz, and Bram Dykstra of an intimate association between death and eroticism.[170]

The association of women with the cemetery was not, however, the product only of artistic imagination. In Angers an association of upper-class women collected money at the Cemetery of the East on

Good Friday, All Saints' Day, and All Souls' Day for masses to be said for the intentions of the dead; young girls from the group volunteered to seek the donations of visitors at their stations in the cemetery. From 1880 until 1914 the account books of the Organization of the Cemetery of the East (Oeuvre du cimetière de l'Est) were carefully maintained, but in 1915 the entries were less carefully made, and there were none at all for 1916, 1917, and 1918. In 1919 the association reconvened, and although the new president noted how difficult it was to recruit volunteers, as late as 1943 members were still request-ing donations at the gates of the cemetery on All Saints' Day.[171] The comforting sight of feminine devotion to the dead withstood the trauma of World War I with great difficulty. At least for a brief period, the cultural assumption that young women had a taste for this work collapsed when many of them had to confront not the image of mourning as presented to them in art and literature but the reality of mourning for the young men killed in the war.

Women may have been presented as privileged keepers of the cem-etery, but we have seen that men as well were expected to visit the dead and be moved and uplifted by the experience. This idea was powerful enough to shape the feelings of someone as proud of his independence and skepticism as Gustave Flaubert. Writing to a friend from his home in 1852, Flaubert noted his disgust at the "gro-tesque funeral" of a distant relation that he was compelled to at-tend—a ceremony that made him think of boring and best-forgotten balls at Rouen. But Flaubert then concludes his letter with a descrip-tion of his visit to the family tomb, a passage in which he in turn accepts, rejects, and then accepts again the sentiments evoked by the visit.

> Since it was the cemetery where my father and sister are buried, the idea took me to go see their tombs. Seeing them moved me hardly at all; there's nothing there that I loved, but only the remains of two corpses which I observed for several hours. But them: they are in me, in my memory. The sight of a piece of clothing that belonged to them has more effect than their tombs. *Idée réçue*, the idea of the tomb! You have to be sad there, that's the rule. Only one thing moved me, seeing inside the little fence a garden stool (similar to those here) that my mother un-doubtedly had brought there. There is a community between this gar-den and that one, an extension of her life over death and a kind of conti-nuity of common existence through these graves.[172]

The idea of passing some time before family tombs may have "taken" Flaubert, but he immediately rejected the sentiments nor-mally associated with the *"idée réçue"* of the visit to the tomb, which he deemed more appropriate for his boring bourgeois acquaintances of Normandy. But just after this remark by which he has apparently distanced himself from conventional feelings, he reverses himself and confesses that he was moved by the sight of a footstool brought there by his mother. The reflection that follows is in fact a highly conventional evocation of the continuity of the family as testified to by the tomb, the kind of cliché that he has just castigated. Flaubert's letter suggests the powerful appeal of the visit to the cemetery and of the sentiments attached to it, which swept over him against his will.

Chapter Six

THE ORIGINS OF COMMERCIAL FUNERALS

IN JANUARY 1986 Lucien Roche, dead at age eighty-one, was brought to the municipal cemetery at Cannes, where his family and friends found that the gates had been locked by city officials to prevent their entry. During the next twenty-four hours his body lay outside the cemetery, watched over by Michel Leclerc, the owner of the undertaking establishment responsible for the funeral arrangements. Finally, after twenty-four hours, the city relented and Roche's casket was allowed into the cemetery, where it was placed in a temporary grave. But the city continued to refuse burial in the family plot, claiming that such an action was illegal.[1]

In the 1980s French newspapers gave frequent coverage to similar incidents, most of them involving Michel Leclerc and his funeral establishments, which numbered eighty by 1986.[2] At issue in Cannes, and elsewhere, was the right of the family to choose an undertaker who had not been approved by the city, which had granted a monopoly on the funeral trade to another corporation. Leclerc, whose family is well known for their chain of discount supermarkets throughout France, offers funerals at 40 percent less than those proposed by firms chosen by city governments. As part of his campaign against the current system of monopolies, Leclerc published advertisements in which he announced that "those who survive must not be forced to submit to a racket. Give them a free choice!"[3] Not surprisingly, Pompes Funèbres Générales, the corporation that dominates the funeral trade in medium-sized French cities, has fought back against the Leclerc initiative. In the spring of 1985 Pompes Funèbres Générales mounted a publicity campaign in which they unveiled a new logo, a white dove taking flight, soaring over the letters PFG. This attempt to improve the image of the dominant firm was published in the major newspapers in full-page ads that combined claims of expertise, a hint of disappointment about the public misunderstanding of their difficult work, and an assertion of pride in a profession that they had practiced for over one hundred years. The advertisement concludes with the new logo and the slogan "The dignity of death, the respect of life." ("*La dignité de la mort, le respect de la vie.*")[4] Both Leclerc and PFG claim, of course, to represent the public interest and to have as their goal providing dignified and fairly priced funerals.[5]

Controversies surrounding the funeral profession are neither recent nor unique to France. Philippe Ariès, inspired by Jessica Mitford's influential polemic *The American Way of Death*, suggests that commercial funerals are an American innovation; others like Thomas Laqueur, and Ruth Richardson have discussed their significance in nineteenth-century England.[6] Despite the recent wave of research on death, however, we know little about how the funeral profession developed in France. In both the United States and England undertakers were able to work in a relatively unconstrained market, and in France as well funeral professionals sought to obtain free access to their clients. Debates that occurred throughout the nineteenth century in France, however, testify to a long struggle in which the clergy and public officials negotiated with each other and with businessmen about regulations that would control the play of the market in the funeral industry. The law that currently regulates French funerals was passed in 1904 following a century in which the Church, the State, and the funeral profession attempted to work out an arrangement that satisfied both public demand for dignified services and their own institutional interests, which were simultaneously political, religious, and financial.

In France, as in England and the United States, funeral professionals evoke complicated responses; they provide a needed service but are resented for the questions about finances that inevitably arise at a time when monetary considerations seem inappropriate. Our ambivalence toward funerals, and toward death, can be illuminated by considering the conflicts and tensions that surrounded the creation of a new method of dealing with the dead in nineteenth-century France. Funeral customs have drawn the interest of historians and anthropologists because they provide a privileged entry point for anyone interested in grasping the fundamental values of a culture.[7] A study of the development of the commercial funeral industry in nineteenth-century France will allow us to see how death was appropriated in the "market culture" emerging at that time.[8]

From the Ancien Régime to the Revolution

The funeral profession in modern France, like the cemeteries examined in the last chapter, grew out of the revolutionary crisis of the late eighteenth century. During the ancien régime funerals in cities were managed by the clergy, elected parish councils (*fabriques*), and the guild of town criers (*jurés-crieurs*). Although several historians have done valuable work on the history of death during the ancien régime, the precise relationship among these different groups remains obscure. By the end of the seventeenth century royal edicts had granted those who purchased the office of town crier a monopoly permitting them to announce a death by means of printed notices, rent the funeral hangings used to decorate the house and the church, provide mourning clothes for the guests, and arrange for the transportation of the body by carriage.[9] The clergy were reimbursed for the religious services, and the parish vestry profited from the sale of candles and the rental of decorations inside the church. The division of labor here was not perfectly clear, but it seems that of the interested parties the town criers received the largest share of the funeral expenses.

The profits gained by the town criers were important enough to provoke both anger among clients and jealousy among potential competitors. At Besançon in 1691 the attempts by the guild to extend its privileges led to accusations that the bodies of the poor were being held hostage because of uncollected fees, and an angry demonstration before the houses of the guild members threatened for a time to turn into a major riot.[10] In Angers the municipal government, seeking to use profits from the funeral industry to support the hospital, purchased the rights to this trade in 1761. An heir to one of the former town criers, however, continued to lay claim to the funeral business in court cases that dragged on for the rest of the century.[11] Other problems for the corporation arose from the jealousy of competitors who sought a share of the lucrative funeral trade. By the end of the eighteenth century Parisian clothiers had won the right to rent funeral garments and printers the right to sell burial notices, thus compromising the guild's monopoly.[12]

By the end of the eighteenth century the funeral trade run jointly by clergy, parishes, and town criers had developed into an elaborate system—but one available only to the aristocracy and the affluent middle class. In principle a distinction was made between religious services, available to everyone regardless of wealth, and funeral pomp, purchased by families with resources. In practice, however, the distinction was difficult to maintain. In Paris, for example, those who could afford nothing and those who purchased the cheapest service at twelve livres were carried directly from home to the cemetery. The twelve-livre service entitled the family to a low mass at the church on the day following the burial.[13] By contrast the funeral for someone of moderate wealth would include printed invitations, candles, decorations of the church and the home, distribution of bread to the poor, the ringing of the church bells, the presence of numerous clergy in the funeral procession, and masses for the repose of the soul. Such a service might cost as much as one thousand livres, and expenses could go as high as four thousand livres for the most elaborate decorations and ceremonies.[14]

In a reaction inspired by the Enlightenment values of "solemnity, restraint, and egalitarian simplicity," the excesses associated with the baroque funeral became less fashionable in the latter part of the eighteenth century, especially among the aristocracy and the clergy.[15] During the revolution this new taste for funereal simplicity acquired the force of law as the system of the ancien régime was attacked in a series of decrees aimed at eliminating social distinctions among the dead.

The most famous example of the revolutionary campaign to enforce simplicity and equality in funerals is the decree of the representative-on-mission Joseph Fouché issued at Nevers in October 1793. According to Article 4 of the decree, "In each municipality, all dead citizens, regardless of sect, will be led twenty-four hours after death, and forty-eight in the case of sudden death, to the place designated for city burials, covered with a funeral veil on which sleep will be painted, accompanied by a public officer, surrounded by their friends in mourning, and a detachment of their brothers in arms."[16] The Parisian prosecutor Anaxagoras Chaumette, inspired by Fouché's example, had a similar measure adopted in Paris in November, which called for the dead to be brought to their graves in a coffin draped with the national colors, led by a man carrying a wooden sign with the inscription "The just man never dies; he lives in the memory of co-citizens."[17]

Despite these attempts at reform, the attachment to traditional rites on the part of French peasants made such decrees difficult to enforce, and many provincial commissioners resigned themselves to tolerating funeral processions conducted with the prayers and songs of the Catholic service.[18] In the cities, on the other hand, traditional practices seem to have been abandoned. In 1795 Gaspard Delamalle described the funeral of his mother, whose coffin was dragged to a miserable grave by disrespectful porters, with neither family nor friends in attendance.[19] For the poor, funerals were even more scandalous. According to one report, their bodies were placed in coffins that were reused several times and carted in wagons that held as many as five or six to cemeteries where their bodies were dumped naked into common graves. Porters were often seen stopping their wagons outside cabarets and were accused of drunkenness.[20] By 1796 these criticisms prompted the Paris municipal council to issue a decree calling for four uniformed porters to carry the coffin from the home to the cemetery and enjoining them, as well as the grave diggers, to respect the dead.[21]

THE ORIGINS OF POMPES FUNÈBRES: PARIS, 1796–1880

The Paris decree of 1796 can be taken as a starting point for the development of the modern system of funerals, in which state regulations designed to ensure equal treatment of all citizens were uneasily combined with the toleration of decorations, vehicles, and coffins that distinguished the funerals of those who could afford to purchase and rent these trappings from entrepreneurs. Following the negotiation of the Concordat reestablishing the Catholic Church in France in 1801, a number of government decrees attempted to regulate the emerging funeral industry and apportion responsibility among the clergy, the parish councils, and the entrepreneurs. These measures failed to reconcile the competing interests, however, and confusion of responsibilities created public controversy over the management and costs of funerals.

Although Paris was the first city where conflicts over the funeral industry emerged, other cities faced similar problems as well. As was true of cemeteries, Paris provided a test case that both the central government and provincial cities used as a model for policy elsewhere in France. As we will see in chapter 7, by the 1850s the commercial funeral industry was spreading rapidly throughout France. The professional undertakers were generally able to satisfy both politicians and the clergy that they could provide a range of services that were sufficiently solemn and also financially advantageous. Consequently, the funeral industry was well placed to take advantage of the renewal of Church-State conflicts that arose toward the end of the century—conflicts that permitted entrepreneurs to assume the dominant role in the provision of funerals that they continue to occupy today.

During the government of the Directory in the last years of the eighteenth century, the Council of 500—acting in response to criticisms about the neglect of the dead during the revolutionary period—took an important first step in reestablishing the legal basis for funeral celebrations. On 7 fructidor, year VII (1799), the Council passed a decree similar to the one issued three years earlier in Paris calling for all citizens to be accompanied to their graves by a municipal officer, family, and friends. Public officials were permitted to have their coffins decorated with civic insignia, and representatives from the appropriate government institution were to take part in the procession. The government of the Directory was still suspicious of the

Church, however, and concerned about the potential offensiveness of funeral pomp. No mention was made of a passage by a church, and no decorations other than the ones mentioned in the decree were to be permitted, so as not to violate the spirit of equality.[22]

This concern for equality implied the resentment of the distinctions between rich and poor that had characterized funerals before the revolution. Egalitarian sentiments continued to be expressed in subsequent decrees, but increasingly they were formulas that had little to do with the developing funeral practices.[23] The decree on funerals in Paris issued by the prefect of the Seine Frochot on 22 ventôse, year IX (12 March 1801), illustrates this ambiguity toward funeral decorations. The regulations that it established governing the funeral industry became a model for subsequent national legislation and allow us to observe the system of commercial funerals in its earliest stage of development.

Frochot's decree of 1801 began with a simple assertion: "Funeral institutions are one of the first needs of a civilization."[24] This claim was a familiar one around the turn of the nineteenth century, as was the introductory analysis of the recent history of funeral practices:

> The institutions which have been abandoned as a result of the Revolution surrounded the funerals of the rich with a last flourish, but accorded to the poor only the sad emblems of misery and abandon. Those which exist today have enveloped both rich and poor in the same indifference; public opinion, in accord with morality, condemns the barrenness of current burials. It is worthy of the first city of the Republic to order, by its example, the decency of burials, and especially to consecrate as an obligation of communal piety the burial of the poor.[25]

This early Parisian legislation emphasized the equal treatment of rich and poor, all of whom would be accorded a solemn funeral administered by state-appointed professionals. In order to ensure that all citizens be treated with dignity, the decree called for a master of ceremonies and at least three porters to be named for each arrondissement. The master of ceremonies was to wear a long black coat, with violet pants and vest, and a three-cornered black hat decorated with a black feather.[26] The porters and coachman were to be outfitted in gray.

Dressed in their distinctive uniform, these early undertakers were responsible for the orderly procession of the dead to the cemetery and for a decent burial ceremony. The law of 1801 established a basic standard that reflects both egalitarian aspirations and a reaction against the abusive treatment of the dead observed during the revolution. Caskets could no longer be reused, and the poor would no longer be unceremoniously dumped into their graves but would have their own shroud and casket, paid for by the city. The carrying of the dead on stretchers was also prohibited; from now on everyone over the age of seven would be brought to his or her grave in a wagon, led by the porters and followed by the master of ceremonies and the family. The wagon was to proceed slowly, and the police were to ensure that it not be stopped on its way to the cemetery. The costs of the standard service were to be kept low, at twenty francs, with the city paying for the poor. Together these measures became a minimum standard for the treatment of the dead that spread from Paris to provincial cities in the course of the nineteenth century.

The decree of 1801 was designed to create a slow pace and solemn atmosphere that would surround all the dead, both rich and poor, but it also included an article that would ultimately undermine the equality aspired to throughout the revolutionary period. According to Article VIII, "The ordinary funeral can be, at the request of the family, augmented by everything they judge appropriate to render it more solemn." No attempt was made to regulate either the number and kind of items available or the prices that could be charged, thus opening the way for the rapid growth of funeral pomp in Paris that was to occur over the next few years and provoke belated attempts to control it.

Frochot's law did not specify who would provide funereal trappings or how the new funerals were to be administered, but it appears that the new system was designed by the prefect after consultation with M. Bobée, an entrepreneur who was eager to invest profits made during the revolutionary wars. In Paris during the Consulate, Bobée was struck by the "indecent manner in which the last duties were rendered to the dearest and most respectable people," and he conceived the idea of a business that would provide a "decent and moral" funeral for everyone.[27] Soon after the decree of ventôse was issued, the Department of the Seine granted Bobée a contract giving him the right to provide the material for Parisian funerals over a period of nine years. According to the terms of the contract, the city would charge citizens a basic fee of twenty francs for every funeral but would exempt the indigent from this tax. The city would in turn reimburse Bobée eight francs for each funeral, whether or not the tax had been paid. In addition the entrepreneur would have the right to collect twenty francs from those who desired presentation of the body in the church before being led to the cemetery. Bobée could also charge additional fees for providing decorations for the house, candles, gloves, printed invitations, inscriptions on tombs, and lead caskets. In return for these privileges Bobée was responsible for the purchase and maintenance of the necessary equipment and for the hiring and supervision of the undertakers, porters, and coachmen placed in each arrondissement.[28]

During his first two years in business Bobée did not make an enormous amount of money, but the accounts that he submitted to the prefect do indicate both the potential profits available and the reviving fashionableness of elaborate funerals. Bobée's initial investment came to about Fr 300,000, including over 100,000 for hearses and carriages for the mourners, and over 100,000 for the materials for the services, including velvet hangings and silver candle holders. Expenses for the first year, including salaries and maintenance, came to Fr 214,395, whereas receipts were only 210,690. During the second year this deficit was turned into a profit with expenses of Fr 308,379 and receipts of 360,508. What is most interesting, however, is the source of the income, which reveals the shifting taste in Paris funerals. Table 6.1 shows the origin of Bobée's receipts over the first two years. These figures indicate the renewal of interest in a church service, as the percentage of those requesting a presentation went from 16 percent to 19 percent. Even more striking, however, is the increase in the amount spent on "accessories," which more than doubled in a single year. Once they were made available people were willing to spend increasing amounts to drape their houses and churches in black crepe, purchase candles, and rent silver ornaments, hearses, and funeral wagons.

Despite the privilege granted to Bobée some competition was tolerated in the early years of the nineteenth century. The merchant Bigot, who identified himself as a tapestry maker/decorator (*tapissier-décorateur*), had begun to provide coffins and hearses and to rent funeral decorations for homes and churches even before Frochot's decree of

TABLE 6.1
Funeral Revenues, Paris

	Year IX	Year X
Burials	12,584	17,071
Burial fees	100,672 frs	136,568 frs
Presentations at church	2,062	3,287
Presentation fees	39,784 frs	63,467 frs
Accessories	70,234 frs	160,473 frs
Total Revenues	210,690 frs	360,508 frs

Source: AN F19 5517. Compte général de l'Entreprise pendant les deux premières années de son exercice; Etat détaillé des recettes et dépenses faites pour le Service des Inhumations, pendant la première année de l'exercice de l'Entrepeneur.

1801. Following the negotiation of the contract between Frochot and Bobée, he stopped providing hearses and coffins but continued to rent and sell ornaments, a practice that was apparently permitted by the department.[29] This competition, combined with the lack of any price control over the decorative objects proposed by the entrepreneurs, provoked administrative concern about the commercialization of the funeral industry. Furthermore, Paris was the only city in which any official regulations had been approved. Provincial cities like Angers were by this time also experimenting with the restoration of funeral ceremonial and were calling on the government to issue national legislation sanctioning this development. In the midst of this revival of funerals the Concordat of 1801, which reestablished an official relationship between Church and State, provided the immediate impetus for redefining an appropriate role for the Church in the conduct and finances of funerals.

The decree of 23 prairial, year XII (1804), which we have already studied as the basic law governing cemeteries, also regulated funerals throughout the nineteenth century.[30] According to this law responsibility for providing and supervising funerals was to be divided between parish councils and cities, and bishops, prefects, and the government ministries in Paris all had the right to approve local regulations. Michel Vovelle has commented that in France the State was "discrete" in its managing of funerals, which were left primarily to the fabriques, elected parish councils responsible for maintaining the church and the material needed for services. According to Vovelle, this privilege was envied by bourgeois entrepreneurs jealous of the potential revenues.[31] The implementation of the decree in Paris during the first half of the nineteenth century suggests, however, a different conclusion. Entrepreneurs were not marginal players in a scene dominated by the parishes but aggressive and successful businessmen who were able to take advantage of the law and organize an increasingly profitable trade in funeral decorations. The decree of 23 prairial attempted to define the respective rights of clergy, communes, parishes, and entrepreneurs; given their varied interests it is unsurprising that this law did not succeed in clearly delineating the division of labor, thus setting the stage for the controversy and debate that surrounded the Paris funeral industry throughout the first half of the century.

Title V of the decree of 23 prairial opened with a clear assertion that the dead had a right to be honored with ceremony, and this was coupled with a statement that families were free to spend what they wanted to on funerals. These expenditures, however, were to be regulated by the local government, which would consult with both the ecclesiastical hierarchy and the central administration. The clergy, for example, were allowed to charge for their participation in processions and religious services requested by the family, with prices to be established by the government acting on the advice of bishops and prefects. The clergy were not to be paid for services for the poor, a reminder of the revolutionary concern for dignified treatment of all citizens.[32]

The decree as it affected the clergy confirmed previous regulations established in Paris following the Concordat. A full year before the law of 23 prairial the government approved the division of clerical services for Paris funerals into five classes, ranging from five to three hundred francs. A first-class service would involve the participation of twenty-five priests, the decoration of the church with funeral crepe and candles, at least eighteen of which would surround the body and be placed on the altar, and a high mass. A fourth-class service, at twelve francs, would have two candles, a low mass, and the participation of three priests in the procession. The price list approved by the government says nothing about the services for a fifth-class funeral, which would cost either five francs or be provided free. It seems likely that at this level the priest accompanied the body to the grave, but without a passage by the church.[33] This careful detailing of services and their prices, and their categorization into clearly defined classes, shows the wide range of clerical ritual available in 1804. Depending on their ability to pay, people could be honored with an elaborate service or dispatched quickly in a perfunctory procession. In chapter 3 I noted how clerical behavior at the deathbed and the collection of mass fees were controversial issues for the clergy, who were resented for charging money for prayers that it was believed should be available to all, regardless of wealth. Funeral charges provoked comparable suspicions because, despite its attempt to provide for clerical participation at all funerals, the Church clearly gave favored treatment to those who could pay.

The law of 23 prairial assigned a key role to local government; mayors were given the right, with the approval of the prefect, to arrange for the most suitable means of transporting bodies to their graves.[34] At the same time, however, the law granted parish councils the right to furnish the carriages, funeral hangings, and other decorations used for funerals and burials. This provision was designed to provide compensation to the fabriques for the income lost as a result of the revolutionary seizure of ecclesiastical property. In providing these services parishes could either exercise their right directly or rent their interest to an entrepreneur, with the approval of the civil authorities.

The provisions of the law of 23 prairial governing funerals, like those regulating cemeteries, involved Church and State in a confusing relationship that neither officials nor the public could easily grasp. Implementation was difficult, especially in the early years, when families and the clergy quarreled over fees and when funeral professionals began to market the funeral as a consumer item. In response to this commercialization of death, Church and State defended their financial interests and institutional prerogatives, while families struggled to assess what kind of funeral they wanted and what they could afford.

The presenting of a bill for a funeral provided the occasion for the parties involved to confront these issues and at times became a painful moment of tension between the clergy and the laity. Some families disputed the fees charged by the clergy and called on civil officials to enforce the prices approved by bishops and the Ministry of Religion. Families also objected when they were presented with two bills, one for religious services paid to the priest and one for the decorations paid to the parish. The government's distinction between the rights of the clergy and the parish councils may have made administrative and financial sense, but it was confusing to those who had to pay, who suspected that they were being double billed. Attempts were made, as we will see, to respond to this complaint, but tension arising from the exchange of money between family and clergy for funeral services was never entirely eliminated, and it contributed to the anticlericalism endemic throughout the century.

The conflicts between families and clergy, however, were not the most severe problem in terms of implementing the decree of 23 prairial. Competition between the Paris fabriques, anxious to take advantage of their new rights, and Bobée, who fought to retain his privileged position in the funeral trade, resulted in a long series of hostile exchanges and administrative infighting. This conflict focused on two key issues that were left unclear in the law of 23 prairial. First, parish councils were given the right to provide all the furnishings that would ensure a decent service, while the cities were charged with regulating the transport of the body to the grave and with setting fees for "printed invitations, funeral hangings, coffins, and the transportation of the body(Arts. 21, 25)." Second, the decree forbade any violation of the rights granted parish councils but did so without prejudice to existing contracts between entrepreneurs and prefects (Art. 24). Massive confusion resulted from this lack of precision, and the problems of Paris early in the century would be repeated elsewhere as the taste for elaborate funerals spread to the provinces. Money was obviously a crucial matter, as profits available from the increasingly lucrative funeral business fueled arguments among parishes, businessmen, and civil officials throughout the century. At the same time that they were fighting about money, the Church and the State were also struggling to assert control over the rituals of death, which were gradually being drawn into the marketplace.

The parishes of Paris were quick to lay claim to the fees permitted them by the new law, hoping to use them to replace the sacred vessels, decorations, and other material seized or destroyed by the revolutionary governments and to make repairs to the churches which had suffered from years of neglect. As the legal commentator Joachim Gaudry pointed out, the "rights over burials and funeral services form the principal revenue of fabriques."[35] Parish councils immediately began negotiating contracts with entrepreneurs who were in direct competition with Bobée. Their intention was to set up a complete service, including the provision of caskets and hearses, that would allow families to choose someone other than the city government's official agent. Bobée's competitors agreed to pay a large proportion of their revenues to the fabriques; the merchant Bigot offered 33 percent, while another entrepreneur, Boulanger, proposed 50 percent.[36]

The prefect Frochot and Bobée immediately moved to defend the current monopoly, arguing that it was a valid contract negotiated by civil officials given broad powers of regulation by the law of 23 prairial. Frochot was able to convince cabinet ministers of the advantages of a monopoly that would eliminate the variation of prices from one parish to another, a situation that would result in public scandal and possible competition among churches. He also argued that allowing parishes to move into the trade would take revenue from the city service that subsidized the funerals of the poor. These arguments were met by the parishes' insistence on the clarity of their rights as outlined in the law, and by accusations of collusion between Frochot and Bobée.

The parish initiative to establish independent contracts with funeral entrepreneurs was foiled by Frochot's decree of 11 vendémiaire, year XIII (1805), which established Bobée's exclusive rights over the "extraordinary services" requested by families and called for the negotiation of a new contract between the parishes and Bobée granting a percentage of his revenues to the churches. Barring an amiable settlement of this issue, the decree set up a system of arbitration. The parishes, looking forward to substantial income, had in mind a percentage comparable to the offers of Bigot and Boulanger. Frochot, however, after two years of bickering, settled on a figure of 16 percent. The parishes were understandably furious with this decision, which they saw as the result of further collusion between Frochot and Bobée, and some of them continued to defy the contract and work with Bigot. The results were exactly what the decree of 23 prairial was designed to avoid: prices for funerals varied from one parish to the next, and the resulting competition confused and angered families faced with choices regarding services for their dead.[37]

The Napoleonic decree of 18 May 1806 responded to the confusion surrounding the implementation of the earlier legislation. The decree also provides a glimpse of how the poor were being treated under the new regime of funerals. Parishes and entrepreneurs were prohibited from removing decorations set up for a family that could afford them during services of a poor person scheduled to follow the paid funeral. By suppressing such behavior, which called attention to the privileges of money and was embarrassing and insulting to the poor, the government hoped to forestall resentment directed against the wealthy and the Church.[38]

The law of 1806 confirmed the rights of parishes to furnish all the decorations for churches and funeral processions, but it also declared that current contracts were to be honored. Bobée had won the right to provide services for the nine years called for in his agreement with Frochot, but following this the parishes would have the right to take their business elsewhere. With this act Napoleon hoped to resolve a simmering feud, but his decree also added an important element that was to shape and trouble funeral practice for the rest of the century.

According to the law of 1806, either the parishes or the entrepreneur that they employed were to establish a price list in which the different funerals were arranged by classes. This list would have to be submitted to city councils and prefects and approved by the minister of religion. Religious services had been divided by classes in Paris since 1803, but Bobée, in carrying out his first contract, had limited himself to a single price list for items under his control. Now the system of classes was to be applied to all aspects of funeral ceremonial. This measure was intended to simplify matters for families, to avoid forcing them to make a long series of choices about the purchase of particular items. Instead it not only resulted in a system that clearly distinguished among the funerals of Parisians on the basis of wealth but also contributed to the formation of attitudes in which the dignity of the service and respect for the dead were associated with the amount of money spent.

Other decisions taken by the emperor and incorporated into the decree of 18 May 1806 were designed to limit the possibility of competition among funeral entrepenuers and between parishes and city governments. In large cities all the parishes were obligated to form a single enterprise, thus preventing individual fabriques or their entrepreneurs from trying to undersell one another. The decree also confirmed the rights of cities to regulate the transport of bodies to their graves and called on city councils to cooperate with parishes in renting this trade to an entrepreneur. Although far from being perfectly clear, these provisions suggested that parishes were primarily responsible for all decorations inside the church and that city councils were charged with the transport of bodies—that is, for the decency of the service outside the church.

The differentiation between inside and outside represented an effort by the government to deal with jurisdictional conflicts over funerals by making a distinction between the private and the public. Religion, which was a matter of individual choice and therefore a private matter, was granted control of home and church; but in moving between home, church, and cemetery, the dead entered the public realm, over which the city claimed control. This set of distinctions between inside and outside, private and public, Church and State, could not be perfectly maintained. Was city or parish responsible for providing decorations for the casket and candles carried by mourners? Parishes clearly had the right to decorate the inside of houses and churches, but what about the external facades? Furthermore, both state officials and clergy were inclined at times to challenge the boundaries. The clergy refused to concede that Catholicism, for example, had no public role to play in managing the dead, and civil officials sometimes defined their sphere of interest as crossing the threshold of houses and churches. The decrees of 23 prairial (1804) and of 18 May 1806 were based on the assumption that clergy, parishes, entrepreneurs, and local and federal officials would work together to provide funerals that would allow those with money to honor their dead with ceremony and ornament, while providing a dignified service for the poor. It was, however, not an easy matter to define the boundaries of Church and State, to reconcile the interests of the several institutions involved, and to organize a funeral service that satisfied both the taste for luxury and the desire for equality.

The parish councils of Paris continued to be dissatisfied with the implementation of the new decrees and were convinced that Bobée and Frochot were conspiring to deprive them of their fair share of revenue. Their pressure led to the first payments by Bobée, who handed over Fr 47,694 for 1806 and 55,863 for 1807. Conflict between the entrepreneur, supported by the prefect Frochot, and the clergy and parishes grew more intense as Bobée's nine-year term approached its expiration in 1812. A decree of 18 August 1811 that established the different classes and prices called for in 1806 aggravated this relationship. According to the decree different services were available, ranging from a first-class funeral costing Fr 4,288 to a sixth-class service for Fr 16. These prices were a maximum, which families could reduce by eliminating some individual items from the list of ornamental objects. The law also required that families be presented with only one bill and assumed that they would choose the same class for both the religious services and the funeral procession. The prices established made clear that it was the entrepreneur who would profit most from the new system. The religious services for the first-class funeral cost Fr 600, whereas the decorations of the house and the church and the rental of the hearse came to Fr 3,688. The disproportion between religious service and funeral pomp was not quite as dramatic for the other classes, but was nonetheless substantial. Religious services for a fourth-class funeral cost Fr 50, whereas the decoration of the house and church were Fr 169. The clergy and parishes were disturbed by this disparity, especially because they received such a small percentage of the revenue for the funeral pomp. Consequently, they permitted families to choose a religious service one class higher than the funeral decorations provided by the entrepreneur. This increased their proportion of funeral revenue but complicated the billing procedure. The standard receipts that grouped religious and funeral services according to class became unusable, and clients were being presented with two separate bills, which led to complaints from both families and the entrepreneur.[39]

The decade of inconclusive decrees and bickering that accompanied the emergence of the Paris funeral industry was finally concluded in 1812, when the parishes considered bids for the provision of funeral services from three different entrepreneurs, including the detested Bobée. All three bid on a schedule of conditions (*cahier des charges*) drawn up by the department that clearly specified the responsibilities of parishes and entrepreneurs. The city of Paris agreed to pay the entrepreneur eight francs for the burial of all those who died at home but were unable to pay for their own funerals; the entrepreneur would also receive a flat rate of six thousand francs for those who died in hospitals, who were to be brought directly to the cemetery, without a passage by the church. For those who could afford to pay, however, the entrepreneur was not to charge an additional fee for bearing the coffin to the church—a provision that suggests that by this time civil burials had become increasingly rare. Special care was taken to monitor the undertakers, who were required to file within twenty-four hours of the burial a receipt with the city listing the furnishings rented for the service.[40]

Bids were submitted to the prefect for the Paris funeral trade on 10 January 1812; Bobée, anxious to retain what was an increasingly profitable business, offered the fabriques 33⅓ percent of the gross receipts, a substantial increase over the 16 percent that he had formerly paid, but still the lowest offer. Nevertheless, the parishes were deeply concerned that his influence with the prefect might gain him the contract, and a joint committee of parish councils wrote the minister of religion to oppose his offer. The parishes also convinced the archbishop of Paris to intervene on their side of the dispute. In February, while the bids were being considered, Cardinal Jean Maury wrote a harsh letter about Bobée to the minister of cults, accusing him of conspiring with public officials and of bad faith. Maury also expressed concern about the threatened publication of a pamphlet by the parishes in which they would expose the "brigandage" of the current entrepreneur, thereby compromising both Church and State in the eyes of the public. Finally, he threatened to raise the issue directly with Napoleon, "and you know he is not very tender toward thieves."[41]

The pressure from the parishes and the archbishop, along with an offer to pay 50 percent of gross receipts to the parishes, led to the award of the contract to M. Labalte. Like Bobée, Labalte ran into some initial problems in working with the parishes, and in June the new entrepreneur wrote to the minister of religion that "the clergy do everything possible to avoid . . . the execution of the decree which grants me incontestable rights, by persuading the families not to adopt the same class of funeral service provided by the 'Enterprise' as chosen for the church, and by furnishing themselves objects which are exclusively given to me."[42] Tight scheduling of processions by the mayors of the twelve arrondissements sometimes led to tension with Labalte, whom families blamed when they were forced to wait for transportation for their dead. The parishes, recalling their unhappy experience with Bobée, were concerned that Labalte did not always deliver the promised percentage of revenues.[43] Despite these problems, however, Labalte's relationship with the parishes and the neighborhoods was relatively calm. The adjudication of 1812 set a model that was followed in Paris for the rest of the century and in provincial cities as well, where secular professionals guaranteed parishes a percentage of revenue in exchange for monopoly rights to the funeral decorations.

The normalization of the funeral trade did not, however, eliminate conflict between the parishes and the entrepreneurs. In subsequent adjudications the percentage granted to parishes fluctuated according to the offers from the entrepreneurs, as shown in table 6.2. The percentage of funeral revenues distributed to the parishes was, however, less difficult to decide than was the issue of how to calculate the gross revenue on which it was to be paid. In the 1830s the entrepreneur Charles Baudouin began offering a number of items apart from the price lists agreed to with the parishes and for which he paid

TABLE 6.2
Percentage of Gross Receipts Paid by Entrepreneur to Parishes

Year	Percentage
1812–20	50%
1821–32	72.5%
1833–42	71.25%
1843–50	71.5%
1853–59	83.5%
1860–69	56%

Source: M. H. Ranvier, *Rapport sur la municipalisation du service des pompes funèbres* (Paris, 1905).

nothing to them. Following several complaints, the government intervened and required Baudouin to include the additional objects when calculating his payment. Beginning in 1842 the entrepreneur was required to pay 50 percent to the fabriques for all objects not included on the official price list and 15 percent on nonrented objects. Baudouin was checked in his desire to increase his revenues at the expense of the parishes, but his effort suggests an aggressive commercialism in the funeral industry that we will see criticized in public debates and literature of the period.[44]

Although constrained by a contract with parishes and checked by government regulation, entrepreneurs including Baudouin were acutely conscious of the potential profits from the funeral business. Figures on the income that the parishes gained from the funeral trade demonstrate how profitable this trade was and also suggest how the taste for funeral ceremony was growing throughout the century, a development that can be confirmed in the comments of journalists and novelists. For the period 1821 to 1832 (the first for which accurate records were kept), the parishes received an average annual payment of Fr 470,854, a figure that dropped to 401,793 for 1833–1842. This decline was due in part to Baudouin's refusal to pay a percentage on new items not covered in the original contract. When an adjustment was made to include these, the income for the parishes rose to an average of Fr 831,472 for the period 1843 to 1850, to 1,108,618 for 1853–1859, and to 1,586,763 for 1860–1870. Income for the parishes reached a peak of Fr 2,481,334 in 1880 and dropped thereafter, averaging 1,833,754 for the last five years (1899–1903) prior to the secularization of the industry. These figures, although they indicate the substantial income available from the funeral trade, do not necessarily reveal its popular appeal, because throughout this period Paris was growing, and the number of deaths and funeral processions in-

TABLE 6.3
Percentage of Parisian Funerals by classes

	Funeral Class		
Years	1, 2, 3	4, 5, 6	7, 8, 9
1832–43	4%	46%	50%
1843–51	5%	57%	38%
1853–59	4%	39%	57%
1860–70	3%	36%	61%

Source: M. H. Ranvier, *Rapport sur la municipalisation du service des pompes funèbres* (Paris, 1905).

creased. Throughout the century there was also a substantial increase in the proportion of Parisians who chose a *service extraordinaire*. Only 19 percent of those who died between 1821 and 1826 chose a service provided by the entrepreneur, but this figure rose to 27 percent for the period 1839 to 1848, 33 percent for 1853–1859, and 40 percent for 1860–1870. Funeral decorations reached the largest proportion of Parisians in 1882, when 49 percent purchased a service extraordinaire. By the end of the century, just before the secularization of the industry, the figures had dropped slightly, averaging 44 percent for the period 1898 to 1903.[45]

In addition to measuring the overall increase in the popularity of commercial funerals, data collected by the city of Paris allow us to form an idea about which category of funerals were most appealing to families. In 1832 a new contract established nine classes of funerals, with prices ranging from Fr 15 to Fr 3,968.[46] By breaking these nine into groups of three, table 6.3 reveals how tastes were changing in the course of the nineteenth century. Those who could afford a funeral, it appears, were primarily interested in the less-expensive variety. Throughout this period it was the modest seventh-class service that was consistently the most popular, an appeal that grew over the decades, increasing its share of Parisian funerals from 35 percent in 1832 to 52 percent in 1870. This service, including the religious ceremonies, cost a minimum of fifty-seven francs, although the family could add a few supplemental decorations to the basic offerings. The differences in the decorations of the hearse and the house of the deceased were illustrated in publicity put out by the entrepreneurs and can give us some visual sense of the services (see illus. 18). Only with a seventh-class service are the horses decorated, and the fringe on the hearse clearly distinguishes it from that of an eighth-class ceremony. Parisians interested in indicating to their neighbors that they could afford to bury their dead decently, though not extravagantly, were thus drawn to this class of service.

The growth of the funeral industry was clearly profitable to both parishes and the entrepreneurs, and the increasing appeal of the service extraordinaire suggests that Parisians responded to the funeral pomp made available to them. Statistics on the income of parishes and the purchase of services, although they demonstrate the growth of the industry, provide only hints about public attitudes toward the commercialization of funerals. A controversy about the marketing practices of the undertaking profession in the 1840s provides more direct evidence of the public's response to the new industry. The pamphlets that recorded this debate describe a public increasingly drawn to funeral display, highly sensitive about the relationship between the expense of the service and the social status of the deceased, and concerned about the abuses that resulted when unscrupulous entrepreneurs attempted to manipulate families anxious to purchase a funeral appropriate to their wealth and position. Some of the great realist literature, especially the work of Balzac and Zola, confirms this interpretation of the public mood. Commercial funerals, including the decorations of the home and the church and the processions to the church and the cemetery, were a carefully scrutinized public representation of the family that allowed friends and neighbors to gauge its wealth and generosity. For those who could afford a service, funerals evoked anxious reflection about how much to spend. These calculations may not have distracted families from the grief that they felt at the loss of a member; but they did become an additional and complicating element in the emotional responses of people in the face of death.

The entrepreneur charged with the service after 1832, M. Baudouin, was an aggressive businessman anxious to increase his revenues. As we have already seen, he angered the parishes by introducing items not included on the price list agreed to in the contract that he had signed with the department of the Seine.[47] Furthermore, during his tenure conflicts began to occur over the right to provide funeral objects. On one occasion Baudouin refused to allow his employees to assist at a funeral in which the deceased had been placed in a coffin made by a competitor, and the body was left in the street while the dispute was resolved. On another occasion he tried to stop a family from decorating the house of the dead (maison mortuaire) and the coffin with medallions produced by M. Pector, a merchant who claimed to be more honest in his dealings with the parishes.[48]

Not surprisingly, the critics anxious to point out the cupidity and dishonesty of Baudouin included his competitors, several of whom

SERVICE ORDINAIRE.

NEUVIÈME CLASSE.

HUITIÈME CLASSE.

QUATRIÈME CLASSE.

TROISIÈME CLASSE.

SEPTIÈME CLASSE.

SIXIÈME CLASSE.

CINQUIÈME CLASSE.

DEUXIÈME CLASSE.

PREMIÈRE CLASSE

18. Parisian hearses, mid-nineteenth century (Source: M. Balard, *Les mystères des pompes funèbres de la ville de Paris dévoilés* [Paris: Allard, 1856]).

19. *The Funeral of Monseigneur Sibour*, archbishop of Paris, 1857. This print from the publisher Pellerin illustrates the pomp available for first-class funerals (Photo: Bibliothèque Nationale).

were eventually to profit from the monopoly rights that they contested during the 1830s. Pector's son Anatole was awarded the service in 1847, and Léon Vafflard, who also competed with the official agents during the 1840s, ran the trade from 1853 to 1875. During the 1840s Baudouin, Pector, Léon Vafflard, and Fréderic Lemaistre engaged in public campaigns to discredit one another. Their attacks and counterattacks cannot be read, of course, as fair-minded reporting, but the language and arguments that they employed, which were designed to mobilize support for their positions, allow us to see the concerns and the quality of the public debate about Parisian funeral practices.[49]

The most characteristic criticism leveled against the undertaking profession had to do with the cupidity of its members and the callousness of their dealings with the families of the dead. Léon Vafflard's pamphlet attacking Fréderic Lemaistre, who ran the Paris funeral trade from 1842 unto 1847, described undertakers waiting impatiently at bedsides for death to arrive and then maneuvering families into excessive purchases in order to make unreasonable profits:

> Can it be that a calculating spirit, with cold heart and dry eyes, should find itself at the deathbed, watching as the soul leaves through the lips, or sitting at the door figuring how much money he would be able to tear away from the regret and pain? . . . Is it possible that men exist who fight over the remains of the dead on their deathbeds, and who see in the *pompes funèbres* less an honor rendered to the memory and virtues of the dead than a means of enriching themselves? Has the unbridled love of gold made us assist at such a sad and shameful debate?[50]

Vafflard's attack assumes an ideal scene in which a tearful family focuses its attention on the last minutes of a beloved member. The presence of a calculating businessman who introduces financial considerations into the family's relationship with the dead is looked upon as a scandal, for Vafflard assumes that his readers share his conviction that money should not be thought about or discussed at such a moment. He is severe in judging the undertaker who carefully assesses the wealth of the family, then takes advantage of their grief to trick them into spending more than they can afford. Vafflard is especially critical of Lemaistre's practice of paying his undertakers by commission rather than a set salary, which led them to increase the pressure that they put on families.

Vafflard's criticisms, and those of others as well, included detailed descriptions of how undertakers manipulated their clients. Appeals were made to the vanity of families, who were told that certain objects had now become so commonplace that to neglect them would be embarrassing. Small medallions, for example, bearing the initials or name of the deceased and sometimes an image representing the person as well were hung on the house, the hearse, and at the church. By the 1840s they were an item pushed hard by the industry and singled out by critics as an unnecessary expense. According to Vafflard, ten of these objects would be sold for two-hundred francs, only 15 percent of which went to the parishes. The entrepreneur was required to pay the full percentage, 71.5 percent for this period, only on rented objects, but the medallions, which became the property of the client, required only the smaller return to the parishes. The undertakers systematically failed to inform the families that the decorations belonged to them, however, and would repossess and reuse them, thus making an enormous profit. Vafflard also noted the practice of encouraging the purchase of items with attractive labels, such as *"draperie antique,"* that cost the entrepreneur very little but brought in large profits. According to Vafflard, the purchase of these "useless" objects was a serious burden to families of modest means.[51]

Finally, according to critics, the undertakers frequently did not provide the services that they had promised and that were required of them under the terms of the contract. Only two porters without a hearse would sometimes arrive for the procession to the church, and their behavior could be disrespectful.[52] In the midst of a mortality crisis, such as the cholera epidemics of 1832 and 1849, the entrepreneur and his undertakers were accused of scandalous neglect. In 1832 porters collected the corpses of five or six children and carried them to the cemetery all at the same time.[53] Coffins fell off the artillery wagons that were used briefly in 1832 to deal with the surfeit of corpses, breaking open and exposing the bodies of the dead on the streets.[54] In 1849 corpses remained unburied for long periods, processions paid for were delayed for hours, sparking terror of contagion, and the families of the poor complained about the improvised vehicles used to transport several bodies at once.[55]

Given the harshness of the criticisms, we might expect that radical solutions would be offered. After all, the revolutionary experiment of the 1790s in which a state-run monopoly provided everyone the same austere service offered an alternative model. But most of the critics were not interested so much in radical reform as they were in sharing in the profits. Vafflard may have been offended by the practices of the undertakers stationed in the twelve city halls of Paris, but his immediate goal was defending his own team of representatives charged with carrying out the wishes of the family. In the mid-1840s, when the funeral industry was growing rapidly and reaching new sectors of the population, families were confused about the possibilities offered to them, a condition apparently exploited by the official entrepreneur and his employees. Into this situation Vafflard introduced a middleman who presented himself as a disinterested party who would represent the family's interests before the official undertakers. By 1844 many families were paying these new funeral professionals, who would then communicate their orders to the official undertakers stationed at the city halls. Lemaistre and Pector, who held the contract for the 1840s, both complained about this practice, but decisions by the prefect of the Seine in 1844 and the conseil d'état in 1848 confirmed the right of Vafflard to provide this intermediate service.[56]

The cycle of criticism continued into the 1850s, but then the revolution of 1848 and the new adjudication of 1853 altered the conditions of the funeral trade in Paris. Anatole Pector, who had replaced Lemaistre in 1847, faced increased competition following the revolution of 1848, and the government, perceiving him as a corrupt holdover from the July Monarchy, was unresponsive to his complaints. Pector was forced to defend himself against attacks that he had become a millionaire by gouging his clients, and he also suffered from an apparent decline in the taste for luxurious funerals following the February Revolution.[57] A commission composed of members of the Paris city council and representatives from the parishes and the archbishop conducted a thorough investigation, then introduced modest reforms designed to end the bickering between competitors and the confusion and anxiety that this caused the families. The reforms consisted of merely placing all the items introduced over the past two decades into one of the nine classes and clearly distinguishing between supplementary and required objects. After revising the cahier des charges to reflect these changes, the department of the Seine accepted bids on the service from entrepreneurs; the contract was awarded to Vafflard, the most vocal critic of the funeral trade during the 1840s.[58]

Under Vafflard's direction, the Paris funeral service ran smoothly throughout the Second Empire. By this time the undertakers and the funerals that they arranged were familiar to Parisians. The controversy surrounding the establishment of the industry and the criticisms of the 1840s suggest, however, that the public, although habituated to commercial funerals, was also suspicious of the undertaking profession. Evidence drawn from nineteenth-century literature offers us another window through which to glimpse the public mood. Of course, the descriptions of deaths and funerals found in Balzac and Zola are imbued with the social attitudes of their authors, novelists whose work appealed to the literate middle classes of France. It was also this group that was targeted by the funeral business, a correspondence that enhances the value of their work. Their portrayals of Parisian funerals allow us to observe closely the practical details that preoccupied families following a death; they also help us sense the values of those interested in funeral display and the doubts that they had about the propriety of such expenditures.

For Balzac funerals were climactic occasions that typified the corruption and venality of the Paris of his day. Briefly in *Père Goriot*, and then at length in *Cousin Pons*, he described how funerals, designed to honor the dead, had become artificial vehicles shamelessly manipulated by socially ambitious families and acquisitive undertakers. Following Goriot's death, his friends Rastignac and Bianchon scrambled to pay for a minimal service. The coffin, covered by a "scanty black cloth," was placed on two chairs outside their rooming house. "A shabby sprinkler lay in a sliver-plated copper bowl of holy water, but no one had stopped to sprinkle the coffin. No attempt had been made even to drape the door with black. The dead man was a pauper, and so there was no display of grief, no friend, no kinsman to follow him to the grave." Only Rastignac and one servant accompanied the hearse and the two porters to the church, where the clergy conducted a hurried service. As the humble procession departed the church, however, "two empty carriages with the coats of arms of the Comte de Restaud and the Baron de Nucingen [the families of Goriot's daughters] arrived, and followed in the procession to Père Lachaise."[59]

Goriot's funeral was obviously a sad affair, but Balzac's text conveys more than melancholy; it expresses a profound ambivalence about the funeral system that was in place in 1834, the year the novel was completed. Balzac was above all offended by the poverty of the funeral. Rastignac tries to persuade one of the daughters, Delphine, to sell some of her jewelry so that her father can be buried "decently," but when no money is forthcoming he is forced to settle for a service that is described as "scanty." The absence of funeral crepe at the home is especially noticed. Of course Balzac was shocked by the absence of Goriot's family, but he seems to accept the expense of the service as the standard by which to measure their affection. That Goriot died poor and abandoned is sad, but that his wealthy family allowed him to be buried without ceremony makes his death even more poignant.

Balzac makes no comment about the last-minute appearance of the funeral carriages bearing the coats of arms of Goriot's relatives, but this final gesture is as empty as the carriages, designed only to save the families from the kind of criticism Balzac himself implied in his earlier description. Goriot's family is condemned first of all for not spending the money needed for a decent burial, and then for substituting a funeral purchase for their own presence. In his account of Goriot's funeral Balzac simultaneously accepts and rejects the commercialization of death that had developed in Paris since the turn of the century.

By the time Balzac wrote *Cousin Pons* in 1846 the funeral industry had, as we have seen, undergone considerable development. His extended description of the death and burial of Sylvain Pons confirms the presence at the deathbeds of Parisians of aggressive and cold-blooded funeral professionals, a group that is perceived as increasingly intrusive upon the grief of the mourners. Balzac elaborates on the standard metaphor of death as a journey to make his point:

> Death, it is often said, is the end of a journey, but few people know how apt this simile is in Paris. A dead man, especially one of standing, is welcomed on the "sombre shore" like a traveler reaching harbor, pestered with recommendations from all the hotel couriers. . . . And so almost all those who lose their fathers, mothers, wives or children are immediately pounced on by funeral touts who batten upon their distress by bullying them into giving an order.[60]

Following Pons's death his loyal friend Schmucke is approached by salesmen who try to induce him to purchase a funeral monument and embalm the deceased. Overcome by grief Schmucke finally consents to hand over all responsibility for the funeral to an intermediary who arranges for a third-class service, which includes a mortuary chapel for the display of the body at the front gate, a hearse, and four mourners' carriages, although only one was needed. The procession to the church is organized and led by one of the official undertakers whose appearance and behavior are scrutinized carefully by Balzac:

> This functionary, magnificently attired in black cloth, black breeches, black silk stockings and white cuffs, adorned with a silver chain to which a medallion was attached, wearing a cravat—such a correct cravat!—of white muslin and white gloves; this incarnation of officialdom, stamped with the very hallmark of public lamentation, was holding an ebony wand, his emblem of office, and, under his left arm, a three-cornered hat, with a tricolor cockade.
>
> "I am the master of ceremonies," said this important person in a soft voice.
>
> This man, whose daily function was to conduct funerals and move among a whole succession of families plunged into one and the same affliction, real or feigned, spoke in low and unctuous tones, like all members of his confraternity. It was his profession to be decorous, polite, seemly, like a statue representing the angel of death.[61]

As described by Balzac, the undertaker of the 1840s had developed a professional manner that recalls clerical behavior and that distinguished him from the more brazen salesmen. When the undertaker notices that Schmucke has no proper mourning clothes, however, his commercial instincts are revealed:

> He cast a glance at Schmucke's clothes, and asked him: "Have you no black suit? . . . I have already told our management," he said, "which has already introduced so many improvements, that it ought to have a wardrobe department and hire mourning to next-of-kin. It is daily becoming more and more necessary."[62]

Balzac's descriptions of the funerals of Père Goriot and cousin Pons provided him an occasion to observe and criticize the commercialization of funerals, a social development that we have seen was affecting increasing numbers of Parisians and provoking public debate and criticism. Balzac's focus on the death of men prevents us from observing whether or not undertakers behaved in a similar fashion toward women. But this focus might also suggest that the death of a man, and particularly of a father, in the case of Goriot, was a crucial social ritual through which values could be observed—a point that confirms what we have seen in cemeteries.

Balzac's descriptions also confirm that only men worked as undertakers in the Paris funeral trade. Women did play an important role in the funeral system of France, however. In the countryside they were frequently charged with preparing the body for burial, and in cities nuns frequently helped the family to bathe and clothe the dead. Women also had a special obligation to mourn for the dead, and were represented in this role in cemeteries. Whereas men mourned their wives for six months in Paris, widows were expected to mourn for a year and six weeks.[63] This private responsibility of women was distinguished from the public profession of undertaker, as only males could perform the latter role. This restriction was uncontroversial at the time and was unexamined in the legislation, public controversies, and literature that provide us with evidence on the funeral trade. Perhaps the restraint expected of the undertaker was assumed to be beyond the capacity of women, who were regarded as emotionally excitable. Certainly the general prejudice against women serving in the public professions contributed to their exclusion from the funeral trade. As a person of authority who would oversee the public procession of the body to the church and the cemetery, the undertaker could only be a man. From its origins in the early nineteenth century, the profession of undertaker was exclusively male, a pattern that reflected and contributed to gender stereotypes and that endures in the modern funeral establishment.

In Balzac's time the system of commercial funerals was struggling to establish itself. By the 1870s, when Emile Zola was writing, the establishment of commercial funerals was essentially complete and is a central element in his presentation of death.[64] The significance of pompes funèbres for Zola is most evident in two works that appeared in 1876. In "How We Die," a series of five sketches first published in the Russian journal Le Messager de l'Europe, he presented a sociology of death in which the habits of the different social classes were minutely observed. These stories show how the class system of funerals corresponded precisely to the class structure of Paris, and they emphasize how this relationship was accepted by families and commented on by relatives and neighbors.

Zola begins his account at the top of the social hierarchy with the death of the Comte de Verteuil, a wealthy and distinguished aristocrat. Although the count disdains the government, his work with the Academy of Moral and Political Sciences and his elevated social position make him a figure of public importance; his death is therefore not just a matter for himself and his family, who are not described as especially moved by his passing. The count is embalmed (the only person discussed in the series to receive this treatment—a fact suggesting that embalming was restricted to the very wealthy), and his room is transformed into a chapel. The procession to the church, with everyone dressed in mourning, proceeds in a showy fashion, stopping all traffic and provoking the curses of coachmen. The count's wife, however, does not assist in the procession but remains in her room daydreaming about her social life. Although it was customary among noble families for women not to assist at funerals, Zola associates the behavior of the countess with an absence of grief.[65] A crowd gathers along the route to watch the hearse, richly decorated with plumes and draped in black with silver fringe. In a detail that recalls Goriot's funeral, the mourners are followed by a long line of black carriages (voitures de deuil), almost all of them empty. The church is also richly decorated, and the two-hour service includes a performance by one of the stars of the opera. Following the procession to the fashionable cemetery of Montparnasse, the coffin is laid before the family's mortuary chapel along a wooded pathway, where four speeches are heard.[66]

In his second story Zola describes the death of Madame Guérard, the wife of a magistrate and a representative of the haute bourgeoisie, who receives a third-class service. The front gate is decorated with black crepe fringed with silver, where the coffin is displayed. The procession to the church is followed by twelve mourning carriages, and Zola notes that "people counted them, and talked about them in the neighborhood." Madame's three sons, who walk behind the

hearse with their heads lowered and their eyes red with tears, are
regarded sympathetically. The other mourners and the watching
crowd judge their behavior according to the money that they have
spent. "For the rest, only one thing was heard: they're burying their
mother in a suitable fashion. The hearse is third class, and must have
cost several thousand francs." The fact that Madame Guérard was
herself very careful about money even provokes a small joke from a
notaire present at the services: "If Mme Guérard had paid for her own
funeral, she would have saved by having only six carriages."[67]

The third family described by Zola falls into the lower middle class
of small shopkeepers. Monsieur and Madame Rousseau have worked
all their lives in their paper store to save enough money for a place in
the country—a plan that is foiled by the death of Madame, apparently
of tuberculosis. Monsieur, although genuinely moved by the death of
his wife, discusses at length the funeral arrangements with the clergy
and the undertakers. He agrees to spend five hundred francs, which
includes one hundred and sixty for the church service, three hundred
for the pompes funèbres, and incidental expenses. Zola remarks that
this attentiveness to financial detail was not a failure to respect his
wife's memory, or the result of suspicions about the clergy and the
undertakers. On the contrary, "He really loved his wife and, if he
could still see her, he is certain that he would make her happy by
haggling with the priests and undertakers. However, he wants, for
the neighborhood, a suitable burial." The funeral he arranges, however, does not come off well. The undertakers, referred to as *croque-
morts* bring a coffin that is too small, forcing the hearse to wait before
the door while they search for another. Because of the delay involved, the coffin rests only ten minutes before the door. The hearse
for the procession is decorated with black cloth with white fringe, and
there are three mourning carriages. At the church Monsieur's sister-
in-law, anxious for an inheritance, "seems to count the candles" and
thinks that "her brother-in-law could have been less ostentatious."[68]

Continuing his descent down the social ladder, Zola next describes
the Morisseaus, a working-class family, the father a mason, the
mother a laundress. Out of work and with all their possessions
pawned, the family struggles through a winter with no work, no
food, and no heat. Because they had worked the previous summer,
they are not immediately eligible for public assistance, and when
their son Charlot falls ill they are unable to provide proper care for
him. They do their best for Charlot, then grieve at his death. The funeral is paid for by the city following an attestation of poverty. The
coffin that is provided consists of four boards poorly assembled. The
procession rushes to the church, where a service is quickly said, and

then the race continues to the cemetery—a muddy, poorly maintained field in which many cheap crosses have been blown over by the wind. On the way back to town Monsieur uses the last of his money to pay for a small party during which he and his friends share two liters of wine and some cheese. "Then the friends took their turn and paid for two more liters. When they got back to Paris, they were quite gay."[69]

Two themes dominate Zola's descriptions of Parisian funerals. First, he emphasizes the transient nature of the grief and how it is diminished by the practical demands that continue even while the dead are still in the same house. The Comtesse de Verteuil is the only character who is indifferent in the face of death; the others all display some form of genuine grief. And yet, the Guérard brothers are concerned about their inheritance, M. Rousseau wishes he didn't have to close his shop on the day of the funeral, and the Morisseaus and their neighbors forget their troubles in an afternoon at a wine shop. Although Zola does not ridicule those who are unable to grieve for more than just a brief moment, their preoccupation with normal routines and with money, does make these Parisians seem callous (illus. 20).

Second, Zola focuses attention on the cost of the funerals and on how important public perception of this has become. The behavior of

20. A *Funeral Procession in Paris*, 1860s. This print by Norbert Goeneutte suggests how funerals were part of the background of the busy streets of Paris. The two men at the left remain absorbed in conversation, and others seem not to notice the passing hearse, but the pedestrian in the center takes a moment to lift his hat to show respect for the dead (Photo: Bibliothèque Nationale).

the family is judged as appropriate if they spend a good amount on decorations, the hearse, and funeral carriages commensurate with their wealth. The mourners were, moreover, conscious of public opinion and responded to it. In "Comment on meurt" the public comments reported by Zola are generally approving of the money spent, but in *L'Assommoir*, which appeared in the same year, Zola suggests that funeral costs could also provoke vicious quarrels, at least in working-class families where resources where scarce. When Madame Coupeau dies, her daughter-in-law Gervaise argues in favor of spending ninety francs—an amount that would pay for a "hearse with narrow hangings":

> We aren't rich, and that's a fact, but still we want to do it decently. Even if Ma Coupeau hasn't left us anything, that's no reason for throwing her into the ground like a dead dog. No, there must be a Mass and a respectable hearse.

But Madame Lorilleux, Coupeau's daughter, angrily resists spending so much, accusing Gervaise of imprudence and vanity:

> "And who's going to pay?" screamed Madame Lorilleux. "Not us, we lost money last week, and not you either, because you are broke. You should just see where you've landed yourselves by trying to impress people." . . .
> "Well, I refuse. Yes, I refuse. It isn't because of the thirty francs [her share of the costs]. I'd give a hundred thousand, if I had it, if it could bring Ma back to life. Only I can't stand pride. You've got a shop and you have dreams of queening it over the whole neighborhood. But we aren't standing for that. We don't want to cut a dash. Oh, you can work it out how you like. Put plumes on the hearse if that amuses you."[70]

When the hearse arrives the next day, it is "the sensation of the whole neighborhood. . . . Everybody was talking about the hangings with white cotton fringes. The Coupeaus would have done better to pay their debts, wouldn't they? But, as the Lorilleux observed, people's pride will out. . . . 'It's disgraceful!' Gervaise was saying at the same moment about the chainmaker and his wife (Lorilleux). 'To think that those skinflints haven't brought even a bunch of violets for their own mother.' "[71] This comment about the flowers suggests another innovation of the funeral entrepreneur. For now, however, the crucial point is that the funeral expenses marked a turning point in Gervaise's life, pushing her further down the social ladder toward complete misery. It is just after the funeral, while the family is eating at the local pub, that Gervaise agrees to give up her lease on her shop, the symbol of her prosperity and respectability.

For Zola, the death of Madame Coupeau is a tragic event. Unlike Balzac, however, he does not focus his criticism on the funeral profession. Undertakers are not accused of trying to gouge their clients; they are portrayed as simple employees in a system that is unquestioned. In another story, first published in 1866, Zola expresses considerable sympathy toward an undertaker, whose profession evokes hatred in the average Parisian.[72] In *L'Assommoir*, however, he describes the profession using a stereotype that dates back at least to the revolutionary era. The undertaker Bazouge, who is responsible for burying Madame Coupeau and later Gervaise, is a drunkard. But he has also become a commentator, whose running patter of commonplaces about death Zola refers to ironically as "philosophical reflections." For Zola, the priest is less important than the undertaker in interpreting death; it is Bazouge who has the last word in *L'Assommoir* as he comes for Gervaise with a pauper's coffin:

> "Ah well, we all go the same way home . . . no need to push and shove, plenty of room for everybody . . . silly to be in a hurry 'cos you don't get there no faster. . . . Now all I want to do is to give people satisfaction. . . . Some are willing, others aren't. . . . Well, let's just see how we can manage it. . . . Here's one who didn't want to go, then she changed her mind. But then she had to wait. . . . Ah well, that's that and she's got what she wanted. . . . Now, upsy-daisy!"
>
> As he seized Gervaise with his big black hands he had a fit of tenderness and gently lifted this woman who had been keen on him for so long. As he laid her in her coffin like a loving father, he burbled on, between hiccups:
>
> "Listen, dear . . . you know . . . it's me, Bibi-la-Gaité, known as the ladies' comforter. . . . There, there, you're all right now. Night-night, my lovely!"[73]

Some of Bazouge's comments recall the fatalism of rural proverbs discussed in chapter 2. Death is inevitable and, therefore, not to be resisted, but it is also a release. This message, carried by the oral culture in the countryside, has been absorbed by urban undertakers, who transmit it along with their professional services. Other evidence also suggests that undertakers may have been perceived in the light of folkloric themes. When Brazier described the coachmen for the hearses of the 1840s in his *Physiology of the Paris Coachman* (*Physiologie du cocher de Paris*), he seems to have drawn on personifications of Death as imperturbable, egalitarian, and terrifying. The coachman who drives a hearse is a kind of urban Ankou: "He is still as death, cold as death; because death is, for him, his life. . . . He doesn't know the corpse he drives, and cares even less what he is: poor, rich, scholar, soldier, or civilian, it's the same to him."[74] This portrayal of the undertaking profession contrasts sharply with the criticisms of venality that date to the early nineteenth century. There is a mythic quality in Brazier's description and in Zola's Bazouge as well.

The evocative power of the undertaker as a symbol of death was clearly evident in one of the most-talked-about paintings of the salon of 1861. In a gigantic work entitled *Ash Wednesday* (*Le Mercredi des Cendres*) the painter, Lambron, shows a croque-mort, a coachman to judge by the whip he carries, greeting Arlequin and Pierrot as they leave a ball in Montmartre (see illus. 21). *Ash Wednesday* evoked extended comments from the influential critics Maxime du Camp and Théophile Gautier and inspired the cover of the popular *Little Magazine of Laughs* (*Petit Journal pour rire*) for its Ash Wednesday edition of 1861.[75] In the painting Pierrot looks away, full of concern and guilty, while Arlequin bows with mock reverence. As Gautier indicated in his reaction to *Ash Wednesday*, Lambron used the croque-mort to personify death in modern Paris:

> Arlequin and Pierrot. . . find themselves face to face with the driver of a hearse, his whip at his shoulder, who seems to say, Get in, bourgeois. . . . Pierrot, faithful to his cowardly character, grimaces and stands still . . . before this somber apparition. The bolder Arlequin, his hand on his heart, bows with an affected graciousness. He assumes a philosophical manner, above superstition. . . . Doesn't he know that the black carriage which you climb only once will bear away all the revelers in the carnival of life, when the Ash Wednesday of life arrives?[76]

For Gautier, Pierrot and Arlequin represent the vanity and shortsightedness of the middle class, who respond to death with either fear or arrogance. Gautier's comment recalls the long tradition of representations of death surprising people in the midst of life, as exemplified in the danses macabres of the Middle Ages. For Gautier and for Lambron, the undertaker has replaced the skeletal figure of Death, but unlike earlier symbolic representations of death, his appearance seems to have neither moral nor religious significance. Gautier's reaction acknowledges the ultimate power of the undertaker, but this figure does not condemn the two clowns, or threaten them; he stands apart with an air of bemused superiority.

In the same room of the salon Lambron presented a smaller painting (*Meeting of the Friends* [*Réunion des amis*]) of a group of croque-morts drinking at a café near a cemetery—a study that played on the contrast between death and the sociability of the living. Gautier noticed that the painting depicted a hierarchy in the undertaking profes-

21. A. Lambron, *Ash Wednesday*, Salon of 1861. Print by Verdeil (Photo: Bibliothèque Nationale).

sion, with a well-dressed coachman condescending to greet a more modestly attired colleague. Maxime du Camp also perceived this distinction; in his study of Paris he described the masters of ceremony, the principal undertakers of the city, as a professional corps who exercised their trade with competence and dignity. They ensured that all the orders for the ceremony were carried out, monitored the other employees to see that they were properly dressed, and tried to control requests for tips. The *ordonnateurs* also avoided the use of jargon as unworthy of their work—an aversion not shared by the porters, who referred to their clients as "a salmon, a herring, or a smelt," by which they meant the body of a rich man, a poor man, or a child. The porters, however, resented being called croque-morts, the common term by which most Parisians knew them. They were familiar not only on the streets of Paris but had become well-known characters in the popular theater. As far as du Camp is concerned, it is the porters who are still guilty of the cupidity that characterized the entire profession earlier in the century; after funerals, despite laws prohibiting the practice, they would seek tips from the family by waiting for them on the street outside the cemetery—a practice that led to several complaints to the police.[77]

By the last decades of the nineteenth century Parisians were accustomed to the system of pompes funèbres that had developed since the Napoleonic Empire. Undertakers had assumed an important role in the management of death, a role that borrowed from the traditions of public service, capitalism, and folklore—a combination that they struggled to work into a professional code. By the latter part of the century some of them, at least, had learned to control the blatant abuses that had been common during the Restoration and July Monarchy. Although accusations directed against greedy undertakers became less common, families were nonetheless still expected to choose from a hierarchy of services based on prices. As a result of this commodification of death, which spread from Paris to other French cities, families learned to translate their affection for the deceased into a specific number of francs and the purchase of a ceremony that would be used to measure both their grief and their status.

Chapter Seven

THE DIFFUSION AND REFORM OF
POMPES FUNÈBRES

PARIS WAS BY FAR the largest city in France, and its symbolic position
as trendsetter matched its physical importance. Not all of France,
however, took advantage of the Napoleonic legislation and adopted
commercial funerals. The results of a government survey in 1894,
which confirms the ethnographic evidence presented in chapter 2,
show that in the villages of France throughout the nineteenth century
neighbors continued to take responsibility for the funeral procession
and the burial of the dead.[1] Still, the same laws that were used to
create the business of pompes funèbres in Paris were increasingly
applied in provincial cities, so that by the end of the century the
commercial funeral industry was a common feature in middle-sized
communities.

The development of pompes funèbres outside of Paris does not
mirror exactly the history of the Paris profession. As with the displacement of cemeteries, provincial cities generally moved more
slowly; by the time they were ready to grant entrepreneurs the rights
to their funeral trade the Parisian profession was already well organized. Agents from Paris, alert to the possibilities offered by the provinces, presented themselves as experienced businessmen capable of
sorting out the complex legislation and providing reasonably priced
services modeled on those of the capital. The spread of pompes
funèbres through urban France in the second half of the nineteenth
century led to the development of an industry linked in a national
network to provide a uniform service. When the Church-State crisis
reached its climax at the turn of the century, the funeral profession
was well established and able to ensure that even after the separation
of Church and State French men and women would be buried with
services that satisfied their demand for decency and dignity.

In the new funeral system, professional undertakers played a role
in which they borrowed much from the clergy. Their dress and their
manner were muted, designed to be reassuring. Unlike the clergy,
however, funeral professionals avoided questions about the meaning
of life and the judgment of the dead. We have seen that clerical motives were frequently impugned, and that the Church had a clear

financial stake in the funeral business. Complaints that undertakers exploited grief for financial gain were also common and were an important element in the debate that led to the reform of the funeral system in 1904. As a result of this law, cities were granted broad powers of regulation over the funeral industry—powers that they continue to wield in contemporary France. Even though the market was not permitted to control the services for the dead, it was understood that businessmen had the right to a reasonable profit. The clergy were no longer the principal figures who dealt with the dead and arranged burials—services that were now regarded, although with much uneasiness, as commodities.

FUNERALS IN THE PROVINCES: ANGERS, 1800–1880

Angers, the capital of Maine-et-Loire, provides a valuable illustration of the diffusion of pompes funèbres in the nineteenth century. The attempts of Angevin officials to create a system that would comply with national legislation foundered throughout the 1840s, but the extensive correspondence that they left allows us to compare the funerals of a provincial capital with those of Paris and other cities. Angevin church officials were especially proud of the solution finally worked out by the 1850s, and some tried to present it as a model to be followed in other communities. The crisis of the end of the century showed that the system could continue to operate without the Church's participation, a development that was not foreseen by those who applied the laws for most of the century.

In the late 1790s Angevin officials, like their Parisian colleagues, were calling on the government to restore dignity to the cult of the dead following the revolutionary era. When the prefect of Maine-et-Loire forwarded to the minister of the interior a petition by a M. Marcombe asking that he be permitted to raise a funeral monument to his wife (an act prohibited during the revolution), he added an appeal for legislation that would end the "neglect of the dead which has characterized the most enlightened and sensitive nation for ten years."[2] After the enabling legislation of 23 prairial was in place, the parishes of Angers arranged to provide funeral palls and decorations for the church doors. Families were permitted to negotiate on their own for the other services, including printed invitations, candles, orphans (who could be hired to walk in the procession), professional mourners, coffins, and the decoration of the church.[3]

In Angers, where candles were traditionally an important part of the funeral celebration, it was the candle makers who were first to take advantage of the new possibilities for an industry of pompes funèbres. By the 1830s individual parishes had established contracts with local tradesmen, a system that caused some public resentment because it meant that funeral costs varied from neighborhood to neighborhood. As in Paris, funerals were priced according to class. At the Angers cathedral of St. Maurice a first-class service included a catafalque and a canopy for the coffin, the decoration of all nine doors, the chairs, fifty pounds of smaller candles, as well as fifteen larger *flambeaux*, four professional weepers, and a procession of orphans from the hospital—all for Fr 988,75. The official price list also notes the inclusion of "death heads and tears" among the decorations, a baroque touch that does not seem to have been present in the Parisian ceremonies. A first-class service in Paris during the same period cost Fr 4,288. At the bottom of the scale, a sixth-class service at St. Maurice, with no decorations, cost Fr 54,45 francs. At the parish of St. Joseph, not far from the cathedral, a first-class service could be purchased for Fr 879,75, while a sixth-class service was available for Fr 64,60.[4]

By the 1830s city officials had grown dissatisfied with the unregulated system run by parishes and candle makers that had developed over the recent decades. In 1832 the mayor of Angers approached the commission that ran the hospital asking if they would consider providing horse-drawn hearses for funerals. The hospital commissioners rejected this idea, fearing it would require them to charge the poor and even prosecute them for nonpayment, which would violate the spirit of charity that was the basis for the hospital.[5] The urban officials of Angers would have preferred to work with colleagues on the hospital commission and to have retained some of the profits for the charitable work of the city. They were forced instead to deal with the fabriques that were charged with the funeral trade by the national legislation and with the candle makers that the parish representatives employed. As in Paris, government officials, clergy, laity, and funeral professionals had difficulty working out an arrangement that was mutually acceptable. In Angers it took almost twenty years before all the parties were able to agree on the division of responsibility and profit.

The first substantial move toward the creation of a uniform system of funerals for Angers was taken by an association of seven candle makers of Angers in 1837, when they signed a contract with the cathedral fabrique granting them a monopoly on services. In order to join the association a candle maker was required to contribute six thousand francs and follow the regulations that defined which decorations were permitted for the different classes of funeral service. The candle makers expected the bishop to encourage the other parishes to adopt the same contract, and they objected when two of them, St. Serge and St. Joseph, signed exclusive treaties with tradesmen who were not part of the association. The point at issue was the percentage that the candle makers would pay to the fabriques. The contract called for 10 percent, whereas St. Serge and St. Joseph were able to negotiate a return of 50 percent. After he learned of the advantageous terms of the new agreements, the bishop was understandably angry with the candle makers, who would apparently be able to reap exorbitant profits as a result of their agreement. He rejected their complaint and argued for a restricted interpretation of the contract, which would permit the association to decorate only church exteriors.[6]

After the contract was signed, the candle makers took another step in 1839 to gain more control over the funeral trade: rather than storing equipment in each parish, the candle makers decided to rent a single house. At this point, the parish porters and grave diggers, who were responsible for bearing the coffins and decorating the houses and churches, complained to the mayor about the inconvenience and proposed that they be given the right to provide funeral decorations in place of the candle makers.[7] Both of these corporations were seeking to position themselves as the professional group most suited to provide for the developing funeral trade.

The aggressive maneuvering of the candle makers, however, cost them the support of the Church and of public opinion as well. Throughout the 1840s, when the parishes and the city council struggled to define a new funeral system, one of the few points on which they consistently agreed was that the candle makers had become abusive in their treatment of the dead. The funeral of a Mademoiselle Chalon illustrates the basis for these complaints. After her death in May 1839 Mademoiselle Chalon's family arranged with M. Gaudron to provide a catafalque and a canopy for the display of the coffin before the home prior to the procession to the church. The regulations established by the association, however, allowed for this display only if the coffin was surrounded by flambeaux; the family requested from Gaudron only smaller and less-expensive candles. When another member of the association noticed this violation, he informed Gaudron that he was liable for a five-hundred-franc fine for violating the convention. Gaudron then went to the home of the Chalon family and, without informing anyone, began dismantling the display and removing the candles. The Chalons lived on the rue St. Aubin, an artisan's street in the center of Angers that leads to the cathedral. Soon an angry crowd gathered and stopped Gaudron, whose intention was to leave the coffin exposed without decoration on the street.[8]

Following a complaint by the family, the police investigated the matter; their report was highly critical of the candle makers, and called on the city administration to intervene in the funeral trade to eliminate such abuses. The current monopoly, according to the police, "is harmful and ruinous for families; because only certain ornaments can be placed with others, people spend much more than they want in order to have their relatives buried in a suitable manner." The report concluded with an appeal for the establishment of a municipally sanctioned service for pompes funèbres, as existed in "all the major cities."[9]

There were other reasons besides the abuses of the candle makers that led the city to begin considering alternative ways of managing funerals. As we have seen, during the 1830s the city council of Angers had begun to negotiate the purchase and development of a new cemetery on the eastern bank of the Maine River (see chapter 5). The opening of this site required a new method of transporting the dead, because it was considered undignified and impractical for the porters to carry coffins on their shoulders for the considerable distances that separated the parish churches from the new cemetery. The introduction of hearses into Angers had already been considered briefly in the early 1830s; the planning of the Cemetery of the East made such an innovation essential.[10]

In the early 1840s the bishop and city administrators collaborated in drawing up a new price list for funeral services that would apply to the entire city; they envisaged a single enterprise charged with transporting the dead, decorating the houses and churches, and providing candles. Six classes of funerals were proposed, and all costs, including those for religious services, were included in a single comprehensive price. Following the consideration of the new price list by a select commission of the city council, it was passed to the prefect, who forwarded it in turn to the Ministry of the Interior for approval.

The minutes of the city council meeting of 10 June 1843 that approved the commission's work reflect a sense of pride and accomplishment, sentiments that the subsequent history of the proposal would show to be naive.[11] The report read by the head of the commission, M. Guillier de la Tousche, presented the new price list as a major reform that would correct the widely acknowledged abuses of the candle makers. By altering the items provided it would also reshape the funeral practices of Angevins, bringing them in line with what was felt to be appropriate to the nineteenth century. The 1843 proposal, in short, provides an excellent vantage point for viewing the financial and aesthetic situation of Angevin pompes funèbres in the first half of the century.

The starting point for the reform was a substantial reduction in the price of each of the six classes of funerals created by the contract with the candle makers of 1837. The average reduction came to 28 percent,

with the largest drop coming in the third class, which went from Fr
527.25 to Fr 227.25. The price reductions called for would not, according to the commission's report, result in any substantial change in the
prayers and decorations that had become customary. Any such innovation would have been opposed by the public, which was understandably pleased by the announcement of the lower prices. The
major savings would come by lowering the prices paid for the candles
and eliminating the large flambeaux. Although the clergy valued the
effect produced by the flambeaux, they were made of poor materials
and emitted a noxious odor.

Reducing the fees charged for candles was not felt to be a hardship,
given the arrangements that existed among parishes, candle makers,
and clergy. Although the family paid a full price for the candles used
at a service, most of them were only partly consumed. Following the
service the fabriques and the clergy divided the remains equally;
the parish used its portion for the regular church services, whereas
the clergy sold theirs back to the candle makers at a rate of Fr 4.50 per
pound. With the new prices, the fabriques and clergy would still have
the same rights as before over the unused candles. Only the unpopular candle makers would suffer; they would receive a lower price for
their product and still be required to buy back the clergy's portion.
These financial details are perhaps arcane, but they illustrate how, by
the 1830s, the funeral trade in Angers had become an important
financial support for the parishes and clergy. The dependence of the
fabriques and the clergy on income derived from pompes funèbres
helps explain the panic among church officials later in the decade,
when a revised version of their reform threatened to eliminate a large
portion of these funds.

Based on the current convention, the commission of 1843 estimated
that of the approximately 1,300 deaths each year 10 individuals would
choose a first-class service, 40 second-class, 90 third-class, and 460 a
fourth-, fifth- or sixth-class service. The city also projected the deaths
of 300 children each year, whose funerals would be simpler and less
expensive than those of adults. It was estimated that 400 poor, or 31
percent of the total dead, would be buried without charge and without pomp, at the city's expense. If these figures are compared with
those of Paris for the same period, it appears that the taste for funeral
pomp was much more widely diffused in Angers than in the capital.
Certainly the large numbers of impoverished Parisians help explain
this difference; but it may also be that in the smaller setting of Angers
the absence of funeral ceremony was more difficult to contemplate.

The reform-minded commissioners also recommended a number of
changes in the personnel and material used in funerals, changes that

reflect the fading of baroque tastes which had survived in Angers after they had disappeared in Paris. The report called for the elimination of the poor children housed at the hospital from funeral processions. The justification for this innovation suggests a new sense of how death was perceived in relationship to the community and provides a revealing glimpse of current funeral practices. According to the commission's report, "childhood, with its gaiety and laughter, makes a painful contrast with the mourning of funerals." Furthermore, by forcing children to adopt a grave countenance, funerals trained them to be hypocritical. Finally, funerals were no place for children, who were placed under the direction of people known to be drunkards (an apparent reference to the porters). Instead of children, the city council approved the hiring of the elderly as professional mourners. This evidence allows us to suggest links between two arguments made by Philippe Ariès. The idea of childhood as a distinct and privileged period emerged in the nineteenth century, a period when death was being redefined as an unbearable rupture in the affectionate relations among family members. In light of these simultaneous developments, Angevin officials came to believe that children, centers and symbols of family intimacy, must be separated from an association with death.

Finally, the commission called for the elimination of the "hideous and repulsive images on the hangings of the church doors and the homes of the dead." No explanation is given for why the skulls and crossbones of the baroque funeral were now regarded with such repugnance. The commissioners use one of the same terms employed by Parisian reformers, "decent," to describe their funereal ideal. Overt reminders of the future state of the human corpse had now become indecent. Of course, this shift in funeral taste was not instantaneous or universal. When Courbet painted a burial scene at Ornans at the end of the 1840s, he depicted a funeral pall still decorated with tears, skull, and crossbones. The suppression of such symbols at Angers corresponds with other changes that we have observed, as well. During the nineteenth century, for example, cemetery regulations ensuring that human remains would be kept out of sight were enforced with increasing vigor. In the second half of the century Catholic preachers made fewer references to the corruption of the corpse. The dead deserved a decent service, and those who could afford it were entitled to a certain luxuriousness in the funeral ritual and monuments that preserved their memory; but the brute fact of their physical decomposition was no longer to be contemplated.[12]

The Angers proposal for reforming the system of funerals was sanctioned by the bishop and by the fall of 1843 was being considered by the minister of the interior.[13] The minister made several objections to the proposal, thus beginning a complicated and protracted set of negotiations involving officials at Paris, the prefect, the city council, the bishop, and the fabriques, all of whom argued with one another for the next ten years. It is easy to understand the exasperation frequently expressed in this correspondence, especially by the Angevins faced with shifting interpretations of the legislation and regulations by ministers in Paris. The officials of the period were continually baffled by the different demands being made on them and plagued by misplaced dossiers and crossing letters. There is no need to trace in detail the development of this dispute, which could serve as a case study in the dysfunction of French bureaucracy in the nineteenth century. But a consideration of the main issues and how they were resolved demonstrates how a national corporation, the society of Pompes Funèbres Générales, was able to emerge as a key institution in the management of death in modern France.

The minister of the interior complained that the Angers proposal was vague and technically deficient. First, it tended to confuse responsibilities that were distinguished in the enabling legislation of 23 prairial, according to which fabriques were responsible for decorating church interiors and city councils for transporting bodies. Furthermore, the new tarif established a single price that included religious services as well as the costs of funeral decorations and transportation. The minister of the interior believed that all these should be clearly distinguished on the price list and, furthermore, that a cahier des charges be drawn up specifying the different tasks to be performed. Finally, provision had to be made for granting the contract for the various services to an entrepreneur.[14]

Over the next two years the city council and the bishop acted to comply with the suggestions from Paris, with no major conflict developing. By 1845 a cahier des charges was ready to be submitted to the Ministry of Interior. This new proposal called for a single enterprise that would provide both for transportation and for the decorations of the churches and houses. As in Paris, the entrepreneur would be chosen based on the percentage that he offered to remit to the fabriques.[15]

The Ministry of Justice and Religion, which shared authority with Interior on this issue, responded to this second proposal from Angers with additional objections. Of these, the most important was the insistence that a coffin be included in the sixth-class service. A later review by the conseil d'état repeated this point, noting that "burying the poor without a coffin is offensive, contrary to public decency and the intent of the law."[16] It was only with the approval of a revised proposal in 1848 that the poor of Angers unable to pay for their own funerals were buried in coffins, a right that Parisians had acquired in the first decade of the century. This practice apparently spread along with the commercial funeral industry, and the willingness of entre-preneurs to provide this service in exchange for the right to profit from the funeral trade was one of the reasons that they were attrac-tive to fabriques and city councils. Coffins performed a number of functions: they protected the corpse from being viewed directly in its final stage before burial; they allowed for the easy transportation of the dead, a matter of increasing importance as cemeteries and churches grew farther apart; and they shielded the buried corpse from direct contact with the soil, suggesting a concern with physical corruption that has become even more pronounced in the twentieth century.[17] In insisting on a coffin for everyone, the French govern-ment was defining a new standard of decency according to which the bodies of all French men and women deserved protection from scru-tiny and decay.

In the 1845 proposal Paris officials also specified some technical problems. The minister noted, for example, that a single price was still called for, thus confusing religious services with external decora-tions. Paris also objected to the inclusion of a carriage to bring the priest to the cemetery in the fifth- and sixth-class services, an extra that added needlessly to the price paid by the poor. In the face of these complaints, the bishop and the mayor continued to insist that single prices be set for the six classes. To do otherwise would compro-mise the relations between the clergy and the public. As the bishop noted, one payment for the hearse, decorations, and candles, fol-lowed by a second for the masses and prayers of the clergy would put the clergy in "a delicate and difficult position." The mayor was more blunt when he wrote that the minister's solution would make it difficult for the clergy to receive their payments and would "compro-mise their dignity and their interests." In defending the proposal both the bishop and the mayor noted that it was the result of an agreement among all the local parties, and that any attempt to intro-duce the distinctions called for by the ministry could disrupt the ac-cord and result in maintaining the status quo, which satisfied no one.[18] The city also insisted that carriages for the priests be main-tained for the fifth- and sixth-class services because, given the dis-tances between churches and the new cemetery, the clergy would not be able to accompany the body on foot. Eliminating the carriages meant denying the poor the presence of the clergy at the grave; such a distinction would be resented and have a negative effect on public opinion.[19]

By 1847 all the parties to these negotiations had agreed to compromises that allowed a third proposal to be officially approved on 18 July of that year.[20] Angers conceded coffins to the poor; Paris allowed for a single price and for the carriages for the clergy. All these issues reveal the concern of local and national officials that a system that established a clear hierarchy of classes not provoke public resentment by denying some people a dignified service. Put in the most general terms, the problem was how to reconcile the freedom of individuals to choose a service commensurate with their wealth with the right of all citizens to equal treatment. This dilemma, inherited from the revolutionary era, was complicated by standards that varied by region and changed over time. Parisians demanded more than Angevins, who aspired to catch up with the capital. The negotiations of the 1840s show how national and local officials worked toward the creation of a national standard of treatment of the dead. In the late 1840s the intervention of the society of Pompes Funèbres Générales at first seemed to complicate the relations between nation and region. By the 1850s, however, it was clear that this private corporation was becoming an important mediator capable of playing an independent role in determining how the French would bury their dead.

Following ministerial approval of the city's proposal, the fabriques and the city council began their search for an entrepreneur willing to fulfill the cahier des charges. The candle makers made an offer and, not surprisingly given the general opprobrium with which they were regarded, it was rejected. Just as the bishop and the mayor began consultations prior to calling for bids for the service, M. Jeramec, an agent from a Paris-based company, arrived in town and met with the vicar-general of the diocese, Abbé Bernier.[21] Within a month he had negotiated a contract with the episcopal officials that was forwarded to the parishes and approved by the end of October. This treaty between the Société des Pompes Funèbres Générales (PFG) and the fabriques was immediately disputed by the city council, marking a break in the local consensus that had held for most of the decade.

The diocesan decision to work with the PFG was based primarily on Jeramec's presentation in late September 1847, in which he demonstrated to episcopal officials that the fabriques of Angers would suffer serious losses of revenues after the new decree was implemented. Jeramec also had a solution, based on the example of the Paris trade over the last two decades. He proposed that the entrepreneur add a list of options beyond the items agreed to by the fabriques and the city council, on the sale of which he would remit 25 percent to the parishes. Part of the appeal of Jeramec's proposal was his argument that with PFG as their entrepreneur the fabriques of

Angers would be able to offer the same material available in Paris, but for 20 percent less. In addition, PFG promised to pay eighteen thousand francs each year to the fabriques, a guaranteed minimum that would help them to maintain church property and conduct services. Abbé Bernier argued that without the funds guaranteed by PFG the dignity of Catholic ritual would be seriously compromised. He also claimed that although the current legislation aimed at ensuring citizens "decent and appropriate services at moderate prices, it was necessary to allow rich or powerful families the possibility of giving to the burials of their relations all the pomp demanded by their rank, their fortune, and their social relations." To do otherwise would be to reintroduce sumptuary legislation contrary to the common law. Finally, Bernier claimed that, based on the examples of Rouen and Orléans, the fabriques were entitled to deal directly with an entrepreneur and were not required to submit their cahier des charges to adjudication.[22]

When the city council met on 15 October 1847, it rejected the contract between the diocese and PFG on the grounds that it violated the decree approved by the king in July. By creating an extensive list of options, the arrangement with PFG opened up the possibility for an abusive entrepreneur to "take advantage of the grief or even of the vanity of families in order to drag them into excessive expenses."[23] Some of the parish councils also expressed concern about this aspect of the treaty. The fabrique from St. Leonard, where many quarry workers resided, indicated that most of their parishioners could not afford the objects available from PFG. Nevertheless, all the parishes—their concerns aroused by a letter from the bishop reporting on their future revenues—ratified the agreement, even as they regretted the disruption in the harmony that had previously existed between religious and civil officials.[24]

As a result of the city's opposition, a deadlock developed over the funeral trade. The diocese insisted on its right to hand the service over to PFG, whereas the city protested that the accord worked on for years by both ecclesiastical and civil officials called for an adjudication of the service in which it would be awarded to the entrepreneur who submitted the best bid. The need to have at least a provisional solution in place because of the opening of the new cemetery led to an agreement to disagree in December 1848. The city granted PFG the right to rent hearses for the funerals at rates set by the city, thus providing for the transportation of the dead, the basic municipal responsibility. At the same time, PFG signed a new contract with the fabriques allowing the company to furnish decorations for the churches and to collect fees for the religious services.[25] In practice this meant that the parishes would not receive any return on the objects used to decorate the hearses, which would go to the city, but they would profit from all the other decorations.

As in Paris, the problems of pompes funèbres were complicated by the revolution of 1848. In Paris, however, the fabriques and the government had already worked out their relationship early in the century, and the major issue was controlling the competition between the professionals. In Angers, where a professional service was still in the process of emerging, the parishes and the city council continued to fight over the control of the trade. As this conflict developed over the next year, the fabriques and the diocese emphasized the need to protect the interests of the Church, while the city and later the national government presented themselves as defenders of the public interest. In the midst of this debate PFG quietly established itself as the sole purveyor of funeral services in Angers. The society's officials were able to work with both the city government and the diocese, without taking sides. Perhaps this is because they knew that no matter which party won the technical dispute about the rights to control the trade, they would stand to profit, assuming that they provided satisfactory services.

The events of February 1848, which brought a new government to Angers as well as to Paris, led to a delay in considering the dossier on pompes funèbres. By September, however, the bishop and the mayor, although still disagreeing about their rights, asked the prefect and the Paris ministries to approve provisionally the treaty between the fabriques and PFG. The mayor conceded that in some ways the contract was an improvement over the current practices. PFG agreed, for example, both to provide coffins to the poor without any charge to the city and to furnish decorations for the funerals of the poor and of children beyond what was called for in the 1847 agreement.[26] However, the new prefect, Georges Bordillon, although he forwarded this proposal to the minister of religion, included with it a letter in which he criticized all the previous accords because they had established distinctions on the basis of wealth. Bordillon's letter is somewhat disingenuous; as a member of the city council in 1847 he wrote a letter of introduction for M. Jeramec from PFG in September, affirming his support of his proposal, which included a distinction by classes. Bordillon had been known, however, for his democratic sympathies—a fact that explains his appointment as prefect—and in September of 1848 he was prepared to defend a radical ideal for the celebration of funerals that recalls the efforts of Fouché and Chaumette in 1793:

The ideal would be that all burials be celebrated in the same way, with dignity and simplicity, whatever be the poverty or wealth of the deceased; the Church should reserve its pomp for solemn feasts common to all citizens, for the commemoration of All Souls' Day, or for the celebration of a service in honor of citizens who died for the fatherland. The classes of prices which now categorize burials on the basis of the fortune of the dead, and which evoke and anticipate all the vanity of the survivors, are far from this ideal, which I persist in believing conforms to Christian beliefs and democratic traditions.[27]

The minister of religion did not go as far as Bordillon. The mood in Paris changed following the bloody June Days, when government troops battled workers in the streets of the capital, and by September ministers were not likely to be sympathetic to the kind of social-democratic rhetoric used by the new prefect. But the minister did agree with the city council and insisted that the parishes had no right to sign an independent contract with PFG without having asked for competitive bids. Furthermore, the optional items in the new treaty had never been reviewed by the ministry and, therefore, could not be approved.

Negotiations began again in 1848, and by 1849 a council of Angevin fabriques had worked out a new price list for the six classes of services that would be high enough to guarantee them sufficient funds. The city council, however, objected to the proposal because the prices were too high, due in part to the inclusion of flambeaux. These large candles, made with the remains of smaller ones, had a "lugubrious and disagreeable appearance" and gave off an odor that was "fetid and nauseating." It was, of course, in the interest of the parishes and the clergy to include as many candles as possible in a service, given the profits that they could make by reselling them to the candle makers. The city's concern to protect the consumer and keep prices low also led officials to complain that the parishes did not intend to decorate the church doors for a fifth-class service. Such decorations were considered crucial for a dignified service; they established a line between those able to bury their dead with decency and those whose poverty made such a show impossible. One city councilor claimed that by eliminating decorations from a fifth-class service parishes would "force families with few resources to take the fourth class."[28]

In addition to these particular objections about services and pricing two issues of principle arose that took two years to resolve and that established a fault line in the dispute between the city and the church over the funeral trade. The parishes claimed the right to establish prices and collect a remittance from the decoration of the house of the deceased, whereas the city argued that the maison mortuaire was in their domain because it was outside the church. This issue, which would come up again in the national debates on funeral reform later in the century, highlights the struggle being fought between Church and State over the space of death. Funerals, like cemeteries, were a source of both financial and symbolic capital, and the houses of the dead were a contested area that, if placed under the jurisdiction of the parishes, would establish Catholicism as still able to control public space during a crucial rite of passage.

The second issue blocking final agreement between Angers and the parishes concerned the mandatory pricing of services. According to the fabriques, the prices for the six classes were set, and families could not be permitted to exclude certain items in order to save money. Such a choice would destroy the sense of a class-based system of funerals and make financial planning impossible. The city defended the rights of individual choice in this matter and argued that the prices for classes were a maximum that could be reduced by allowing families to exclude items. A decision on this issue would, of course, have an important effect on funeral revenues, with the fabriques' interpretation leading to substantially higher income.[29]

By 1852 all these problems had been resolved by negotiations between the fabriques and the city council, with the minister of the interior playing the role of final arbiter. The bishop successfully defended the use of flambeaux as customary in Angers, arguing that the "families have always considered them the most imposing part of the service within the church." By supporting this claim the minister of interior responded to the weight of local custom and simultaneously added to the revenues of the parishes and clergy. The parishes conceded the decoration of the church for a fifth-class service and even allowed this for a sixth-class service. Only the indigent were buried with no hangings at the church and at home, and officials agreed that these would constitute one-third of the burials in Angers. Finally the minister of interior ruled that the city had the right to regulate the decoration of the maison mortuaire and that the fabriques' interpretation of the price list should be adopted. Those who chose a certain class would be obligated to pay the entire fee set by the tarif.

In 1852, ten years after Angevin officials had begun their work, a modern funeral service was finally established in Angers. A contract with PFG was quickly signed, and from that point on the correspondence shows none of the bureaucratic skirmishing that attended the establishment of the funeral trade. The contract was renewed periodically with only brief and polite exchanges until the end of the century. In 1888, when the city council was asked to ratify another nine-year term, one member objected that he didn't know what he was approving. The mayor responded that there was no need to explore the issue because the system had worked well for over thirty years, and the current contract saved the city from burying the poor at its own expense.[30]

The system finally agreed to in 1852 resembles in many ways what had already been established in Paris. The entrepreneur agreed to remit 40 percent of the revenue on rented objects and 10 percent on material purchased outright to the fabriques. These percentages were significantly lower than those paid by Paris entrepreneurs, but PFG could argue in turn that the prices at Angers were much lower for services that were roughly comparable. A first-class service in Angers, according to the contract, would cost only Fr 712, compared to almost Fr 4,000 in Paris. Angevins interested in an even more lavish service could add additional plumes for the horses, fancier clothes for the porters, coats of arms, gloves for the mourners, and expensive invitations; but even if they chose all the options available, their costs would not have approached those of the Parisians.[31]

There was, however, one major difference between Paris and Angers. In Angers the fabriques retained relatively more control over the funeral system. Technically, a council of representatives from the parishes was charged with the service, but these men in fact did very little. This fiction allowed the fabriques to rent their interest in the funeral trade directly to a contractor without having to go through an adjudication. The parishes named a managing director charged with supervising the personnel of PFG, thus providing in principle for local control over the national corporation.

The first director named by the council of fabriques in Angers was Xavier Riobé, who remained in his post until the 1880s. Under his leadership funerals were conducted smoothly, and by the 1860s he was proposing that the Angers system be adopted as a model by other cities. According to Riobé, whose pamphlets appeared in Angers and Paris in the 1860s, funerals were the only means of support for parishes because all other sources of income, such as pew rentals, were diminishing with the decline of religious zeal. Based on his observations in Angers and elsewhere in France Riobé argued that "wherever care has been taken to offer the public the means to celebrate their funerals with brilliance, important results have been immediately obtained, and the fabriques have gathered in unhoped-for fruits."[32]

Riobé presented himself as a defender of the interests of the fabriques, and it is certainly the case that the financial situation of the parishes of Angers improved as a result of the funeral system that he managed. Revenue from the funeral trade received from PFG rose from nine thousand francs in 1849 to fifty thousand in 1890.[33] Although he was a native of Angers, during his tenure as director-general Riobé came to identify himself as a professional undertaker and a proponent of PFG, which published and distributed one of his pamphlets. Although the fabriques technically retained control, Riobé's service operated just as the Paris enterprise did, taking orders from families and distributing the revenues based on the agreed percentages. The advantages claimed by Riobé for the Angers system were the same that would result if PFG were to run the service directly. In both cases the lay undertakers saved the clergy the embarrassing task of collecting fees for services, while providing the parishes sufficient funds for maintaining the cult. And in both cases cities profited from the system by freeing themselves of the charge of burying the poor. Riobé pointed out an additional advantage of commercial funerals. By increasing the revenues for the parishes, city governments would free themselves of potential expenses, because the law controlling municipalities made them liable for any deficits run up by the fabriques. Finally, in proposing a cooperative arrangement between parishes and PFG Riobé did not neglect an argument that had become a standard of the Paris funeral profession early in the century: commercial funerals not only provided families that could afford them the opportunity to celebrate their dead with the desired pomp but also guaranteed that some of the proceeds from this service would pay for the decent burial of the poor.[34]

Throughout the 1850s these same arguments were made by PFG in provincial cities throughout France. From its origins in the Paris region in the 1840s PFG showed itself to be an aggressive firm, always looking for ways to expand into new markets. Already charged with the funeral service for the suburbs of Paris, by 1847 PFG was competing with the official firm of Paris, underselling the entrepreneur Pector in providing luxury-quality coffins and decorative emblems. Pector complained about this competition from PFG as a violation of his contractual rights, just as PFG complains today when faced with competition from Michel Leclerc.[35] There are other parallels between PFG in the 1850s and Leclerc's funeral business of the 1980s; in both cases, for example, the newer firms actively and successfully marketed themselves on a national level. The entrepreneurs of PFG used Angers as a reference when they approached other cities in western France. Officials from Cherbourg, Le Havre, Le Mans, and Tours consulted with colleagues from Angers before eventually signing contracts with PFG. By the end of the century cities as far away as Dijon and Montpellier were corresponding with Angers. These requests for information reveal the continuing spread of practices first introduced in Paris early in the century. Tours, like Angers, introduced hearses and commercial funerals in the 1850s following the construction of a new cemetery outside of town. Not every city that corresponded with Angers chose to employ PFG, but by the end of the century the firm was established in twenty-five provincial cities in addition to the Paris region.[36] The firm that today dominates the funeral trade owes its early success to its ability to cooperate with the fabriques charged with responsibility for the cult of the dead. When a reform of pompes funèbres was discussed in the latter part of the nineteenth century both undertakers and fabriques were criticized, but the final law passed in 1904 was directed primarily against the parishes. The laymen of the funeral profession were suspect, but their services were indispensable.

THE REFORM OF POMPES FUNÈBRES: 1880–1904

The treatment of the dead was among the most emotionally charged issues dealt with in the wave of anticlerical legislation that followed the republican victory in 1876. Avner Ben-Amos and James Lehning have shown how the issue of funerals was a central issue in the political disputes between republicans and anticlericals that led to the secularization of cemeteries in 1881 (see chapter 5) and the right to choose a civil rather than a religious burial in 1887 (see chapter 3).[37] A reform of the system of pompes funèbres was originally seen as a logical corollary to the cemetery and funeral legislation passed in the 1880s. Reforming pompes funèbres was much more problematic, however, and the anticlerical majority was able to overcome its internal divisions only in 1904, at the height of the conflict that resulted in the separation of Church and State. This delay was due to a confusion in the debate; the language of anticlericalism and Church State conflict that shaped discussion of this issue was inadequate to capture and express the sentiments of politicians who desired to preserve the religious dimension of funerals even while they restricted the role of Catholicism. The debates also reveal a long struggle to address the financial aspect of the funeral trade, as bourgeois politicians sought to reconcile the legitimate interests of businessmen with the need to keep the profane market a safe distance from the sacred corpse. Other historians have used the reports and debates on pompes funèbres to trace the development of anticlericalism, but a close reading of these texts also reveals how politicians worked to preserve the religious atmosphere of the cult of the dead, which was threatened by capitalist motives and secular ideology.

The first proposal for a reform of pompes funèbres, introduced in 1879, called for a transfer of the parishes' right to control the funeral trade to city governments. This law was withdrawn in May 1881 as time was running out for the legislative session, but a similar bill was reintroduced in December 1881 by M. Lefebvre, a deputy from Seine-et-Marne. Lefebvre was motivated by a recent incident in his department in which a parish refused to provide the funeral pall for someone who had chosen to be buried without a church service. Evidence from Angers suggests that the clergy sought to limit access to the traditional decorations to those who died after the Last Sacraments had been administered, a tactic designed to pressure families into accepting the priest's presence at the deathbed.[38] The chamber commission's report on this law, submitted in 1882, made "liberty of conscience" the primary argument in favor of a reform:

> To surrender the management of a public service which concerns all citizens, regardless of their philosophic or religious belief, to the representatives of a particular religion, makes the respect for the dead and the decency of funerals depend on the good will of a minister and the conformity of his opinions with those of the deceased. [Such a system also] permits the corpse of a dissenter to be branded with a mark of infamy by refusing him the honors that ordinarily accompany burial.[39]

According to the commission, the legislation of 23 prairial erred in confusing the religious services that are the proper domain of the Church, which can rightfully be claimed by believers, with the decency that ought to surround the burial of all citizens, regardless of creed. The legislators who examined the new measure were certainly correct in perceiving that the Napoleonic law identified decent burial with a religious service, but they were perhaps too optimistic about how easy it would be to separate these two concepts.

The argument that the parish monopoly over the funeral trade violated the liberty of conscience was repeated in a variety of forms for the next twenty-five years. Proponents of a reform of pompes funèbres insisted that they occupied the moral high ground in their desire to prevent the Church from abusing its privilege by refusing funeral decorations to unbelievers. The particular form of this argument shifted, however, in part as a result of a second set of considerations. In addition to the moral argument, politicians were forced to deal with the financial realities of the funeral trade. Once the fabriques were denied their monopoly, who would provide for pompes funèbres? Entrepreneurs were available, of course, and many already had contracts with the parishes, especially in the cities of France. But the commissioners reporting on the Lefebvre bill in 1882 unequivocally rejected the surrender of the funeral trade to the free market: "These are not things to be traded, nor abandoned to chance." Furthermore, simply to open up the trade to all comers would only ensure the survival of the status quo, because the fabriques which already possessed the material for funerals would be at a clear advantage in such a competitive situation.

The solution proposed by the Lefebvre bill of 1881 was to grant communes a monopoly over the material necessary for a burial and to permit the families of the dead to add to this whatever religious or philosophical emblems they desired. The parishes retained the right to decorate churches. In practice, this bill would require cities to acquire hearses or stretchers for the transport of the dead, material for decorating them, and funeral palls to cover the coffins. Not surprisingly, conservatives responded with a defense of the fabriques' monopoly; but some republicans also objected to the reform, arguing that a communal monopoly would be as expensive and abusive as the one granted to parishes. Instead, they offered a counterproposal in which the funeral trade would be deregulated and surrendered to a free market.

Henri Giraud was the principal spokesman for those who sought to eliminate all monopoly privileges in the provision of funerals. Like the proposals of those who supported transferring the monopoly to communes, his argument drew on both moral and financial considerations, but the latter were given relatively more attention by Giraud and reveal a resentment against the entrepreneurs who cooperated with the fabriques. Giraud argued that any monopoly, including a communal one, violated the rights of groups to provide for the burial of their members. He was referring specifically to mutual-aid societies, which had grown rapidly since the 1850s. These organizations, designed early in the century to ensure a decent burial to their members, were in the process of transforming themselves into life-insurance companies that would provide for survivors as well as bury the dead.[40] The older task of assisting at the burial of their members was still part of the charter of many societies and led at times to conflicts when both members and entrepreneurs claimed the responsibility for bearing the dead in procession.[41] According to Giraud, transferring monopoly rights over funerals to communes would still lead to the unfair restriction of the rights of society members to conduct their own funerals, and he therefore proposed the elimination of all such privileges.

Giraud spent most of his time in the debates over funeral reform criticizing the financial consequences of the current system, which resulted in high prices and the unjustified limitation of commerce. According to Giraud, parishes generally contracted out their funeral rights to entrepreneurs for remittances of 50 to 75 percent. Lefebvres's bill, by transferring monopoly rights to communes, would result in similar contracts, because mayors and city councils would naturally exploit the trade as a source of revenue. Giraud presented himself as a defender of the consumer and argued that deregulation and a free market in funerals would lower prices: "You're putting into the hands of the city council the means to enrich itself, but what will become of the inhabitants forced to bear this heavy burden?" To support his argument Giraud pointed to entrepreneurs at Toulouse and Le Havre who took advantage of their monopoly to sue competitors and force them out of the market. As his argument reached its climax, a republican colleague interjected a cry that reveals succinctly the mood informing his presentation. When Giraud claimed that even the poor had to spend seven hundred francs to be buried, Gustave Rivet yelled out: "At these prices we can't afford to die!" ("*A ce prix, on ne peut plus mourir!*")

Giraud concluded by arguing that the elimination of the funeral monopoly would create a system comparable to the one in England; lower prices would be charged because undertakers would reduce their prices by the percentages currently paid to fabriques. As he closed his address Giraud shifted his argument from a financial to a moral focus: he described the current system as one of "pillage and shameless exploitation" based on the "inventive genius of people who rack their brains creating all this decorative jumble as subtle as it is useless." Giraud did not explain how such abuses would be avoided in the free market that he favored, and opponents of deregulation consistently argued that it would in fact encourage the aggressive marketing of funeral decorations.

Giraud's position, repeated and modified when pompes funèbres were again debated early in the twentieth century, reveals some of the unresolved and contradictory concerns regarding funerals within the republican majority. Some republicans believed that people had the right to be buried by friends and associates if they so desired. This freedom of choice would have the added advantage of permitting all interested entrepreneurs a share in the market, and the resulting competition would in turn lower prices. This liberal vision of politicians like Giraud, however, was combined with a resentment of entrepreneurs who exploited the grief of families in order to increase their profits. Other republicans such as Lefebvre appreciated the contradiction implicit in Giraud's argument and hoped that a communal monopoly would check the abuses in the present system.

The conservative response to the reform of pompes funèbres was delivered by Monseigneur Charles Freppel, the bishop of Angers and the leading spokesman for the defense of Church privileges threatened by the anticlerical majority. He acknowledged that "liberty of conscience" was a legitimate concern and conceded that the fabriques in some villages had acted intolerantly, but he insisted that a ministerial circular emphasizing their obligation to bury all citizens was the appropriate solution. Paris provided Freppel an example of how the current system could work without difficulty; there the fabriques never refused the material requested and made no inquiry into the religious convictions of the deceased.[42]

According to Freppel, the proposed reform posed a serious threat to the dignity of funerals prized by the French. From his perspective the procession now to be regulated exclusively by the commune was part of the religious service, and he compared the Lefebvre reform with the attempt to secularize funerals during the revolution, an experiment that he assumed all agreed had resulted in lack of respect for the dead. The poor would in practice be denied access to the consolation of religion under the new measure, because they would not be able to rent religious symbols to go along with the neutral material provided by communes. (A deputy from the Left shouted at this point: "You'll furnish them free!"—a comment suggesting that the Church's financial interests in the funeral trade took precedence over its charitable obligations.) The funeral pall was the key item here, according to Freppel, for traditionally this was a black cloth that bore a large white cross. The elimination of this symbol of death and resurrection, which was so much a part of the culture of death in France, would be catastrophic: "The decency of funerals disappears when the idea of the immortality of the soul is absent, and it is religion alone which can guarantee the respect due to the dead."[43]

The reporter for the Lefebvre bill in the Chamber, M. de la Porte, knowing that he had a strong majority, limited himself to brief responses. To Giraud he emphasized that a free market would result in the maintenance of the status quo, as the parishes would profit from their material advantages in the trade. To Freppel he responded that the fabriques would still have the right to income from the decoration of the churches, and he reported two complaints from the diocese of Angers about the intolerance of fabriques, suggesting that the bishop was either naive or deceptive in minimizing the Church's abuses. The Lefebvre bill passed easily over the objections of Giraud and Freppel, and on 12 November 1883 the Chamber approved by a vote of 346 to

102 the transfer of monopoly rights over pompes funèbres to the communes.[44]

When Lefebvre's bill reached the Senate, however, it met with substantial opposition. The reporter for the commission that examined the measure, M. Garrisson, emphasized the need to balance family and civic interests on "this difficult and delicate question." In his view, the Chamber reform was correct in attempting to control the funeral trade, for "absolute liberty is incompatible with French manners." Garrisson, like other republicans, objected to the high prices that he blamed on the current monopoly, and he was explicitly critical of undertakers who exploited the grief of families in order to make a profit. By passing the trade exclusively to the communes, however, the Chamber threatened the free choice of families, which might object to handing over their dead to a communal representative, a political agent who had no place in the cult of the dead. Consequently, the Senate Commission rewrote the law to allow both communes and fabriques to provide the material for pompes funèbres. In order to protect the rights of non-Catholics to a decent burial in cases where cities did not take advantage of their new rights, the Senate bill allowed communes to requisition material from the fabriques in cases when they refused to provide it.[45]

Although the Senate version was much more generous toward the fabriques, the right still opposed it with arguments extending points made by Freppel in the Chamber. Senator Allou's comments are especially revealing because he concentrated on the danger of dividing the funeral service into two distinct parts. Such a split would result in "disorder and confusion" in the cult of the dead, which demanded "unity." Under the terms of the reform, for example, he asked who would be responsible for decorating the maison mortuaire. Who would provide for the holy water and candles and for the chapel sometimes erected in the room of the deceased? All this was part of the "exterior" service, but Allou found it inconceivable that communes rather than parishes would be allowed access to this material. Allou was not apparently bothered that the entrepreneurs who were already managing funerals in cities had access to holy water, candles, and other material. His argument was based on an appeal to family sentiments that favored Church control of funerals. Whereas Church control was still common in the villages of France, Allou's argument was anachronistic for the cities that were the focal point of the debate on the reform: in urban France, secular entrepreneurs had already replaced fabriques and clergy. Anticlericals were quick to point this out, but they were unable to form a coherent judgment about the commercialization that had occurred because they were unsure whether or not the market had a legitimate claim on the cult of the dead.[46]

Republican ambivalence toward commercial funerals is evident in Garrisson's defense of his proposal against the right, which favored continuing the monopoly granted to the parishes. According to Garrisson, allowing both the communes and fabriques to provide funeral material would bring prices down. But on this point Garrisson ran into trouble because he was in effect defending the value of competition in the funeral trade, which elsewhere he attacked as a violation of the French spirit. His discomfort was evident when he tried to describe how his proposal would lower prices: "If there was—I don't want to use a word with commercial significance, I don't want to say competition—but if there was 'emulation' between the two exterior services, this would lead necessarily to the reduction of prices that the commission desires. . . ."[47] When challenged about the financial consequences of his project, Garrisson again showed his discomfort and quickly moved the debate to a moral plane, including a defense of the religious significance of funerals:

> The figures don't matter: it's not a question of money but of principle, a question which is much higher. What is being proposed to you? After overturning one monopoly to establish another. . . . to break abruptly with our most respected customs, habits, and traditions at the risk of violating our conscience, and nothing, you know, is more delicate than a conscience. It is proposed that the commune be given all the rights and to reserve nothing to that represented by the religious element, whose role however is so considerable in all societies, that it would be insane not to take it into account (*Très bien! Très bien!* on the right); if not from the point of view of sentiment, at least from the point of view of reason, of politics. It is impossible to regard the religious element as a negligible quantity.

Garrisson had previously acknowledged the abuses that sometimes occurred under the current system and had complained strenuously about the high costs of current funerals. When challenged that his reform would not solve these problems, he shifted to an argument that appealed to the French tradition of religious services. The decoration of the house, the hearse, and the coffin with religious symbols created a sacred atmosphere around the body that was threatened by a communal monopoly. Carried away by his rhetoric, and by encouragement from the center and the right of the Senate, Garrisson insisted that it was necessary to take from the past that which "experience has consecrated." He concluded with a variation on the theme of the importance of tradition: "A nation has its manners, its traditions, its beliefs, its intimate sentiments, which must not be crushed."[48]

Garrisson did not explicitly defend Catholicism or its doctrines in trying to preserve the rights of fabriques, but a careful examination of his rhetoric shows an interesting turn. He began his speech by evoking custom, habit, and tradition, but in the end he added to this litany belief as well. Garrisson did not specify which beliefs were threatened, but the tenor of his remarks aligns him with the deputy in the Chamber who shouted at one point that a communal monopoly amounted to "obligatory atheism."[49] Monsignor Freppel knew what he was doing when he closed his speech to the Chamber by appealing to the commitment of the French to the cross, the symbol of resurrection, as an essential decoration of the funeral pall, because even republicans like Garrisson were offended by the idea of a religiously neutral funeral procession.

In January 1886 the Senate approved the version of the reform proposed by its commission, which would permit both communes and fabriques to provide funeral decorations. The Chamber failed to take up this measure, and the fabriques thus continued to exercise their rights over the funeral trade for the rest of the century. No consensus between Chamber and Senate emerged on the proposed reform of pompes funèbres; the debates reveal that republican politicians, who enjoyed a majority in both houses, found it difficult to reconcile the conflicting interests involved in the issue. Catholic intolerance and high prices were resented, but despite these abuses the status quo preserved the right of families to use religious symbols and protected them from unregulated competition in the delicate matter of funerals. The republican newspaper Le Temps, generally sympathetic to anticlerical causes, typified the hesitancy on this issue when it reported on the Senate debate: "It seems that the calm and serenity that ought to surround death must not be confused with politics."[50] The right was no more able to formulate a clear position than were the anticlericals, and at times they described a system of funerals that bore little resemblance to the commercial practices in place in urban centers.

One final reason can be given for the failure of a reform of pompes funèbres in the 1880s. As Emile de Marcère, one of the last speakers in the Senate debate, pointed out, neither the Chamber nor the Senate was well informed about the funeral practices in the cities and towns of France. In a number of large cities, including Lyon and Lille, the fabriques had never taken advantage of their rights over pompes funèbres, limiting themselves to the interior of churches. The law allowed for villages where families took responsibility for funerals to continue to provide for pompes funèbres, but no one knew how common this practice was. In fact, there was no study by the government of the consequences of either the Chamber or Senate reform. Confused about the conflicting values that they perceived in the issue and uninformed about essential facts, French politicians placed the reform of pompes funèbres low on their agenda throughout the 1890s.[51]

The Church-State crisis of the early twentieth century brought the issue of pompes funèbres back to the floors of the Chamber and the Senate. The reports and debates of this period reveal important changes in both the facts and attitudes concerning funerals: the argument based on "liberty of conscience" had receded by the 1900s, and financial and market considerations became much more central. In particular, the argument in favor of the "absolute liberty" of the market that had been rejected easily in the 1880s was pressed hard and at one point was apparently accepted in the Chamber. The strength of this position was derived in part from the changing conditions of the funeral trade. By the 1900s businessmen with interests in commercial funerals were making their presence felt by lobbying sympathetic lawmakers. Despite this pressure in favor of deregulation, the idea of a communal monopoly finally triumphed because the majority remained sensitive to the argument that death ought in principle not to be subject to the competition of the marketplace. The debates demonstrate how politicians accepted that even under the new reform commercial enterprises would play a crucial role in the provision of pompes funèbres.

In 1900 a Chamber commission assigned a bill similar to Lefebvre's proposal of 1881 expressed confidence that the time had finally come to finish the work begun two decades earlier: "If the status quo has some defenders," read the commission report, "it is for form, for honor. These intransigents well know that they support a lost cause that is moreover unjust. They protest, but they concede. They are too few."[52] In arguing for their reform, however, anticlericals were forced to acknowledge an important change in the behavior of the fabriques: they no longer refused to bury freethinkers. Despite this evidence of Catholic tolerance, anticlericals still maintained that the current system violated the liberty of conscience. In its new version, however, this argument combined financial and moral themes that had been separated in the debate of the 1880s:

> The fabriques bury freethinkers now despite themselves, for they alone have the right to bury them; they alone profit from the price of a burial. And Gambetta, for whom "clericalism was the enemy," and Hugo, who refused "the prayers of all churches," and Quinet, and Michelet, and Renan, have paid in dying a tax to all these different cults that they equally rejected.[53]

In both the 1880s and the 1900s anticlericals objected to the fabriques' monopoly as a violation of the rights of freethinkers, but the shape of this argument changed radically over two decades. In the earlier period, the complaint was that parishes refused to provide freethinkers the material needed for a decent burial, thus putting unfair pressure on them and their families to violate their conscience and accept a church service. Liberty of conscience was still an issue in the 1900s, but by then the focus of the complaint had become the obligation of anticlericals to contribute financially to churches that they rejected. In the 1880s anticlericals argued that fabriques forfeited the right to provide pompes funèbres because they failed to fulfill their moral and legal obligation to bury the dead. Twenty years later parishes were acting with the tolerance asked for by critics, but anticlericals nonetheless sought to take away their rights, an inconsistency that the Catholics pointed to in opposing the reform.[54]

In resisting the reform in the early 1900s Catholics raised another issue, one that had formerly not been part of their repertoire and that showed how they also were influenced by arguments in favor of the marketplace. According to Suchetet, communes, in taking over the funeral trade, would be violating the rights of businessmen to compete for profits: "The commune, in effect, has no more right to bear the dead to their graves than it has the right to transport merchandise. . . . We would fall thus into state socialism." The conservative Groussau threw the anticlericals into confusion when he pressed the issue by asking supporters of the bill whether communes would be obligated to establish monopolies. He pointed out that in many towns where the fabriques had never exercised their rights over pompes funèbres, entrepreneurs had recently established themselves; their new businesses would be threatened by the communal monopoly. The republican deputy M. Bepmale challenged Groussau, arguing that the law permitted but did not require communal monopolies. When asked to clarify the matter the reporter Rabier responded ambiguously, apparently unsure about the implications of the law that he was proposing.

The right had scored a point in the debate, but it was not one that they could take advantage of without defending merchants who operated in competition with the fabriques. In the closing decades of the nineteenth century commercial funerals were increasingly available in the cities and towns of France, but in many cases these were offered by businessmen who had not entered into any formal agreements with the parishes. In those cities where the fabriques granted their rights to a single entrepreneur, other businessmen began asserting their rights to a share in the market. The introduction of new fu-

neral objects not formerly included in official price lists allowed an
entry point for merchants. Flowers became an increasingly important
object, perhaps at the expense of candles. Crowns of flowers, either
real or ceramic, to be placed on coffins and graves became an essential part of the funeral service. In Paris one company began renting
omnibus funéraires so that large groups of mourners could ride rather
than walk to the church and cemetery. These innovations led to a
large number of suits in which entrepreneurs sought to defend their
monopoly rights.[55] By 1900 the judgments in these cases were increasingly favorable to competition. The appeals court at Lyon, for
example, ruled that the fabriques' right to a monopoly could only be
exercised directly; once the parishes contracted out their rights, other
entrepreneurs could enter into the funeral market.[56]

Although the right had introduced the issue of free trade as an argument in favor of the status quo, it was a proponent of reform, the
deputy Fleury-Ravarin, who most clearly and consistently advocated
liberty of commerce for the funeral industry. In his amendment to the
Senate bill, Fleury-Ravarin proposed that the reform restrict the communal monopoly to the transport of the body and give all merchants
the right to compete for the rest of the funeral business. He based his
argument on the case of Lyon, where the fabriques had never taken
up their rights and the city provided for the transportation of the
body, leaving all decorations to family choice and private industry.
When a deputy on the right interrupted with a slogan intended
to mock the speaker—"Freedom for the coffin!" (*"La liberté au
cercueil!"*)—he drew laughs from his colleagues, and Fleury-Ravarin
responded quickly that he was defending *"la liberté de commerce."*
When asked if this meant that people would have the right to pur
chase their coffins from anyone whom they chose, he took up the
previous witticism and made it his own: "We demand the freedom of
the coffin." This exchange is revealing because the right had hoped to
ridicule Fleury-Ravarin's argument for "absolute liberty" of the market, but after a moment's hesitation Fleury-Ravarin acknowledged
and accepted the implications of his proposal for the placing of funerals on the open market.[57]

The amendment proposed by Fleury-Ravarin called for the restriction of the communal monopoly to transporting the body and for the
guarantee of free trade in coffins and funeral decorations. When his
amendment passed, however, Fleury-Ravarin was apparently taken
by surprise. Concerned that the vote applied only to restricting communal governments, without guaranteeing the rights of entrepreneurs, he called for a second vote. At this point the debate became
very confused, and no one seemed entirely sure of what it was that

they had actually approved. The reporter argued that voting twice on the same amendment violated parliamentary procedure and threatened to invalidate the bill. Fleury-Ravarin nonetheless insisted, and when the votes were cast the second part of his amendment was defeated by a tie vote, 269 to 269. As the senators who took up the measure in the following year pointed out, the meaning of these votes was unclear. It may be that some deputies did not favor the explicit guarantee to free trade called for by Fleury-Ravarin, or perhaps they were simply annoyed by his excessive maneuvering. As passed to the Senate the bill called for the abolition of the fabriques' monopoly and the establishment of a communal service for the transport of the body.

The Senate report on the Chamber bill and the debate that followed in the summer of 1904 constitute the last stage in the history of the reform of pompes funèbres. The revisions introduced and approved by the Senate were adopted without change by the Chamber in December 1904. The report prepared by the Senate commission chaired by M. Milliès-Lacroix represents a break with previous parliamentary handling of the reform in that it made a serious effort to determine how many fabriques actually took advantage of their monopoly rights. The results of the inquiry showed that parishes exercised control over pompes funèbres in 47 of 86 departmental capitals, 75 of 275 subprefectures, and 198 of 545 other urban centers. The report does not specify in how many cases these fabriques granted their rights to an entrepreneur, but the spread of the Société des Pompes Funèbres Générales in the second half of the century suggests that such contracts were common. In the cities where fabriques did not manage the funeral trade either directly or indirectly private firms existed to serve the public, a development discussed in the Chamber debates of 1903 and again in the Senate discussion of 1904. The figures gathered by the Senate commission undercut the argument of the right about the importance of pompes funèbres to parish life; the reformers could argue that in most places the fabriques had demonstrated their ability to function without these revenues. At the same time the Senate report highlighted the role of private firms, which assumed a central place in the subsequent debate.[58]

The Senate introduced one major modification to the Chamber bill: instead of merely granting communes the right to transport bodies, it specified exactly what would be included in the new monopoly:

> The exterior service of pompes funèbres, including the transport of bodies, the furnishing of hearses, coffins, hangings for the homes of the dead, mourning carriages, as well as the furnishings and personnel nec-

essary for burials, exhumations, and cremations, belong to communes, as part of a public service. These can assume the service directly, or grant it to an enterprise, in conformity with the laws and regulations controlling the adjudication of public works.

A substantial portion of the report and the debate that followed centered on this article. Although the reform was part of the anticlerical movement, the Senate debates indicate that the key conflict was no longer between cities and parishes but between cities and entrepreneurs.

Both in his commission's report and in his opening speech on the reform, Milliès-Lacroix presented himself as a defender not only of commerce but also of the rights of families, which deserved protection from the scandalous marketing of funeral objects. This familiar argument was answered by Alfred Girard, who introduced Fleury-Ravarin's Chamber amendment on the Senate floor. Girard accepted the need to laicize funerals, but once the fabriques were removed from the trade he insisted that the "liberty of commerce" should prevail. In his defense of this principle he went much further than Fleury-Ravarin in proclaiming the advantages of the marketplace for the cult of the dead. As a result of the competition that would follow from his amendment the public would profit from lower prices, whereas a communal monopoly would continue the high costs established by the fabriques. Girard admitted that clients might be badgered as a result of this competition, but he refused to see this as a sufficient reason for establishing a communal monopoly:

> Badgering is the result of competition; the more lively the competition is the more the client is badgered. But this doesn't only happen with pompes funèbres. As troublesome as the entrepreneurs in this trade are, they are not so insistent as wine merchants, for example; and you don't contemplate the establishment of a wine monopoly in order to prevent the clientele from being troubled and subjected to "mercantile speculation."[59]

Girard's comparison of the funeral trade with commerce in wine suggests how far the debate on pompes funèbres had progressed over the past two decades; no one prior to him had attempted to assert that funerals were a business like any other and, therefore, required no special treatment from civil authorities. The only legitimate interests recognized by Girard are those of the marketplace, where entrepreneurs have a right to sell their wares and buyers the right to choose. He concluded his speech with an appeal to antimonopolist and anti-Parisian sentiment: the creation of communal monopolies, which would then grant their rights to a single merchant, would favor the large firms of Paris. And just as the national railroad system and the department stores of Paris were destroying local clothing industries, the domination of Paris—an obvious reference to PFG— would destroy the local funeral trades:

> Thus the clientele of the living increasingly escapes to Paris. There remains the clientele of the dead who—until the present at least, I don't guarantee the future—don't have themselves buried in Paris, nor buried locally by Parisians. Don't let this resource be stolen from our merchants, our provincial retailers. . . . (*Très bien! Très bien!* from many sections)

With Girard the focus of the debate on pompes funèbres has clearly shifted from "liberty of conscience" to "liberty of commerce." The rights of merchants and the freedom of the marketplace were the primary values to be defended in reforming the funeral system.

The centerpiece of Milliès-Lacroix's response to the free marketers was a long citation from a letter by the mayor of Lyon, M. Augagneur, a professor on the faculty of medicine. Lyon had been described by both Fleury-Ravarin and Girard as a model for how well competition could work in the funeral trade, but Augagneur presented a very different picture. The fabriques had never used their monopoly rights in the city, and the commune had restricted itself to providing for the transportation of the body, leaving to private industry the provision of the coffin and decorations. But the result was, according to the mayor, a situation that compromised public health. Greed and the desire to cut costs led to the delivery of unacceptable coffins, which leaked during the processions. The employees of several firms scandalously intruded on the grief of families to sell their wares. One firm, the Société des Pompes Funèbres Générales of Lyon, dominated the trade and was now spreading throughout the south, where it was competing with the Paris company. Like PFG of Paris, the Lyon firm was known at times to encourage fabriques to assume their rights, then establish itself as the privileged entrepreneur. These firms, which now lobbied for free trade, were actually interested in protecting the de facto monopolies that they had achieved when neither fabriques nor communes controlled the profession. By the end of the century the major firms had, in fact, become active lobbyists defending their rights, and their letters were taken seriously by politicians on all sides of the issue. Their argument that free trade would lead to lower prices was invalid, according to Milliès-Lacroix, because it would result not in competition but in unregulated monopolies that would gouge the public. Finally, he raised an old argument dating from the revolutionary period: the communal monopoly would allow cities to raise sufficient revenues to bury the poor decently, whereas with free trade the rich would choose private firms, leaving the cities with inadequate funds and thus denying the poor access to a proper service.[60]

In the Senate, amendments proposed by defenders of the status quo were defeated easily by voice vote, but the Girard amendment favoring free trade drew enough support to require individual balloting. In the end, however, senators voted to support the bill calling for communal control over the *service extérieure*, defined broadly to include coffins, hearses, and decorations. The bill was then returned to the Chamber, and despite a close vote defeating Fleury-Ravarin's amendment in favor of free trade (297 to 258) the Senate version of the bill, which grants communes monopoly rights, was passed into law.

Markets, Mass Consumption, and Funerals

In nineteenth-century France, urban funerals were increasingly assimilated into what William Reddy has described as the "market culture" of the time. In Paris early in the century, and then in Angers and other cities, merchants collaborated with churchmen to turn funerals into commodities—objects that were priced, categorized, and sold to whomever could afford them. Thomas Laqueur has noted a similar development in England, where undertakers succeeded in turning funerals into "a consumption good whose cost was clearly evident and could be matched with exquisite precision to the class and degree of 'respectability' . . . of the deceased."[61] The marketing techniques employed by undertakers were comparable to those used by other successful entrepreneurs. Like the department stores that became fashionable in this era, funeral companies such as PFG offered concentrated services at fixed prices, and their spread led to a homogenization of funereal style.[62] The growth and spread of the funeral trade accompanied the broader development of mass consumption, in which increasing numbers of men and women aspired to possess objects formerly restricted to an aristocratic elite.[63]

Although this analysis suggests that capitalism increasingly controlled the cult of the dead, the growth and regulation of commercial funerals that we have observed can yield more than this facile generalization. Entrepreneurs created new products, sold them in expanding markets, and in general took responsibility for the cult of the dead that had formerly been in the hands of the Church and the State. As they pushed forward, however, funeral professionals met with sub-

stantial resistance in the form of public opinion and government regulation, which attempted to restrict the play of market forces in the
provision of funerals. William Reddy's understanding of the concept
of "market culture" is useful here. He emphasizes its prescriptive dimension as a set of ideas and assumptions resisted by those who insisted on introducing a moral dimension that could not be quantified
into their social relations.[64] Similarly, I propose that the commodification of funerals was resisted as an unacceptable intrusion of the marketplace into a sphere that ought to be protected from considerations
of money. As Viviana Zelizer has suggested, social scientists have in
the past been too eager to employ market models to explain a constantly expanding terrain of human behavior. Her research exploring
how children came to be understood as "priceless" individuals calls
attention to another area in which markets were seen as an inappropriate intrusion into the nonmarket values of family life.[65] More im-
portantly here, however, her work also emphasizes the ambiguity
and tension that people felt as they confronted the marketplace. Even
though families may have resented having to place a monetary value
on children, or on their dead, by the end of the nineteenth century
they were compelled at times to put a price on such priceless commodities.

The spread of commercial funerals in urban France illustrates the
way in which attitudes toward death were shaped not so much by the
marketplace as by the battle between market and nonmarket values
centered on the dead and their families. This struggle was complicated by religious and political considerations. One of the advantages
perceived by Catholic parishes in letting entrepreneurs exploit their
rights over funerals was the insulation that this afforded them from
accusations of market-minded venality. Their hopes on this matter
were not realized, however. Perhaps individual clients were not always conscious of how the Church profited from funerals, but anticlerical politicians and their supporters made funeral revenues one of
the issues with which to attack their clerical opponents. The abolition
of the parish monopoly forced politicians, however, to consider alternative methods of providing for funerals, and here their values led
them in different directions. Liberalism pushed them toward the acceptance of the marketplace as the fairest and most efficient instrument for determining the quantity and quality of pompes funèbres,
but a residue of revolutionary egalitarianism made them fear the consequences of this for the poorest citizens. The class system introduced early in the century inevitably led to the introduction of social
distinctions into funerals, but complete liberty might result in the
total abasement of the poor. It was not primarily because of the poor,

however, that the Third Republic rejected, narrowly and after careful consideration, a free market in funerals.

The politicians of the Third Republic were drawn to the idea of a communal monopoly because it was judged to be an effective check on acquisitive impulses that had to be excluded from the cult of the dead. There was concern about the actual consequences of a monopoly and evidence that it did not always prevent the abusive treatment of families feared by critics throughout the century. Despite substantial support, however, the alternative of complete deregulation was rejected. The motives for the adoption of communal control over funerals were complex and include a statist commitment to the control of public ceremonies, a need to protect the health of the community, and a desire to gain access to revenues that could guarantee respectful treatment of all the dead. Underlying these motives, however, was a sense that the French should not allow the spirit of calculation to assume a predominant role in the cult of the dead. The development of family sentiment in the nineteenth century included a devotion to the dead, whose memories were to be cherished by visits to cemeteries. Funerals were key rituals in initiating these family cults, and the atmosphere of recollection and regret that they called for was incompatible with monetary considerations.

Despite government intentions families could not be fully protected in the funeral market. The experience of the nineteenth century illustrates this fact; and the law passed in 1904, although it transferred regulatory control from parishes to communes, had little effect on the growth of the commercial funeral industry, which continues to prosper. All that was required was that firms satisfy communal expectations, and their experience with fabriques and city councils in the nineteenth century prepared them to do so. As some defenders of free trade predicted, the system of communal monopolies has favored the growth of a single enterprise whose wealth and experience have allowed it to underbid potential competition. The Société des Pompes Funèbres Générales has provoked public resentment, and appeals for free trade and the abolition of the monopoly of 1904 can be heard. The death of Lucien Robbes with which I opened my treatment of pompes funèbres illustrates these complaints, but perhaps another contemporary example is needed to help explain why the system endures despite these criticisms. Anne Philippe describes her exchanges with an undertaker in a *mémoire* describing her mother's death in the 1980s.[66] *Monsieur le directeur*, as she calls him, is courteous and efficient and makes no effort to influence the choices that she has to make about the coffin, the hearse, and the service. Although her mother was an unbeliever, the curé makes a brief appearance, but it is clearly the undertaker who is in charge of the funeral, which is conducted with a quiet dignity. Of course, Anne Philippe had no trouble paying for the funeral, which made her choices less difficult than they might be for others. There is some tension in the conversations between the client and undertaker, who adopts an unctuous and ministerial manner, somewhat like Balzac's professional of the 1840s. The author has trouble concentrating as they leaf through the catalogue together, and she almost laughs as she contemplates the "class" of the coffin and the hearse. Despite the slight edge of discomfort, however, the relationship between family and undertaker is one of respect and restraint. This story contrasts sharply with the death of Robbes, with its public confrontation between competitors, and perhaps it is the desire to limit such scenes that explains why the 1904 law is still in effect.

COURBET'S *BURIAL AT ORNANS* AND THE CULT OF THE DEAD

Since the time when it was presented at the Salon of 1851 Gustave Courbet's *Burial at Ornans* has had a provocative effect on both viewers and critics, who continue to debate its meaning (see illus. 22). The generally hostile reception of the painting at the time focused on the "ugliness" of Courbet's subjects, and on the absence of the pious atmosphere that generally characterized such genre scenes. Courbet's few defenders praised the accuracy of his representation and associated the painter's "realism" with the democratic and socialist ideals that he shared with them.[1] As T. J. Clark has shown, these contemporary readings interpreted Courbet's *Burial* in the context of the tense environment that followed the revolutionary year of 1848. Clark's own interpretation, based in part on the findings of recent social history, has refined and extended this view. For Clark the indeterminate social class of the participants at the *Burial* reflects the ambivalent social position of Courbet's family, somewhere between peasant and bourgeois. More generally, the painting reveals "the equivocal position of the bourgeoisie itself in 1850": the situation of Courbet— "building a bourgeois identity, . . . exchanging his smock for his dress-coat and spats"—was a familiar one in mid-century France.[2]

Clark's view of the *Burial* has been widely cited, and its powerful argument is difficult to resist. Recently, however, Michael Fried has criticized Clark for being too exclusively concerned with social context and insufficiently attentive to the painting itself.[3] From Fried's perspective the *Burial* exemplifies Courbet's attempt "to establish a particular relationship, antitheatrical in essence, between painting and beholder. . . . [F]acilitating the quasi-corporeal merger of beholder into painting . . . was a fundamental object, perhaps *the* fundamental object of Courbet's enterprise."[4] The sophisticated readings of Fried and Clark have a great deal to offer, and I do not wish to dispute the social and aesthetic meanings that they have found in the *Burial at Ornans*. For both of these critics, however, the fact that Courbet chose to paint a burial is of secondary importance. To them, the scene is primarily a vehicle through which the artist expressed his ambivalent and complex attitudes about social class (in the case of

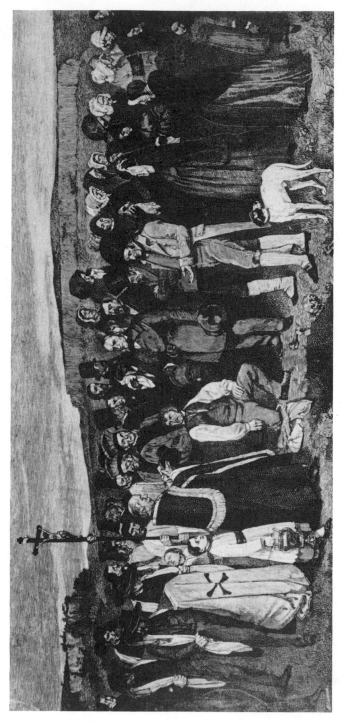

22. Gustave Courbet, *The Burial at Ornans*, Salon of 1851. Print.

Clark) and aesthetic experience (in the case of Fried). Even if we accept these interpretive emphases, it seems fair to ask why Courbet chose to express his vision by depicting a crowd of mourners gathering in a country cemetery around an open grave. Death and burial are not peripheral to this painting; they are what it is about, and if Courbet was able to generate meanings beyond the event depicted on his canvas these are nonetheless inescapably bound by and to the overt content.

For Clark the "emotional organization" of the *Burial* is set by Courbet's refusal to emphasize a sacramental moment. "In the *Burial* there is no single focus of attention, no climax toward which the forms and faces turn. Least of all is the picture organized around the sacrament of burial: hardly a single face, save perhaps the grave digger's, is turned toward the priest, and the line of heads at the right of the picture looks the other way entirely—away from the coffin and the crucifix."[5] Linda Nochlin, like Clark, has noted "The psychological and pictorial disassociation of the figures from each other in Courbet's *Burial*," which helps to demonstrate that "for him the transcendent meaning of funerals in general is completely unimportant . . . ."[6] The responses of Clark and Nochlin, like those of many critics of the time, however, are based on unfulfilled conventional expectations about the emotional and religious mood believed to be characteristic of a funeral. In rejecting these conventions Courbet was also playing off them, and the "emotional organization" of the *Burial* therefore builds on its denial of the consolation of sacramental transcendence. But this denial is accompanied by a continued reliance on Catholic ritual: the priest still officiates, and the processional crucifix still dominates the horizon, present to the viewer even if not a focal point for the mourners. Courbet's painting can bear interpretation as a commentary on social structure and aesthetic relationships, but it is more immediately and self-evidently a response to the problematic nature of death as it was experienced within French culture during the nineteenth century.

Pierre-Joseph Proudhon commented at length on the gap between expectation and image in Courbet's *Burial*, and his analysis can carry us further into the paradoxical nature of the painting, and of the status of death in France. Proudhon begins with an extended observation that could have been written by a pious Catholic, or by a spiritualist such as Victor Cousin:

> Of all the acts of life, the most serious, the one which lends itself least to irony is the one which ends it, death. If something must remain sacred, for the believer as well as for the unbeliever, it is the last moments, the

will, the solemn farewells, the funeral, the tomb. All peoples have felt the majesty of these scenes; all have surrounded them with religion. In all periods the same sentiment has inspired artists who, in this case, perhaps the only one, have been able both to follow the ideal of their age and remain faithful to the eternal truth of their mission. It seems that no artistic distortion of this tragic solemnity would be possible, where a family, surrounded by friends and neighbors, assisted by the clergy, is going to place the seal on the great separation, in returning to the earth the body of a husband, a father.[7]

It was exactly this kind of rhetoric, which we have met on several occasions throughout this book, that informed the development of the cult of the dead in France. Even the detail that identifies the object of the cult with a husband and father can be observed in the images and language that portrayed death and the dead. Proudhon, however, sets up this ideal only to emphasize what he believes was the subversive and sacrilegious intent of Courbet. The grotesque features and emotional indifference of the official party and the mourners in the *Burial* point up the hypocrisy of the ritual and stimulate an assault on the cult of the dead in which he enumerates each of its elements:

> We have lost the religion of the dead; we no longer understand this sublime poetry with which Christianity surrounded it; we have lost faith in prayers, and we mock the next life. The death of a man today, in the thoughts of everyone, is like that of a beast: *Unis est finis hominis et jumenti*; and despite the *Requiem*, despite the catafalque, despite the bells, despite the church and all its *décorum*, we treat the remains of one like those of the other. Why the funerals? Why the burials? What do these marble tombs, these crosses, these inscriptions, these crowns of *immortelles* mean? Wouldn't it be enough for you that a cart, ordered by the police, would take the body and lead it to . . . the garbage dump at Montfaucon?[8]

Proudhon's identification of his radical critique with "the thoughts of everyone" is clearly false, and in his use of "we" he projects a bitter personal skepticism onto a generalized public opinion. It is precisely the prayers, bells, funeral decorations, church services, burials, crosses, and marble tombs that distinguish the death of a person from that of an animal. Here as well Proudhon's concerns were close to those of the clergy, such as Bishop Charles Freppel and Monseigneur Jean-Joseph Gaume, who made similar observations about the loss of faith in the context of the debates about cemetery reform in the 1880s (see chapter 5). The details of the cult that Proudhon lists so carefully contradict his assertion that the French have lost the religion of the dead and suggest a conclusion more in keeping with the prior (and more orthodox) sentiments that he believed Courbet was undermining. Proudhon, along with many Catholics, had elevated expectations about the atmosphere that ought to characterize a religious funeral. His response to the *Burial*, like the painting itself, turns on a familiarity with the conventional rituals and their meanings, whose power is thereby acknowledged and implicitly confirmed.

Courbet's acquaintance with the rituals of death was derived in part from his experience of growing up in a devout family.[9] The *Burial* also suggests, however, the influence of a number of iconological traditions, which have been carefully traced by art historians. These images are significant not only because they provided sources for Courbet's painting but also because they helped shape the perceptions and emotional responses of viewers. Popular prints depicting the funerals of Marlborough and Napoleon, *souvenirs mortuaires* used by families to commemorate deaths, and representations of the stages of life all influenced Courbet's thematic and stylistic choices.[10] But souvenirs mortuaires generally included prayers for the repose of the soul of the dead, and the funerals of heroes were rituals conducted with dignity and respect. In prints showing the stages of life (*degrés des âges*) individuals or couples ascended and descended steps that mark ten-year intervals, while beneath them the artists rendered a vision of eternity. In the ancien régime this was generally a scene of Heaven and Hell, and such references to the Catholic afterlife were still available in the nineteenth century. In Courbet's time, however, the central images in ages of life tended to show scenes of peaceful repose, of tombs surrounded by a loving family.[11] Art historians may be correct in arguing that the structure of Courbet's *Burial* was influenced by images of the degrés des âges, because in both the figures are displayed around a central area that refers to human mortality. But viewers of the degrés des âges were assured that they could expect a long life and some form of survival beyond the grave as well, either in an afterworld or in the memory of their family. There is no such reassurance in the open grave of the *Burial*, a fact that might help explain its disturbing effect on viewers.

Paintings aimed at the middle-class audience that frequented the salons illustrate Proudhon's observation that other artists who dealt with death were frequently content to portray orthodox religious sentiments. A purposeful stroller through the Musée d'Orsay can confirm this insight by looking, for example, at Isidore Pils's painting of *The Death of a Sister of Chairty* (*La Mort d'une soeur de charité*), also shown at the Salon of 1851. Pils shows Sister Saint-Prosper, who died in 1846, on her deathbed, smiling slightly, at peace and resigned to her fate. She is apparently consoled by her religious faith (she is holding a rosary in her hands) and by her life of charity, represented by the poor who have entered the room to pray for her. Critics at the time praised both the execution of this painting and its "ability to convey uplifting sentiments to the poor."[12] Nicolas-André Monsiau's painting of the *Devotion of Monseigneur de Belzunce (Dévouement de Monseigneur de Belzunce)*, presented at the Salon of 1819, is an even clearer affirmation of the power of the Catholic rituals of death (illus. 23). This painting claims to describe a historical event, the bishop of Marseille administering the Last Sacraments to victims of the plague of 1720. Like Courbet, Monsiau shows a cross piercing the horizon on the left side of the painting and, like Courbet, he places a dog into the lower right foreground. The dying and those assisting them in Monsiau's painting, however, are linked in a moment of ritual fervor as they raise their eyes to the clergy and their arms in prayer, pleading for assistance and salvation. The dying woman being given communion looks at the bishop and beyond him at the cross. The dying woman on the left looks at the Franciscan assisting her, and the cross is in her line of vision as well. For Monsiau, the sacraments of the Church and the symbol of the cross are potent forces, filling people with hope in their last moments.[13]

Cemeteries as well as scenes of death were the occasion for pious reflections. As Linda Nochlin has pointed out, Augustin Roger's *A Village Burial (Un enterrement de village)* (Salon of 1822) exemplifies the genre's emphasis on mourners who are sad, attentive, and prayerful, in contrast with those of Courbet's painting.[14] In *The Grave Digger (Le Fossoyeur)*, a painting presented at the Salon of 1843, Eugène Poittevin posed a reflective grave digger next to an open grave, while on the opposite side his three children look on (illus. 24). The critic in *Le Magasin pittoresque* praised this painting for its edifying qualities and noted the reassurance provided by the parish cross that rises on the left side, just as in Monsiau's *Devotion* and Courbet's *Burial*.[15] We have seen that the Church continued to serve as a mediator between life and death in the experience of most people in the nineteenth century. Conventional paintings of death and burial allowed the clergy to appear as devoted, even heroic, confident in their sacramental powers and in the salvation that they implied. The laity may be saddened by death, but they are consoled by the presence of the priest and by the cross. Courbet gives us the priest, the cross, and the people; but despite Proudhon's comment that such scenes defied ironic representation, it is fair to say that the *Burial* is full of irony. Proudhon, and perhaps Courbet, share a view of what the nature of

23. Nicolas-André Monsiau, *The Devotion of Monseigneur de Belzunce, Bishop of Marseille, Salon of 1819* (The Louvre, Photo courtesy of Réunion des Musées Nationaux).

24. Eugène Poittevin, *The Grave Digger*, Salon of 1843. Print by Girardet.

this occasion should have been and, apparently, some indignation that it falls short of that ideal.

Conventional images reflected the cult of the dead as it was idealized by the clergy, politicians, and businessmen who were formally charged with its administration and whose attitudes and practices have been examined in the preceding chapters.[16] We have seen, however, that this ideal was challenged throughout the century. Elites engaged in conflicts for control of a ritual that was able to generate both money and meaning, and their battles could not fail to include and agitate the popular audience served by the cult. The city council of Ornans battled for thirty years over the creation of a new cemetery, and, in fact, Courbet's *Burial* may represent the first interment to have taken place at the new site.[17] As we saw in chapter 3, such disputes were common in France in the first half of the century, as people struggled to redefine their relationship with the dead and with the clergy and civil officials who mediated between the living and the dead. Parisians who viewed Courbet's *Burial* could reflect on recent controversies surrounding the funeral industry which, as we have seen in chapter 6, was under attack for price gouging and for failing in its responsibility to provide a dignified service during the cholera epidemic of 1849.[18] Also, throughout the first half of the century socialist theorists with whom Courbet was familiar had expressed public doubts about the claims of Catholic orthodoxy and the efficacy of clerical ritual. After his own death Courbet's family, all of whom were practicing Catholics, was torn by a conflict over the painter's request for a civil burial, and his father refused to attend the services after failing to nullify the will of his son.[19] A burial scene may have provided Courbet with the best possible occasion for portraying the tensions within a rural community at mid-century, but noting this point should alert us as well to the cultural significance of burial and to the social messages imbedded in it. As Fried argues, a serpentine funeral procession and an open grave may be particularly capable of drawing in the viewer, but these are not only formal devices; they are also substantive references to human mortality, a condition common to subjects and audience that was increasingly problematic in the nineteenth century. The ambivalent emotions of the mourners, which constitute what Clark calls the "affective atmosphere" of the painting, are less the result of some veiled conflict between bourgeois and peasant, or a clever play between art and audience, than they are the result of anxiety and doubts about the meaning of the rituals of death that were being contested and reshaped throughout the century.

Reconsidering some of the details in Courbet's painting may suggest additional reasons for regarding *Burial at Ornans* as a comment on the cult of the dead. In 1850 Max Buchon proposed that the *Burial* was a contemporary *Dance of Death*, for like its medieval antecedents it suggested the equality of all the "oppressors of the poor world" before death.[20] According to Buchon, Courbet achieved his results without abandoning a commitment to "absolute realism"; the skull that lies just to the right of the grave, however, cannot have been a "realistic" detail. The uncovering of bones was not uncommon in the overcrowded urban cemeteries that were the focus of reform efforts in the first half of the century, but because the cemetery of Ornans was new the skull must be considered an invention of Courbet, an heir to the *memento mori* common in baroque art.[21] This association with baroque themes is reinforced by the clearly defined black crossbones on the funeral pall that covers the casket, and Courbet may have inverted the colors of this decoration explicitly to call attention to it. The "vague oppression" that Buchon noted as a characteristic response to the *Burial* can be related to its unequivocal evocation of human mortality and decomposition, but without the standard compensations available in orthodox art.

The parish crucifix, which pierces the horizon and dominates the upper third of the *Burial*, provides a cue that viewers might look to in seeking relief from the evidence of mortality, and from the distracted and ambivalent emotions of the processional party. Hélène Toussaint goes so far as to argue that the crucifix calls to mind the hopes among some socialists following the revolution of 1848 that Christianity would provide the basis for national unity and social regeneration. Toussaint, however, seems to be extending the optimistic atmosphere of the spring of 1848 (before the massacre of June and the election of Louis Napoleon in December) into 1849 and 1850, by which time reconciliation had given way to repression. Crosses and crucifixes dominate the tops of many French paintings that have death as their theme, including Monsiau's *Devotion* and Poittevin's *Grave Digger*. Courbet's crucifix, however, cannot bear Toussaint's interpretation, nor is it a standard reference to the Christian hope for salvation implicit in Christ's sacrifice. There is no connection whatsoever between the mourners and the crucifix, a point that Courbet emphasized by having the choirboy beneath it look up, but only to meet the regard of one of the pallbearers. This disassociation, which contrasts sharply with the intimate relationship between Church and people depicted by Monsiau and in paintings by Jules Breton, is as telling as that which separates the mourners from one another, for Courbet allows the viewer no consolation from either the solidarity of family and friends or from religious symbol and belief.[22]

Comparing conventional images with Courbet's *Burial* yields one final point that helps us understand contemporary reactions to the painting. James Rubin has pointed out that Courbet chose to capture the scene just as the final participants were approaching the grave and before the ritual prayers led by the priest have begun.[23] As a consequence, Courbet has emphasized "our own experience of an uncomfortable moment in the proceedings, a moment during which ritual is suspended . . . during which the continuum of meaning so amply filled by the rhetoric of ceremony has temporarily given way to a vacuum."[24] The art historians are right to argue that Courbet's *Burial* conveys none of the transcendent meaning typically associated with Christian death and burial, but this "vacuum" could only be created by carefully recording the preritual moment. Once the priest has found his place in the book, once the crowd of mourners has settled down and collected itself, then the uneasy period of anticipation might give way to prayers murmured together, a sense of community, recollection, and even belief. Courbet denies his viewers the comfort of this moment and implicitly places a higher value on the preceding ambivalence of a nonritualized experience. Looking at the *Burial* the viewer knows that the proper ceremonies are about to take place, but Courbet suggests that they will be momentary and artificial rather than deeply, personally, and lastingly felt. He thus adheres to and in a perverse way expresses the nineteenth century's high standards of personal belief.

We have seen how intensely the French of the nineteenth century were committed to ritualizing death, through folk practices, Christianity, civil cemeteries, and commercial funerals. All these aspects of the cult of the dead were surrounded by debates and conflicts that were unresolved for most of the century. These were painful to the French, and many of the images about death that they admired understandably concentrated instead on the ritual moments that generated meaning and transcendence. Courbet's evocation of a nonritualized experience reminded some critics that their cult of the dead was a fragile construction vulnerable to conflict, avarice, and disbelief. Proudhon saw it that way and expressed satisfaction that Courbet had shown the collapse of the religion of the dead. But we should also recall his prior appeal that "if something must remain sacred, for the believer as well as for the unbeliever, it is the last moments, the will, the solemn farewells, the funeral, the tomb." This affirmation runs counter to Proudhon's criticism of the cult of the dead and may have been inspired by values that are echoed more than they are denied in Courbet's painting. Proudhon and Courbet were engaged in the religious and social controversies of nineteenth-century France and were pleased to observe what they felt was an erosion of belief in traditional Catholic ritual. They also shared with Catholics a sense that death should be surrounded by a sacred atmosphere and an anxiety that it was threatened by the profanity of the modern world. Courbet's *Burial at Ornans* and Proudhon's reaction to it thus reflect ambivalence and uneasiness about the cult of the dead—feelings that this book suggests were shared by many French men and women of their time. If my reading of Courbet is correct, his painting also reveals some of the deepest commitments that the French had, which they struggled to express in belief and ritual throughout the nineteenth century.

NOTES

INTRODUCTION

1. For the medical profession see Sydney H. Wanzer, M.D., et al, "The Physician's Responsibility Toward Hopelessly Ill Patients," *New England Journal of Medicine* 310 (12 April 1989): 955–959. For a review of the issues involved in defining death in the current medical environment: see Karen Grandstrand Gervais, *Redefining Death* (New Haven: Yale University Press, 1986); Samuel Gorovitz, *Drawing the Line: Life, Death, and Ethical Choices in an American Hospital* (New York: Oxford University Press, 1991). On death and religion see the essays in Ronald Numbers and Darrel Amundsen, eds., *Caring and Curing—Health and Medicine in Western Religious Traditions* (New York: Macmillan, 1986). In France research on death and dying has been encouraged by the Société de thanatologie, founded in 1966, whose journal began appearing in 1974. For a history and summary of the work of the Société see *Les Français et la mort—Enquêtes et témoignages* (Paris: Société de thanatologie, n.d.). Louis-Vincent Thomas, an anthropologist who has worked on death in Africa, has summarized contemporary discussion of death in France in *Rites de mort—Pour la paix des vivants* (Paris: Payot, 1985). For a survey of recent work on the sociology of death see Michael Kearl, *Endings—A Sociology of Death and Dying* (New York: Oxford University Press, 1989). For a cross-cultural analysis that surveys much recent research and places contemporary American funerals in a broad anthropological context, see Richard Huntington and Peter Metcalf, *Celebrations of Death—The Anthropology of Mortuary Ritual* (Cambridge: Cambridge University Press, 1979). Recent anthropological studies include: Ellen Badone, *The Appointed Hour: Death, Worldview and Social Change in Brittany* (Berkeley: University of California Press, 1989); Paul Barber, *Vampires, Burial, and Death—Folklore and Reality* (New Haven: Yale University Press, 1988); Gail Kligman, *The Wedding of the Dead: Ritual, Poetics, and Popular Culture in Transylvania* (Berkeley: University of California Press, 1988); Loring Danforth and A. Tsiaras, *The Death Ritual of Rural Greece* (Princeton: Princeton University Press, 1982); Lawrence Taylor, ed., "The Uses of Death in Europe," special issue of *Anthropological Quarterly* 62 (1989). David E. Stannard, *The Puritan Way of Death—A Study in Religion, Culture, and Social Change* (New York: Oxford University Press, 1977) is a provocative and widely cited historical essay.

2. Nancy Gibbs, "Love and Let Die," *Time* 135 (March 19, 1990), 62–70. The daily press has also paid significant attention to the problems of the terminally ill; see Susan Okie, "A Slow Death Amid Doctor-Family Conflict." *Washington Post*, June 16, 1991, A1–A14. Suicide and doctor-assisted death for the terminally ill are also subjects of current interest, to judge by the attention

paid to Derek Humphry and the Hemlock Society and to Dr. Jack Kevorkian. For a recent review of Humphry's suicide manual, *Final Exit*, and a number of other works on death and medicine, see David Rothman, "Rationing Life," *New York Review of Books* (39) 5 March 1992: 32–37.

3. Elisabeth Kübler-Ross, *On Death and Dying* (New York: Macmillan, 1970). Ernest Becker also contributed to the heightened public consciousness about death in a work that combined psychological theory and philosophical reflection, *The Denial of Death* (New York: Free Press, 1973).

4. For the fullest statement of Ariès's position see *The Hour of Our Death*, trans. Helen Weaver (New York: Knopf, 1981). But see also Philippe Ariès, *Western Attitudes toward Death: From the Middle Ages to the Present*, trans. Patricia Ranum (Baltimore: Johns Hopkins University Press, 1974); the French version of this essay, along with some briefer pieces, appeared in Ariès, *Essais sur l'histoire de la mort en Occident* (Paris: Seuil, 1975); see also Ariès, *Images of Man and Death*, trans. Janet Lloyd (Cambridge: Harvard University Press, 1985). The French historian Michel Vovelle has also been an important influence on the study of death, but much of his work has been more specialized than that of Ariès, and the absence of translations into English have limited his impact in the United States. For his major synthesis which is intended to rival Ariès's work, see Michel Vovelle, *La Mort et l'Occident de 1300 à nos jours* (Paris: Gallimard, 1983). For comparisons of the work of Ariès and Vovelle, see Robert Darnton, "The History of Mentalities," in *The Kiss of Lamourette* (New York: Norton, 1990), 268–290; Thomas Kselman, "Death in Historical Perspective," *Sociological Forum* 2 (1987): 591–597.

5. For reactions to Ariès's work, in addition to Darnton, "The History of Mentalities," and Kselman, "Death in Historical Perspective," see Lawrence Stone, "Death and Its History," *New York Review of Books*, 12 October 1978, 22–32; Paul Robinson, "Five Models for Dying," *Psychology Today* 15 (March 1981): 85–91; Joachim Whaley, "Introduction," in J. Whaley, ed., *Mirrors of Mortality—Studies in the Social History of Death* (New York: St. Martin's Press, 1981), 4–9; Badone, *The Appointed Hour*, 11–15; and Allan Mitchell, "Philippe Ariès and the French Way of Death," *French Historical Studies* 10 (1978): 684–695.

6. Philippe Ariès, *Centuries of Childhood*, trans. Robert Baldick (New York: Vintage, 1962).

7. Lawrence Taylor, "The Uses of Death in Europe," *Anthropological Quarterly* 62 (1989): 150. Some of what I attempt to accomplish addresses issues raised by Mitchell, "Philippe Ariès and the French Way of Death."

8. Stone, "Death and Its History;" Vovelle, *La Mort et l'Occident*, 8–9.

9. See, for example, the statement of Bishop Austin Vaughan, who said Governor Mario Cuomo of New York was in "serious risk of going to hell" because of his stand on abortion. *New York Times*, 4 Feb. 1990, "The Week in Review," 5.

10. François Lebrun, *Les Hommes et la mort en Anjou au 17e et 18e siècles* (Paris: Mouton, 1971). This region is also familiar to many through the influential study of Charles Tilly, *The Vendée* (New York: Wiley, 1967).

CHAPTER ONE

1. Achille Guillard, *Eléments de statistique humaine; ou démographie comparée, où sont exposés les principes de la science nouvelle, et confrontés d'après les documents les plus authentiques, l'état, les mouvements généraux et les progrès de la population dans les pays civilisés* (Paris: Guillaumin, 1855), xxvi. For brief descriptions of Guillard's career see Jacques et Michel Dupâquier, *Histoire de la démographie* (Paris: Perrin, 1985), 401–403, and Michel Dupâquier, "La Famille Bertillon et la naissance d'une nouvelle science sociale: la démographie," *Annales de démographie historique* (1983): 293–311.

2. Dupâquier, *Histoire de la démographie*, 174–188; J. Bourgeois-Pichat, "The General Development of the Population of France Since the Eighteenth Century," in *Population in History*, ed. D. V. Glass and D.E.C. Eversley (Chicago: Aldine Publishing Company, 1965), 480. John McManners, *Death and the Enlightenment* (New York: Oxford University Press, 1981), 94–111. In the seventeenth century a number of Englishmen, including the same Edmond Halley who gave his name to the comet, were already looking for regularities in the vital events of birth, marriage, and death. See Michael Cullen, *The Statistical Movement in Early Victorian Britain* (New York: Barnes and Noble, 1975); Dupâquier, *Histoire de la démographie*, 199–250. The context for developments in seventeenth-century England is thoroughly explored in Charles Webster, *The Great Instauration: Science, Medicine, and Reform, 1626–1660* (New York: Holmes and Meier, 1976), esp. 422–423, 444–446.

3. Pierre Chaunu, "Préface," of Dupâquier, *Histoire de la démographie*, 7–8.

4. On the distinction between the history of demographic facts and the history of demographic ideas see: B.P. Lécuyer, "Démographie, statistique et hygiène publique sous la monarchie censitaire," *Annales de démographie historique* (1977): 215–245; Marc Penin, "Les Questions de population au tournant du siècle à travers l'oeuvre de Charles Gide (1847–1932)," *Histoire, Economie, et Société* 5 (1986): 137–158. For the history of demographic knowledge in the nineteenth century see Jacques Dupâquier and René Le Mée, "La Connaissance des faits démographiques de 1789 à 1914," in *Histoire de la population française*, vol. 3, ed. Jacques Dupâquier (Paris: Presses Universitaires de France, 1988), 15–61. Dupâquier and Le Mée concentrate, however, on the institutional context rather than public opinion. Dupâquier, *Histoire de la démographie*, is a valuable survey of the history of demographic technique, but he does not deal with the findings of the demographers he studies.

5. Michael W. Flinn, *European Demographic System, 1500–1820* (Baltimore: Johns Hopkins University Press, 1981), 47.

6. Medical and demographic historians continue to debate the explanation for the decline in mortality rates. According to Maurice Garden, "the Dossier is not closed for the partisans of social-economic factors, of biological explanations, or, more precisely, of genetic evolution." "Avant-Propos," "Le déclin de la mortalité," *Annales de démographie historique* (1989). This issue includes a series of articles that review some of the competing explanations for the decline of mortality. See also Alain Bideau, Jacques Dupâquier, Jean-Noël

Biraben, Jacques Léonard, and Bernard-Pierre Lécuyer, "La mortalité," in *Histoire de la population française*, ed. Dupâquier, 3: 279–349. For an influential account that stresses the importance of improved nutrition and public hygiene see Thomas McKeown, *The Modern Rise of Population* (New York: Academic Press, 1976). For a valuable critique of McKeown see P. B. Medawar, "In Defense of Doctors," *New York Review of Books*, 15 May 1980, 6–12. A more moderate view distinguishes between the gradual decline in mortality of the nineteenth century and the rapid progress of the twentieth, with the latter resulting from advances in bacteriology and medical science that began in the 1870s with the work of Louis Pasteur and Robert Koch. For an overview of the advances in public health see Bernard-Pierre Lécuyer and Jean-Noël Biraben, "L'Hygiène publique et la révolution pastorienne," in *Histoire de la population française*, ed. Dupâquier, 3:321–343. Bruno Latour, *The Pasteurization of France*, trans. Alan Sheridan and John Law (Cambridge: Harvard University Press, 1988) provides an idiosyncratic account which stresses the importance of social context rather than individual achievement. Samuel Preston and Etienne van de Walle, "Urban French Mortality in the Nineteenth Century," *Population Studies* 32(1978): 291, confirm McKeown's argument for the nineteenth century but note that medical improvements became increasingly important starting in the 1890s. Similarly, Jacques Léonard, *La France médicale au XIXe siècle* (Paris: Gallimard, 1978) suggests that preventive medicine proposed by those in favor of public hygiene was significant but discounts the impact of medical science before the end of the century. See also William H, McNeill, *Plagues and Peoples* (Garden City, N.Y.: Anchor Books, 1976), 230, 236. Finally, Fernand Braudel summarized long-term demographic changes in *The Identity of France*, vol. 2, *People and Production* (New York: Harper Collins, 1990), 167–202. According to Braudel's periodization, French population has been on an upswing since 1450, based first of all on changes in disease patterns and diet, and since 1850 on improvements in medicine.

    7. McManners, *Death and the Enlightenment*, 92.

    8. Bourgeois-Pichat, "Population of France," 506. For recent surveys see Alain Bideau, Jacques Dupâquier, and Jean-Noël Biraben, "La Mortalité de 1800 à 1914," in *Histoire de la population*, ed. Dupâquier, 3:279–298; Jacques Vallin, "La Mortalité en Europe de 1720 à 1914: Tendances à long terme et changements de structure par sexe et par âge," *Annales de démographie historique* (1989): 31–54.

    9. Bourgeois-Pichat, "Population of France," 504–505; McManners, *Death and the Enlightenment*, 93. Etienne Van de Walle reports an increase in female life expectancy from 35.6 for 1801–1805 to 47.2 for 1896–1900 in *The Female Population of France in the Nineteenth Century* (Princeton: Princeton University Press, 1974), table 8.1, 191–195. For an overview see André Armengaud, "Un Siècle délaissé: Le XIXe Siècle (1815–1914)," *Annales de démographie historique* (1971): 299–310;

    10. André Armengaud, *La Population française au XIXe siècle*, 2d ed. (Paris: Presses Universitaires de France, 1976), 121.

    11. J.P. Graffenauer, *Topographie physique et médicale de la ville de Strasbourg* (Strasbourg: Levrault, 1816), 105. See also Claude Lachaise, *Topographie médi-*

cale de Paris (Paris, 1822). The eighteenth-century demographer Antoine De-
parcieux argued that cities had higher mortality rates than the countryside,
but others, including Messance, believed that urban areas encouraged population growth. McManners, *Death and the Enlightenment*, 102. For assessments
of the work of some early demographers see: Lécuyer, "Démographie,
statistique, et hygiène publique sous la monarchie censitaire"; Edmonde
Vedrenne-Villeneuve, "L'Inégalité sociale devant la mort dans la première
moitié du XIXe siècle," *Population* 16 (1961): 665–679.

Nineteenth-century demographers had much less to say about the countryside, which was assumed to be healthier and have lower mortality rates
than urban areas. They based their conclusions primarily on an examination
of urban and departmental statistics rather than on an analysis of specific
villages. Villermé's study of Haut-Rhin, for example, showed a life expectancy of 7.5 years at birth for the city of Mulhouse and 13.5 years for the
rest of the department but made no distinctions between any of the towns
and villages outside the major urban center. See L.R. Villermé, *Tableau de
l'état physique et moral des ouvriers employés dans les manufactures de coton,
de laine, et de soie*, 2 vols. (Paris: Renouard, 1840), 2: 251. For a similar reliance
on urban and departmental data see J.B.F. Demonferrand, *Essai sur les lois de
la population* (Paris, 1838), 287; Emile Levasseur, *Population française*, 3 vols.
(Paris: Rousseau, 1889–1891), 2: 155. Contemporary historians, working
from civil registers that provide evidence on particular communes, are more
sensitive to the variations between regions; some rural areas experienced
mortality rates that were above the national average. Compare, for example,
the life-expectancy table for Marlhes, a village in the department of the Loire,
in James Lehning, *The Peasants of Marlhes* (Chapel Hill: University of North
Carolina Press, 1980), 56–57, with the national figures in Bourgeois-Pichat,
"Population of France," 504–505. Similarly, the crude death rates from three
villages in Languedoc reported by Leslie Moch, *Paths to the City* (Beverly
Hills: Sage, 1983), 47, 57, 64, are higher than the figures in Bourgeois-Pichat,
506. Certainly historians today are more likely to stress the importance of
local conditions—the climate, the water supply, the economic circumstances
of the population—rather than to make blanket judgments about the health
of the country as opposed to the city. For some demographic studies of
villages in the nineteenth century see: Reymond Deniel and Louis Henry,
"La Population d'un village du Nord de la France," *Population* 20 (1965):
563–602; J. Houdaille, "La Population de Boulay (Moselle) avant 1850,"
Population 22 (1967): 1055–1084; Christian Poitou, "La Mortalité en Sologne
orléanaise de 1670 à 1870," *Annales de démographie historique* (1978): 235–
264. Jean-Claude Sangoï, *Démographie paysanne en Bas Quercy, 1751–1872*
(Paris: C.N.R.S., 1988); Jean-Claude Farcy, *Vivre et mourir en Eure-et-Loir au
XIXe siècle* (Chartres: C.D.D.P., 1979); Jacques Thomé, *Douceur angevine?
Naître, vivre, et mourir à Avrillé, 1532–1980* (Maulévrier: Hérault, 1986).
Those historians who aggregate their data into regions also stress the varia-
tions between rural areas; see Gregor Dallas, *The Imperfect Peasant Economy:
The Loire Country, 1800–1914* (New York: Cambridge University Press, 1982),
180–190.

12. William Coleman, *Death Is a Social Disease: Public Health and Political Economy in Early Industrial France* (Madison: University of Wisconsin Press, 1982), 162. Villermé's methods became a model for others interested in acquiring a precise knowledge of mortality. At Nantes A. Guépin and E. Bonamy acknowledged his influence and went on to note that when applied to Nantes, Villermé's techniques showed a situation that "surpassed our expectations; this research reveals frightening facts." See A. Guépin and E. Bonamy, *Nantes au XIXe siècle* (Nantes: Sebire, 1835), 454.

13. Louis Chevalier, *The Laboring Classes and Dangerous Classes* (Princeton: Princeton University Press, 1981), 50–53.

14. "Lois de la population et de la mortalité," *Le Magasin pittoresque* 15 (May 1847): 149–152.

15. L.R. Villermé, "De la mortalité dans les divers quartiers de Paris," *Annales d'hygiène publique et de médecine légale* 3 (1830): 334. Chevalier, *Laboring Classes*, 327, notes but quickly dismisses the optimism about long-term decline in mortality rates; Pierre Guillaume, *Du désespoir au salut: les Tuberculeux aux 19e et 20e siècles* (Paris: Aubier, 1986), 15, notes Villermé's conviction that mortality had declined but overinterprets this point when he asserts that only at the end of the nineteenth century was "the accent placed on the perverse role of the city that ruins the health of the worker." Guépin and Bonamy, *Nantes au XIXe siècle*, 492, point out the long-run decline in mortality for their city despite the unhealthy conditions that they describe.

16. Lambert A. J. Quetelet, *A Treatise on Man*, trans. Solomon Diamond (Edinburgh: William and Robert Chambers, 1842), 43–44.

17. Eugène Buret, *De la misère des classes laborieuses en Angleterre et en France*, 2 vols. (Paris: Paulin, 1840), 2: 124–125, cited in Coleman *Death is a Social Disease*, 278.

18. See the comments by the minister Forcade de la Roquette, *Journal Officiel*, 25 February 1869, 243.

19. "Mortalité," in *Grand Dictionnaire universel du XIXe siecle*, vol. 11 (Paris: Larousse, 1874), 592.

20. Gustave Lagneau, "Population de Paris; remarques démographiques sur l'habitat urbain," *Bulletin de l'Academie de Médecine* (1893): 740–760. For a current review of the patterns of urban mortality see Preston and van de Walle, "Urban French Mortality."

21. Alfred Legoyt, *La France et l'étranger: Études de statistique comparée*, 2 vols. (Paris: Berger-Levrault, 1870).

22. Legoyt, *La France et l'étranger*, 2: 287–309; Levasseur, *Population française* 2: 137–139, is much more sanguine in his analysis of accidental deaths, in part because they seem to have stabilized in the 1870s.

23. Lisa Lieberman, *Une Maladie Epidémique: Suicide and its Implications in Nineteenth-century France* (Ph.D. diss., Yale University, 1987), 203–204.

24. In the extensive bibliography of nineteenth-century sources in Lieberman, *Une Maladie Epidémique*, twice as many come from the period 1851–1914 as from 1800–1850; see 230–240; for publicity about suicide early in the century see Chevalier, *Laboring Classes and Dangerous Classes*, 280–284.

25. Legoyt, *La France et l'étranger*, 2: 561–574. For the theme of social dissolution and its relation to studies of suicide see Steven Lukes, *Emile Durkheim:*

His Life and Work (New York: Penguin, 1973), 194–199. Levasseur, *Population française* 2: 125–137, while he notes the social causes, also suggests that drunkenness, madness, and an inherited "germ" account for suicide. For an analysis of the contending explanations see Lieberman, *Une Maladie Epidémique.*

26. Emile Durkheim, *Revue philosophique* 26 (1888): 446–463. Steven Lukes calls attention to this article in *Emile Durkheim*, 194–195.

27. Emile Durkheim, *Suicide: A Study in Sociology*, trans. J. A. Spaulding and G. Simpson (New York: Free Press, 1951). For the reactions to *Suicide* see Lukes, *Emile Durkheim*, 199–225; Lieberman, *Une Maladie Epidémique*, 203–229.

28. Yves Charbit, *Du Malthusianisme au populationnisme—Les Économistes français et la population, 1840–1870* (Paris: Presses Universitaires de France, 1981), 26–27.

29. Mary Lynn McDougall, "Protecting Infants: The French Campaign for Maternity Leaves, 1890s–1913," *French Historical Studies* 13 (1983): 79–105, provides a useful summary of the public discussion concerning infant mortality. See also: Charbit, *De Malthusianisme au populationnisme*, 156–158; Joseph Spengler, *France Faces Depopulation*, 2d ed. (Durham, N.C.: Duke University Press, 1979), 225–231; George D. Sussman, *Selling Mother's Milk: The Wet-Nursing Business in France, 1715–1914* (Urbana: University of Illinois Press, 1982), 121–126.

30. Jacqueline Hecht, "L'Evaluation de la mortalité aux jeunes âges dans la littérature économique et démographique de l'ancien régime," in *La Mortalité des enfants dans le monde et dans l'histoire*, ed. M. Boulanger and D. Tabutin (Liège: Ordina, 1980), 29–79.

31. Quetelet, *A Treatise on Man*, 31.

32. Villermé, "De la mortalité dans les divers quartiers de Paris," 329–331; McManners, *Death and the Enlightenment*, 100–102; Chevalier, *Laboring Classes and Dangerous Classes*, 331.

33. Sussman, *Selling Mother's Milk*, 110–117.

34. Rachel Fuchs, *Abandoned Children: Foundlings and Child Welfare in Nineteenth-Century France* (Albany: State University of New York Press, 1984), 142–144.

35. Sussman, *Selling Mother's Milk*, 117, 181; Fuchs, *Abandoned Children*, 144; Berlanstein, *The Working People of Paris, 1871–1914* (Baltimore: Johns Hopkins University Press, 1984), 60–62; M. V. Beaver, "Population, Infant Mortality, and Milk," *Population* 25 (1970): 243–255; Ann F. La Berge, "Mothers and Infants, Nurses and Nursing: Alfred Donné and the Medicalization of Child Care in Nineteenth-Century France," *The Journal of the History of Medicine and Allied Sciences* 46 (1991): 20–43; Spengler, *France Faces Depopulation*, 234–235, 240–250; Poulain and Tabutin, "Mortalité aux jeunes âges," 147.

36. Ariès, *Images of Man and Death*, 246–252.

37. Archives nationales (hereafter AN), FI² 106²⁶. For Paris see Chevalier, *Laboring Classes and Dangerous Classes*, 332–336; for the government campaign in the provinces see Evelyn Ackerman, *Village on the Seine: Tradition and Change in Bonnières, 1815–1914* (Ithaca: Cornell University Press, 1978), 42–46; Alain Bideau, Guy Brunet, and Roger Desbos, "Variations locales de la mor-

talité des enfants: L'Éxemple de la Chatellenie de Saint-Trivier-en-Dombes (1730–1869)," *Annales de démographie historique* (1978): 7–29; for a general history of the disease and its control see Pierre Darmon, *La Longue Traque de la variole* (Paris: Perrin, 1986).

38. McNeill, *Plagues and Peoples*, 223.

39. Ibid., 231.

40. For a general study that focuses on the demographic patterns see Patrice Bourdelais and Jean-Yves Raulot, *Une Peur bleue—Histoire du choléra en France, 1832–1854* (Paris: Payot, 1987). For a review of the literature on cholera, including the work of Bourdelais and Raulot, see Richard Evans, "Blue Funk and Yellow Peril: Cholera and Society in Nineteenth-Century France," *European History Quarterly* 20 (1990): 111–125. For popular responses to the outbreak see François Delaporte, *Disease and Civilization: The Cholera in Paris, 1832*, trans. A. Goldhammer (Cambridge: MIT Press, 1986), 47–72; George David Sussman, *From Yellow Fever to Cholera: A Study of French Government Policy, Medical Professionalism and Popular Movements in the Epidemic Crises of the Restoration and July Monarchy* (Ph.D. diss. Yale University, 1971), 245–259; 278–309; Louis Chevalier, ed., *Le Choléra: La Première Épidémie du XIXe siécle* (La Roche-sur-Yon: Imprimerie Centrale de l'Ouest, 1958), 14–20, 93–95, 108; Ackerman, *Village on the Seine*, 46–50; Dallas, *Imperfect Peasant Economy*, 184–188; Pierre Guillaume, *La Population de Bordeaux au XIXe siècle* (Paris: Presses Universitaires de France, 1972), 178–196; for the response to the outbreak of 1854 see Jean-Yves Bousique, "L'Epidémie, l'objet de l'histoire: La Choléra dans le canton de Cabanes," *Annales du Midi* 97 (1985): 411–426. For a masterful account of cholera placed in its political and social context see Richard Evans, *Death in Hamburg: Society and Politics in the Cholera Years, 1830–1914* (New York: Penguin, 1990).

41. Delaporte, *Disease and Civilisation*, 33–45; Sussman, *From Yellow Fever to Cholera*, 310–329.

42. For attitudes toward doctors and hospitals see Jacques Léonard, *La Médecine entre les savoirs et les pouvoirs* (Paris: Aubier Montaigne, 1981), 106–107; Sussman, *From Yellow Fever to Cholera*, 275–276; Matthew Ramsey, *Professional and Popular Medicine in France, 1770–1830* (New York: Cambridge University Press, 1988), 122–124. For Sue see *The Mysteries of Paris*, 2 vols. (New York: International Book Company, n.d.), 2: 102–103. For similar suspicions in England see the brilliant study of Ruth Richardson, *Death, Dissection, and the Destitute* (New York: Penguin, 1989).

43. McNeill, *Plagues and Peoples*, 151. Later in this same work McNeill speculates that the absence of the plague helps explain the rise of deism during the Enlightenment: "A world in which lethal infectious disease seldom seized a person suddenly in the prime of life no longer stood so much in need of Divine Providence to explain such deaths (228)."

44. For the figures for Paris see Chevalier, *Laboring Classes*, 323–325; the table on 325 of Chevalier mistakenly gives the 1832 figures for 1833. For the 1832 epidemic in France, see Catherine Rollet and Agnès Souriac, "Epidémies et mentalités: Le Choléra de 1832 en Seine-et-Oise," *Annales—économies, sociétés, civilisations* 29 (1974): 935–965; Patrice Bourdelais and Jean-Yves

Raulot, "La Marche du choléra en France, 1832 et 1854," *Annales—économies, sociétés, civilisations*, 33 (1978): 125–142. For annual mortality rates see Mitchell, *European Historical Statistics*, 18–21.

45. Pierre Guillaume, *La Population de Bordeaux au XIXe siécle* (Paris: Colin, 1972), 149–157; Guillaume *Du Désespoir au salut*, 136–141, 147–149; Allan Mitchell, "Obsessive Questions and Faint Answers: The French Response to Tuberculosis in the Belle Epoque," *Bulletin of the History of Medicine* 62 (1988): 215–235; Levasseur, *Population française*, 2: 117–118.

46. Guillaume, *Du Désespoir au salut*, 108–114.

47. Cited in ibid., 123.

48. Ibid., 155–169.

49. Matthew Ramsay, *Professional and Popular Medicine in France, 1770–1830*; Léonard, *La France médicale au XIXe siècle* (Paris: Gallimard, 1978); Léonard, *La Médecine entre les savoirs et les pouvoirs*; Léonard, *La Vie quotidienne du médecin de province au XIXe siècle* (Paris: Hachette, 1977); Jan Goldstein, *Console and Classify: The French Psychiatric Profession in the Nineteenth Century* (New York: Cambridge University Press, 1987); Evelyn B. Ackerman, *Health Care in the Parisian Countryside, 1800–1914* (New Brunswick: Rutgers University Press, 1990); P. Calbo, "Médecins en Sarthe dans la seconde moitié du XIXe siècle," *Annales de Bretagne et du pays de l'ouest* 92 (1985): 209–224; Olivier Faure, "Lyons Doctors in the Nineteenth Century: An Exceptional Social Union," *Journal of Social History* 10 (1977): 508–523. For a valuable review of the recent literature see Olivier Faure, "The Social History of Health in France: A Survey of Recent Developments," *Social History of Medicine* 3 (1990): 437–451.

50. The number of hospitals increased in France by 43 percent between 1853 and 1911; during the same period the annual number of patients cared for in hospitals increased 73 percent. See Biraben and Léonard, "Les Maladies et la médecine," 315. John Weiss estimates that there were 1,500 hospitals operating in France in the 1870s, which treated over 400,000 patients a year. See his "Origins of the French Welfare State: Poor Relief in the Third Republic, 1871–1914," *French Historical Studies* 13 (1983): 51. For the importance of hospitals see: Olivier Faure, *Genèse de l'hôpital moderne—Les Hospices civils de Lyon de 1802 à 1845* (Lyon: Presses Universitaires de Lyon, 1982); S. Borsa and C.P. Michel, *La Vie quotidienne des hôpitaux en France au XIXe siècle* (Paris: Hachette, 1985). For the influence of the medical profession on public policy see Robert A. Nye, *Crime, Madness, and Politics in Modern France—The Medical Concept of National Decline* (Princeton: Princeton University Press, 1984); Goldstein, *Console and Classify*, 276–321.

51. For an example of antimedical propaganda from the end of the century see Toby Gelfand, "Medical Nemesis, Paris, 1894: Léon Daudet's *Les Morticoles*," *Bulletin of the History of Medicine* 60 (1986): 155–176. For the continuing fear of hospitals see Lucien Gaillard, "La Misère et l'assistance à Marseille sous la second Empire et les premières années de la IIIe République," *Provence Historique* 27 (1977): 341–363.

52. In 1810 35 per cent of the deaths recorded on the état civil held in the municipal archives of Angers took place in hospitals; in 1884 the figure had

declined to 21 percent. The declarations of death were frequently made by hospital personnel rather than family members, suggesting the isolation of the hospitalized.

53. For Villermé see Coleman, *Death Is a Social Disease*; William Sewell, Jr., *Work and Revolution in France* (Cambridge: Cambridge University Press, 1980), 223–234; and Lécuyer, "Démographie, statistique, et hygiène publique sous la monarchie censitaire." For the pioneering work of the Belgian statistician Quetelet, see Dupâquier, *Histoire de la démographie*, 393–398 and Theodore M. Porter, *The Rise of Statistical Thinking, 1820–1900* (Princeton: Princeton University Press, 1986), 47–49, 100–109.

54. Dupâquier and Le Mée, "La Connaissance des faits démographiques"; Hervé Le Bras, "La Statistique générale de la France," in *Les Lieux de mémoire*, vol. 2, pt. 2, *La Nation*, Pierre Nora, ed. (Paris: Gallimard, 1986), 317–353.

55. *Recherches statistiques sur la ville de Paris et sur le département de la Seine*, vol. 1 (Paris: Ballard, 1821); Chevalier, *Laboring Classes and Dangerous Classes*, 44. For the origins of statistical publications see also Coleman, *Death Is a Social Disease*, 141–148.

56. Le Bras, "La Statistique générale de la France," 317, 340–344.

57. René Le Mée, "La Statistique démographique officielle de 1815 à 1870 en France," *Annales de démographie historique* (1979): 252–279; Dupâquier, *Histoire de la démographie*, 268–269, 292–296; Le Meé and Dupâquier, "La Connaissance des faits démographiques," 34–35; Spengler, *France Faces Depopulation*, 13.

58. B.G.F. Bausset-Roquefort, *Etude sur le mouvement de la population depuis la commencement du XIXe siècle* (Marseille: Roux, 1862), 2.

59. J.B.F. Demonferrand, *Essai sur les lois de la population et de la mortalité en France* (1838), 291–292; Louis-René Villermé, "Des Sociétés de prévoyance ou de secours mutuels," *Annales d'hygiène publique* (1845): 94–111; Bausset-Roquefort, *Etude sur le mouvement de la population*, 62–74; Legoyt, *La France et l'étranger*, 1: 547–566. For the growth in life insurance, which evolved out of mutual-aid societies, see Biraben and Léonard, "Les Maladies et la médecine," 3: 317–318.

60. Dupâquier, *Histoire de la démographie*, 300–316.

61. Gerald Geison, ed., *Professions and the French State, 1700–1900* (Philadelphia: University of Pennsylvania Press, 1984).

62. *L'Univers*, 27 January 1852, 1.

63. Legoyt, *La France et l'étranger*, 1: vi; Dupâquier and Le Mée, "La Connaissance des faits démographiques," 40–41. According to Le Bras, the Statistique générale de la France lost popular support in the latter part of the nineteenth century, in part because of a new emphasis on biological variables that were not part of its official program; see Le Bras, "La Statistique générale de la France," 344–346.

64. Ackerknecht, "Hygiene in France, 1815–1848"; Porter, *The Rise of Statistical Thinking*, 42, 48; Coleman, *Death Is a Social Disease*, 250–256.

65. Cited in Docteur Duché, *Quelques Particularités sur le mouvement de la population dans le département de l'Yonne* (1864), 4. For Süssmilch see: Jacqueline Hecht, "Johann Peter Süssmilch: Point alpha ou omega de la science

démographique naive?" *Annales de démographie historique* (1979): 101–134; Dupâquier, *Histoire de la démographie*, 166–172; Porter, *The Rise of Statistical Thinking*, 21–23.

66. Guillard, *Eléments de statistique humaine*, 272.

67. Legoyt, *La France et l'étranger*, 1: 403. Villermé took a similar position; see Coleman, *Death Is a Social Disease*, 181.

68. Legoyt, 1: 573.

69. Charbit, *Du malthusianisme au populationnisme*, 157; for a general account of this shift in liberal ideology in favor of more active social reform see Sanford Elwitt, *The Third Republic Defended—Bourgeois Reform in France, 1880–1914* (Baton Rouge: Louisiana State University Press, 1986).

70. Guillard, *Eléments de statistique humaine*, v.

71. McManners, *Death and the Enlightenment*, 94, 105.

72. Levasseur, *Population française*, 3: 110.

73. McManners, *Death and the Enlightenment*, 100.

74. For a good example of the treatment of AIDS in the contemporary French press see "Sida: Le Ghetto?" *L'Express*, 12 June 1987, pp. 19–28. According to Guy Herzlich, the French are particularly inclined to discuss demographic matters in a political context; see "L'Obsession démographique," *Le Monde*, 17 May 1990, which examines the recent debate about natality.

CHAPTER TWO

1. According to William Sewell, "It is a well-known fact of demographic history that urbanization proceeded more slowly in France than in most other countries that industrialized in the nineteenth century." *Structure and Mobility: The Men and Women of Marseille, 1820–1870* (Cambridge: Cambridge University Press, 1985), 2–4. For overviews on urban growth see Maurice Garden, "Le Bilan global," in *Histoire de la population française*, ed. Dupâquier, 3:129–135; Georges Dupeaux, "La Croissance urbaine en France au XIXe siècle," *Revue d'histoire économique et sociale* 52 (1974): 73–89; Eugen Weber, *Peasants into Frenchmen: The Modernization of Rural France* (Stanford: Stanford University Press, 1976), 8. For the relationship between country and city see Leslie Moch, *Paths to the City: Regional Migration in Nineteenth-Century France* (Beverly Hills: Sage Publications, 1983) and Sewell, *Structure and Mobility*, 159–212.

2. Eugène Polain, *Il était une fois. . . . Contes populaires entendus en français à Liège et publiés avec notes et index* (Paris: Droz, 1942), 25. But Polain also heard tales from his bourgeois grandfather, who learned them from Perrault. Perrault himself probably learned many of his tales from his son's nurse; see Robert Darnton, *The Great Cat Massacre* (New York: Basic Books, 1984), 11. For the development of the discipline of folklore see Paul Delarue, *Le Conte populaire français*, vol. 1, nouvelle ed. (Paris: Maisonneuve et Larose, 1976), 30–31; Michael Marrus, "Folklore as an Ethnographic Source: A 'Mise au Point,' " in Jacques Beauroy, Marc Bertrand, Edward Gargan, eds., *The Wolf and the Lamb—Popular Culture in France from the Old Regime to the Twentieth Century*

314 NOTES TO PP. 37–39

(Saratoga, Cal.: Anma Libri, 1977), 109–125; Richard Dorson, foreword to Geneviève Massignon, *Folktales of France* (Chicago: University of Chicago Press, 1968). In reviewing the different versions of the tale "Godfather Death," Emmanuel Le Roy Ladurie establishes the importance of the late nineteenth century for ethnographic research. *Love, Death and Money in the Pays d'Oc* (New York: Penguin, 1984), 164, 182–183, 430–431. Charles Rearick traces the growing interest of historians such as Michelet and Thierry in folklore early in the nineteenth century in *Beyond the Enlightenment: Historians and Folklore in Nineteenth-Century France* (Bloomington: Indiana University Press, 1974). But the intellectuals described by Rearick did very little ethnographic research, which did not flourish until the end of the century.

3. Françoise Cachin, "Le Paysage du peintre," in *Les Lieux de mémoire*, ed. Pierre Nora, vol. 2, *La Nation*, pt. 1 (Paris: Gallimard, 1986), 435. See also Raymond Grew, "Picturing the People: Images of the Lower Orders in Nineteenth-Century French Art," *Journal of Interdisciplinary History* 17 (1986): 206–207. Writing in 1851, George Sand regretted the disappearance of rural traditions: "A year or two more, perhaps, and the railways will pass their levels over our deep valleys, sweeping away, with the swiftness of lightning, our ancient traditions and our marvelous legends." *The Haunted Pool* (San Lorenzo, Cal.: Shameless Hussy Press, 1976), appendix.

4. Anatole Le Braz, *La Légende de la mort chez les bretons armoricains*, 5th ed., 2 vols. (Paris: Champion, 1928). The 1928 edition was reprinted in 1982 by Lafitte, of Marseille, which published a single-volume abridgement the same year.

5. For the definition of a *veillée* see Badone, *The Appointed Hour*, 9. For the influence of Le Braz's literary tastes on his presentation of the tales see Georges Dottin, "Préface," *Légende de la mort*, 1: 12, and François Postic, "Des antiquaires aux folkloristes: Découverte et promotion des littératures orales," in *Histoire littéraire et culturelle de la Bretagne*, 2 vols., ed. Jean Balcou and Yves Le Gallo (Paris: Champion, 1987), 2:355–365. Ruth Richardson deals with the issue of bias in ethnographic materials in *Death, Dissection, and the Destitute*, 12–13.

6. Jean Delumeau, *Le Catholicisme entre Luther et Voltaire* (Paris: Presses Universitaires de France, 1971); this work has now been translated as *Catholicism between Luther and Voltaire: A New View of the Counter-Reformation* (Philadelphia: Westminster Press, 1977). See also Delumeau, *La Peur en Occident (XIVe-XVIIIe siècles)* (Paris: Fayard, 1978) and Delumeau *Le Péché et la peur—La Culpabilisation en Occident (XIIIe-XVIIIe siècles)* (Paris: Fayard, 1983), translated as *Sin and Fear: The Emergence of a Western Guilt Culture* (New York: St. Martin's Press, 1990). For a similar approach to popular culture see Robert Muchembled, *Culture populaire et culture des élites dans la France moderne (XVe-XVIIIe siècles)* (Paris: Flammarion, 1978). For a critical review of the literature on popular culture see Stuart Clark, "French Historians and Early Modern Popular Culture," *Past and Present* no. 100 (August 1983): 62–99.

7. Peter Burke, *Popular Culture in Early Modern Europe* (New York: Harper and Row, 1978). Burke has also reviewed a number of recent works on popular culture; see his "From Pioneers to Settlers: Recent Studies of the History of Popular Culture," *Comparative Studies in Society and History* 25 (1983): 181–

187. For a critical review of the category of popular religion as applied to the Middle Ages see John Van Engen, "The Christian Middle Ages as an Historiographical Problem," *American Historical Review* 91 (1986): 519–552.

8. Ellen Badone, personal communication, March 2, 1990. Badone spells out her position on the interrelations between popular and official religion in the introduction to the anthology that she edited, *Religious Orthodoxy and Popular Faith in European Society* (Princeton: Princeton University Press, 1990), 3–23.

9. Le Braz, *Légende de la mort*, lxxv–lxxvii.

10. Ibid., lxxxi.

11. Ibid., xliii–l. Jean Markale, *Contes de la mort* (Etrépilly: Presses du village, 1986), 9–11. Markale's introduction to this collection repeats many of the ideas that guided ethnographic research in the nineteenth century. Markale has a reputation as a popularizer rather than as a scholarly ethnographer, but in this collection of tales he clearly identifies the sources of his texts, which were originally collected by reputable ethnographers, including Le Braz.

12. Gilbert Durand, "Préface," in Paul Sébillot, *Le Ciel, la nuit, et les esprits de l'air* (Paris: Imago, 1982), 10–11. This work first appeared as part of Sébillot's *Le Folklore de France*, 4 vols. (Paris: Guimolto, 1904–1906). The new edition by Imago reflects the continuing interest in folklore in contemporary France as a way of rediscovering its rural past; see review of Sébillot by Jacques Lacarrière, *L'Express*, 24 August 1984, 50–52. On the relationship of folklore studies to modernization see also Catherine Bertho, "L'Invention de la Bretagne: Genèse soicale d'un stéréotype," *Actes de la recherche en science sociale* 35: 45–62. French interest in folklore developed later than in Germany. For a discussion of how aesthetic and political ideas shaped the renewal of interest in central European folklore see Burke, *Popular Culture in Early Modern Europe*, 3–22.

13. Henry Cormeau, *Terroirs mauges. Miettes d'une vie provinciale*, 2 vols. (Paris: Georges Crès, 1912), 2: 332. Jacques Léonard, *La France médicale au XIXe siècle* (Paris: Gallimard, 1978), 20; Weber, *Peasants into Frenchmen*, 153–154.

14. Aimé de Soland, *Proverbes et dictons rimés de l'Anjou* (Angers: Lainé, 1858), 124. According to another version, from the early twentieth century, "Mort désirée, longue durée." A.J. Verrier and Onillon, *Glossaire etymologique et historique des patois et des parlers de l'Anjou* (Angers: Germain et Grassin, 1908), 510.

15. Soland, *Proverbes de l'Anjou*, 163.

16. Verrier and Onillon, *Glossaire etymologique*, 510.

17. Ibid., 3.

18. Ibid., 135.

19. Arnold Van Gennep, *Manuel de folklore français contemporain*, (Paris: Picard, 1943), 1:660–663; Sébillot, *Le Ciel, la nuit, et les esprits de l'air*, 81, 165; Jean-Pierre Pinies, *Figures de la sorcellerie languedocienne* (Paris: CNRS, 1983), 207–209; Judith Devlin, *The Superstitious Mind: French Peasants and the Supernatural in the Nineteenth Century* (New Haven: Yale University Press, 1987), 94, 96.

20. Paul Sébillot, *Le Ciel, la nuit, et les esprits de l'air*, 68, 164–165; Camille Fraysse, *Le Folk-lore du baugeois* (Baugé: Dangin, 1906), 87–88; Markale, *Contes de la mort*, 48–50; for an extensive list of omens from Brittany see Le Braz, *La Légende de la mort*, 1:1–14. In some cases omens of death such as these were related to beliefs about the presence of the dead or of a personified figure of Death. The dog howled, for example, because he could see the figure of Death approaching.

21. Martine Segalen, "Le Mariage," in *Histoire de la population française*, ed. Dupâquier, 3:428; Segalen, *Love and Power in the Peasant Family* (Chicago: University of Chicago Press, 1983), 28–30.

22. Badone, *The Appointed Hour*, 309.

23. Ibid., 311, 315.

24. Delarue, *Le Conte populaire français*, 1: 147–149. Folklorists and anthropologists generally distinguish between legends, which are set in historical time in a world similar to that of the teller and in which the characters are predominantly human, and folktales, which are set in a temporal and spatial context that is removed from normal time and space. I employ both of these concepts but will also use the generic term "narrative" on occasion. For these categories see William Bascom, "The Forms of Folklore: Prose Narratives," in *Sacred Narrative—Readings in the Theory of Myth*, ed. Alan Dundes (Berkeley: University of California Press, 1984), 5–13.

25. Bruno Bettelheim, *The Uses of Enchantment—The Meaning and Importance of Fairy Tales* (New York: Vintage, 1977); Eugen Weber, "The Reality of Folktales," *Journal of the History of Ideas* 42 (1981): 93–113; Robert Darnton, "Peasants Tell Tales: The Meaning of Mother Goose," in *The Great Cat Massacre*, 9–72. Weber's argument that folktales reflect the concrete circumstances of peasant life is also stated in *Peasants into Frenchmen*, 424–427. Judith Devlin takes a similar position in *The Superstitious Mind*, 189–190. A more extreme statement of this position derived from a Marxist perspective can be found in Jack Zipes, *Breaking the Magic Spell—Radical Theories of Folk and Fairy Tales* (Austin: University of Texas Press, 1979). Le Roy Ladurie explores the complex relationship between folktales, literature, and social reality in *Love, Death and Money in the Pays d'Oc*.

26. The story of Bluebeard was known through a popular print distributed by Pellerin of Epinal as well as through oral transmission; a copy of this broadsheet is preserved in the Cabinet des estampes of the Bibliothèque nationale, Li 59, T. I, microfilm B7. For several versions of the tale see Delarue, *Conte populaire*, 1:189–198.

27. Le Braz, *Légende de la mort*, 1: 111–118, 132–136; Sébillot, *Le Ciel, la nuit, et les esprits de l'air*, 173–178; Badone, *The Appointed Hour*, 160–162. For the importance of the Ankou in the early twentieth century see Pierre-Jakez Hélias, *The Horse of Pride—Life in a Breton Village* (New Haven: Yale University Press, 1978), 100–103.

28. Le Braz, *Légende de la mort*, 1: 161–163. For an eighteenth-century edition of the *danse macabre* see Robert Favre, ed., *La Fin dernière* (Paris: Montalba, 1984), 71–165.

29. Le Roy Ladurie, *Love, Death and Money*, 536 n. 61. See also André Varagnac, *Civilisation traditionnelle et genres de vie* (Paris: Albin Michel, 1948),

213. Robert Darnton, on the other hand, tends to discount evidence from Brittany, whose emphasis on magic and the supernatural does not accord with his general view of French folk narratives. See *The Great Cat Massacre*, 50.

30. Delarue, *Conte populaire*, 1: 367–372. Le Roy Ladurie, *Love, Death and Money*, provides an extended structural analysis of a number of versions of Godfather Death. Le Roy Ladurie's purpose is to link the folktale with the eighteenth-century Occitan novel, *Jean-l'ont-pris*, written by Abbé Jean-Baptiste Castor Fabre. See also Polain, *Il était une fois*, 101–103.

31. Markale, *Contes de la mort*, 278–283. On the theme of egalitarianism in folk narratives see also Devlin, *The Superstitious Mind*, 24–32.

32. Le Roy Ladurie, *Love, Death and Money*, 161–164; Delarue, *Conte populaire*, 1:371.

33. Markale, *Contes de la mort*, 289–290.

34. Delarue, *Conte populaire* 1: 346–349. For Darnton's interpretation of this tale see his "Peasants Tell Tales," 60.

35. Markale, *Contes de la mort*, 291–293.

36. Delarue, *Conte populaire*, 2: 157–168. See also "L'Homme qui ne voulait pas mourir," in Markale, *Contes de la mort*, 305–309. For similar tales collected in Flanders and Corsica see ibid., 299–304, 309–313.

37. Edmund Leach, *Claude Lévi-Strauss* (New York: Penguin, 1976), 62.

38. Badone, *The Appointed Hour*, 77–78, describes how this distinction between urban and rural funerals still functions in contemporary Brittany.

39. Janine Brouard, *La Naissance, le mariage, la mort en Anjou dans la première moitié du XXe siècle*, Cahiers de l'I.P.S.A., no. 8 (Angers: Université catholique de l'ouest, 1984). I am grateful to Mme. Brouard for giving me access to the full texts of the interviews on which this publication is based. In Brittany change has come even slower; in one of the villages studied by Badone, the percentage of those who died in a hospital did not exceed 15 percent until 1971. See Badone, *The Appointed Hour*, 45.

40. Van Gennep, *Manuel de folklore français*, 1:662.

41. Ibid., 664–666.

42. Arnold Van Gennep, *The Rites of Passage* (Chicago: University of Chicago Press, 1960), 146–147. Louis-Vincent Thomas, *Rites de mort* (Paris: Fayard, 1985), 111–128. Thomas, although he draws heavily from Van Gennep, emphasizes the psychological function of traditional rites and contrasts their efficacy with the deritualization he believes to be characteristic of the modern world. For the influence of Van Gennep on contemporary anthropological work on death see Huntingon and Metcalf, *Celebrations of Death*, 8–16. Badone, *The Appointed Hour*, 51–102, provides an excellent account of death rituals in contemporary rural Brittany.

43. *Death, Dissection, and the Destitute*, 28.

44. Van Gennep, *Manuel de folklore français*, 1: 671–675. See also Hélias, *Horse of Pride*, 107–108; Emile Guillaumin, *The Life of a Simple Man* (Hanover, N.H.: University Press of New England, 1983), 54–55; Judith Devlin, *The Superstitious Mind*, 50; Badone, *The Appointed Hour*, 61–62.

45. Van Gennep, *Manuel de folklore français*, 1: 690–698 provides details on the regional variations of the *glas*.

46. Brouard, *La Naissance, le mariage, la mort en Anjou*, 126; the comments about the use of the shroud are found in the full texts of the interviews. For a discussion of superstitions surrounding the use of the shroud and its replacement by clothes see Van Gennep, *Manuel de folklore français*, 1: 710–715. For the importance of women in caring for the dead see: Marie-France Gueusqin, "Gardiennes et portefaix—De la prééminence de la femme dans le travail funéraire d'une commune rurale de la Nièvre," *Ethnologie française* 13 (1983): 129–138; Jean-Louis Maigrot, "Les Gestes des funérailles en Haute-Marne," *Ethnologie française* 6 (1976): 381–386; Badone, *The Appointed Hour*, 58–61. On the bathing habits of the French see Eugen Weber, *France—Fin de Siècle* (Cambridge: Harvard University Press, 1986), 58–60.

47. Van Gennep, *Manuel de folklore français*, 1: 704. See also Hélias, *Horse of Pride*, 110–111; Maigrot, "Les Gestes des funérailles," 384; Badone, *The Appointed Hour*, 63–68.

48. Hélias, *Horse of Pride*, 112. According to Badone, *The Appointed Hour*, 69–70, the last of the *diseurs de grâces* died in the early 1970s.

49. Van Gennep, *Manuel de folklore français*, 1: 708–710. For the final viewing in England during this period see Richardon, *Death, Dissection, and the Destitute*, 24–25.

50. Van Gennep, *Manuel de folklore français*, 1: 718–725; Weber, *Peasants into Frenchmen*, 373; Devlin, *The Superstitious Mind*, 90.

51. James F. Romano, *Death, Burial, and Afterlife in Ancient Egypt* (Pittsburgh: Carnegie Museum of Natural History, 1990).

52. Martine Segalen, *Les Confrèries dans la France contemporaine* (Paris: Flammarion, 1975), 30–35, 51–67, 72–76; Michel Bée, "La Révolte des confrèries de charité de l'Eure en 1842–1843," *Annales de Normandie* 24 (1972): 89–115. In Brittany, according to Badone, *The Appointed Hour*, 79, pallbearers were chosen of the same age and sex of the dead, a custom that is now dying out.

53. Van Gennep, *Manuel de folklore français*, 1: 726–750. This and related issues about the costs of funerals will be discussed in chapters 6 and 7.

54. Ibid., 751–753. See also Badone, *The Appointed Hour*, 75–84.

55. Van Gennep, *Manuel de folklore français*, 1: 759–761. See the epilogue for a more extended discussion of Courbet's painting.

56. Cormeau, *Terroirs mauges*, 282.

57. Badone, *The Appointed Hour*.

58. Ibid., 2; Philippe Ariès, *The Hour of Our Death* (New York: Knopf, 1981), 9–10.

59. Guy de Maupassant, *Contes de jour et de la nuit* (Paris: Garnier/Flammarion, 1977), 101–111.

60. Guillaumin, *The Life of a Simple Man*, 53–56.

61. Cormeau, *Terroirs mauges*, 18. In most versions of this tale the hero has a number of other adventures and claims that he will not marry until he has been frightened. After Jean-sans-peur saves a princess from the devil a grateful king hides a pigeon in a pie, which frightens Jean and allows him to marry the girl. See Delarue, *Conte populaire*, 1: 293–305.

62. Delumeau, *La Peur en Occident*, 110.

63. Devlin, *Superstitious Mind*, 90–91.

64. Carlo Ginzburg, *Night Battles—Witchcraft and Agrarian Cults in the Six-teenth and Seventeenth Centuries* (New York: Penguin, 1985), 47–49.

65. Sébillot, *Le Ciel, la nuit, et les esprits de l'air*, 189–190.

66. For the identification of the horde with the condemned see Fraysse, *Le Folk-lore de Baugeois*, 48–49. Pinies, *Figures de la sorcellerie*, 241–254.

67. Pinies, *Figures de la sorcellerie*, 241–254.

68. Agricol Perdiguier, *Mémoires d'un compagnon* (Paris: Maspero, 1977), 64; Badone, *The Appointed Hour*, 287.

69. René Laurentin, *Lourdes—Dossier des documents authentiques* (Paris: Le-thielleux, 1957) 1:143–145, 169. For a useful summary of the apparitions at Lourdes see Sandra L. Zimdars-Swartz, *Encountering Mary—From La Salette to Medjugorje* (Princeton: Princeton University Press, 1991), 43–57.

70. Writing about English folk practices in the early nineteenth century, Ruth Richardson has suggested that "the significance of the human corpse in popular death culture . . . seems to have been coloured by a prevailing belief in the existence of a strong tie between body and personality/soul for an un-defined period of time after death. . . . The result was an uncertain balance between solicitude toward the corpse, and fear of it." *Death, Dissection, and the Destitute*, 7.

71. Delarue, *Conte populaire* , 2: 157–162.

72. Delarue, *Conte populaire* , 1: 388–392; see also Markale, *Contes de la mort*, 153–156.

73. Markale, *Contes de la mort*, 232–239. For similar tales told in Brittany see ibid., 230–231, 240–242.

74. For other popular tales concerning Paradise and Hell see Delarue, *Conte populaire*, 4:170–181.

75. Delarue, *Conte populaire*, 1:161–171. See also ibid., 4: 254–256.

76. Markale, *Contes de la mort*, 179–181.

77. Markale, *Contes de la mort*, 126–127. In a similar tale from Brittany a priest who refused to carry the Last Sacraments to a dying person on Christmas Eve cannot be saved until he finds someone alive willing to re-ceive Communion from him. Le Braz, *Légende de la mort*, 2: 64–67. See also Markale, *Contes de la mort*, 228–229. Alphonse Daudet, "Les Trois Messes basses," in *Lettres de mon moulin* (Paris: Livre de Poche, 1982), 142–153.

78. Sébillot, *Le Ciel, la nuit, et les esprits de l'air*, 169; Le Braz, *Légende de la mort*, 2: 28–29.

79. Varagnac, *Civilisation traditionnelle et genres de vie*, 212.

CHAPTER THREE

1. See, for example, the holy card of the crucifixion published in *L'Image de piété en France, 1814–1914* (Paris: Musée Galerie de la Seita, 1984), 153. Nu-merous examples of such images can be found in Cabinet des estampes, Bi-bliothèque nationale, Rc mat 6B, which includes almost two hundred sheets of pious images on the theme of death; for a good example of a late-nineteenth-

century crucifixion image available on the microfilm collection of the Cabinet des estampes see Rc mat 5b, R 2896.

2. Michael Phayer, "Politics and Popular Religion: The Cult of the Cross in France, 1815–1840," *Journal of Social History* 11 (1978): 346–365.

3. AN BB 30 198 (3). Letter from Royal Prosecutor of Baugé to Minister of Justice, 3 February 1824.

4. Jacques Le Goff, *The Birth of Purgatory* (Chicago: University of Chicago Press, 1986), 1–2.

5. Le Goff, *The Birth of Purgatory*; Michel and Gaby Vovelle, *Vision de la mort et l'au-delà en Provence d'après les autels des âmes du Purgatoire* (Paris: Colin, 1970); D.P. Walker, *The Decline of Hell—Seventeenth-Century Discussions of Eternal Torment* (Chicago: University of Chicago Press, 1964); Colleen McDannell and Bernhard Lang, *Heaven—A History* (New Haven: Yale University Press, 1988). See also: Piero Camporesi, *The Fear of Hell—Images of Damnation and Salvation in Early Modern Europe* (University Park: Pennsylvania State University Press, 1991); Geoffrey Rowell, *Hell and the Victorians—A Study of the Nineteenth-Century Theological Controversies Concerning Eternal Punishment and the Future Life* (Oxford: Clarendon Press, 1974); Michael Wheeler, *Death and the Future Life in Victorian Literature and Theology* (Cambridge: Cambridge University Press, 1990). For an interesting work comparing near-death experiences, including glimpses of the afterworld, in medieval and modern times, see Carol Zaleski, *Otherworld Journeys* (New York: Oxford University Press, 1985). Zaleski, however, passes very quickly over the nineteenth century. For a contemporary theological perspective see Hans Küng, *Eternal Life? Life After Death as Medical, Philosophical, and Theological Problem* (Garden City, N.Y.: Doubleday, 1984). Popular interest in the afterlife can be gauged by the enormous popularity of Raymond Moody's work on near-death experiences, *Life after Life* (Atlanta: Mockingbird Press, 1975), which has sold over seven million copies since its appearance in 1975. See also Verlyn Klinkenborg, "At the Edge of Eternity: Learning from Encounters with Death," *Life* 15 (March 1992): 64–73.

6. John McManners, *Death and the Enlightenment* (Oxford: Clarendon Press, 1981), 161.

7. Michel Vovelle, *La Mort et l'Occident de 1300 à nos jours* (Paris: Gallimard, 1983), 532.

8. Jean Guerber, *Le Ralliement du clergé français à la morale liguorienne* (Rome: Università Gregoriana, 1973); Gérard Cholvy and Yves-Marie Hilaire, *Histoire religieuse de la France contemporaine, 1800–1880* (Paris: Privat, 1985), 154–159; Philippe Boutry, *Prêtres et paroisses au pays du Curé d'Ars* (Paris: Cerf, 1986), 408–422; Ralph Gibson, *The Social History of French Catholicism, 1789–1914* (New York: Routledge and Kegan Paul, 1989), 260–265.

9. Harry S. Stout, *The New England Soul—Preaching and Religious Culture in Colonial New England* (New York: Oxford University Press, 1986), 3.

10. Maurice Agulhon, *La République au village* (Paris: Seuil, 1970); Barnett Singer, *Village Notables in Nineteenth-Century France* (Albany: SUNY Press, 1983); Martyn Lyons, *Le Triomphe du livre—Une Histoire sociologique de la lecture dans la France du XIXe siècle* (Paris: Promodis, 1987).

11. Boutry, *Prêtres et paroisses*, 598–599.

12. My findings here parallel much of what Ralph Gibson has to say about manuscript sermons he found in Périgord from the same period. See his "De la prédication de la peur à la vision d'un dieu d'amour—La prédication en Périgord aux XVIIe-XIXe siècles," in *Le Jugement, le ciel, et l'enfer dans l'histoire du christianisme*, Actes de la Douzième rencontre d'Histoire Religieuse tenue à Fontevraud les 14 et 15 octobre 1988 (Angers: Presses de l'Université d'Angers, 1989), 153–167; and "Hellfire and Damnation in Nineteenth-Century France," *Catholic Historical Review* 74 (1988): 388–389. For general descriptions of Catholic piety during this period see Claude Langlois, "Permanence, renouveau et affrontements (1830–1880)," in *Histoire des catholiques en France du XVe siècle à nos jours*, ed. François Lebrun (Paris: Privat, 1980), 314–318; Cholvy and Hilaire, *Histoire religieuse, 1800–1880*, 58–66. According to Jean Delumeau and Piero Camporesi, fear is the principal motif of Counter-Reformation Catholicism. See Jean Delumeau, *Le Péché et la peur—La Culpabilisation en Occident, XIIIe—XVIIIe siècles* (Paris: Fayard, 1983); Camporesi, *The Fear of Hell*.

13. All these sermons are now stored at the Archives d'Evéché of Angers. For Bourg see Archives d'Evéché d'Angers (hereafter AEA), P12, for St. Germain des Près, AEA, P63, and St. Michel, AEA, P62. The authorship of these sermons cannot be determined with certainty. The curés in office at the time when they were preached seem to be the most likely candidates, though this assumes that the sermons found in the rectories were preached there and not brought in later. In the case of St. Germain, there seems little doubt that Laroche was the author. The sermon "Sur la mort du juste" found in that town includes a reference to the patron of the parish, St. Germain, and lists delivery dates of 1823, 1826, 1828, and 1831, years in which Laroche was curé. Père Pouplard, the archivist of the diocese of Angers, was especially helpful in my consultation of these documents.

14. François Lebrun, *Paroisses et communes de France—Maine-et-Loire* (Paris: Ecole pratique des hautes etudes, 1974), 340, 369, 401–402. AEA, 3F3.

15. AEA, Dutertre, René Marie, and Laroche, Joseph, in *fichier* of parish clergy. For the clergy of Anjou and the oath see Timothy Tackett, "The West in France in 1789: The Religious Factor in the Origins of the Counterrevolution," *Journal of Modern History* 54 (1988): 715–745.

16. AEA, P63. Several of the sermons from Bourg also list two dates on which they were delivered; see AEA, P12.

17. François Lebrun, *Parole de Dieu et Révolution—Les sermons d'un curé angevin avant et pendant la guerre de Vendée* (Paris: Imago, 1988; first edition, 1979), 20. On eighteenth-century sermons see also Marie-Claude Leleux, "Les Prédicateurs jésuites et leur temps—à travers les sermons prononcés dans le Paris religieux du XVIIIe siècle, 1729–1762," *Histoire économique et sociale* 8 (1989): 21–44; according to Leleux, death "totally obsessed the religious discourse" of the sermons (33).

18. Gibson, "De la prédication de la peur à la vision d'un dieu d'amour," 154–155. On this point see also: Robert Favre, introduction to *La Fin dernière* (Paris: Montalba, 1984), 37–43; McManners, *Death and the Enlightenment*, 132.

Both Favre and McManners stress that the preaching of hellfire was accompanied by more hopeful messages of union with God.

19. Ernest Sevrin, *Les Missions religieuses en France sous la Restauration*, 2 vols. (Saint Mandé et Paris: Vrin, 1948–1959); Devlin, *The Superstitious Mind*, 33–36.

20. McManners, *Death and the Enlightenment*, 144–145, notes that some of the parish clergy in the eighteenth century were critical of the hellfire preaching of Capucin missionaries. The revolution, however, may have persuaded the curés of the need for taking a harsher line.

21. James Joyce, *A Portrait of the Artist as a Young Man* (New York: Huebsch, 1916), 127–153.

22. Laroche began with this text in his sermon "Sur la mort du juste," which he preached in 1823, 1826, 1828, and 1831; AEA P63. Dutertre cited it in his sermon "Sur la mort," preached on 15 March 1846; AEA P12.

23. Jacques Brydaine, *Sermons du Père Brydaine*, 5 vols., 4th ed. (Paris: Lecoffre, 1867). The devotional works of the seventeenth-century priest Paul de Barry also continued to appear in the nineteenth century; see his *Pensez-y bien, réflexions sur les quatre fins derniers* (Paris and Troyes: Société de Saint-Victor pour la propagation des bons livres, 1857). Camporesi, *The Fear of Hell*, provides extensive quotations from hellfire preaching (mostly Italian) in the seventeenth and eighteenth centuries.

24. AEA P12, Dutertre, "Sur la mort du pécheur et du juste."

25. Gibson, *A Social History of French Catholicism*, 180–190.

26. AEA P12, Dutertre, "Sur la mort du pécheur et du juste."

27. AEA P63, Laroche, "Sur la mort du juste."

28. Ibid.

29. Robert Favre, ed., *La Fin dernière*, 51–52.

30. For some examples of the baroque emphasis on the corruption of the flesh see Delumeau, *Le Péché et la peur*, 404–406; Vovelle, *Mourir autrefois*, 63–64.

31. Caroline Bynum, "Bodily Miracles and the Resurrection of the Body in the High Middle Ages," in *Belief in History*, ed. Thomas Kselman (Notre Dame: University of Notre Dame Press, 1990); Richardson, *Death, Dissection, and the Destitute* 76–77.

32. McManners, *Death and the Enlightenment*, 125–126.

33. AEA P62, Thoré, "Instruction sur les indulgences."

34. AEA P12, Dutertre, "Sur la mort."

35. Gibson, "De la prédication de la peur," 156. See also Gibson, "Hellfire and Damnation," 384, for a selection from Bridaine describing the pains of hell.

36. Gibson, "Hellfire and Damnation," 390. Other examples of this technique are cited by Devlin, *The Superstitious Mind*, 35–36.

37. Albert Camus, *La Peste* (Paris: Gallimard, 1947), 91–95.

38. Archives départementales de Maine-et-Loire (hereafter ADML), 5 V 32 includes correspondence from mayors concerned about the sermons preached in the midst of the cholera epidemic of 1832; see also Devlin, *The Superstitious Mind*, 33, 36.

39. Elizabeth Germain, *Parler du salut? Aux origines d'une mentalité religieuse* (Paris: Beauchesne, 1967).

40. *Catechisme du diocèse d'Angers* (Angers: Pavie, 1815), 58.

41. Marcel Launay, *Le Diocèse de Nantes sous le Second Empire* (Nantes: Cid, 1982), 1: 466; Christianne Marcilharcy, *Le Diocèse d'Orléans sous l'épiscopat de Mgr Dupanloup* (Paris: Plon, 1962), 289.

42. "Sur la mort" can be found in: *Cantiques à l'usage de la mission donnée dans l'Eglise Cathédrale en décembre 1807* (Angers: Pavie, 1807), 37–38; *Cantiques à l'usage des missions et des retraites* (Angers: Mame, 1828), 26–27; *Chants pieux ou choix de cantiques* (Paris: Poussielgue, 1861), 232–233.

43. For other images evoking death see *Un Siècle des images de piété*, 22–24. Selections from the colportage literature on death and salvation can be found in: Geneviève Bollème, *La Bible bleue: Anthologie d'une littérature populaire* (Paris: Flammarion, 1975), 67–139; Favre, ed., *La Fin dernière*.

44. For an eighteenth-century version of *Le Miroir du pécheur* see Favre, ed., *La Fin dernière*, 293–314. The image included in this 1754 edition seems somewhat cruder than that of the nineteenth century. The demons are larger and more malignant, and the condemned man is drawn more simply; see ibid., 297. These images were still common in Brittany into the twentieth century, where they are recalled to this day by some of the elderly; see Ellen Badone, *The Appointed Hour*, 179–182.

45. AEA P63, Laroche, "Sur la mort du juste." Thoré, in his sermon for All Saints' Day (AEA P62), referred to the "games, diversions, licentiousness, pleasures of the cabaret" that typified feast days.

46. AEA P63, Laroche, "Sur l'enfer." Thoré's sermon "Sur l'enfer" (AEA P62) includes a similar passage.

47. AEA P12, Dutertre, "Sur la mort des pécheurs."

48. Bibliothèque nationale, Cabinet des estampes, Oa 22, M 143250.

49. Walker, *The Decline of Hell*; McManners, *Death and the Enlightenment*, 176–190.

50. Gustave de Ravignan, *Conférences du Révérend Père de Ravignan de la compagnie de Jésus prêchées à Notre-Dame de Paris*, 4 vols. (Paris: Poussielgue, 1860); Ravignan did, however, preach one sermon on the eternity of punishment, a doctrine that seems to have been particularly doubted by his audience. Henri de Lacordaire, *Conférences de Notre Dame*, 3 vols. (Paris: Poussielgue, 1861). For the importance of Lacordaire see Cholvy and Hilaire, *Histoire religieuse*, 1:94–95.

51. A dossier of sermons preached by various clergy at the cathedral of St. Maurice, Angers, in 1862–1863 can be found in the Archives d'Evéché of Angers; these had not been catalogued when I consulted them in 1982.

52. AEA P 121, Sermons of Guillaume Rochard (1807–1863).

53. Gibson, "Hellfire and Damnation," 383.

54. Gibson, "De la prédication de la peur," 162–163.

55. Ibid., 164. Some passages from sermons earlier in the century that describe the death of a just man also refer to the happiness that awaits him in Heaven. But in these, such as Abbé Thoré's sermon "Sur la mort du juste et du pécheur," the contrast with the death of the sinner who dies in fear was designed to prevent the confidence that was typical of the later preaching.

56. Claude Savart, *Les Catholiques en France au XIXe siècle—Le Témoignage du livre religieux* (Paris: Beauchesne, 1985), 483–484.

57. *L'Ami du clergé paroissial*, 13 (1901), 1031, 1033. I found no sermon in either volume 3 (1891) or in volume 13 (1901) dedicated to the death of the sinner, the small number of elect, or Hell. This confirms Ralph Gibson's findings for the journal, which he reviewed for the period 1898–1903; see Gibson, "Hellfire and Damnation," 397–398. Abbé Lelandais balances his collection with two sermons each on Heaven, Hell, and Purgatory, a judiciousness that was not observed earlier in the century; see his *Choix de la prédication contemporaine*, 7th ed., 4 vols. (Paris: Bloud et Barral, 1885), 1: 504–624. F. X. Schouppe, *Short Sermons for the Low Masses of Sunday*, trans. from the French (New York: Benziger, 1883), 106–109, 195–200, 281–285, 370–374; Schouppe's collection of brief sermons was a response to the declining numbers who attended the high mass on Sunday, and in the short time available at the low masses it was impossible for him to elaborate with any detail on the Hell preached earlier in the century.

58. Robin Briggs, *Communities of Belief—Cultural and Social Tension in Early Modern France* (Oxford: Clarendon Press, 1989), 285–293; Boutry, *Prêtres et paroisses*, 406; Guerber, *Le Ralliement du clergé français à la morale liguorienne*, 21–93.

59. For a detailed study of this work and its influence see Guerber, *Le Ralliement du clergé français*, 208–367. Boutry, *Prêtres et paroisses*, 408–422 traces the effects of the ligourian morality on the diocese of Belley.

60. Boutry, *Prêtres et paroisses*, 420; Philippe Boutry and Michel Cenquin, *Deux Pèlerinages au XIXe siècle: Ars et Paray-le-Monial* (Paris: Beauchesne, 1980), 61–69. For Vianney's early sermons and their sources in a number of rigorist manuals see Jacqueline Genet, *L'Enigme des sermons du curé d'Ars* (Paris: L'Orante, 1961).

61. Thomas Allies, *Journal in France* (London, 1849), 279.

62. Yves Lambert, "Crise de la confession, crise de l'économie de salut: Le Cas d'une paroisse bretonne de 1900 à 1982," in *Pratiques de la confession—Des Pères du désert à Vatican II* (Paris: Cerf, 1983), 267. For an extended discussion on changed attitudes concerning the afterlife see Yves Lambert, *Dieu change en Bretagne* (Paris: Cerf, 1985), 355–383; Badone, *The Appointed Hour*. For improved material conditions see Weber, *France—Fin de Siècle*.

63. Badone, *The Appointed Hour*.

64. AEA P62, Thoré, "Sur le paradis."

65. See, for example, "Bonheur du ciel," and "Désirs du ciel," in *Cantiques à l'usage des missions*, 41–43; "Le ciel," in *Chants pieux*, 114–115.

66. McManners, *Death and the Afterlife*, 124, 131.

67. McDannell and Lang, *Heaven—A History*, 181–275.

68. Jean Cuisenier, *French Folk Art* (New York: Kodansha, 1977), 163.

69. Pierre Blot, S.J., *Au ciel on se reconnaît*, 38e ed. (Paris, 1902).

70. "Les Consolations du culte des morts—La Réunion," in *L'Ami du clergé paroissial* 13 (1901): 785–788.

71. AEA P12, Jean-Jacques Dutertre, "Sur l'enfer."

72. Christianne Marcilharcy, *Le Diocèse d'Orléans sous l'épiscopat de Mgr Dupanloup* (Paris: Plon, 1962), 326–327. The figure for the Last Sacraments is from 1858 rather than 1868, but Marcilharcy's analysis suggests that there was little change in the attachment to these rites during the Second Empire. See also Gibson, *Social History of French Catholicism*, 163–165.

73. Pierre Pierrard, *La Vie quotidienne du prêtre français au XIXe siècle* (Paris: Hachette, 1986), 355; François Isambert, *Christianisme et classe ouvrière* (Paris: Castermann, 1961), 88–114.

74. *Le Médecin des pauvres* (Rouen: Surville, 1851), 6. The same pamphlet includes an image of the wound in Christ's side with the guarantee that whoever carries it will not die a "bad death."

75. ADML 2 V 2, file 2, Béhuard. Similar complaints can be found in the correspondence from St. Jean de la Croix, St. Sigismund, Chavaignon, Douée, and Epinal. For similar concerns in the department of Ain see Boutry, *Prêtres et paroisses*, 465.

76. ADML 2 V 2, Angers.

77. Ariès, *Images of Man and Death*, 102–103, argues that the disappearance of the priest from several deathbed scenes presented by artists suggests that "the solemn rites of a Christian death, deemed superstitious, were now avoided." But a number of the images presented by Ariès, such as François Brillaud's *Last Rites in the Vendée* (1910), reveal the continuing appeal of clerical presence.

78. *Rituel du diocèse d'Angers*, 3 vols. (Angers: Mame, 1828), 2:17. For a good overview of the clerical ministry to the sick in Roman Catholicism see Pierre Guillaume, *Médecins, église et foi, XIXe-XXe siècles* (Paris: Aubier, 1990), 15–25; see also Marvin O'Connell, "The Roman Catholic Tradition since 1565," in *Caring and Curing—Health and Medicine in the Western Religious Traditions*, ed. Ronald Numbers and Darrel Admundsen (New York: Macmillan, 1986), 122 123.

79. *Rituel du diocèse d'Angers*, 2:22. For the prevalence of this belief in the ancien régime see Jean-Baptiste Thiers, *Traité des superstitions qui regardent les sacremens*, 4 vols. (Paris, 1751), 4:385. François Isambert, "Les Transformations du rituel catholique des mourants," *Archives de sciences sociales des religions* 39 (1975): 89–100, compares the administration of the Last Sacraments as regulated by the decrees of the Council of Trent with the practices called for by Vatican II.

80. *Rituel du diocèse d'Angers*, 2:22–23.

81. Even the Last Sacraments, however, could be used to make a mean-spirited joke at the expense of an enemy. At Longué (Maine-et-Loire) in 1866, M. Aubrun, the secretary of the mayor, sent two girls to ask the curé to go to the home of M. Plès, where someone had just died. Plès, an officer of the fire department and an enemy of the mayor, had just been fired, and the curé complained of the joke to the bishop of Angers, who took the issue up with the prefect. See ADML 1 M 6/48.

82. Boutry, *Prêtres et paroisses*, 209–226; Pierrard, *La Vie quotidienne du prêtre français au XIXe siècle*, esp. 381–404; Launay, *Le Diocèse de Nantes*, 2:521–537.

83. AMA, cimetières, Letter of M. Adville to the mayor of Angers, 5 June 1832. Adville was complaining about the lugubrious effect produced by Catholic death ritual, and perhaps he exaggerated the number of those who followed the priest, but even so it must have been a substantial crowd.

84. Gustave Flaubert, *Madame Bovary* (New York: Universal Library, n.d.), 353–356. Disrespect for the priest while he was carrying the viaticum was prosecuted during the Restoration; see AN BB 30 198(1), which reports the case of two civil servants who refused to take their hats off as the sacrament passed by them in the village of Longué (Maine-et-Loire) in 1822.

85. For the shift from public to private see McManners, *Death and the Enlightenment*, 235–237, 255–258. Ariès provides an extended treatment of the deathbeds of the La Ferronays, an aristocratic family firmly attached to Catholic ritual in *The Hour of Our Death*, 412–431. For clerical practice see *Rituel d'Angers*, 3:3–4; R. P. Le Vavasseur, *Cérémonial selon le Rit Romain*, 5th ed. (Paris: Lecoffre, 1876), 647–648; R.P.A. Velgre, *Cours élémentaire de liturgie sacrée*, 6th ed. (Paris: Lethielleux, 1896), 382–385. In 1901 the clergy of Toulouse appealed to the conseil d'état to defend their right to be accompanied by "un certain nombre de personnes" when they bore the Eucharist to the sick and dying, suggesting that the practice still occurred. The practice was also still common in Brittany into the mid-twentieth century; see Badone, *The Appointed Hour*, 44–45.

86. The *Rituel d'Angers*, 3:25, encouraged the practice of administering the viaticum after extreme unction but acknowledged that this variation from the traditional sequence might provoke opposition, in which case the priest was to concede to the wishes of the dying person and the family. Velgre, *Cours élémentaire*, 386, affirms the pattern of confession, viaticum, and extreme unction. Although ideally the last two were to be administered during separate visits, in fact the delays of the family in calling the priest generally led to the grouping of the three in a single ritual pattern. For the significance of this sequence and its alteration under the reforms of Vatican II, see Isambert, "Les Transformations du rituel catholique des mourants," 89–90.

87. Boutry, *Prêtres et paroisses*, 465.

88. *L'Ami du clergé*, 10 (1888): 596.

89. For an excellent summary of the *levée*, the funeral, and burial see R. P. Huguet, *Mois consolateur des âmes du Purgatoire* (Paris: Perisse, 1864), 10–22. See also *Rituel d'Angers*, 3:57–63; Velgre, *Cours élémentaire*, 389–400.

90. Allies, *Journal in France*, 101.

91. AMA, cimetières, Letter of M. Adville to mayor of Angers, 5 June 1832. The fear that funeral services would depress the sick and thereby hurt their chances for survival was not unique, and government regulations sometimes limited the sounding of the death knell in order to lessen anxiety; see AN F 19 5513, "Sonnerie des cloches pendant les épidémies," circular from minister of interior to prefects, 20 January 1806.

92. Cited in O'Connell, "The Roman Catholic Tradition Since 1545," 134. For the prayers and songs said at funeral masses and offices for the dead see "Commun des saints," in *Offices de l'église du matin et du soir suivant le rit romain* (Paris: Lecoffre, 1858), 102–146. Those who assisted at funerals with the

missals that were increasingly widespread in the nineteenth century would be able to follow the prayers and songs in French as well as Latin; see Michel Albaric, Barnard Ardura, et al., *Histoire du missel français* (Paris: Brepols, 1986), 131–146.

93. René Laurentin and Bernard Billet, eds., *Lourdes—Documents authentiques* (Paris: Lethielleux, 1957), 1:143–145, 169; Thomas Kselman, *Miracles and Prophecies in Nineteenth-Century France* (New Brunswick: Rutgers University Press, 1983).

94. McManners, *Death and the Enlightenment*, 191–197.

95. Ibid., 245–248.

96. Abbé Uzureau, "Mort chrétienne de Benaben," *Andegaviana*, 3e série (Angers, 1905), 386–392.

97. See, for example, *L'Ami de la religion* 25 (1820): 52, 58; (1829): 73–74, 78; (1834): 376. M. Patricia Dougherty, O.P., "Constitutional Bishops and the Catholic Press During the Early July Monarchy: Grégoire and Talleyrand," *Proceedings of the Annual Meeting of the Western Society for French History* 17 (1991): 305–314, discusses press coverage of the deaths of Grégoire in 1831 and Talleyrand in 1838. Grégoire received the last rites but Archbishop Quélen refused him a Catholic burial; Talleyrand received the last rites and was buried as a Catholic layman. For a detailed account of Talleyrand's conversion see F. Lagrange, *Vie de Mgr Dupanloup*, 3 vols. (Paris: Poussielgue, 1884), 1:222–257. Catholic fiction writers were also fond of conversion stories. See Mathilde Tarweld, "Clementine," *Le Magasin catholique* 6 (1855): 150–151.

98. Abbé Edmond Lambert, *Histoire de l'église de Notre-Dame des Victoires* (Paris: Curot, 1872), 290–292; *Le Salut facilité aux pécheurs*, 4th ed. (Angers: Launay-Gagnon, 1842), 8–9.

99. C. F. Chevé, *Dictionnaire des conversions ou Essai d'Encylopédie historique des conversions au Catholicisme depuis le dix-huitième siécle* (Paris: Migne, 1852), vol. 3 of *Nouvelle Encyclopédie théologique*, 677–678. For other accounts of deathbed conversions in this volume see 202, 827, 1025. Evelyn Waugh's *Brideshead Revisited* can be read as an elaborate variation on this theme of the aging man converted by his family on his deathbed.

100. Jean-Jacques Rousseau, *Julie ou La Nouvelle Héloïse* (Paris: Garnier-Flammarion, 1967), 545; for the death of Julie see Jean Starobinski, *Jean-Jacques Rousseau—Transparency and Obstruction* (Chicago: University of Chicago Press, 1988), 113–121. McManners emphasizes the death of Julie as "the supreme manifesto of sentimental and moralizing deism against hierarchical and sacramental Catholicism." See his *Death and the Enlightenment*, 257.

101. On nursing sisters see S. Borsa and C.-R. Michel, *Des hôpitaux en France au XIXe siècle* (Paris: Hachette, 1985), 161–171; Guillaume, *Médecins, église et foi*, 22–24.

102. ADML, H suppl., L 40; AEA, 5 K 4.

103. For Paris see Guillaume, *Médecins, église et foi*, 82–86; Fénélon Gibon, *La Laicisation des hôpitaux de Paris* (Paris: Poussielgue, 1888). For a similar controversy in Marseille see Lucien Gaillard, "La Misère et l'assistance à Marseille sous le Second Empire et les premières années de la IIIe République," *Provence historique* 27 (1977): 341–363. The Conseil supérieure de l'as-

sistance publique passed a regulation that gave ministers access to the sick, but only if authorized by the hospital administration; public prayers were prohibited. See AN F19 5615, file on "Dispositions réglementaires concernant le service des Cultes dans les hôpitaux et hospices."

104. P. Debreyne, *La Théologie morale et les sciences médicales*, 6th ed. (Paris: Poussielgue, 1884). In an earlier work, *Etude de la mort* (Paris: Poussielgue, 1845), ii-iii, Debreyne summarized for the clergy the signs of imminent death on the basis of the latest medical science. Debreyne's motive was to arm the priest with the information that he needed in terms of when to provide the Last Sacraments, because the largely unbelieving medical corps could not be relied on to warn the patient and the priest that death was near. For the growing power of the medical profession in their relationship with the sick and dying see Guillaume, *Médecins, église et foi*, 75.

105. Debreyne, *La Théologie morale et les sciences médicales*, 229.

106. Ibid., 230.

107. Michel Vovelle, *Piété baroque et déchristianisation en Provence au XVIIIe siècle* (Paris: Seuil, 1978); Pierre Chaunu, *Mourir à Paris—16e, 17e, 18e siècles* (Paris: Fayard, 1978); Jean de Viguerie, "Les Fondations et la foi du peuple chrétien—Les Fondations des messes en Anjou aux XVIIe et XVIIIe siècles," *Revue Historique* 156 (1977): 289–320.

108. Boutry, *Prêtres et paroisses*, 422.

109. M. Faugeras, "Les Fondations dans le diocèse de Nantes de 1800 à 1850," in *Histoire de la messe, XVIIe–XIXe siècles* (Angers: Presse de l'Université d'Angers, 1980), 141–153.

110. AN F 19 5712, petition of people of Douce for the removal of their *desservant* submitted to the subprefect of Saumur, 20 May 1831. For other examples of complaints see: *L'Ami de la religion* 74 (1832): 373; Faugeras, "Les Fondations dans le diocèse de Nantes," and Boutry, *Prêtres et paroisses*, 423–433. A file of the applications for foundations from Maine-et-Loire can be found in AN F 19 4180.

111. See clipping in AN F 19 5720. The son of Deligmère, however, disputed this account, which he attributed to an anticlerical son-in-law.

112. R. W. Franklin, *Nineteenth-Century Churches—The History of a New Catholicism in Württemberg, England, and France* (New York: Garland, 1987), 407–410.

113. *Journal des Débats*, 22 August 1843, clipping found in AN F 19 5712. See also ADML 1 N 39, which includes the minutes of an 1839 meeting of the general council at which Bordillon pushed through a motion that called the attention of the government to the dangerous consequences of the growth of religious congregations, which he accused of taking advantage of the dying.

114. *Le Temps*, 20 April 1879, 2.

115. Dale Van Kley, *The Damiens Affair and the Unraveling of the Ancien Régime (1750–1770)* (Princeton: Princeton University Press, 1984).

116. AN F 19 5523.

117. For a brief account of Montlosier's political significance see Guillaume de Bertier de Sauvigny, *The Bourbon Restoration* (Philadelphia: University of Pennsylvania Press, 1966), 382–384. For the debate on the affair in the Cham-

ber see *L'Ami de la religion* 100 (1839): 18–20, 148, 156. For extensive citations from the newspaper coverage of the affair see ibid., 99 (1838): 518, 529–530, 536–537, 550–552, 581–582; and 100 (1839): 247. Louis-Maire Cormenin, an important publicist whose pamphlets generally opposed the July Monarchy, defended the bishop of Clermont-Ferrand on the principle of the need to separate spiritual from temporal affairs. See his *Défense de l'évêque de Clermont, traduit pour cause d'abus devant les révérends Pères du Conseil d'Etat*, 2d ed. (Paris: Pagnerre, 1839). The decision of the conseil d'état condemning the bishop can be found in AN F 19 6115.

118. Jules Michelet, *Mother Death—The Journal of Jules Michelet, 1815–1850*, trans. and ed. Edward Kaplan (Amherst: University of Massachusetts Press, 1984), 126. François Truffaut provides a recent example of resentment of the clerical role at death in his film *La Chambre verte*. When the priest tries to console Mazet, whose wife has just died, with assurances that they will see each other again, his friend Davenne responds angrily that "the only thing we want from you is to say 'Rise and walk' and to have the dead get up and walk. If you can't revive Geneviève Mazet, today, now, at this very second, there's nothing for you to do here. . . . Get out! Get out!" See the screenplay published in *L'Avant-Scène* 1 November 1978, 8.

119. Jules Michelet, *Du prêtre, de la femme, de la famille* (Paris: Hachette, 1845). For a study of the development of Michelet's ideas on religion that stresses the importance of the death of Mme Dumesmil see José Cabanis, *Michelet, le prêtre et la femme* (Paris: Gallimard, 1978), 108–118.

120. Jacqueline Lalouette, "Les Enterrements civils dans les premières décennies de la Troisième République," *Ethnologie française* 13 (1983): 111–128; Patrick Hutton, *The Cult of the Revolutionary Tradition: The Blanquists in Politics, 1864–1893* (Berkeley: University of California Press, 1981), 53–55; Thomas Kselman, "Funeral Conflicts in Nineteenth-Century France," *Comparative Studies in Society and History* 30 (1988): 312–322. For another example of the successful resistance of clerical pressure see *L'Electeur*, 18 March 1885, clipping in AN F 19 5776.

121. AEA, O (Broc).

122. Roger Martin du Gard, *Jean Barois* (1913; New York: Bobbs-Merrill, 1969), 255.

123. Avner Ben-Amos, "Les Funérailles de Victor Hugo," in *La République*, vol. 1 of *Les Lieux de mémoire*, ed. Pierre Nora (Paris: Gallimard, 1984), 473–522; Philippe Regnier, "L'Enterrement du siècle," in *Tombeau de Victor Hugo*, ed. André Comte-Sponville, Emmanuel Fraisse, Jacqueline Lalouette, and Philippe Regnier (Paris: Quintette, 1985), 28–29.

124. For other examples of conversions see Louis Pérouas, *Refus d'une religion, religion d'un refus* (Paris: Ecole des hautes études en sciences sociales, 1985), 178–179. In some cases family members acted discreetly to allow the visit of a priest, as in the village of Sceaux, Maine-et-Loire, where the curé reported that an anticlerical had left the house for a few days hoping that the sacraments would be administered and the death occur in his absence, a scenario that in fact took place; see ADML 1 M 6/48.

125. François Mauriac, *The Inner Presence* (New York, 1968), 58–59.

126. Joachim Gaudry, *Traité de la législation des cultes*, 3 vols. (Paris: Durand, 1856), 1: 204–210; 545–547; Abbé Craisson, *De la sépulture ecclésiastique*, 2d ed. (Poitiers: Oudin, 1868); *Rituel du diocèse d'Angers*, 2:22. For a more extended discussion of the problems involving funerals see Kselman, "Funeral Conflicts in Nineteenth-Century France."

127. The decree of 23 prairial, along with other decrees and circulars on the refusal of sacraments, can be found in AN F 19 5512 and F 19 5513.

128. ADML 5 V 30, letter of the mayor of Varennes to the subprefect of Saumur, 30 Dec. 1828.

129. Agulhon, *La République au village*, p. 183. See also Berenson, *Populist Religion and Left-Wing Politics in France* 66–67; Singer, *Village Notables*, 69. Jews also sometimes became engaged in conflicts with their rabbis; see the case of Rabbi Cohen, of Rouen, who refused to bury the daughter of a member of his congregation because the family chose the less-expensive communal cemetery rather than the Jewish burial ground. AN F 19 11032.

130. See, for example, the circular letters from the minister of interior to the prefects of 8 Messidor, year XII; 26 Thermidor, year XII (AN F 19 5513). In a letter from the prefect of Seine-et-Oise to the subprefects and mayors of his department, dated 24 September 1838, he noted "serious difficulties" between mayors and curés over the administration of the decree of 23 prairial. Similar problems were addressed in a letter from the minister of religion to the bishops of 28 June 1838; a letter from the minister of justice and religion to the bishops of 16 December 1844; and a letter from the minister of justice and religion to the bishops and prefects of 25 June 1847 (AN F 19 5512). In general these administrative letters urged bishops and prefects to encourage a tolerant attitude on the part of the clergy with regard to religious services for the dead. But they also discouraged municipal authorities from directly challenging clerical authority by forcing their way into churches when a refusal had taken place.

131. François Lebrun, *Les Hommes et la mort en Anjou au 17e et 18e siècles* (Paris: Mouton, 1971), 418; Marcilharcy, *Le Diocèse d'Orléans*, 321.

132. Abbé Juin, *Lettre au clergé français, ou conseils touchant les refus de sépulture* (Paris: Leclerc, n.d.), 25–28. For an excellent overview of the different attitudes toward suicide in the nineteenth century see Lisa Jo Liberman, *Une Maladie Epidémique*.

133. "Des suicides: Resumé de la législation ancienne et moderne sur l'inhumation des personnes que se donnent volontairement la mort," in file on "Suicides," AN F19 5514. Michael MacDonald has noted the popular resistance to burying suicides in consecrated ground in nineteenth-century England. See "The Secularization of Suicide in England, 1660–1800," *Past and Present* 111 (May 1980), p. 88.

134. AEA, O (Champtoceaux).

135. Avner Ben-Amos, "Molding the National Memory: The State Funerals of the French Third Republic" (Ph.D. diss., University of California, Berkeley, 1988), 49–86, 155–157, provides a number of additional illustrations of the political nature of civil burials.

136. AEA, O (Gennes). Documents on similar cases are collected in AN F

19 5519 and F 19 5520, and in the Archives de la Préfecture de la Police, Paris, BA 494–495. For rituals similar to Besnard's see: Lalouette, "Les Enterrements civils," 111–114; Pérouas, *Refus d'une religion*, 180–181; Boutry, *Prêtres et paroisses*, 468–469; Gérard Cholvy, *Religion et société au XIXe siècle: Le Diocèse de Montpellier*, 2 vols. (Lille, 1973), 2:1256–1258. The ceremonies used at civil burials in the Third Republic resemble those of the *compagnons* earlier in the century; see the descriptions in Agricol Perdiguier, *Mémoires d'un compagnon* (Paris: Maspero, 1977), 193–195, 341–342. The *compagnons*, however, insisted on a church service as well.

137. Ben-Amos, "Les Funérailles de Victor Hugo"; Ben-Amos, *Molding the National Memory*, 178–197, 299–314; André Comte-Sponville, et al., *Tombeau de Victor Hugo*.

138. This shift from community to association as the source of funeral conflicts reflects a general trend in the history of collective action. See Charles Tilly, *The Contentious French* (Cambridge: Harvard University Press, 1986).

139. Toward the end of the century Church-State conflict on the death-ritual issue revolved around the management of pompes funèbres, which will be considered in chapters 6 and 7.

140. AN F 19 10172, a file from the Gard includes a case in which a Protestant minister replaced a priest at a funeral following clerical refusal in 1875. See also general file, letter from the minister of education and religion to the prefect of Seine-Inférieur, 31 August 1855, on the question of Protestant ministers replacing Catholic priests.

141. Ben-Amos, *Molding the National Memory*, 154.

142. *Journal Officiel* (hereafter *JO*) *Chambre*, 25 June 1873, 4163–4174. For a thorough discussion of these cases see Ben-Amos, *Molding the National Memory*, 163–178.

143. *JO Chambre*, 11 November 1876, 8620.

144. Ben-Amos, *Molding the National Memory*, 177.

145. For the initial proposal see *JO Chambre*, 10 June 1880, 6314. For subsequent amendments see *JO Chambre Documents* August 1881, annexe no. 3982, 1405–1410; February 1882, annexe no. 332, 203–205; April 1882, 853–855; June 1882, annexe no. 914, 1566–1567; *JO Sénat Documents*, May 1883, annexe no. 143, 731–734. For debates on the issue see *JO Chambre*, 2 February 1882, 71–72; 7 May 1882, 512–519; 28 June 1882, 1063–1066; 14 February 1886, 212–218; 18 February 1886, 230–243, 30 March 1886, 607–618, *JO Sénat* 11 May 1883, 470–475. For a brief review of the legislative history of this proposal see Louis Capéran, *Histoire contemporaine de la laïcité française* (Paris: Nouvelles Editions Latines, 1961), 3: 98–104.

146. *JO Chambre Documents*, February 1882, annexe 332, 204.

147. See, for example, the debate involving Msgr Freppel and Clovis Hughes, *JO Chambre*, 7 May 1882, 502–519.

148. See, for example, the case of Mme Bouvet, who died in Saumur in 1885, and whose parents desired a Catholic service whereas her husband insisted on a civil burial; AEA, 6 G 1. See also *La loi*, 25 May 1889, which reports a trial in Carcassone in which the Catholic and freethinking children of François Caut argued over his burial; F 19 5520. When the positivist Paul Bert

died while serving as an administrator in Vietnam in 1886 some Catholic papers reported that he had converted on his deathbed, a story that was denied in the liberal papers, which in this case were accurate; see *Le Temps*, 24 December 1886, 2; 29 December, 1–2.

149. For the passage of the final version of the law see *JO Chambre Débats*, 29 October 1887, 1898, 1907.

150. AN F 19 6115. For example, see cases involving parishes of Chateau-Regnault and Nouyon (Ardennes), St. Roman de Malegarde (Vaucluse).

151. Abbé Alfred Monnin, *Le Curé d'Ars*, 2 vols. (Paris: Douniol, 1863), 2: 193–199; Abbé Sanson, *Purgatoire et ciel* (Paris: Bray et Retaux, 1875), 183–184.

152. Allies, *Journal in France*, 217.

153. Ariès, *The Hour of Our Death*, 154–159; Vovelle, *Piété baroque*; Chaunu, *Mourir à Paris*. For contemporary practice in Brittany see Badone, *The Appointed Hour*.

154.
> "Sir Deceased, I'll have from you
> Cash; for candle wax you'll pay;
> And other minor expenses, too."
> Now he could buy a small cask he'd wanted to get
> Of the very best regional wine.
> A pretty niece, who was his pet,
> And also his maid, Paquette,
> In brand-new skirts would shine.

From *The Complete Fables of Jean de la Fontaine*, ed. and trans. Norman B. Spencer (Evanston: Northwestern University Press, 1988), 322–323.

155. P. Boissonnade and Léonce Cathelineau, eds., *Cahiers de doléances de la Sénéchaussée de Civry* (Niort: St. Denis, 1925), 34. For an assessment of the importance of the *casuel* in the eighteenth century see Philippe Loupès, "Le Casuel dans le diocèse de Bordeaux aux XVIIe et XVIIIe siècles," *Revue d'histoire de l'église de France* 57 (1972): 19–52.

156. *Journal de Denis Boutroue, curé-cultivateur (1783–1817)*, vol. 12 of *Le Folklore de la Beauce*, ed. Charles Marcel-Robillard and René Rivet (Paris: Maisoneuve et Larose, 1978), 11–61.

157. *L'Office des morts* (Laval: Godbert, 1859), 65. F. X. Schouppe, *Purgatory* (Rockville, Ill.: Tan 1973; first published in France, 1893), 155, writes that "of all that we can do in favor of the souls in Purgatory, there is nothing more precious than the immolation of our Divine Saviour upon the altar."

158. Christianne Marcilharcy, *Le Diocèse d'Orléans au milieu du XIXe siècle* (Paris: Sirey, 1964), 374; Yves-Marie Hilaire, *Une Chrétienté au XIXe siècle?* (Villeneuve-d'Ascq: Université de Lille, 1977), 1:189; for Angers see the correspondence in AEA 1 L 8.

159. Hilaire, *Une Chrétienté au XIXe siècle?*, 1:188–189. See also: Boutry, *Prêtres et paroisses*, 327–332; Bernard Delpal, *Entre paroisse et commune—Les Catholiques de la Drôme au milieu du XIXe siècle* (Valence: Editions Peuple Libre, 1989), 56–59. For the casuel in the diocese of Angers see "Etat du casuel," in AEA, 1 L 8.

160. In the more solemn service the priest would chant a portion of the office of the dead at the conclusion of the mass, which could take as much as an additional fifteen minutes.

161. All the correspondence on the proposed *tarif* of 1843 that I cite can be found in AEA, 1 L 8. On declining numbers of requests see the letter from the curé of Durtal and from the clergy of the canton of Baugé, who wrote that "honoraria for masses are diminishing noticeably everywhere, and some curés have hardly thirty masses a year." For an analysis of the different relations between clergy and community that characterized the diocese of Angers see Timothy Tackett, "The West in France in 1789."

162. AEA 1 L 8. Letter from René Grange, Noellet. For the requests of *trentaines* see the letter in the same file from the clergy of Cholet.

163. AEA 1 L 8, Letter from the clergy of Vihiers.

164. AEA 1 L 8 (1843). Letter from the curé of Allonnes.

165. AN F 20 573. Table of average salaries, by canton, of Maine-et-Loire.

166. *L'Univers*, 28 November 1857, 1.

167. For a thorough discussion of the kinds of issues raised by the clergy see M. Collet, *Traité des saints mystères ou l'on résout les principales difficultés que se rencontrent dans leurs célébration*, 10th ed., 2 vols. (Paris: Méquingnon, 1828), 1:50–86. At the end of the century the clerical review *L'Ami du clergé* provided a forum for discussing *honoraires*; see *L'Ami du clergé* 10 (1888): 209, 391, 557, 594.

168. AEA 1 L 8. Letter from the curé of La Jumeilière to the bishop of Angers, 19 August 1863.

169. For the case of Gelineau see AEA 6 G 1; AN F 19 5776. For a similar conflict in the town of Broc see AEA 1 L 8. A correspondent from Marseille wrote the minister Combes in 1903 to ask that the sale of masses and prayers be forbidden as part of the anticlerical legislation being considered; F 19 5520. Clerical venality could provoke a satirical response as well; see the poem published in Beziers, 1843, cited by Cholvy, *Religion et société au XIXe siècle*, 1:429–430. Income from the casuel could also poison relations between the clergy of the same parish, as is evident in the dispute between the curé and assistant of Brissac over the mass fees in 1881–1882; see AEA, 1 L 8.

170. AEA 1 L 8, Letter of Curé Ribert of Brissac to the bishop of Angers, 30 November 1882. Ribort had just arrived in the parish, a delicate time for a curé. When the curé of Thouarcé arrived at his parish in 1870 he made a similar decision to continue with the established prices "out of fear, perhaps excessive, of causing murmurs." AEA, 1 L 8.

171. In 1880 low masses in Anjou were listed at one franc, fifty centimes, and simple sung masses at two francs, rates that resemble those of Paris during the same period. See AEA, 1 L 8. Tarif des oblations, 1880; Joseph Rogé, *Le Simple Prêtre* (Paris: Casterman, 1965), 209–210.

172. AEA, 6 G 1, Letter of the bishop to the clergy of the diocese of Angers, 10 September 1889.

173. *Marthe* (Paris: Seuil, 1982), 21–26, 308–309.

174. Mary McCarthy, "In the Family Way," *New York Review of Books*, 8 December 1983, 17. It seems likely that the Montbourgs reminded Mc-

Carthy of the narrow piety and penny-pinching of her own early years, which she bitterly recounts in *Memoirs of a Catholic Girlhood*.

175. Philippe Ariès, *The Hour of our Death*, 412–439.

176. *Marthe*, 299.

177. Ibid., 379–390.

178. Honoré de Balzac, "La Messe de l'athée," in *French Stories/Contes Français*, ed. Wallace Fowlie (New York: Bantam, 1960), 79–81.

179. Michel Winock, "Un Avant-goût d'apocalypse: L'Incendie du Bazar de la Charité," in *Edouard Drumont et Cie: Antsémitisme et fascisme en France* (Paris: Seuil, 1982), 13–34; John McManners, *Church and State in France, 1870–1914* (New York: Harper Torchbooks, 1972), 124.

180. R. R. Huguet, *Mois consolateur des âmes du Purgatoire* (Paris: Perisse, 1864), v; Louis Rouzic, *Le Purgatoire—Pour nos morts et avec nos morts*, 3e ed. (Paris: Tequi, 1922), preface.

181. Roland Bainton, *Here I Stand—A Life of Martin Luther* (New York: Abingdon, 1950), 74–78.

182. Alexis Lépicier, *Les Indulgences—Leur origine, leur nature, leur développement*, 2 vols. (Paris: Lethielleux, 1903), 2:236–241.

183. Thiers, *Traité des superstitions*, 4:1–320.

184. Jean Bouvier, *Traité dogmatique et pratique des indulgences, des confréries, et du Jubilé* (Le Mans: Monnoyer, 1826), x. Bouvier's work profited from his being named bishop of Tours; it went through ten editions between 1826 and 1855 and was the most influential French work on the question in the nineteenth century. Other works on Purgatory include: Abbé Louvet, *Le Purgatoire d'après les révélations des saints*, 3d ed. (Albi, 1899); R. P. Hamon, *Au delà du tombeau*, 3rd ed. (Paris: Tequi, 1912); Père Alexis Ségala, *Le Purgatoire—Dogme, suffrages, pratiques*, 2d ed. (Paris: Poussielgue, 1880); Abbé Henry Boco, *Nos communications avec les morts* (Paris: Haton, 1903); Schouppe, *Purgatory*; Huguet, *Mois consolateur des âmes du Purgatoire*.

185. Lépicier, *Les Indulgences*, 2:250. For the decrees of the Sacred Congregation see Josephus Schneider, S.J., *Rescripta authentica sacrae congregationis indulgentiis sacrisque reliquiis* (Rome, 1885).

186. Lépicier, *Les Indulgences*, 1:103–133; Bouvier, *Traité dogmatique*, 77–81.

187. *Recueil des scapulaires* (Paris: Agence ecclésiastique et religieuse de Rome, 1862), 9.

188. *Un Siècle d'images de piété* traces the history of the production of holy cards during the nineteenth century. A good selection of this material is on microfilm at the Bibliothèque nationale, Cabinet des estampes, Rc mat 5b, R593–3858.

189. For a collection of *images mortuaires* see Bibliothèque nationale, Cabinet des estampes, Rc mat 6B. See also *Un Siècle d'images de piété*, 181, where the editors note that beyond these specialized images "death is present everywhere, all the pious imagery develops *sub specie ae eternitatis*; it is its profound *raison d'être* to manifest here-below the reality of the beyond."

190. Schouppe, *Purgatory*, 198, mentions this prayer first on his list of indulgences that are easy to gain.

191. *L'Ami du clergé* 1 (1879): 489; Bouvier, *Traité dogmatique*, 166–208, 304–319; Paul Parfait, *L'Arsénal des dévotions* (Paris: Decaux, 1876), 71–141. The

members of the Confraternity of Our Lady of Mount Carmel believed that wearing the scapular protected them from a sudden death, based on promises made by the Virgin to St. Simon Stock in the thirteenth century; see "Notre Dame du Carmel et le scapulaire," *Semaine religieuse* Angers, 3 July 1864, 567–568.

192. Abbé Vivent, *Petit manuel du pelèrinage de Lourdes* (Paris: Chance, 1874), 124–125. For the development of Marian piety in the nineteenth century see Kselman, *Miracles and Prophecies in Nineteenth-century France*.

193. Abbé Cloquet, *Les Plus Faciles Indulgences à gagner*, 4th ed. (Lyon, n.d.); an 1872 edition of this work carried the approval of the Sacred Congregation of Indulgences. *Le Moyen d'aller droit au ciel*, 4th ed. (Lyon: Rougier, 1870). Both of these are cited in Parfait, *L'Arsenal de dévotion*, 366–367. The works of Msgr Méric were also frequently recommended; Méric edited a monthly journal, *Revue du monde invisible*, and was the author of: *L'Autre Vie*, 2 vols.; *Les Élus se reconnaitront au ciel*; and *Spiritualisme et spiritisme*. See *L'Ami du clergé paroissial* 16 (1904): 114, 140.

194. P. Gay, *Neuvaine en l'honneur des âmes du Purgatoire*, 2d ed. (Paris: Enault et Mas, n. d.), 48; cited in Parfait, *L'Arsenal de dévotion*, 87–88.

195. Lépicier, *Les Indulgences*, 2:256.

196. Vovelle, *Vision de la mort et l'au-delà en Provence d'après les autels des âmes du Purgatoire*.

CHAPTER FOUR

1. I do not mean to imply that orthodox Catholicism was uniformly and unquestioningly accepted by everyone but the *philosophes* during the eighteenth century. Jacques-Louis Ménétra, a glassworker who toured France in the second half of the eighteenth century and who left a manuscript journal that has recently been edited, was suspicious of the clergy and critical of what he called "fanaticism and superstition." Ménétra mentions some of Rousseau's works, and his attitudes toward religion seem in general to resemble those current among intellectuals of the period. Ménétra also prayed, however, went to mass, and offered no systematic alternative to the Catholicism that he still practiced. See Jacques-Louis Ménétra, *Journal of My Life*, introduction and commentary by Daniel Roche (New York: Columbia University Press, 1986), 19–21, 32–34, 55–56, 73, 78–79, 93 94, 159–160, 255. Ménétra, for all his skepticism, never imagined the kind of unorthodox cosmology developed by Menocchio, the Italian miller of the seventeenth century whose ideas are familiar through Carlo Ginzburg, *The Cheese and the Worms: The Cosmos of a Sixteenth-Century Miller* (Baltimore: Johns Hopkins University Press, 1980). For the presence of skepticism and atheisim among the common people of England see Keith Thomas, *Religion and the Decline of Magic* (New York: Scribners, 1971), 166–173.

2. F.A. Aulard, ed., *La Société des Jacobins—Recueil des documents* (Paris: Cerf, 1897), 6:280.

3. Nicole Bossut, "Aux origines de la déchristianisation dans la Nièvre: Fouché, Chaumette, ou les Jacobins?" *Annales historiques de la Révolution française* 264 (1986): 181–202; Richard Etlin, *The Architecture of Death—The*

Transformation of the Cemetery in Eighteenth-Century Paris (Cambridge: MIT Press, 1984), 236–238. The impact of this decree on government policy regarding cemeteries and funerals will be discussed in chapters 5 and 6.

4. There is some possibility of terminological confusion, because in France *spiritualisme* describes something very different from American and English "spiritualism." Because French philosophers such as Cousin had already adopted the term *spiritualisme*, those in France interested in communication with the dead chose *spiritisme* to describe their philosophy. On the choice of terms see Allan Kardec, *Le Livre des esprits*, 15th ed. (Paris: Didier, 1865), iii–v.

5. Albert Mathiez, *La Théophilanthropie et le culte décadaire* (Geneva: Slatkine-Margolis Reprints, 1973; first published 1903). For a brief summary of the movement of dechristianization see Emmet Kennedy, *A Cultural History of the French Revolution* (New Haven: Yale University Press, 1989), 338–353. Suzanne Desan, *Reclaiming the Sacred: Lay Religion and Popular Politics in Revolutionary France* (Ithaca: Cornell University Press, 1990), shows how villagers in the department of the Yonne resisted dechristianization by appealing to the same liberties advocated by the revolutionaries.

6. The followers of Louis-Auguste Blanqui also associated the atheism of Chaumette and the Terror, but from their perspective Chaumette was a hero; see Patrick Hutton, *The Cult of the Revolutionary Tradition: The Blanquists in French Politics, 1864–1893* (Berkeley: University of California Press, 1981), 51–53, 71.

7. Alan Spitzer, *The French Generation of 1820* (Princeton: Princeton University Press, 1987), 90. James Kloppenberg, *Uncertain Victory: Social Democracy and Progressivism in European and American Thought, 1870–1920* (New York: Oxford University Press, 1986), describes Cousin's philosophy as "a thin verbal wallpaper covering the cracks between science and religion. (17)" For a more generous assessment see William Logue, *From Philosophy to Sociology— The Evolution of French Liberalism, 1870–1914* (Dekalb: Northern Illinois University Press, 1983), 17–19.

8. For Cousin's career and influence see Spitzer, *The Generation of 1820*, 71–96; Doris Goldstein, "Official Philosophies in Modern France: The Example of Victor Cousin," *Journal of Social History* 1 (1968): 259–279; Phyllis Stock-Morton, *Moral Education for a Secular Society* (Albany: State University of New York Press, 1988), 30–40. Georges Weill, *Histore de l'idée laïque au dix-neuvième siècle* (Paris, 1925), 75–80; D.G. Charlton, *Secular Religions in France, 1815–1870* (New York: Oxford University Press, 1963), 96–102. Two of Cousin's students who had distinguished careers in education and public service have also left accounts of his work: Jules Simon, *Victor Cousin* (Paris: Hachette, 1887); Paul Janet, *Victor Cousin et son ouevre* (Paris: Calmann-Lévy, 1885).

9. Victor Cousin, *Du vrai, du beau, et du bien* (Paris, 1856), 413.

10. Ibid., 416.

11. Victor Cousin, *Philosophie populaire* (Paris: Didot, 1848), 17–18.

12. Ibid., 4,8.

13. ADML, 1 N 48. Minutes of meeting of 1 December 1848.

14. Cousin published Rousseau's *Confession of a Savoyard Vicar* as part of *Philosophie populaire*. For Rousseau see Robert Favre, *La Mort au siècle des*

lumières (Lyons: Presses Universitaires de Lyons, 1978), 200–202. Cousin's focus on a spiritual self resembles in some ways the philsopher Maine de Biran's concept of a *sens intime*; see Maurice Mandelbaum, *History, Man, and Reason: A Study in Nineteenth-Century Thought* (Baltimore: Johns Hopkins University Press, 1971), 283–287.

15. Cousin, *Du vrai*, 334–335, 360.

16. Romantic ideas about the self are discussed in Meyer Abrams, *Natural Supernaturalism: Tradition and Revolution in Romantic Literature* (New York: Norton, 1971) and Paul Benichou, *Le Temps des prophètes: Doctrines de l'âge romantique* (Paris: Gallimard, 1977).

17. For a discussion of the second generation of spiritualists see Logue, *From Philosophy to Sociology*, 19–50. See also: Stock-Morton, *Moral Education*, 47–59; Weill, *L'Idée laïque*, 106–108, 132–142. Catholics during the Second Empire were increasingly sympathetic to Cousin; see the review of his *Du vrai* in *L'Ami de la religion* 162 (1853): 541–547.

18. Phillip Bertocci, *Jules Simon: Republican Anticlericalism and Cultural Politics in France (1848–1886)* (Columbia: University of Missouri Press, 1978), provides an excellent introduction to the ideas and political engagement of Simon. See also Logue, *From Philosophy to Sociology*, 41–47.

19. Jules Simon, *La Religion naturelle*, 4th ed. (Paris: Hachette, 1857), 369. Simon also defended the doctrine of immortality in his work on moral philosophy, *Le Devoir* (Paris: Hachette, 1854), 495–520; a selection on the immortality of the soul from this book was reprinted in the popular journal *Le Magasin pittoresque* 22 (1854): 74–75. For a brief summary of the argument of Simon see Bertocci, *Jules Simon*, 87–90.

20. Marcel Méry, *La Critique du christianisme chez Renouvier*, 2 vols. (Paris: Ophrys, 1963), 1:62–77. Méry's work, which is a detailed analysis of every stage of Renouvier's philosophy, also establishes the influence of Saint-Simon and Comte on him during this period. The distinctions I draw between the alternative afterlives should not be taken as excluding the possibility of cross-fertilization, which was especially the case in the first half of the century. On Renouvier see also Logue, *From Philosophy to Sociology*, 51–72.

21. Charles Renouvier, *Essais de critique générale: Deuxième Essai* (Paris: Ladrange, 1859), 565–689. Méry, *La Critique du christianisme*, 1:197–206. In his last years Renouvier continued to defend the concept of immortality, but he expressed this doctrine in more mystical language and integrated it into a philosophical system that he called Personalism, which he hoped would serve as the religion for a reformed world. See Charles Renouvier, *Les Derniers Entretiens* (Paris: Vrin, 1930).

22. Stock-Morton, *Moral Education*, 43, 55, 193; Weill, *L'Idée laïque*, 106–108.

23. Gérard Gayot, *La Franc-Maçonnerie française* (Paris: Gallimard, 1980), 27, 223–226.

24. Stock-Morton, *Moral Education*, 45–55, 69–72; Weill, *L'Idée laïque*, 182–183.

25. The French text reads: "*Je crois fermement à une autre vie, puisque Dieu qui est souverainement juste, nous en a donné l'idée; dans cette autre vie, à la rémunération du bien et du mal, puisque Dieu nous a permis de les distinguer et nous a donné la liberté de choisir; mais au-delà de ces notions claires, tout ce qui dépasse les*

bornes de ce monde me parait enveloppé de ténèbres qui m'épouvantent." In Alexis de Tocqueville, *Oeuvres complètes* (Paris: Gallimard, 1983), 14:315.

26. Emile Ollivier, the liberal prime minister during the closing days of the Second Empire, expressed sentiments similar to those of de Tocqueville in his will, where he wrote that "reason is the only revelation accorded to man by He who is" and that "formal religions are merely mythologies." But these mythologies were useful in consoling "those who are impatient for precise information about the life to come, of the existence of which reason assures us, without having the power to lay bare its mysteries." See Jacques Gadille, "On French Anticlericalism: Some Reflections," *European Studies Review* 13 (1983): 138. Even the most militant of anticlericals sometimes accepted spiritualist ideas, as may have been the case with Emile Combes. See Alec Mellor, *Histoire de l'anticléricalisme français* (Paris: Veyrier, 1978), 360–362.

27. Favre, *La Mort au siècle des lumières,* 203–211; McManners, *Death and the Enlightenment,* 160–166; Michael J. Buckley, *At the Origins of Modern Atheism* (New Haven: Yale University Press, 1988).

28. Hutton, *The Cult of the Revolutionary Tradition,* establishes the connections between revolutionary atheism and Blanquist socialism in the nineteenth century.

29. Claude Henri Saint-Simon, *The New Christianity,* in Albert Fried and Ronald Sanders, eds., *Socialist Thought—A Documentary History* (Garden City, N.Y.: Anchor Doubleday, 1964), 91.

30. Maurice Mandelbaum, *History, Man, and Reason,* 63–64.

31. The standard biography of Comte remains Henri Gouhier, *La Vie d'Auguste Comte* (Paris: N.R.F., 1931). For a brief introduction see Frank Manuel, *The Prophets of Paris* (New York: Harper and Row, 1965), 249–296. For a collection of critical essays, including a brief recapitulation of his life by Gouhier, see *Auguste Comte—Qui êtes-vous?* (Lyons: La Manufacture, 1988).

32. Auguse Comte, *The Positive Philosophy of Auguste Comte,* trans. Harriet Martineau (London: Trubner, 1853); cited in Henry Aiken, ed., *The Age of Ideology* (New York: Mentor, 1956), 124.

33. Auguste Comte, *Testament avec les documents qui s'y rapportent* (Paris, 1896), 146. This recollection, written in 1848 does not seem to have exaggerated the significance of the meeting, to judge by the letter Comte wrote the following day; see *Testament,* 247–250. For Comte's religious doctrine see the collection of his work edited by Gertrud Lenzer, *Auguste Comte and Positivism—The Essential Writings* (New York: Harper, 1975), 393–398, 442–476.

34. Henri Gouhier, "La Vie d'Auguste Comte—esquisse," in *Auguste Comte—Qui êtes-vous?,* 70.

35. Steven Vincent, *Pierre-Joseph Proudhon and the Rise of French Republican Socialism* (New York: Oxford University Press, 1984), 81. For an excellent summary of the ambiguity of Proudhon's position see ibid., 102–106. See also: Théodore Ruyssen, "La Religion dans la vie de Proudhon," in *Oeuvres complètes de P.-J. Proudhon—Ecrits sur la religion* (Paris: Rivière, 1959), 7–76; Stock-Morton, *Moral Education,* 62–68. For Proudhon's reference to himself as an antitheist rather than an atheist see *Ecrits sur la religion,* 217.

36. On Blanqui see Maurice Dommanget, *Les Idées politiques et sociales d'Auguste Blanqui* (Paris: Rivière, 1957), 271–303 and Alan Spitzer, *The Revolution-*

ary Theories of Louis-Auguste Blanqui (New York: Columbia, 1957), 29, 47–64. In his last years Blanqui developed a theory in which he proposed that events on earth, including the details of individual lives, are repeated infinite numbers of times in a material universe of infinite extent; see A. Blanqui, *L'Éternité par les astres* (Paris: Baillière, 1872). This text is discussed in Stanley Jaki, *Science and Creation—From Eternal Cycles to an Oscillating Universe* (New York: Science History Publications, 1974), 314–318. On Cabet see Christopher Johnson, *Utopian Communism in France—Cabet and the Icarians, 1839–1851* (Ithaca: Cornell University Press, 1974), 95.

37. See Bertocci, *Jules Simon*, 94–104.

38. Gayot, *Franc-Maçonnerie française*, 31, 226–237; Stock-Morton, *Moral Education*, 68–72.

39. Katherine Auspitz, *The Radical Bourgeoisie—The Ligue de l'Enseignement and the Origins of the Third Republic, 1866–1885* (Cambridge: Cambridge University Press, 1982); Stock-Morton, *Moral Education*, 73–75, 114–122.

40. Extensive excerpts from Ferry's speeches to the Masons can be found in Pierre Chevallier, *La Séparation de l'église et l'école* (Paris: Fayard, 1981), 88–100.

41. René Rémond, *L'Anticléricalisme en France de 1815 à nos jours* (Brussels: Comlexe, 1985; first published 1976), 192.

42. For a summary of the debates on this issue see Louis Capéran, *Histoire contemporaine de la laïcité française*, vol. 2, *La Révolution scolaire* (Paris: Rivière, 1960).

43. *JO Sénat*, 3 July 1881, 1002.

44. For a detailed review of the parliamentary debates and maneuvering see Chevallier, *La Séparation de l'église de l'école*, 319–338. For Simon's last speech defending religious instruction see *JO Débats*, 12 March 1882, 170–174. Chevallier, *La Séparation*, and Louis Capéran, *Histoire de la laïcité républicaine: La laïcité en marche* (Paris: Nouvelle Editions Latines, 1961) 243–254, see Ferry as duplicitous in the debate over moral instruction.

45. Ernest Renan, *L'Avenir de la science*, in *Oeuvres complètes* (Paris: Calmann-Lévy, 1949), 3:991–992.

46. Ibid., 992–993. For an example of the kind of cynical manipulation of the afterlife condemned by Renan see the remarks of the materialist Senator in Victor Hugo, *Les Misérables*, trans. Charles Wilbour (New York: Random House Modern Library, n.d.; first published, 1862). "[I]t is necessary there should be something for those who are below us, the bare-foots, knifegrinders, and other wretches. Legends and chimeras are given them to swallow, about the soul, immortality, paradise, and the stars. They munch that; they spread it on their dry bread. He who has nothing besides, has the good God—that is the least good he can have. . . . The good God is good for the people (27)."

47. The Catholic writer Ernest Hello described this paradox in *M. Renan, l'Allemagne, et l'athéisme au XIXe siècle* (Paris: Douniol, 1859). See also Charlton, *Secular Religions*, 106–113. Renan's own description of his youth, much of which was spent in Catholic seminaries, is beautifully recalled in his *Souvenirs d'enfance et de jeunesse* (Paris: Gallimard, 1983; first published 1883).

48. For a brief introduction to these criticisms see J. Alexander Gunn, *Modern French Philosophy* (London: Fisher Unwin, 1922), 110–131. The

flattering preface to this book written by Bergson suggests its accurate representation of his position. See also Harry Paul, *The Edge of Contingency* (Gainesville: University of Florida Press, 1979). Roger Martin du Gard, *Jean Barois*, provides an excellent introduction to the personal and professional troubles experienced by convinced positivists during the early twentieth century.

49. Georges Clemenceau, *In the Evening of My Thought*, 2 vols., trans. Charles Thompson and John Heard (New York: Houghton-Mifflin, 1929). For Clemenceau's analysis of death see 2:479–523.

50. Cited in Stock-Morton, *Moral Education*, vi, 174. For an extensive treatment of the ideas of Buisson and others who advocated a morality independent of religion see Clive Castaldo, *La Foi Laïque and Its Critics: Secular Humanism After the Dreyfus Affair* (Ph.D. diss., Cambridge University, 1985).

51. Emile Durkheim, *Moral Education* (New York: Free Press, 1973), 3.

52. Ibid., 248.

53. Ibid., 79

54. On Durkheim's moral theory see Stock-Morton, *Moral Education*, 139–153; Auspitz, *The Radical Bourgeoisie*, 171–175.

55. The political and social implications of the cult of the dead as developed over the past three centuries are treated in a number of the essays in the recent collections edited by Pierre Nora. Although the work of Nora and his collaborators is scholarly in its design and presentation, it can also be seen as the latest manifestation of the cult of the dead that it examines. See Mona Ozouf, "Le Panthéon—l'École normale des morts," in Pierre Nora, ed., *Les lieux de mémoire*, vol. 1, *La République* (Paris: Gallimard, 1984), 139–166; Jean-Claude Bonnet, "Les Morts illustres—Oraison funèbre, éloge académique, nécrologie," in Pierre Nora, ed., *Les lieux de mémoire*, vol. 2, pt. 3, *La Nation* (Paris: Gallimard, 1986), 217–241; June Hargrove, "Les Statues de Paris," in ibid., 243–282. For an overview of the political uses made of funerals from the revolution through the Third Republic see Ben-Amos, *Molding the National Memory*. For the revolution see also Albert Soboul, "Sentiment religieux et cultes populaires pendant la révolution: Saintes, patriotes et martyrs de la liberté," *Archives de sociologie des religions* 1 (1956): 73–87.

56. Ben-Amos, *Molding the National Memory*, 215.

57. Auguste Comte, *Catéchisme positiviste* (Paris: Garnier-Flammarion, 1966), 182. The priests of the Religion of Humanity would be charged with the administration of the sacrament and, in exceptional cases, would designate those who were unworthy to be placed in the "desert of the condemned."

58. Mona Ozouf, "Le Panthéon—l'École normale des morts"; Kselman, "Funeral Conflicts in Nineteenth-Century France."

59. Jean Tulard, "Le Retour des Cendres," in *Les Lieux de mémoire*, vol. 2, pt. 3, *La Nation*, ed. Pierre Nora (Paris: Gallimard, 1986), 81–110.

60. Maurice Agulhon, "La 'Statuomanie' et l'histoire," *Ethnologie française* 8 (1978): 145–172; William Cohen, "Symbols of Power: Statues in Nineteenth-Century Provincial France," *Comparative Studies in Society and History* 31 (1989): 491–513. Ben-Amos, *Molding the National Memory*. The socialists also

made substantial contributions to the civil cult of the dead; see Hutton, *The Cult of the Revolutionary Tradition*, 51–58, 119–142.

61. Ralph Giesey, *The Royal Funeral Ceremony in Renaissance France* (Geneva: Droz, 1960).

62. Auguste Comte, *Testament*, includes the daily prayers and all the confessions, as well as a selection of the correspondence between Comte and Mme de Vaux.

63. Ernest Renan, *The Life of Jesus* (New York: Random House, 1927; first published 1867).

64. R. Laurence Moore, *In Search of White Crows—Spiritualism, Parapsychology, and American Culture* (New York: Oxford University Press, 1977); Janet Oppenheim, *The Other World—Spiritualism and Psychical Research in England, 1850–1914* (New York: Cambridge University Press, 1985). On English spiritualism see also: Logie Barrow, *Independent Spirits—Spiritualism and English Plebians, 1850–1910* (New York: Routledge and Kegan Paul, 1986); Alex Owen, *The Darkened Room: Women, Power and Spiritualism in Late Victorian England* (London: Virago, 1989). For a survey of the movement that concentrates on revealing the fraudulent practices of the mediums see Ruth Brandon, *The Spiritualists* (New York: Knopf, 1983).

65. Oppenheim, *The Other World*, 59.

66. Paris was the site, in 1900, of a "Congrès spirite et spiritualiste" that drew an international audience, including the biologist Alfred Russell Wallace, the British scientist credited along with Darwin for discovering the principle of natural selection. See *Le Temps*, 19 September 1900, 4.

67. Henri Bergson, "Fantômes de vivantes," in *Melanges* (Paris: PUF, 1972), 1002–1019. For Bergson's involvement with the controversial medium Eusapia Palladino see ibid., 673–674.

68. For the occult aspects of the Enlightenment see Robert Darnton, *Mesmerism and the Enlightenment in France* (New York: Schocken, 1970); Auguste Viatte, *Les Sources occultes du Romantisme*, vol. 1 (Paris: Champion, 1965); Clark Garrett, *Respectable Folly—Millenarianism and the French Revolution in France and England* (Baltimore: Johns Hopkins University Press, 1975). On spirit possession see Clark Garrett, *Spirit Possession and Popular Religion—From the Camisards to the Shakers* (Baltimore: Johns Hopkins University Press, 1987). For the Renaissance see D.P. Walker, *Spiritual and Demonic Magic—From Ficino to Campanella* (Notre Dame: University of Notre Dame Press, 1975).

69. The expansion of knowledge about Eastern religions constitutes another strain of thought that helps explain the emergence of spiritism. A review of the index in the basic work by Raymond Schwab, *The Oriental Renaissance—Europe's Discovery of India and the East, 1680–1880* (New York: Columbia University Press, 1984; first published in French, 1950) suggests that virtually every thinker considered in this chapter was influenced by the texts of Indian religion that began appearing in the late eighteenth century and that gave added support to the doctrine of metempsychosis. Alphonse de Lamartine was strongly influenced by these materials, as can be seen in his *Opinions sur Dieu, le bonheur, et l'éternité d'après les livres sacrés de l'inde*

(Paris: Sand, 1984; first published 1856). Herbert Juin's introduction to this volume provides a brief summary of the translation and reception of Eastern texts in the first half of the nineteenth century. For the career of Anquetil-Duperron, whose translations of the Upanishads began appearing in 1786, see Jean-Luc Kieffer, *Anquetil-Duperron—L'Inde en France au XVIIIe siècle* (Paris: Les Belles Lettres, 1983).

70. Jules Fleury, *Souvenirs et portraits de jeunesse* (Paris, 1872), 132–133. On Hoene-Wroński (1776–1853), see Andrzej Walicki, *Philosophy and Romantic Nationalism: The Case of Poland* (Oxford: Clarendon Press, 1982), 107–121.

71. *Oeuvres complètes de Charles Baudelaire—Traductions: Histoires extraordinaires par Edgar Poe* (Paris: Conard, 1932), 269–283, 456.

72. For general treatments of the Romantic era and its religious preoccupations see Bénichou, *Le Temps des prophètes*; Abrams, *Natural Supernaturalism*; Georges Gusdorf, *Du néant à Dieu dans le savoir romantique* (Paris: Payot, 1983); Bernard M. G. Reardon, *Religion in the Age of Romanticism* (Cambridge: Cambridge University Press, 1985). For a more idiosyncratic view of the period, stressing the importance of concerns about transcendence and the afterlife, see Philippe Muray, *Le 19e Siècle à travers les âges* (Paris: Denoel, 1984). For the influence of spiritual currents on particular authors see Jacques Borel, *Séraphita et le mysticisme balzacien* (Paris: Corti, 1967); Auguste Viatte, *Victor Hugo et les illuminés de son temps* (Montréal: Les Editions de l'Arbre, 1942).

73. William H. Sewell, *Work and Revolution in France—The Language of Labor from the Old Regime to 1848* (Cambridge: Cambridge University Press, 1980); Bernard Moss, *The Origins of the French Labor Movement: The Socialism of Skilled Workers, 1830–1914* (Berkeley: University of California Press, 1976); Christopher Johnson, *Utopian Communism in France*.

74. Edward Berenson, *Populist Religion and Left-Wing Politics in France, 1830–1852* (Princeton: Princeton University Press, 1984).

75. Alphonse Esquiros, *De la vie future au point de vue socialiste* (Paris: Comon, 1850). For a recent study of Esquiros's literary work see Anthony Zielonka, *Alphonse Esquiros (1812–1876)—A Study of His Works* (Paris: Champion-Slatkine, 1985). For biographical details see J. P. Van der Linden, *Alphonse Esquiros, de la bohème romantique à la république sociale* (Paris: Nizet, 1948).

76. Esquiros, *De la vie future*, 110.

77. Ibid., 119, 121.

78. Jonathan Beecher, *Charles Fourier—The Visionary and His World* (Berkeley: University of California Press, 1986), 318–352. For a concise presentation of his ideas about immortality see Charles Fourier, *Théorie de l'Unité Universelle*, in *Oeuvres complètes* (Paris, 1841), 3:304–346. Michel Nathan, in *Le Ciel des Fourièrists—Habitants des étoiles et réincarnations de l'âme* (Lyon: Presses Universitaires de Lyon, 1981), traces the influence of Fourier on later thinkers. Some Catholic thinkers were pursuing similar lines of thought during this period, including the influential philospher Ballance. See Bernard Reardon, *Liberalism and Tradition: Aspects of Catholic Thought in Nineteenth-Century France* (Cambridge: Cambridge University Press, 1975), 56.

79. *Théorie de l'Unité Universelle* in *Oeuvres complètes* (Paris, 1841), 3:309.

80. Fourier's dependance on an argument that moves from the subjective experience of a human sentiment to an affirmation of a supernatural truth identifies him with a Romantic theological tradition that can be seen clearly in the work of Chateaubriand. Fourier's argument here resembles Chateaubriand's defense of the immortality of the soul; see *Génie du christianisme* (Paris: Flammarion, 1966; first published 1802), 1:197–220.

81. Ralph Locke, *Music, Musicians, and the Saint-Simonians* (Chicago: University of Chicago Press, 1986), 65–66, 116, 335 n. 28.

82. Jules Michelet, *Mother Death—The Journal of Jules Michelet, 1815–1850*, 73. Jean Reynaud, *Terre et ciel* (Paris: Furne, 1854). This book went through three editions in the 1850s and was considered serious enough to be condemned by a church council at Périgueux in 1857. See Jean Reynaud, *Réponse au concile de Périgueux* (Paris: Furne, 1858).

83. Jacques Viard, *Pierre Leroux et les socialistes européens* (Paris: Actes Sud, 1982); Viard, "Les Origines du socialisme républicain," *Revue d'histoire moderne et contemporaine* 33 (1986): 133–147. For Leroux's role as cofounder of the influential journal *Le Globe* see Spitzer, *The French Generation of 1820*, 97–128. For the influence of Leroux on writers including George Sand and Victor Hugo see David Owen Evans, *Le Socialisme romantique—Pierre Leroux et ses contemporains* (Paris: Rivière, 1948).

84. Pierre Leroux, *De l'humanité, de son principe, et de son avenir* (Paris: Perrotin, 1840).

85. Leroux, *De l'humanité*, 1:242.

86. Ibid., 244.

87. Ibid., 289–290.

88. Garrett, *Respectable Folly*, 106–109; Viatte, *Les Sources occultes du romantisme*, 1:71–103; Darnton, *Mesmerism*, 132. For a selection of his work in English see George F. Dole, ed., *Emmanuel Swedenborg—The Universal Human and Soul-Body Interaction* (New York: Paulist Press, 1984). McDannell and Lang have now provided an able summary of Swedenborg's system in *Heaven: A History*, 181–227. See also Borel, *Séraphita et le mysticisme balzacien*, 129–160.

89. *L'Apocalypse réveilée*, trans. J. P. Moet and J.A.T. Tull (Paris: Treuttel et Wurtz, 1823).

90. *Arcanes célèstes*, 7 vols. (St. Amande et Paris, 1841–1854).

91. *L'Apocalypse réveilée* (St. Amande et Paris, 1856), 1:153.

92. Cited in Borel, *Séraphita et le mysticisme balzacien*, 143.

93. Darnton, *Mesmerism*, 67–72; Viatte, *Victor Hugo et les illuminés*, 10–25.

94. An initial report to the Academy of Medicine in 1831 had been favorable, but skeptics succeeded in preventing its publication. See: Elie Méric, *Le Merveilleux et la science—Étude sur l'hypnotisme* (Paris: Letouzey, 1887), 143–155; Darnton, *Mesmerism*; Christopher McIntosh, *Eliphas Lévi and the French Occult Revival* (New York: Weiser, 1974), 54–55.

95. Marie-Anne-Adélaïde Lenormand, *Les Oracles sibyllins* (Paris: chez l'auteur, 1817); Lenormand, *Arrêt suprème des dieux d'olympe* (Paris: chez l'auteur, 1833). For a review of Mlle Lenormand's early career see Jean Mabire, "Marie

Lenormand, devineresse—Les Habiletés d'une 'grosse normande,' " *Historia* 466 (October 1985): 90–96.

96. Viatte, *Victor Hugo et les illuminés de son temps*, 33–53; Frank Paul Bowman, "Illuminism, Utopia, Mythology," in *The French Romantics*, ed. D.G. Charlton (Cambridge: Cambridge University Press, 1984), 1:8; Borel, *Séraphita et le mysticisme balzacien*.

97. Louis Alphonse Cahagnet, *Arcanes de la vie future dévoilés* (Paris: Baillière, 1848).

98. Emma Hardinge Britten, *Nineteenth Century Miracles* (New York: Lovell, 1884), 42–44.

99. For the history of spiritism see Jean Vartier, *Allan Kardec—La Naissance du Spiritisme* (Paris: Hachette, 1971). David Hess provides a useful discussion of the context of the French movement in *Spirits and Scientists: Ideology, Spiritism, and Brazilian Culture* (University Park: Pennsylvania State University Press, 1991). Hess's concern with French spiritism, and particularly with Allan Kardec, is based on the importance of the movement in modern Brazil, where Kardec's version of spiritism is a major force in the religious life of the country. For critical comments on the movement from contemporaries see: Emile Littré, "Du tables parlantes, des esprits frappeurs et autres manifestations de ce temps-ci," *Revue des deux mondes* 1 (1856): 847–872; Adrien Delandre, "La Magie et les magiciens au XIXe siècle," *Revue contemporaine* 32 (1857): 5–32, 251–284; for the responses of the Church see Abbé J. Cognat, "De l'évocation des esprits," *L'Ami de la religion* 163 (14 January 1854): 109–115; Louis Veuillot, *L'Univers*, 26 July 1852; P. A. Matignon, S.J., *Les Morts et les vivants* (Paris: Le Clère, 1863).

100. For a complete edition of the texts and a useful introduction by Jean and Sheila Gaudin see Victor Hugo, *Oeuvres complètes*, ed. Jean Massin, vol. 9, pt. 2 (Paris: Le Club Français du Livre, 1971), 1167–1492. For a brief narrative of the events see Hubert Juin, *Victor Hugo, 1844–1870* (Paris: Flammarion, 1984), 297–329. Hugo's experiments are also treated in Maurice Levaillant, *La Crise mystique de Victor Hugo (1843–1856)* (Paris: Corti, 1954).

101. For the fears that the tables would distract the Hugo circle from its political responsibilities see Hugo, *Oeuvres complètes*, vol. 9, pt. 2, 1185.

102. Ian Dowbiggin, "French Psychiatry and the Search for a Professional Identity: The Société Médico-Psychologique, 1840–1870," *Bulletin of the History of Medecine* 63 (1989): 350–351. Dowbiggin cites an article by Baillarger and Brierre de Boismont, "D'une tendance particulière de l'esprit au merveilleux à l'époque des grands commotions," *Annales médico-psychologiques* (1853): 711–715; see also Henri Ellenberger, *The Discovery of the Unconscious: The History and Evolution of Dynamic Psychiatry* (New York: Basic Books, 1970), 225–226.

103. For the connection between Fourier and *Démocratie pacifique* see the edition of 8 April 1847. One of Edgar Allan Poe's first stories to appear in France was also published in this paper; see "Le Chat noir," *Démocratie pacifique*, 27 January 1847. For the experiments of the editors see Eugène Nus, *Choses de l'autre monde*, 5th ed. (Paris: Librairie des sciences psychologiques et spirites, n.d.). Another editor of the paper, Victor Hennequin, was also converted to spiritism and became a militant advocate of the movement

in the 1850s; see Nathan, *Le Ciel des fourièrists*. Although there is no evidence that he consulted mediums, Alphonse de Lamartine, in *Opinions sur Dieu, le bonheur, et l'éternité*, published in 1856, also found consolation for his recent political failure by contemplating the ideas about human struggle and immortality that he found in the literature of the Orient.

104. Hugo, *Oeuvres complètes*, vol. 9, pt. 2, 1233. See also Victor Hugo, *Les Contemplations* (Paris: Gallimard, 1973; first published, 1856), in which Hugo presents his ideas about expiation and reincarnation.

105. Hugo, *Ouevres complètes*, vol. 9, pt. 2, 1170.

106. Ibid., 1174. See also Léon-Paul Fargue, preface of Victor Hugo, *Les Contemplations*, 16: "The revelations of the turning tables . . . taught Hugo nothing which he didn't already know; the spirits limited themselves to repeating dogmas from the 'religion' that Hugo had already developed, and which he was in the process of completing and explaining, and which resembles the 'religions' which were constructed throughout this half-century in the zone where utopian socialism met the occult."

107. Hugo, *Oeuvres complètes*, vol. 9, pt. 2, 1181, 1255.

108. Hugo, *Les Contemplations*. See in particular "Pleurs dans la nuit (306–328)" and "Ce que dit la bouche d'ombre (386–409.)"

109. Hugo wrote on 17 December 1854: "*Ce monde sublime veut rester sublime; mais ne veut pas devenir exact, ou du moins il veut que son exactitude sublime ne nous apparaisse qu'énorme et confuse dans de prodigieuses échappées d'ombre et de lumière; il veut être notre vision et non notre science. . . . Dès que nous commençons à voir un peu distinctement, le monde mysterieux se ferme. Il faut que nous ne soyons surs de rien, c'est là l'expiation humaine. Chaque fois que l'homme, submergé à vau-l'eau dans les ténèbres, ruisselant de toutes les écumes de l'abime et de la nuit, parvient à se cramponner au bord de la barque de foi et sort de l'obscurité à mi-corps, l'ombre qui est dans la barque lui fait lacher prise, et le rejette au gouffre, et lui dit: Va, homme, lutte, souffre, roule, nage, doute! E pur si muove! Et pourtant je crois! et pourtant je crois! et pourtant je crois! a toi, mon âme, a vous, mon Dieu!*" Hugo, *Oeuvres complètes*, vol. 9, pt. 2, 1178.

110. *Lettres familières de l'Impératrice* (Paris: Le Divan, 1935), 1:141–142; Dr. E. Barthez, *The Empress Eugénie and her Circle* (New York: Brentano's, 1913), 137–143.

111. According to Flaubert, the popularity of the turning tables was encouraged by the press that reported the events as a serious matter. See *Bouvard et Pécuchet* (Paris: Gallimard, 1979), 277–301. Spiritism and the related systems of Swedenborgianism and mesmerism also were frequent elements in the popular genre of the *conte fantastique*. See Pierre-Georges Castex, *Le Conte fantastique en France de Nodier à Maupassant* (Paris: Corti, 1982).

112. For a brief description of the Davenports' performances see Arthur Conan Doyle, *The History of Spiritualism* (New York: Doran, 1926), 211–229. Doyle, of course, was an advocate of the Davenports, but his remarks are nonetheless of interest, for he points out that their public performances marked an important stage in the diffusion of the movement to a mass audience.

113. *Le Temps*, 19 September 1865, 1.

114. Vartier, *Allan Kardec*, 27–39; Yvonne Castellan, *Le spiritisme*, 5th ed. (Paris: Presses Universitaires de France, 1974).

115. According to the *Catalogue des imprimés* of the Bibliothèque Nationale, *Le Livre des esprits* went through thirty-five editions between 1857 and 1889. For an extensive analysis of the content see Hess, *Spirits and Scientists*, 59–79. According to Hess *Le Livre des esprits* can be seen as a kind of "Pestalozzian textbook." A condensed version of this work, published as *Qu'est-ce que le spiritisme* went through fourteen editions between 1859 and 1881. Kardec also published a guide for mediums, *Le Livre des médiums*, which went through eighteen editions between 1861 and 1885. Other popular works include: *Caractères de la révélation spirite*, thirty-one editions between 1868 and 1881; *L'Evangile selon le spiritisme*, fourteen editions between 1864 and 1880; *Résumé de la loi des phénomènes spirites*, thirty-one editions between 1864 and 1881; and *Le Spiritisme à sa plus simple expression*, thirty-three editions between 1862 and 1884.

116. Camille Flammarion, *Mémoires* (Paris: Flammarion, 1911), 494–498.

117. Flammarion, *Mémoires*.

118. See, for example, Camille Flammarion, *La Pluralité des mondes*, 33d edition (Paris: Flammarion, 1885?), 315–329. For the publishing history of this work, which went through at least thirty editions between 1862 and 1882, see Michael Crowe, *The Extraterrestrial Life Debate, 1750–1900* (Cambridge: Cambridge University Press, 1986), 652.

119. Flammarion, *Mémoires*, 298–300, 325–332. See also Crowe, *Extraterrestrial Life Debate*, 378–386, 612–613, who notes that *Astronomie populaire* went through seventy editions by 1885. In *Récits de l'infini*, 11th ed. (Paris: Flammarion, 1885), Flammarion presents his ideas in the form of dialogues between Lumen, a spirit who describes the universe and the afterlife, and his earthbound friend, Quaerens. This work went through twelve editions between 1873 and 1892. Flammarion also published *Les Habitants de l'autre monde* (Paris: Ledoyen, 1862), a work that presents messages from spirits including Socrates, Lammenais, and Delphine de Girardin. See also his *L'Inconnu et les problèmes psychiques: manifestations des mourants, apparitions, télépathie, communications psychiques, suggestion mentale, vue à distance; le monde des rêves, la divination de l'avenir* (Paris: Flammarion, 1900). The title of this work suggests the range of evidence that Flammarion thought could be brought to bear on the question of the afterlife. Flammarion also believed that haunted houses proved the existence of a spirit world, and he engaged in a public controversy with the composer Camille Saint-Saëns, who disputed the possibility of a personal soul, in the *Nouvelle revue*, 15 Dec. 1900. See Flammarion, *Haunted Houses*, (New York: Appleton, 1924). In his final work, *La Mort et son mystère*, 3 vols. (Paris: Flammarion, 1920–1922), Flammarion continued to argue for the existence of an immortal soul on the basis of ghostly apparitions and occult phenomena, which he believed should be understood as natural rather than supernatural manifestations.

120. Another influential figure was Louis Figuier, a doctor who, like Flammarion, gained a reputation as a popularizer of modern science. Following

the death of his son Figuier was converted to spiritism, and his work, *Le Lendemain de la mort, ou la vie future selon la science* (Paris: Hachette, 1871), went through ten editions by 1894. For other works in the tradition of Flammarion and Reynaud see Crowe, *Extraterrestrial Life Debate*, 407–423.

121. Castellan, *Le Spiritisme*, a contemporary apology for spiritism published in the "Que sais-je?" series of the Presses Universitaires de France, treats Kardec as the founder of the movement, as does Vartier, *Allan Kardec*.

122. See, for example, *Le Livre des esprits*, 331, where Kardec comments on a spirit communication: *"L'humanité progresse par les individus qui s'améliorent peu à peu et s'éclairent; alors, quand ceux-ci l'emportent en nombre, ils prennent le dessus et entrainent les autres."* From Kardec's perspective, social progress would result primarily from individual enlightenment rather than collective action.

123. Allan Kardec, "Propagation du Spiritisme," *Revue spirite*, 1858, pt. 1:241. Hess notes the importance of working-class members, especially in Lyon, *Spirits and Scientists*, 61–62.

124. Kardec, *Le Livre des esprits*, 58–62; Allan Kardec, *Qu'est-ce que le Spiritisme?*, 19th ed. (Paris: Librairie des sciences psychologiques, n.d.), 113.

125. Kardec, *Le Livre des esprits*, 88.

126. Ibid., 79–81.

127. Caroline Bynum, "Bodily Self and the Resurrection of the Body in the High Middle Ages," in Thomas Kselman, ed., *Belief in History—Innovative Approaches to European and American Religion* (Notre Dame: University of Notre Dame Press, 1990). See also Caroline Bynum, *Holy Feast and Holy Fast—The Religious Significance of Food to Medieval Women* (Berkeley: University of California Press, 1987), esp. 299–302.

128. Flammarion reveals a similar distaste for corporal existence in his obsessive preoccupation with the image of a female eating, a sight that never failed to disgust his spiritual contacts. Michel Nathan, "Les Métamorphoses de la féminité dans l'oeuvre de Camille Flammarion," in *La Femme au XIXe siècle*, 2d ed. (Lyons: Presses Universitaires de Lyons, 1979), 123–136.

129. On the importance of the sidereal revolution see Crowe, *Extraterresital Life Debate*, 41. Blanqui, *L'Éternité par les astres*, also accepted the existence of life on other planets but not the idea of reincarnation. According to Blanqui, as a result of evolution and the existence of an infintely extended universe, the events of this world were destined to be repeated endlessly on countless other worlds.

130. Oppenheim, *The Other World*, esp. 67–85. In France the Protestant aristocrat Agénor Etienne de Gasparin argued that the evidence from the turning tables confirmed basic Christian doctrine, but Catholics were generally unpersuaded by this position. See Gasparin, *Science vs. Modern Spiritualism: A Treatise on Turning Tables, the Supernatural in General, and Spirits*, trans. E. W. Robert (New York: Kiggins and Kellogg, 1858); Vartier, *Allan Kardec*, 102–107.

131. Flammarion, *Mémoires*, 168–188.

132. Flammarion was active in Jean Macé's anticlerical Ligue de l'Enseignement in the late 1860s; see his *Mémoires*, 384–385. Léon Denis, who succeeded

Kardec as the leader of the spiritist organization, was overtly hostile to Catholicism; see Castellan, *Le Spiritisme*, 70-72.

133. Jules Eudes de Mirville, *Pneumatologie: Des esprits et de leurs manifestations fluidiques*, 6 vols. (Paris: Vrayet de Surcy, 1863-1864). On Mirville see Vartier, *Allan Kardec*, 93-102. For the psychiatrists see Dowbiggin, "French Psychiatry," 351.

134. Vartier, *Allan Kardec*, 263-275; Abbé Henry Bolo, *Nos communications avec les morts*, 6th ed. (Paris: Haton, 1903), 75-82.

135. *Le Temps*, 18 July 1899, p. 2.

136. Brandon, *The Spiritualists*, 96-97, 132-147. Charles Richet, "Du somnambulisme provoqué," *Revue philosophique de la France et de l'étranger* 5 (1880): 337-374, 462-484. The *Revue philosophique* in the 1880s gave extensive coverage to the experiments of the English Society of Psychic Research; see Méric, *Le Merveilleux et la science*, 321-323.

137. A. Girard and J. Stoetzel, "Les Français et les valeurs du temps présent," *Revue française de sociologie* (January-March, 1985): 3-31. Jean Prieur has presented and defended spiritist beliefs in a number of works; see, for example, *Les Témoins de l'invisible* (Paris: Fayard, 1972), a work for which Gabriel Marcel agreed to write a preface. See also Hélène Renard, *L'Après-Vie* (Paris: Philippe Lebaud, 1985).

138. For a brief introduction to these questions see Dominick La Capra, *History and Criticism* (Ithaca: Cornell University Press, 1985). For a collection of essays on the theory and practice of the new intellectual history see Dominick La Capra and Steven Kaplan, *Modern European Intellectual History* (Ithaca: Cornell University Press, 1982). Michael Ermath, "Mindful Matters: The Empire's New Codes and the Plight of Modern Intellectual History," *Journal of Modern History* 57 (1985): 506-527 offers a critical and somewhat hostile appraisal of the new approaches. For a more sympathetic reading of a number of recent works in the field see John Toews, "Intellectual History after the Linguistic Turn: The Autonomy of Meaning and the Irreducibility of Experience," *American Historical Review* 92 (1987): 879-907.

139. Flammarion, *La Mort et son mystère*, 1:19, reports having received 4,106 letters between 1899 and 1919, many of which were reproduced in this three-volume work.

140. "Confessions d'un curé de village," in *De la vie future*, 9-59.

141. Nathan, *Ciel des fouriéristes*, 32.

142. *Conte fantastique*, 8.

143. *Introduction à la littérature fantastique* (Paris: Seuil, 1970), 29.

144. For some recent collections of these see: Charles Nodier, *La Fée aux Miettes, Smarra, Trilby* (Paris: Gallimard, 1982); Prosper Mérimée, *Carmen* (Paris: Flammarion, 1973), which includes the *conte fantastique*, "Les Ames du Purgatoire"; Théophile Gautier, *La Morte amoureuse, avatar, et autre récits fantastiques* (Paris: Gallimard, 1981); Guy de Maupassant, *Contes fantastiques complets* (Paris: Marabout, 1983).

145. Baudelaire, *Histoires extraordinaires par Edgar Poe*.

146. Théophile Gautier, "La cafetière," in *La Morte amoreuse*, 47-57. This story first appeared in *Le Cabinet de lecture*, 4 May 1831.

147. Flammarion, *Récits de l'infini; L'Inconnu, La Mort et son mystère*.

148. Robert Isherwood, *Farce and Fantasy: Popular Entertainment in Eighteenth-Century Paris* (New York: Oxford University Press, 1986), 51–55.

CHAPTER FIVE

1. Madeleine Rebérioux, "Le Mur des Fédéres," in *Les Lieux de mémoire*, ed. Pierre Nora, vol. 1, *La République* (Paris: Gallimard, 1984), 619–649. For the habits of contemporary Parisians, who continue to visit their cemeteries, see Jane Kramer, "Letter from Europe," *The New Yorker*, 20 May 1985, 102. For an evocative essay see Frederick Brown, *Père Lachaise—Elysium as Real Estate* (New York: Viking, 1973).

2. Nicole Bossut, "Aux origines de la déchristianisation dans la Nièvre: Fouché, Chaumette, ou les Jacobins?" *Annales historiques de la Révolution française* 264 (1986): 181–202; Richard Etlin, *The Architecture of Death—The Transformation of the Cemetery in Eighteenth-Century Paris* (Cambridge: MIT Press, 1984), 236–238. For the adoption of a similar measure in Beauvais see Maurice Dommanget, "La Déchristianisation à Beauvais, les sacrements civiques," *Annales révolutionnaires* 11 (1919), 181–188.

3. Emmet Kennedy, *A Cultural History of the French Revolution* (New Haven: Yale University Press, 1989), 206–212; Michel Ragon, *The Space of Death: A Study of Funerary Architecture, Decoration, and Urbanism* (Charlottesville: University Press of Virginia, 1983), 221–224. The scene is also described by John McManners, *Death and the Enlightenment* (New York: Oxford University Press, 1981), 353–354. The desecration of the royal tombs was used by Chateaubriand to illustrate the contempt for the dead that he believed was characteristic of the Enlightenment and the revolution. See *Génie du christianisme*, 2 vols. (Paris: Garnier/Flammarion, 1966), 2:99–101.

4. Daniel Ligou, "L'Evolution des cimetières," *Archives de sciences sociales des religions* 39 (1975): 72.

5. Etlin, *The Architecture of Death*, 238. For similar sentiments see the pamphlet written by the revolutionary commissioners of Lyon in 1794, *Les Commissaires aux inhumations, aux citoyens maire et officiers municipaux de Commune-Affranchie* (Lyons, 1794).

6. G. G. Delamalle, *Réflexions sur l'enterrement de ma mère*, 2d ed. (Paris: Librairie Chrétienne, an IV [1796]), 5. This pamphlet has also been used by Etlin, *The Architecture of Death*, 246; for similar descriptions see Ariès, *The Hour of Our Death* 504–506; Chateaubriand, *Génie du christianisme*, 2:95–96, n. 2.

7. Madeleine Fosil, "Les Attitudes devant la mort au XVIIIe siècle: Sépultures et suppressions de sépultures dans le cimetière parisien des Saint-Innocents," *Revue historique* 510 (1974): 303–330; John Freeman and Roger Williams, *How Modernity Came to a Provençal Town—Citizens and Clergy of Grasse* (Lewiston, N.Y.: Mellen, 1988), 130–136; Etlin, *The Architecture of Death*, 22–26; Ariès, *The Hour of Our Death*, 479–496.

8. Ligou, "L'Evolution des cimetières," 72–73.

9. Ozouf, "Le Panthéon," 139–166.

10. Jacques-Michel Coupé, *Des sépultures en politique et en morale* (Paris: Imprimerie Nationale, Thermidor an IV [1796]), 10.

11. P.B.F. Bontoux, *Des devoirs á rendre aux morts* (Paris: Imprimerie Nationale, Prairial, an IV [1796]), 3. For other public statements condemning the current state of cemeteries see Etlin, *The Architecture of Death*, 251–253.

12. Coupé, *Des sépultures*, 5.

13. Bontoux referred to the funeral monuments destroyed by Fouché as "the sweet illusions of hope." (*Devoirs*, 3.) Coupé, in *Des sépultures*, 5, writes that "nature has given us some illusions, and . . . a sound policy knows how to make use of them." A few pages later he argued that people be permitted to pray for the dead, "to console themselves in their fugitive existence . . . through their illusions." (Coupé, *Des sépultures*, 9.)

14. Jacques Coupé, *De la moralité des sépultures et de leur police* (Paris: Vallant, an IX [1801]), 20.

15. The prefect of Maine-et-Loire expressed this fear in a letter to his subprefects in 1805 concerning epidemics: "I remind you on this subject of the necessity of strictly enforcing the imperial decree on cemeteries, especially the provisions on placement and the renewal of graves. It will be sufficient for me to observe that the gas released by cadavers is an extremely energetic and dangerous poison, and that of all the emanations that harm the air and compromise public health, none is perhaps as dangerous as those from burial sites." See ADML, 46 M 1, letter of prefect of Maine-et-Loire to subprefects, 10 messidor, year XIII.

16. Etlin, *The Architecture of Death*, 299. The opening of new cemeteries had been discussed throughout the 1790s; see ibid., 249–250. See also Léon Vafflard, *Notice sur les champs des sépultures anciennes et modernes de la ville de Paris* (Paris: Librairie Internationale, 1867), 16–25.

17. Montmartre was originally opened in 1798, but its poor condition led to its closing for several years prior to the definitive reopening in 1825; see Etlin, *The Architecture of Death*, 251.

18. Jules Michelet, *Histoire de la Révolution française* (Paris: Laffont, 1979), 2:842–848. In the 1790s citizens from the second arrondissement complained about the closing of the cemetery of Monceau in favor of St. Roch; see ADS, VD* 3538–3547. The decision to open the cemetery of Montmartre in 1798 was designed to resolve the conflict between these two neighborhoods; see Etlin, *The Architecture of Death*, 250.

19. François Lebrun, *Les Hommes et la mort en Anjou aux 17e et 18e siècles* (Paris: Mouton, 1971), 484–486; F. Uzureau, "Les Cimetières d'Angers," *L'Anjou historique* 24 (1924): 132–136. For the opening of cemeteries in Orléans, Nantes, Tours, and Rouen, see: *Notice historique sur l'ancien grand cimetière et sur les cimetières actuels de la ville d'Orléans* (Orléans, 1824); Marcel Launay, "Le Cimetière comme élément de la nouvelle sensibilité funèbre au XIXe siècle: Un Exemple nantais," *Bulletin de la Société archéologique et historique de Nantes et de Loire-Atlantique* 119 (1983): 180; Madeleine Lasserre, "La Loi et les morts: La Difficile Création du cimetière général de Tours au XIXe siècle," *Annales de Bretagne et des Pays de l'Ouest* 98 (1991): 303–312; Jean-Pierre Chaline, *Les Bourgeois de Rouen: Une Élite urbaine au XIXe siècle* (Paris: Presses

de la Fondation nationale des sciences politiques, 1982), 287. In Provence new cemeteries were created in most cities during the Restoration or in the early years of the July Monarchy; see Régis Bertrand and Michel Vovelle, *La Ville des morts—Essai sur l'imaginaire d'après les cimetières provençaux* (Paris: CNRS, 1983), 24.

20. Archives municipales d'Angers (henceforth AMA), DD 16.

21. AMA 37 M 1, Report of the mayor to the prefect, 1808. Rouen also went through a second stage of *translation*; see Chaline, *Les Bourgeois de Rouen*, 287–288.

22. Lebrun, *Les Hommes et la mort*, 173–174; Serge Chassagne, "Une Ville provinciale à l'heure de la croissance (1815–1901)," in *Histoire d'Angers*, ed. F. Lebrun (Paris: Privat, 1975), 203–207, 224, 230. The location of the Hôtel-Dieu (municipal hospital) and the *hôpital général* (which received the impoverished elderly and abandoned children) in this neighborhood, both of which had high mortality rates, helps explain the high percentage of deaths.

23. Uzureau, "Les Cimetières d'Angers," 133.

24. AMA 37 M 5 (cemetery of Guinefolle), letter of Citizen Michel to the city council, 1806.

25. AMA, 37 M 7, prefect to mayor, 7 August 1802 (19 thermidor an X).

26. AMA, 37 M 7, prefect to mayor, 14 nivoise, an XIII.

27. AMA, 37 M 7, Petition to Prefect of Maine-et-Loire, 13 nivoise, an XIII.

28. AMA 37 M 7, mayor to prefect, 19 nivoise, an XIII; petition of St. Laud to municipal council, 11 May 1808.

29. AMA 37 M 12, letter of curé of St. Maurice to mayor, 15 May 1823. For another criticism of the cemetery "le Clon" see the report that the commissioner of police Chesnau sent to the mayor of Angers, AMA—"Cimetières," report of 30 July 1825.

30. AMA 37 M 10, petition of inhabitants of faubourg St. Michel to minister of interior, 10 November 1828.

31. When the city purchased land for the Cemetery of the East in 1834, it paid almost Fr 10,000 per hectare; for the enlargement of the Cemetery of the West agreed to at the same time the price was only Fr 5,600 per hectare. See AMA 37 M 7, Registre des délibérations du conseil municipal, 11 June 1834.

32. R. Bertrand, "Cimetières marseillais aux XVIIIe et XIXe siècles," *Provence historique* 92 (1973): 217–246, esp. 233. The cemetery of Saint-Charles proved too small to serve the growing city and was closed in 1876; the major cemetery still used in Marseille, Saint-Pierre, was opened in 1853; Bertrand and Vovelle, *La Ville des morts*, 27.

33. AMA 37 M 12, letter of curés of St. Serge and Notre Dame to mayor, undated, probably 1823.

34. Alain Lottin, "Les Morts chassés de la cité—'Lumières et Préjugés': Les Émeutes à Lille et à Cambrai lors du transfert des cimetières," *Revue du Nord* 60 (1978): 73–117.

35. AMA 37 M 12, petition of parishioners of St. Serge and Notre Dame, July 27, 1829. This line of argument carried weight with the prefect, who wrote the mayor that "considerations based on religious morale might argue

in favor of conserving this burial place." AMA 37 M 12, letter of prefect of
Maine-et-Loire to mayor of Angers, 13 January 1829.

36. AMA 37 M 12, Letter of curés of St. Serge and Notre Dame to mayor of
Angers, [1823].

37. AMA 37 M 10, petition of inhabitants of faubourg St. Michel to minister of interior, 10 November 1828.

38. AMA 37 M 12, letter of prefect of Maine-et-Loire to mayor of Angers,
17 October 1820; letter of minister of interior to prefect of Maine-et-Loire, 14
January 1823; prefect to mayor, 13 January 1829; prefect to mayor, 26 March
1831. It was the prefect's letter of 1829, which was prompted by a citizens'
petition of 1828, that finally led the city council to vote the closing of the
cemetery of St. Michel.

39. Chassagne, "Une Ville provinciale (1815–1901)," 218–219.

40. AMA 37 M 10, petition from inhabitants of faubourg St. Michel to
mayor, 25 June 1832.

41. AMA 37 M 47, Avis du maire, 4 April 1835; AMA 37 M 1, extract from
register of city-council meeting, 11 June 1834. The relation between epidemic
disease and the closing of cemeteries can also be established for the city of
Pouancé, where an outbreak of dysentery in 1811 led to the creation of a new
burial ground; ADML, 46 M 1, mayor of Pouancé to subprefect, 9 November
1811. For the fear of infection from cemeteries see also ADML, 46 M 1, letter
from prefect of Maine-et-Loire to subprefects, 10 messidor, year XIII.

42. AMA 37 M 1, extract from meeting of city council, 11 June 1834; 37 M
47, Avis du maire, 4 April 1835.

43. AMA 37 M 47, Avis du maire, 4 April 1835.

44. Cimetières communaux—Ordonnance royale—Instructions (Angers, 1844);
Ligou, "L'Évolution des cimetières," 73.

45. AN F19 5532. Circular of prefect of Orne, 14 thermidor, year 12.

46. See for example AN F19 5532, letter of minister of interior to minister
of ecclesiastical affairs, 11 February 1829, and royal ordinance of 15 February
1829, which discuss the petition of the family of Marquis de Dreuz-Brezé for
the right to bury him in the family chapel of the parish church. For another
example of burial in a private chapel see the documents on Charles-Auguste
Leclerc, who was buried in the church at Verzin (Maine-et-Loire) in 1806,
before being exhumed by order of the government; AN F19 5523.

47. ADML 5 V 30, report of lieutenant stationed at Segré, 10 April 1827. In
a letter to the prefect of Maine-et-Loire requesting that the deceased curé
Pierre-Charles Fleury be buried in his parish church, the mayor of Chalonnes
noted that "many exceptions to the law of 23 prairial have been made."
ADML 5 V 30, mayor of Chalonnes to prefect of Maine-et-Loire, 28 September 1826.

48. ADML 7 V, Circular from minister of education and religion to prefects, 14 December 1831. See also F19 5532, "Note pour Monsieur le Garde des
Sceaux sur les inhumations et la translation dans l'églises des restes mortels de personnes décédées depuis plus ou moins temps."

49. Ariès, The Hour of Our Death, 337.

50. Michel Bée, "Les Cimetières de Calvados en 1804," in Mentalités religieuses dans la France de l'ouest aux XIXe et XXe siècles (Caen, 1976), 18–20. Bée

reports, on the basis of a prefectoral study, that one-third of the cemeteries were still within the commune and another third a short distance away.

51. Philippe Boutry, *Prêtres et paroisses au pays du curé d'Ars* (Paris: Cerf, 1986), 153.

52. AN F19 4378, letter from prefect of Pyrénées-Orientales to minister of education and religion, June 1832.

53. P. M. Jones, *Politics and Rural Society* (Cambridge: Cambridge University Press, 1985), 136. Boutry also notes the resistance to *translation* in the department of Ain, *Prêtres et paroisses*, 168–177. Boutry, however, sees this attitude emerging only in the 1860s. For the existence of churchyards in Provençal villages, see Bertrand and Vovelle, *La Ville des morts*, 32–33, who relate this resistance to change to rural depopulation.

54. Claudette Mainzer, *Gustave Courbet, Franc-Comtois: The Early Personal History Paintings* (Ph.D. diss., Ohio State University, 1982), 49–74. For a description of a *translation* of a village cemetery, see Emile Zola, *La Fortune des Rougon* (Paris: Denoel, 1984; first published 1871), 50–51.

55. Jones, *Politics and Rural Society*, 137.

56. Boutry, *Prêtres et paroisses*, 173. For a similar conflict in Anjou see AEA, O—St. Hilaire-St. Florent, which describes a conflict in 1804 between the villages of St. Hilaire and St. Florent over whether or not they would be permitted separate cemeteries.

57. Jones, *Politics and Rural Society*, 136–137; see also his essay, "Parish, Seigneurie and the Community of Inhabitants in Southern Central France During the Eighteenth and Nineteenth Centuries," *Past and Present* 91 (1981): 99–100. For the concept of "memory place" see Pierre Nora, "Entre mémoire et histoire," in *Les Lieux de mémoire, vol. 1, La République*, ed. Pierre Nora (Paris: Gallimard, 1984), xvii–xlii. See also Françoise Zonabend, "Les Morts et les vivants—Le Cimetière de Minot en Chatillonnais," *Etudes rurales* 52 (1973): 7–23; Zonabend *The Enduring Memory—Time and History in a French Village* (Manchester: Manchester University Press, 1984). For the continuing attachment to cemeteries in contemporary Brittany see Badone, *The Appointed Hour*, 131–157.

58. AN F19 5727, "Police des cultes, Clermont-Ferrand," clipping from *Courrier de la Limagne* (Journal de Riom), 28 December 1839. For other examples of clergy-led opposition to new cemeteries see AN F19 5512, documents on 1831 conflict in the village of Vittefleur (Seine-Inférieur); AN F19 4378, documents on the 1849 conflict in the village of Bernard (Vendée); AEA, OP25, documents on the 1835 conflict in the village of Aviré; AEA O—Champtoceaux, documents on the 1859 conflict in this village.

59. Christianne Marcilharcy, *Le Diocèse d'Orléans sous l'épiscopat de Mgr Dupanloup, 1849–1878* (Paris: Plon, 1962), 236. This adaptation of the former churchyard for "*usages profanes*" is also noted by clerical opponents in the department of Ain; see Boutry, *Prêtres et paroisses*, 174–175.

60. Monseigneur Gaume, *The Christian Cemetery in the Nineteenth Century; or The Last War-Cry of the Communists*, trans. from French by Rev. Richard Brennan (New York: Benziger, 1874), 29.

61. AN F19 4378, letter from Mgr Bourret to procureur général, 10 May 1876. The incident is briefly described by Jones, *Politics and Rural Society*, 138.

Jones dates the event on May 26, but the bishop's letter says it occurred on April 26. Mgr Bourret responded to the riot by placing an interdict on the cemetery, which he withdrew only three months later. Boutry points out that the curé d'Ars was instrumental in the decision to move the cemetery out of his town in 1855; see his *Prêtres et paroisses*, 172. For an example of clerical support for a *translation* in Anjou see AEA, O-Montreuil-Bellay, letter from curé to bishop, 22 April 1850.

62. *L'Ami du clergé* 1 (7 August 1879): 550–551; 9 (2 June 1887): 271.

63. *Le Temps*, 15 April 1863, 1.

64. Norbert's painting, *Vue générale de Paris—Prise de l'Observatoire, en ballon, 1855*, can be seen at the Musée d'Orsay, Paris.

65. *Le Temps*, 7 January 1868, 1.

66. David H. Pinkney, *Napoleon III and the Rebuilding of Paris* (Princeton: Princeton University Press, 1958), 145–148; Ariès, *The Hour of Our Death*, 538–547.

67. Maxime du Camp, *Paris—Ses organes, ses fonctions, et sa vie* (Paris: Hachette, 1875), 6:212, 220–224; *Le Temps*, 2 July 1874, 2; *Le Temps*, 6 April 1881, 2.

68. Ariès, *The Hour of Our Death*, 541–545; *Le Temps*, 17 April 1874, 3.

69. Marcel Launay, "Le Cimetière comme élément de la nouvelle sensibilité funèbre au XIXe siècle," 181; Bertrand, "Cimetières marseillais," 244. In Marseille and Grasse city councils were forced to open new cemeteries when the older ones were filled because urban growth made it impossible to extend the existing sites. See Bertrand and Vovelle, *La Ville des morts*, 26–28; Freeman and Williams, *How Modernity Came to a Provençal Town*, 464–468.

70. ADML 7V, petition from Chanzeaux to prefect of Maine-et-Loire, 13 March 1868. Laurence Wylie, ed. *Chanzeaux: A Village in Anjou* (Cambridge: Harvard University Press, 1966).

71. J.-F.-E. Chardouillet, *Les Cimetières de Paris—Sont-ils foyers d'inféction?* (Paris, 1881), cited in Ariès, *The Hour of Our Death*, 540.

72. Alain Corbin, *The Foul and the Fragrant—Odor and the French Social Imagination* (Cambridge: Harvard University Press, 1986), 222–223.

73. Dr. Paul Brouardel, *Sépultures—Projet de revision du décret du 23 prairial an XII* (Paris: Melun, 1896). A copy of this report to the Comité consultatif d'hygiène publique de France is filed in AN F19 4378.

74. Richard Etlin makes a similar point in the conclusion of his important study, *The Architecture of Death*, where he writes that "the cemetery in those times always furnished a landscape, either architectural or horticultural, as well as metaphysical, which reflected the underlying bonds and tensions of social and individual life (368)."

75. Ariès, *The Hour of Our Death*, 56–59, 272–273, 516.

76. Article 4 of the law reads: "*Chaque inhumation aura lieu dans une fosse séparée; chaque fosse qui sera ouverte aura un mètre cinq décimètres à deux mètres de profondeur sur huit décimètres de largeur et sera ensuite remplie de terre bien foulée.*"

77. Article 10 of the law of 23 prairial.

78. Article 11 of the law of 23 prairial, an XII reads: "*Ces concessions ne seront néanmoins accordées qu'à ceux qui offriront de faire des fondations ou donations en*

faveur des pauvres et des hôpitaux, indépendamment d'une somme qui sera donné à la commune, et lorsque ces fondations ou donations auront été autorisées par le Gouvernement, dans les formes accoutumées, sur l'avis des conseils municipaux et la perception des préfets."

79. For a discussion of this policy see Alphonse Esquiros, "Les Cimetières de Paris," *Revue de Paris* (Feb.–Mar. 1844): 261–266; see also Etlin, *The Architecture of Death*, 310–312.

80. J.-A. Dulaure, *Histoire physique, civile et morale de Paris* (Paris: Furne, 1838), 53. In an attempt to limit their sale, the government increased the price of permanent concessions in 1829; see Esquiros, "Les Cimetières de Paris," 264.

81. Etlin, *The Architecture of Death*, 340.

82. Esquiros, "Les Cimetières de Paris," 252.

83. Chaline, *Les Bourgeois de Rouen*, 288; Bertrand, "Cimetières marseillais," 237–238; Bertrand and Vovelle, *La Ville des morts*, 35–38; *Administration des fabriques de la ville d'Angers—Règlement pour les concessions de terrains dans les cimetières* (Angers, 1842). In Angers a sliding scale was adopted, so that the price for every additional square meter increased.

84. AMA 37 M 47, register of city–council meeting, 13 October 1876; AMA—cimetières, concessions in cemeteries, 1889–1893.

85. Bertrand and Vovelle, *La Ville des morts*, 63, 179; Ariès, *The Hour of Our Death*, 517.

86. *Cimetières communaux—Ordonnance royale—Instructions* (Angers, 1844), 75–76. See also the letter of the minister of the interior to prefects, July 1841, printed in Vafflard, *Notice sur les champs de sépultures*, 52–53.

87. *Le Temps*, 7 October 1868, 3.

88. AMA 37 M 47, register of city–council meeting, 13 October 1876. For Père Lachaise see Etlin, *The Architecture of Death*, 360, 367.

89. Ariès, *The Hour of Our Death*, 533–534; Etlin, *The Architecture of Death*, 366–368; Bertrand and Vovelle, *La Ville des morts*, 28–30, 98–101.

90. *Cimetières communaux—Ordonnance royale—Instructions* (Angers, 1844), 79. This understanding of property recalls some of the restrictions common during the ancien régime. See William H. Sewell, *Work and Revolution in France: The Language of Labor from the Old Regime to 1848* (Cambridge: Cambridge University Press, 1980), 114–142, for the shift from this older sense to the modern concept of "absolute private property (115)."

91. *Le Temps*, 12 January 1868, 1. For other articles on this affair see *Le Temps*, 7 January 1868, 1; 15 January 1868, 3; 30 January 1868, 1. See also Pinkney, *Napoleon III and the Rebuilding of Paris*, 69. For a similar case twenty years later see *Le Temps*, 29 January 1888, 3.

92. AMA, Cimetières, letter of Mme Josephine Malton to mayor, 14 February 1874.

93. ADML 7 V 6, letter of Prefect Georges Bordillon to minister of religion, 4 September 1848.

94. Jacques Fernand, *Les Cimetières supprimés* (Paris: Vanier, 1873), filed in AN F19 4379. Edmond and Jules de Goncourt express a similar point of view in their description of the cemetery of Montmartre, *Germinie Lacerteux* (New York: Penguin, 1984; first published 1864), 167–170.

95. Sir Francis Head, *A Faggot of French Sticks or, Paris in 1851* (New York: Putnam, 1852), 455; for similar descriptions see Esquiros, "Les Cimetières de Paris," 269–270; the Goncourts, *Germinie Lacerteux*, 168.

96. Bertrand and Vovelle, *La Ville des morts*, 109–110, 172, 180, present graphs showing the predominance of family concessions in the second half of the century. For a discussion of practices in contemporary Brittany, where families place individual coffins in their vaults, see Badone, *The Appointed Hour*, 138–149. See also Zonabend, "Les Morts et les vivants," for the practice of burying family members on top of each other.

97. John Merriman, "The Demoiselles of the Ariège, 1829–1831," in *1830 in France*, ed. John Merriman (New York: Franklin Watts, 1975), 87–118; Ted Margadant, *French Peasants in Revolt* (Princeton: Princeton University Press, 1979), 45–46.

98. In its first draft of the law of 23 prairial the section de l'intérieur of the conseil d'état suggested that no cult should be able to claim ownership of cemeteries, which were defined as communal property. Those desiring a consecrated burial space could have their grave blessed individually, but the Catholic clergy would not be allowed to bless the entire cemetery, an act that would imply proprietary rights. Although Paris eventually adopted the practice of individually consecrated graves, this proposal was rejected by the Council of State. The law also gave parish councils the right to gather and sell *produits spontanés* (wood, fruit, seeds, etc.) from the cemeteries, a provision that led to frequent arguments between cities and parishes.

99. Léon Baratte, *Rapports de l'autorité civile et de l'autorité religieuse en matière de sépulture* (Le Mans: Drouin, 1904), 115–116.

100. Ligou, "L'Evolution des cimetières," 74–75; Bertrand and Vovelle, *La Ville des morts*, 86–91.

101. AN F19 5514, letter of minister of justice and religion to all bishops, 1 July 1845; ibid., prefect of Aube to minister of education and religion, 16 September 1878, establishes that government policy required a separate burial space only when a religious congregation met regularly at a determined site.

102. Kselman, "Funeral Conflicts in Nineteenth-Century France."

103. See ADML, 5 V 34 for correspondence regarding the issue of creating separate sections in the cemeteries of Maine-et-Loire, which was raised in a number of communes in 1837. For evidence from other departments see AN F19 5514, file on *mort-nés*. See also: AN F19 4378, letter of bishop of Meaux to minister of religion, 10 July 1841; AN F19 5512, letter from prefect of Vosges to subprefects, 18 June 1839. Also in AN F19 4378 see two pamphlets: *Des sépultures* (Epernay: Fiévet, s.d.); *Note sur cette question: Quelle est l'autorité préposée aux lieux de sépulture?* (Epernay: Fiévet, 1838).

104. ADML 5 V 34, letter of minister of justice and religion to prefect of Maine-et-Loire, 21 March 1838.

105. AN F19 5504. None of the funeral conflicts that I discovered in the first half of the nineteenth century in the department of Maine-et-Loire concerned the burial of infants in unconsecrated ground; see Kselman, "Funeral Conflicts."

106. AN F19 5514, file on mort-nés.

107. Visitors to cemeteries in Maine-et-Loire will notice that special sections still exist for infants and very young children. However, instead of being relegated to isolated corners, children are frequently buried in a central area. Their tombs are not marked with the large gray stones that decorate the graves of adults but with small white crosses and angels. Since the nineteenth century, children have been moved from unblessed and isolated corners to privileged sections where their purity and perfection are memorialized.

108. AN F19 5530. For the mounting tension between confessions that informed these disputes see Natalie Isser, "Protestants and Proselytization During the Second French Empire," *Journal of Church and State* 30 (1988): 51–70.

109. AN F19 5530, letter of M. Vaurigaud to minister of education and religion, 25 September 1858.

110. See, for example, the letter from the minister of justice and religion to the bishops, 1 July 1845, which notes that as a result of burial in unconsecrated portions reserved for unbaptized children and suicides, "the feelings of Protestants have been wounded and, in the name of the freedom of religion, they have protested against burials they consider offensive to their religious community." AN F19 5514. For other cases in which Vaurigaud protested the placement of a Protestant grave see AN F19 5531.

111. For this case and others see the Chamber report on reforming the law on cemeteries in *JO Chambre*, 5 July 1880 (séance du 12 juin), 7596–7600.

112. AN F19 4379, Letter of Msgr Landriot, the bishop of La Rochelle, to the minister of religion, 29 June 1866. According to Landriot, "It is a custom consecrated by pious tradition not to separate after death spouses or children who have lived in the same home, although their religious convictions were not the same."

113. AEA, 6 G 1, letter of Msgr Bouvier to bishop of Angers, 8 March 1851.

114. AEA, O   St. Florent. See also AN F19 5514, file on morts-nés, for the case of the village of Balledent (Haute-Vienne) in 1873. There a Catholic family was refused the right to bury a stillborn infant in their family grave, a decision that they first accepted but subsequently refused following conversations with the Protestant mayor. The burial then proceeded to take place in the family concession, in consecrated ground, leading to a protest by the curé. In Paris the minister of the interior at first supported the mayor, whereas the minister of religion defended the curé; by the time these ministries were able to agree that the law was on the side of the Church, the cemetery had been placed under interdict. The clerical victory, however, was only apparent. The mayor still refused to carry out the exhumation, and the family, a prominent one, had now begun worshiping with the Protestants, who made up about eighty of a population of seven hundred. In this situation, to avoid losing parishioners to the Protestants, the Church backed down. The bishop agreed to lift the interdict and permit Protestants to be buried in what he had previously regarded as the "Catholic" cemetery.

115. Fred Licht, "Tomb Sculpture," in *The Romantics to Rodin: French Nineteenth-Century Sculpture from North American Collections*, ed. Peter Fusco and

H. W. Janson (Los Angeles: Los Angeles County Museum of Art, 1980), 96–108, esp. 100.

116. AN F19 5514.

117. For the Gasnier case in addition to documents in AN F19 5514 see AEA, OP 28; *Le Temps*, 11 April 1880, 3; 18 April 1880, 2.

118. See, for example, the speech of Ferdinand Boyer, *JO Chambre Débats*, 23 January 1880, 618: *"Jusqu'à cette époque néfaste, leur lieu (des Catholiques) de repos avait été respecté; les catholiques dormaient dans leur cimetières leur dernier sommeil."*

119. *JO Chambre Débats*, 8 March 1881, 433.

120. Gaume, *The Christian Cemetery*, 73. In the village of St. Julien-de-Lampon, in the Dordogne, the curé used his pulpit to condemn the burial of a suicide in consecrated ground and anticipated a time when dogs and other animals would be buried in the cemetery; see AN 4378, letter from minister of interior to minister of religion, 8 March 1865.

121. *JO Chambre—Annexes*, 7 March 1879, annexe no. 1170. "Proposition de loi ayant pour objet l'abrogation de l'article 15 du décret du 23 prairial an XII relatif aux cimetières," 1776–1777.

122. *JO Chambre—Annexes*, 7 March 1879, annexe no. 1170.

123. *XIXe Siècle*, 1 January 1877, clipping in AN F 19 5514.

124. Léon Vafflard, *Notice sur les champs de sépultures anciens et modernes de la ville de Paris* (Paris: Librairie Internationale, 1867), 32–33, provides a figure of 73,125 during a week in November; this study was part of Haussmann's investigation into the feasibility of a new cemetery at Méry-sur-Oise. According to *Le Temps*, 17 April 1874, 68,035 Parisians visited their cemeteries during the week of December 1–7, 1873. The same article estimated 370,000 visitors on All Souls' Day of that year. *Le Temps* of 3 November 1891 estimated crowds of 400,000 for the previous day.

125. AEA, 2K8, *Souscription pour la construction d'une chapelle dans le cimetière de l'Est* (Angers, 1867). Guides to cemeteries include: P. de Saint-A., *Promenade aux cimetières de Paris, aux sépultures royales de Saint-Denis, et aux catacombes* (Paris, 1816); G.G., *Promenade sérieuse au cimetière du Père Lachaise, ou de Mont-Louis près de Paris* (Paris, 1826); M. Richard, *Le véritable conducteur aux cimetières du Père Lachaise, Montmartre, et Vaugirard* (Paris, 1836). These and other material on the popularity of Parisian cemeteries are cited in Etlin, *The Architecture of Death*, 340–358. A tourist guide to Marseille described the picturesque qualities of the "cimetière Saint-Charles" in 1840; see M. Richard, *Conducteur de l'étranger dans Marseille* (Marseilles, 1840), 54; cited in Bertrand, "Cimetières marseillais," 243–244. A. Guépin and E. Bonamy demonstrated similar pride in the "cimetière de Miséricorde" of Nantes; see their *Nantes au XIXe siècle* (Nantes, 1835).

126. AEA, O—Meigné-le-Vicomte. Letter from curé to bishop, 24 June 1854; Bertrand and Vovelle, *La Ville des morts*, 42–43.

127. ADS, VD6 7, no. 2, arrêté de 14 septembre 1850. ADML, 6 Fi 299, Arrêté de 1 mars 1865; Bertrand and Vovelle, *La Ville des morts*, 43.

128. AMA, Cimetières/pompes funèbres.

129. Pinkney, *Napoleon III and the Rebuilding of Paris*, 94–102.

130. ADS, VD4, 2725, 2783, 2803.

131. ADS, VD6, 7, prefect of the Seine, arrêt of 14 September 1850.

132. Ariès, *The Hour of Our Death*, 533; Vovelle, *La Mort et l'occident*, 631–632; Bertrand and Vovelle, *La Ville des morts*; Etlin, *The Architecture of Death*, 366–367.

133. Bertrand and Vovelle, *La Ville des morts*, 114–115; Ariès, *The Hour of Our Death*, 535–536; Etlin, *The Architecture of Death*, 366.

134. Michel Vovelle has made a similar argument based on his examination of the *faire-part*, the announcements of death circulated by families, which printed longer and longer lists of those relatives who were close enough to the deceased to merit inclusion. See "Le deuil bourgeois. Du faire-part à la statuaire funéraire," in Michel Vovelle, *Histoires figurales—Des monstres médiévaux à Wonderwoman* (Paris: Sogedin, 1989), 239–252.

135. Bertrand and Vovelle, *La Ville des morts*, 112–113, 177.

136. See the illustrations in A. Pugin, *Paris and Its Environs*, 2 vols. (London: Jennings and Chaplin, 1831), 2: 104, 129, 149. Of the tombs depicted by Pugin only General Foy's bears a small cross. For other illustrations of Père Lachaise see Richard Etlin, *The Architecture of Death*, 345–354; note especially the print of Civeton (349), which shows a wooden cross in the foreground against a setting of monumental tombs, most of which do not include a cross. Civeton presents a woman and child mourning before the wooden cross, a theme that was to become a commonplace of funerary art in the nineteenth century. The cemetery of Montmartre, as depicted by Schaal in 1824, included a section of ordinary graves marked by wooden crosses in the lower portion and stone monuments on the slope of the hill; see ibid., 338. The lithograph of the *Cimetière St. Jean* published in *Notice historique sur l'ancien grand cimetière et sur les cimetières actuels de la ville d'Orléans* (Orléans, 1824) shows a number of small crosses scattered among the larger monuments, one of which is surmounted by a cross. See also the description in the Concourts, *Germinie Lacerteux*, 168.

137. AEA, 2K8, *Souscription pour la construction d'une chapelle dans le cimetière de l'Est* (Angers, 1867).

138. AMA, Cimetières, letter of M. Faribault Entrepreneur des monuments funèbres, to mayor of Angers, 7 May 1902; Rapport du service de la Voirie municipale, 15 May 1902.

139. Bertrand and Vovelle, *La Ville des morts*, 113, note that this style is rare in Provence.

140. For Marian devotions in the nineteenth century see Thomas Kselman, *Miracles and Prophecies in Nineteenth-Century France* (New Brunswick: Rutgers University Press, 1983).

141. For the increasing use of "incorporated" crosses in Provence after 1900 see Bertrand and Vovelle, *La Ville des morts*, 113, 177.

142. Aries, *The Hour of Our Death*, 276. Ariès acknowledges the importance of the cross but breaks his account off in the early nineteenth century. Michel Vovelle sees evidence for the rechristianization of death in the second half of

the nineteenth century in the ceramic funeral plaques of Limoges; see his " 'Ici repose . . .'—Les Plaques funéraires peintes du cimetière de Limoges," in *Histoire figurales*, 253–259.

143. Ariès, *The Hour of Our Death*, 216–233.

144. Vovelle, *La Mort et l'occident*, 613–614; Bertrand and Vovelle, *La Ville des morts*, 118–120, 187.

145. Comte F. de Gramont, *Comment on vient et comment on s'en va*, (Paris: Lévy, 1858), 219–220; R. R. Madden, *The Shrines and Sepulchres of the Old and New World* (London: Newly, 1851), 2:439.

146. Ariès, *The Hour of Our Death*, 529.

147. Epitaphs seem to have been fairly evenly distributed between men and women, to judge by the research of Bertrand and Vovelle, *La Ville des morts*, 121. In 1825 in the cemetery of Orléans there were 96 epitaphs for women, and 114 for men. See *Notice historique sur l'ancien grand cimetière . . . d'Orléans*.

148.

> Ci Git
> Laurette Courtigne née le
> 20 8bre 1818, décédée le 1 juin
> 1832
>
> Elle fut un modèle de piété
> et d'amour filial
>
> Hélas! Dans l'âge le plus tendre
> Peine et soins n'ont pu la défendre
> Des coups de la cruelle mort
> O passant, priez sur sa tombe
> Ou ses parents plaignent le sort

149.

> La mort a moissonné cet enfant au berceau,
> Mort impitoyable et barbare,
> Ah! c'est en vain que ta faux nous sépare,
> Henri parle à nos coeurs, du fond de son tombeau

This epitaph, written in 1818 for Nicolas Henri Légier, seems to have inspired another, written for Claude Marie Benoist, the father of a family who died in 1822:

> C'est en vain que la mort en moissonant les jours,
> Croit dissoudre Benoist les noeuds de notre amour;
> Tu vivras parmi nous. Ta mémoire chérie.
> Du fond de ton tombeau le rappelle à la vie.

All the epitaphs from the early period of the cemetery of St. Vincent were published in *Notice historique sur l'ancien grand cimetière et sur les cimetières actuels de la ville d'Orléans*, 58–71.

150. *Images of Man and Death*, 247.

151. Bertrand and Vovelle, *La Ville des morts*, 182.

152. *Notice historique sur l'ancien grand cimetière . . . de la ville d'Orléans*, 56–75.

153. See also Bertrand and Vovelle, *La Ville des morts*, 183, which shows the decline of the phrase "Rest in Peace," which appeared on about 50 percent of the epitaphs in 1870, but which has virtually disappeared from contemporary tombs in Provence. Ibid., 185, shows the decline in religious references in epitaphs.

154. Ariès, *The Hour of Our Death*, 230.

155. Chateaubriand, *Génie du christianisme*, 2:89–101.

156. Fustel de Coulanges, *The Ancient City* (Garden City: Anchor Doubleday, 1955; first published 1864), 15–39; passage cited from 36. Fustel noted, however, that ancient tombs were generally near home and not gathered in cemeteries.

157. For an account of the disaster and the responses to it see *Journal de Maine-et-Loire*, 16, 17, 19, 22, 23, 24, 25 April 1850, 7, 13, 15, 16 May 1850.

158. Prost, "Les Monuments aux morts"; David Troyansky, "Monumental Politics: National History and Local Memory in French *Monuments aux Morts* in the Department of the Aisne since 1870," *French Historical Studies* 15 (1987): 121–141; David Troyansky, "The Monument Wars of Saint-Quentin in the Third Republic," in *La Cérémonie du pouvoir: Rituels politiques du pouvoir d'état en France de la Révolution à nos jours*, ed. Antoine de Baecque (forthcoming).

159. Aimé Feutry, "Le Temple de la mort," in *Opuscules poétiques et philologiques* (La Haye, 1771), 36–38; Philippe Bridel, "Le Cimetière," in *Poésies helvétiennes* (Lausanne, 1782), 1. These and other examples are cited in Michel Vovelle, *Mourir autrefois—Attitudes collectives devant la mort aux XVIIe et XVIIIe siècles* (Paris: Gallimard, 1974), 213–217. For a thorough examination of the English poets and their Continental imitators see Paul Van Tieghem, *Le Préromantisme*, vol. 2 (Paris: Sfelt, 1929).

160. Jacques Delille, *Les Jardins*; cited in Ariès, *The Hour of Our Death*, 526.

161.
> *Non! tu vis, tu m'entends, tu me réponds, tu m'aimes;*
> *Nos places ont changé, nos rapports sont les mêmes.*
> *Ame qui fus ma mére, oh! parle! parle-moi!*
> *Ma conversation est au ciel avec toi.*

From Alphonse de Lamartine, *Jocelyn* (Geneva: Editions au Grand Passage, n.d.), 146. For the importance of *Jocelyn* see Virgil Nemoianu, *The Taming of Romanticism—European Literature in the Age of Biedermeier* (Cambridge: Harvard University Press, 1984), 87.

162. ADS, 4 AZ, no. 763. Letter of Michelet to prefect of the Seine, 23 August 1839.

163. Michelet, *Mother Death*, 45.

164. A number of poems from *Les Contemplations* conclude with notes indicating their association with cemeteries. See "Pleurs dans la nuit," "Cadaver," "Ce que c'est que la mort," in Victor Hugo, *Les Contemplations* (Paris: Gallimard, 1973; first published 1856), 306–328, 341–343, 361–362.

165. Speech before the Senate, *Journal Officiel*, 29 June 1868, clipping in Collection Lazare ADS D. Z. vol 27, no. 1990.

166. Rebérioux, "Le Mur des fédéres." See also Hutton, *The Cult of the Revolutionary Tradition*.

167. For other examples of such images see Michelle Perrot, ed., *A History of Private Life*, vol. 4, *From the Fires of Revolution to the Great War* (Cambridge: Harvard University Press, 1990), 178, 333. See also the painting by William Bouguereau of two women consoling each other at a cross reproduced in Ariès, *Images of Man and Death*, 265. Bertrand and Vovelle, *La Ville des morts*, 135, refer to the omnipresence of representations of women in funeral sculpture in Provence. Ellen Badone, *The Appointed Hour*, 252, notes the role of women in caring for the cemetery. For an ethnographic account of the role of women in the mourning rituals of contemporary rural Greece see Loring Danforth and Alexander Tsiaras (photographs), *The Death Rituals of Rural Greece* (Princeton: Princeton University Press, 1982). For the position of women in nineteenth-century France, see Bonnie Smith, *Ladies of the Leisure Class—The Bourgeoises of Northern France in the Nineteenth Century* (Princeton: Princeton University Press, 1981); James McMillan, *Housewife or Harlot—The Place of Women in French Society, 1870–1940* (New York: St. Martin's Press, 1981).

168. Martine Segalen, "Le Mariage," in *Histoire de la population française*, ed. Jacques Dupâquier (Paris: Presses Universitaires de France, 1988), 3:428.

169. For similar images see the cover of *Le Soleil du Dimanche*, 4 Nov. 1900, and the color illustration of a cemetery in Brittany in *Le Petit Journal*, 31 Oct. 1897. The images from *Le Soleil du Dimanche* can be located in the Bibliothèque Nationale, Cabinet des Estampes, series Oa, microfilm M 143070, M143071.

170. Ariès, *Images of Man and Death*, 176–181; Ariès, *The Hour of Our Death*, 369–381, 392–395; Mario Praz, *The Romantic Agony* (New York: Meridian, 1956); Bram Dijkstra, *Idols of Perversity—Fantasies of Feminine Evil in Fin-de-Siècle Culture* (New York: Oxford University Press, 1986), 51–63.

171. AEA, 2K8, Documents on "Oeuvre du cimetière de l'Est."

172. "*Comme c'était au cimetière où sont mon père et ma soeur, l'idée m'a pris d'aller voir leurs tombes. Cette vue m'a peu ému; il n'y a là rien de ce que j'ai aimé, mais seulement les restes de deux cadavres que j'ai contemplés pendant quelques heures. Mais eux: ils sont en moi, dans mon souvenir. La vue d'un vêtement qui leur a appartenu me fait plus d'effet que celle de leurs tombeaux. Idée reçue, l'idée de la tombe! Il faut être triste là, c'est de règle. Une seule chose m'a ému, c'est de voir dans le petit enclos un tabouret de jardin (pareil à ceux qui sont ici) et que ma mère, sans doute, y a fait porter. C'est une communauté entre ce jardin-là et l'autre, une extension de sa vie sur cette mort et comme une continuité d'existence commune à travers les sépulcres.*"

Gustave Flaubert, *Correspondance*, vol. 2, *1852* (Paris: Conard, 1926–1954), 35. For a similar reaction by a contemporary author during a visit to her mother's tomb see Marguerite Yourcenar, *Souvenirs pieux* (Paris: Gallimard, 1974), 56–59.

CHAPTER SIX

1. *Libération*, 17 January 1986, 23.

2. For other incidents involving Leclerc see *Courrier de l'Ouest*, 14 October 1984; *Libération*, 26 January 1985, 40; for a brief overview of the conflict see *Newsweek* (international edition), 1 April 1985, 43.

3. *"Ceux qui restent ne peuvent être soumis au Racket, donnons leur le libre choix!"* See *Le Quotidien de Paris*, 26 November 1984, 1.

4. The text of the advertisement reads: *"Et pour que la vie, justement, soit préservée, respectée; pour aider les vivants à honorer leurs morts, il existe des professionels qui prennent en charge, avec pudeur et savoir-faire, les problèmes; tous les problèmes d'organisation qui se posent lors d'un décès. Nous, les hommes et les femmes des PFG, nous sommes là pour apporter à ceux qui restent avec leur peine une assistance totale et souvent méconnue. Nous sommes 5300 en France à exercer un métier plus difficile que les autres; ce métier, nous y sommes fidèles depuis plus d'un siècle. Et nous en sommes fiers."* Le Monde, 7 May 1985, 9.

5. For criticisms of the French funeral industry see Jacques Potel, *Mort à vain, mort à vendre* (Paris: Desclée, 1970); "Les Obsèques, commerce ou service publique?" *Le Monde*, 21, 22 October 1970; Louis-Vincent Thomas, *Rites de mort—Pour la paix des vivants* (Paris: Fayard, 1985), 46–49; Marc-Ambroise Rendu, "Le Funéraire nouveau," *Le Monde* 27–28 December 1987, 5, which reviews the controversy between PFG and Leclerc.

6. Ariès, *The Hour of Our Death*, 596–600; Thomas Laqueur, "Bodies, Death, and Pauper Funerals," *Representations* 1 (1983): 109–131; Richardson, *Death, Dissection, and the Destitute*, 272–275. See also Vovelle, *La Mort et l'occident*, 621–630; Joachim Whaley, "Symbolism for the Survivors: The Disposal of the Dead in Hamburg in the Late Seventeenth and Eighteenth Centuries," in *Mirrors of Mortality—Studies in the Social History of Death*, ed. Joachim Whaley (New York: St. Martin's Press, 1981), 80–105.

7. Huntington and Metcalf, *Celebrations of Death*; French scholars from the nineteenth and early twentieth centuries may have been led to see the cultural significance of funerals by observing customs in their own country; see Fustel de Coulanges, *The Ancient City*; Robert Hertz, *Death and the Right Hand*, trans. Rodney and Claudia Needham (Glencoe, Ill.: Free Press, 1960; first published 1907, 1909).

8. For the concept of "market culture" see William Reddy, *The Rise of Market Culture: The Textile Trade and French Society, 1750–1900* (New York: Cambridge University Press, 1984). See also Laqueur, "Bodies, Death, and Pauper Funerals," who argues that in nineteenth-century England undertakers succeeded in turning funerals into "a consumption good whose cost was clearly evident and could be matched with exquisite precision to the class and degree of 'respectability . . . of the deceased (114)."

9. Jacqueline Thibaut-Payen, *Les Morts, l'église, et l'état dans le ressort du parlement de Paris aux XVIIe et XVIIIe siècles* (Paris: Lanore, 1977), 62–77; Lebrun, *Les Hommes et la mort en Anjou aux 17e et 18e siècles*; Pierre Chaunu, *La Mort à Paris 16e, 17e, 18e siècles* (Paris: Fayard, 1978), 351–352; Vovelle, *La Mort et l'occident* 457–461; McManners, *Death and the Enlightenment*, 281–288.

10. Charles Tilly, *The Contentious French* (Cambridge: Harvard University Press, 1986), 18.

11. Uzureau, "Les Pompes funèbres à Angers avant la Révolution," *Anjou historique* (1912–1913): 142–143.

12. René de Lespinasse, *Les Métiers et corporations de la Ville de Paris* (Paris: Imprimerie Nationale, 1897), 3:171, 435. Competition among guilds for a share in the funeral trade has been observed elsewhere in Europe as well; see

Whaley, "Symbolism for the Survivors: The Disposal of the Dead in Hamburg in the Late Seventeenth and Eighteenth Centuries."

13. *Mémoire sur le service et les frais d'inhumations dans la Ville de Paris, sur leur produit, sur leur emploi* (Paris, [1804]); Ranvier, *Rapport au nom de la 2e commission sur la municipalisation du service des pompes funèbres* (Paris, 1905; filed in AN F2 2762), 22. These two reports do not cite any direct testimony from the eighteenth century, but the first is persuasive because it was so close in time to the events described and displays no anticlerical prejudice. See Thibaut-Payen, *Les Morts, l'église, et l'état*, 72, for a suggestion that services were provided freely to the poor. Thibaut-Payen uses the price list proposed by the parish of Saint-Eustache in Paris to the Parlement of 1763, which may or may not actually describe funeral practice.

14. McManners, *Death and the Enlightenment*, 284–286. For the costs of funerals in seventeenth-century Paris, see Chaunu, *La Mort à Paris*, 360–361.

15. McManners, *Death and the Enlightenment*, 299; see also Ariès, *The Hour of Our Death*, 322–324; Michel Vovelle, *Piété baroque et déchristianisation en Provence au XVIIIe siècle* (Paris: Seuil, 1978), 85–100; Vovelle, *La Mort et l'occident*, 457–460; Etlin, *The Architecture of Death: The Transformation of the Cemetery in Eighteenth-Century Paris*, 99.

16. Vovelle, *La Mort et l'occident*, 492; Etlin, *The Architecture of Death* 236–238; Nicole Bossut, "Aux origines de la déchristianisation dans la Nièvre." This was the same decree that included the provision for cemeteries to announce at their entrances "Death Is an Eternal Sleep." See chapters 4 and 5.

17. *Le Moniteur*, 18 (23 November 1793): 482. Ranvier, *Rapport sur la municipalisation du service des pompes funèbres*, 25. For the adoption of a similar measure in Beauvais see Maurice Dommanget, "La Déchristianisation à Beauvais, les sacrements civiques," *Annales révolutionnaires* 11 (1919): 181–188. Michelet notes the "equality of burials" as one of the achievements of the Revolutionary Commune; Jules Michelet, *Histoire de la Révolution française* (Paris: Laffont, 1979), 2:628. Revolutionaries anxious to inspire patriotic fervor among the living created more elaborate ceremonies to honor revolutionary martyrs, and memorial services and funerals were important civic festivals in 1792 and 1793. Parodic funerals were employed to symbolize the passing of the ancien régime and the defeat of the enemies of the revolution. See Mona Ozouf, *La Fête révolutionnaire* (Paris: Gallimard, 1976), 95–97, 106–114. For an analysis of some of the songs and speeches used to celebrate revolutionary funerals see George Armstrong Kelly, *Mortal Politics in Eighteenth-Century France* (Waterloo: University of Waterloo Press, 1986), 238–260, 271–280.

18. Ozouf, *La Fête révolutionnaire*, 318–320.

19. G. Delamalle, *Réflexions sur l'enterrement de ma mère*; Delamalle was still being cited by critics of the revolution in the early twentieth century. For an extensive citation from the pamphlet see the speech by M. Dominique Delahaye, *JO Sénat Débats*, 11 July 1904, 827; Delahaye was attempting to block the secularization of the funeral industry, a reform that will be discussed in the following chapter.

20. Ranvier, *Rapport sur la municipilisation du service des pompes funèbres*, 22. For additional evidence on the conduct of funerals during the revolution see Ariès, *The Hour of Our Death*, 504–506.

21. Etlin, *The Architecture of Death*, 249.

22. Ranvier, *Rapport sur la municipilisation du service des pompes funèbres*, 25. For a discussion of funerals and burials during the Directory see: Kelly, *Mortal Politics*, 288–291; Pascal Hintermeyer, *Politiques de la mort* (Paris: Payot, 1981); Etlin, *The Architecture of Death*, 245–254.

23. For an example of the desire to combine decency and equality see the speech by the member of the Directory, Louis-Marie Lavellière-Lépeaux at the Institut national, 12 floréal, year VI, in *Mémoires de Lavellière-Lépeaux* (Paris: Plon, n.d.), 3:19–21. See also Kelly, *Mortal Politics*, 285–287.

24. AN, F19 5517, *Arrêté du préfet du département de la Seine concernant les inhumations*; another copy of this can be found in ADS, VD4, 2679.

25. For a similar expression see ADS, VD4, 2682, letter of Frochot to mayors of arrondissements, 29 germinal year XII (19 April 1802).

26. Soon after the initial decree Frochot changed the dress code so that the ordonnateurs would be dressed entirely in black; instead of with a feather their hats were to be decorated with black crêpe that would hang from one side; see ADS VD4, 2692, *Arrêté* of 29 germinal, year IX (19 April 1802).

27. AN F19 5517, letter from Bobée to conseil d'état, undated [1812].

28. For the 1801 agreement between Paris and Bobée see ADS, VD4, 2679, 2683, 2686.

29. *Reclamation par Louis-Auguste Bigot, marchand tapissier-décorateur, premier entrepreneur des cérémonies religieuses et Pompes Funèbres à Paris . . . contre le prétendu privilège de Sieur Bobée concernant les Pompes et Ornements des Inhumations dans la Ville de Paris* (Paris, n.d.); see also letter from Bigot to mayors of twelve Paris arrondissements, ADS, VD4, 2694.

30. In its original form the proposal assigned responsibility for pompes funèbres to the hospital administrations of the cities of France. This was intended to eliminate the "sordid speculations" that were observed in the emerging industry in Paris and elsewhere. The *idée sage* of granting control over prices and objects to the hospitals was to "turn the last prodigalities of the rich to the profit of the poor, and . . . under a virtuous administration lighten the expenses poor families judge indispensable not because of vanity, but because of decency." The goal of controlling the costs of funerals and of using the fees paid for elaborate ceremonies to cover expenses of the poor was incorporated into the decree issued the following year, and employing the hospital as the institution best equipped to take on the task of managing funerals was an idea that led to a number of experiments later in the century. In its final form, however, the decree of 23 prairial did not make hospitals the beneficiaries of the new industry. See AN F19 5517, Comte Ségur, *Rapport sur les sépultures* (Paris, an XI).

31. Vovelle, *La Mort et l'occident*, 557.

32. The French text of Article 20 of the law of 23 prairial reads: "*Les frais à payer aux ministres des cultes et autres individus attachés aux églises et temples, tant pour leur assistance aux convois que pour les services requis par les familles, seront*

réglés par le Gouvernement, sur l'avis des éveques, des consistoires et des préfets et sur la proposition du ministre des Cultes. Il ne leur sera rien alloué pour leur assistance à l'inhumation des individus inscrits au role des indigents."

33. AN F19 5517. *Casuel à percevoir dans les paroisses et succursales de Paris* (Paris, an XI). The charges for the different classes cannot be calculated exactly since they would vary depending on how many clergy and candles the family chose. The absence of a passage by the church for a fifth-class service is implied by later regulations that explicitly call for such a service if desired by the family; see Article 12 of the Decree of 18 May 1806.

34. Article 21: *"Le mode le plus convenable pour le transport des corps sera réglé, suivant les localités, par les maires, sauf l'approbation des préfets."*

35. Gaudry, *Traité de la législation des cultes*, 2: 614

36. Ranvier, *Rapport sur la municipilisation du service des pompes funèbres*, 32; AN F19 5517, letter of fabriques of Paris to minister of cults, 11 February 1812; *Reclamation par Louis-Auguste Bigot* (Paris, 1807).

37. Ranvier, *Rapport*, 32; the conflicts of this period are treated in a number of letters and printed complaints filed in AN F19 5517, "Pièces relatives aux demandes particulières des Sieurs Bigot, Fremont, et Boulanger." See also ADS, VD4, 2705 for Frochot's decree setting the rate of return to fabriques at 16 percent.

38. AN F19 5517, Decree of 18 May 1806.

39. The prices established in 1811 are listed in Ranvier, *Rapport sur la municipilisation*, 37–38. AN F19 5517, contains copies of printed receipts used by Bobée. For the controversy surrounding the prices see AN F19 5517, letter from the minister of religion to the archbishop of Paris concerning the burial of the mother-in-law of Monsieur Girard, chef du secrétariat du Corps Legislatif; and "Observations présentées à Son Excellence le Ministre des Cultes sur l'inexécution du décret impérial du août 1811." For an advertisement in which Bobée listed the services he provided see ADS, D10, AZ 542.

40. *Cahier de charges de l'entreprise générale du service des inhumations* (Paris, 1811).

41. AN F19 5517, letter of Cardinal Maury to the minister of religion, 12 February 1812.

42. Labalte complained, for example, that fabriques rather than the entrepreneur were renting the *drap mortuaire* for the memorial services conducted for the dead nine days and one year after their burial. AN F19 5517, letters of Labalte to the minister of cults, 14 and 28 June, 1812.

43. ADS, VD4, 2651, letter of Labalte to the mayor of the eleventh arrondissement, 7 February 1813; VD4 2652, prefectural decree of 1823 requiring mayors to schedule funeral processions at least two hours apart; AN F19, 10168, extract from the minutes of a meeting of secretaries of state attached to the Ministry of Religion, 4 July 1815, requiring Labalte to pay 50 percent of gross revenues to fabriques.

44. For Baudouin's practices see: Léon Vafflard, *De l'intérêt que le public a ce que le bail actuel des pompes funèbres peut expirer depuis 3 ans* (Paris: Lacombe, 1842); Anatole Pector, *Précis sur le service des inhumations et des pompes funèbres de la ville de Paris* (Paris: Duberger, 1842). Both of these pamphlets are located

in ADS, VD4, 2782, 2786. See also Ranvier, *Rapport sur la municipalisation du service des pompes funèbres*, 42–43.

45. Data for 1821–1826 and 1839–1848 reported in Adeline Daumard, *La Bourgeoisie parisienne de 1815 à 1848* (Paris: SEVPEN, 1963), 11. For the rest of the century see Ranvier, *Rapport sur la municipilisation du service*, 49–50, 98.

46. *Rapport au Roi* (Paris: Ministry of the Interior, 1840), filed in AN F19 5518 (2). These figures could be substantially increased by the purchase of optional items.

47. See references in note 45; see also Ranvier, *Rapport sur la municipalisation du service des pompes funèbres*, 41; *Observations présentées au nom des fabriques sur les modifications à apporter aux conditions prochaines de l'adjudication du service des pompes funèbres* (Paris: Gros, n.d.).

48. *Refutation de la Calomnie dirigée contre M. Pector par le Sieur Charles Baudouin* (Paris: Duverger, 1842); copies of this pamphlet are filed in AN F19 5518 (2) and ADS, VD4, 2792.

49. A number of pamphlets and newspaper articles from the 1840s were collected and published together by M. Balard during the Second Empire. See M. Balard, *Les Mystères des pompes funèbres de la ville de Paris dévoilés par les entrepreneurs eux-mêmes* (Paris: Allard, 1856).

50. Léon Vafflard, *Observations sur le service des inhumations et pompes funèbres de la ville de Paris* (Paris, 1847).

51. Vafflard, *Observations sur le service des inhumations et pompes funèbres*. For a similar critique of the undertakers, see M. Balard, *Aperçu sur quelques améliorations importantes à introduire dans le service des pompes funèbres de la ville de Paris et de ses dépendances* (Paris: Stahl, 1845). Balard was himself an under-taker and therefore familiar with the practices of his colleagues, which he considered abusive. See also articles published in the Parisian journal *Lucifer* in 1847, reprinted in Balard, *Mystères des pompes funèbres*, 212–223, and a letter from Dr. Felix Gannal to the prefect of the Seine, published in *Le Constitution-nel*, 18 January 1848. Gannal, who was an embalmer, criticized the undertak-ers for pushing the services of the brother-in-law of Pector, who had as-sumed the Paris contract by the late 1840s. See also Léon Vafflard, *De l'intérêt que le public a ce que le bail actuel des pompes funèbres peut expirer depuis 3 ans*, and Pector, *Précis sur le service des inhumations et des pompes funèbres*.

52. Vafflard, *Observations sur le service des inhumations et pompes funèbres*.

53. ADS, VD4, 2753, letter of prefect to mayors of twelve arrondissements, 6 February 1832. For additional complaints during the cholera epidemic see ADS, VD4, 2755, letter of prefect to mayors, 10 April 1832; 2757, letter of pre-fect to mayors, 13 April 1832.

54. Esquiros, "Les Cimetières de Paris," 260.

55. Fréderic Lemaistre, *Réforme administrative*, 14 June 1849; 28 June 1849; 5 July 1849; 12 July 1849; 19 July 1849. Of course, Lemaistre's complaints were inspired in part by his resentment about being replaced as the entrepreneur. For the prefect of the Seine's response to these criticisms see *La Patrie*, 4 July 1849, and *Le Moniteur*, 17 July 1849.

56. For the prefectural decree of 1844 see Vafflard, *Régulateur général des convois*, 14–17. For the decision of the conseil d'état see Balard, *Mystères*, 33–

38. The issue is dealt with in *Lettre adressée à MM. les maires de Paris sur l'entre-prise des pompes funèbres* (Paris, 1842), filed in AN F19 10168, "Consistoire de l'église réformé de Paris, projet pour l'établissement pour le service des pompes funèbres."

57. Anatole Pector, *Exposé des causes qui ont influé* . . . (Paris, 1849).

58. Ranvier, *Rapport sur la municipilisation du service*, 45–51.

59. Honoré de Balzac, *Old Goriot* (Baltimore: Penguin, 1971), 302–304.

60. Honoré de Balzac, *Cousin Pons* (Baltimore: Penguin, 1968), 288. For government decrees designed to control the harassment of families see ADS, VD4 2696, prefectural warning to be posted in all city halls, 1832.

61. Balzac, *Cousin Pons*, 294. Balzac was not the only writer to notice the black dress of the undertakers in 1846. In his essay on the Salon of 1846 Charles Baudelaire called attention to the middle-class fashion of dark clothes, which he compared with the uniforms of undertakers and professional mourners: "But all the same, has not this much abused garb its own beauty and its native charm? Is it not the symbol of our suffering age, which wears the symbol of a perpetual mourning even upon its thin black shoulders? Note, too, that the dress-coat and the frock-coat possess not only their political beauty, but ther poetic beauty, which is an expression of the public soul—an immense cortège of undertaker's mutes (mutes in love, political mutes, bourgeois mutes). We are each of us celebrating some funeral." Cited in Michael Fried, *Courbet's Realism* (Chicago: University of Chicago Press, 1990), 116.

62. Balzac, *Cousin Pons*, 296.

63. Martin-Fugier, "Bourgeois Rituals," 335.

64. Emile Zola, *Oeuvres complètes* (Paris: Cercle du Livre Précieux, 1968), 9:679.

65. Ariès, *The Hour of Our Death*, 419.

66. Emile Zola, "Comment on meurt," *Oeuvres complètes*, 9:559–564.

67. Ibid., 567–568.

68. Ibid., 570–574.

69. Ibid., 575–579.

70. Emile Zola, *L'Assommoir* (Baltimore: Penguin, 1970), 292.

71. Ibid., 300–301.

72. Emile Zola, "Un croque-mort," *Oeuvres complètes*, 9:252–256.

73. Zola, *L'Assommoir*, 422–423.

74. Brazier, *Physiologie du Cocher de Paris*, cited in *Magasin catholique illustré* 2 (1851): 14–15. For the popularity of this genre see Jerrold Seigel, *Bohemian Paris* (New York: Pantheon Books, 1986), 28–29.

75. Maxime du Camp, *Le Salon de 1861* (Paris: Bourdilliat, 1861), 107–109; Théophile Gautier, *Abécédaire du salon de 1861* (Paris: Dentu, 1861), 246–248; A. Grévin, "Un Dessin pour le mercredi des cendres," *Petit Journal pour rire*, vol. 7 (1861), no. 315.

76. Gautier, *Salon de 1861*, 247.

77. Maxime du Camp, *Paris—ses organes, ses fonctions et sa vie dans la seconde moitié du XIXe siècle* (Paris: Hachette, 1875), 152–155. The long series of governmental decrees designed to prohibit requests for tips suggests that the

practice was common throughout the century; see ADS, VD4, 2719 (1812); 2725 (1817); 2753 (1832); 2762 (1843). For a complete list of the employees of the Paris funeral profession see AN F19 2762.

CHAPTER SEVEN

1. AN F19 5520.

2. ADML, 1M1/1. Letter from the prefect of Maine-et-Loire to the minister of the interior, 11 messidor, year X.

3. Decorating the interior was apparently unusual and expensive in Angers early in the century. See AMA, files on cimetières/pompes funebrès. Letter of the vicar-general to the mayor, 10 September 1806. Many of these files remain uncatalogued; I will refer to them as AMA, cimetières. I am grateful to the archival services at Angers for allowing me access to this material.

4. See AMA, cimetières. Posters listing funeral costs for the parishes of St. Maruice and St. Joseph.

5. This suggestion that the hospital should play a role in organizing funerals recalls the original proposal for reform discussed in Paris before the decree of 23 prairial. In the nineteenth century several cities experimented briefly with having their hospitals manage funerals, and at Nantes they provided coffins to the city for most of the century. In these measures we can see the survival of the impulse to ensure that the expenditures of the wealthy on funeral pomp would support charitable institutions. In Angers, however, this proposal was quickly dismissed as impractical, and elsewhere hospitals were replaced by entrepreneurs by the 1830s. For Nantes see AMA, cimetières. Letters from the mayor of Nantes to the mayor of Angers, 3 April 1832, and 6 April 1841. The Nantes hospitals briefly ran the funeral trade in 1803–1804. In Dunkirk the hospitals were responsible for the *convois funèbres* in the 1820s. See AN F19 5513. Minutes of the city council of Dunkirk, 7 January, and 19, 24 February 1834.

6. AEA, 6G1. Plainte des ciriers d'Angers contre les curés de St. Serge et St. Joseph au sujet des tentures funèbres, January 1839. AMA, cimetières. Letter of Charles Poisson, *cirier*, to the mayor of Angers, 5 June 1839.

7. AMA, cimetières. Plainte des fossoyeurs contre les ciriers à l'occasion de la mise à exécution du nouveau mode de transport arrêté par le maire, 13 Murch 1839.

8. AMA, cimetières. Letter of Mathurin Chalon to the commissaire of police, 31 May 1839.

9. AMA, cimetières. Letter from the bureau de police to the mayor, 6 June 1839.

10. AMA, cimetières. Correspondence of M. Collet-Lecuyer, Orléans, with the mayor of Angers concerning the establishment of a municipal service for pompes funèbres, 1839; projet d'un établissement de corbillards pour la ville d'Angers, présenté le 15 juillet par M. Salgnes.

11. ADML, 7V6.

12. For the increasing desire to prevent physical decomposition in contemporary France see Badone, *The Appointed Hour*, 151.

13. ADML, 7V6. Episcopal decree of 13 September 1843.

14. ADML 7V6. Letter from the minister of the interior to the prefect of Maine-et-Loire, 27 October 1843.

15. ADML 7V6. Guillet de la Tousche's report to the city council, 22 August 1845.

16. ADML 7V6. Avis du conseil de l'Intérieur du Conseil d'Etat sur un projet de règlement, 7 February 1847. Angevin officials defended the omission of the coffin from the price list for the sixth-class service by arguing that they were trying to save the poor an expense; see ADML 7V6, letter of the mayor to the bishop, 19 October 1846. In the smaller towns of Maine-et-Loire as late as the 1860s it was still common for the poor who died in public institutions to be buried without their own coffins; see AN F15 3721. Questionnaire sur les hospices, 1864, Durtal.

17. Badone, *The Appointed Hour*, 150.

18. ADML 7V6. Letter from the bishop of Angers to the minister of justice and religion, 24 March 1846; letter from the mayor of Angers to the prefect of Maine-et-Loire, 14 March 1846.

19. ADML, 7V6. Minutes of the city council, 20 March 1847.

20. ADML, 7V6. Royal decree, 18 July 1847.

21. AMA, cimetières. Letter of the bishop of Angers to the mayor, 24 September 1847. The best summary of the diocesan negotiations with Jeramec is found in ADML, 7V6, "Notes à consulter sur la question relative à l'établissement d'un nouveau service de pompes funèbres pour la ville d'Angers," prepared by the vicar-general Abbé Bernier, 4 October 1847.

22. ADML, 7V6. Bernier, "Notes à consulter sur les questions relative à . . . pompes funèbres."

23. ADML, 7V6. Meeting of *conseil municipal* of Angers, 15 October 1847.

24. ADML, 7V6. Letter of the bishop to the fabrique of St. Jacques; reports on meetings of fabriques, 1847.

25. AMA, cimetières. Arrêté du Maire d'Angers, 20 December 1847. ADML 7V6. Contract between Pompes Funèbres Générales and fabriques of Angers, 23 December 1847.

26. ADML, 7V6. Letter of the mayor of Angers to the prefect of Maine-et-Loire, 2 September 1848.

27. ADML, 7V6. Letter of the prefect of Maine-et-Loire to the minister of religion, 4 September 1848.

28. AMA, cimetières. Minutes of Angers city council, 24 June 1850.

29. ADML, 7V6. Minutes of Angers city council, 14 March 1851; letter of the mayor of Angers to the prefect, 19 April 1851.

30. ADML, 7V6. Minutes of Angers city council, 4 June 1888.

31. For the complete price list see *Administration des fabriques de la ville d'Angers* (Angers, n. d. [1862]).

32. Xavier Riobé, *Note à consulter pour l'établissement d'un mode régulier d'inhumuation et de pompes funèbres* (Paris: Entreprises des Pompes Funèbres Générales, n. d.), 2. See also *Pompes funèbres—Observations sur l'administration des fabriques en matière de pompes funèbres* (Angers: Lemesle, 1865).

33. AEA, 6 G 1. Entreprise des Pompes funèbres générales. Réponse au

projet présenté par la Commission des Fabriques d'Angers pour le renou-vellement des Pompes funèbres, 7 September 1897.

34. *"En un mot, on offre aux familles qui le désirent les moyens de déployer du luxe et de l'éclat dans les funérailles, et on assure un convoi décent et économique à celles qui ne peuvent ou ne veulent pas faire de dépenses."* Riobé, *Note à consulter*, 10.

35. Anatole Pector, *Exposé des causes qui ont influé sur la situation de l'entre-prise des pompes funèbres de la ville de Paris* (Paris: Bénard, 1849), included in Balard, *Les mystères des pompes funèbres de la ville de Paris dévoilés* (Paris: Allard, 1856) 157. See also Ranvier, *Rapport sur la municipilisation du service des pompes funèbres*, 45.

36. AN F19 5519. Report on PFG. For the correspondence between Angers and other cities on the establishment of commercial funerals see AMA, ci-metières, file on "autre villes."

37. Avner Ben-Amos, *Molding the National Memory*; James Lehning, "Death and the Republic: Political Funerals in the Early Third Republic," *Proceedings of the Annual Meeting of the Western Society for French History*, 18 (1991): 205–214.

38. AEA, 6 G 1. Rapport fait à Monseigneur l'Evèque sur les plaintes des catholiques et les réformes que leur foi réclame au sujet des pompes funèbres, 17 May 1873.

39. *JO Chambre Documents*, 26 July 1882, report on Lefebvre's bill.

40. Resources for mutual-aid societies grew from Fr 741,000 in 1856, to 19 million in 1871, and to 41 million in 1881. During the period 1871–1881 1,224 new societies were formed. *JO Chambre Débats*, 13 November 1883, 2296, 2308. Debate on law on Sociétés de secours mutuels.

41. *JO Chambre Débats*, 28 October 1883, 2148–2149. Giraud's speech on the reform of municipalities.

42. It is worth noting that Freppel here used the lack of confessional dis-tinctions in Paris funerals as a model to be emulated, whereas in the debates on cemeteries he had argued that it was an exception to be avoided. See chap-ter 5.

43. *JO Chambre Débats*, 30 October 1883, 2164–2168; 13 November 1883, 2192. Freppel probably based his speeches on an extensive report on the bill prepared by his vicar-general, "Observations critiques sur le projet de sécu-larisation au profit des communes du monopole des pompes funèbres," found in AEA, 6 G 1. By the 1880s the administrators of the fabriques respon-sible for the funeral trade in major cities such as Bordeaux and Marseilles were actively lobbying politicians for the maintenance of the status quo. See correspondence with Angers in AEA, 6G1.

44. *JO Chambre Débats*, 13 November 1883, 2318.

45. *JO Sénat Débats*, 19 November 1885, 1181–1182.

46. *JO Sénat Débats*, 19 November 1885, 1185–1187.

47. *JO Sénat Débats*, 29 November 1885, 1195. The commission's report, however, was less reticent in using the word *competition* (*concurrence*) to de-scribe its proposal; see the citation of the report in Martin's speech, *JO Sénat Débats*, 29 November 1885, 1198.

48. *JO Sénat Débats*, 29 November 1885, 1198–1199.

49. *JO Chambre Débats*, 13 November 1883, 2318.

50. *Le Temps*, 21 November 1885, 3.

51. The Chamber assigned commissions to consider the Senate proposal in the 1890s, but their reports never reached the floor; the issue had not therefore been entirely forgotten, but in the climate of the *ralliement* of the 1890s anticlericals were unable to gain serious consideration for a reform. The best brief legislative history of the bills for reforming pompes funèbres can be found in the reports of the Chamber and Senate commissions, which took up the measure again in the early twentieth century. See *JO Chambre Documents*, 28 May 1900, annexe no. 1658, 1122–1124; *JO Sénat Documents*, 31 May 1904, annexe no. 144, 225–229. The minister of the interior did conduct a survey in 1894 to try to determine how a communal monopoly would affect the conduct of funerals throughout France. The responses from the prefects, although inconsistent and confusing, demonstrated that commercial funerals could generally be purchased in the largest cities of each department; elsewhere families and parishes provided coffins, transportation, and simple decorations including the funeral pall at little or no expense. The results of this survey are filed in AN F19 5520. The circular from the Ministry of the Interior asked prefects to report whether communes, ecclesiastical establishements, municipalities, or families were in charge of pompes funèbres. The responses suggest that prefects had trouble distinguishing among families, parishes, and communes. In many villages of France these institutions cooperated in the provision of funerals, and the sharp distinctions assumed by the ministerial circular could not be applied.

52. *JO Chambre Documents*, 23 May 1900, annexe 1658, 1122.

53. Ibid., 1122.

54. *JO Chambre Débats*, 29 December 1903, 3440, speech of deputy Lerolle.

55. For the increasing competition between the fabriques' entrepreneurs and other merchants see the file on the 1904 reform in AN F19 5520, which includes references to twenty-six cases of litigation between 1889 and 1903. See also AEA, O (Baugé), for an exchange in which the city council in 1897 tried to force an adjudication of the *service extérieur* to give all merchants a right to compete for the trade, monopolized currently by a candle maker working for the fabriques.

56. AN F19 5519, file on pompes funèbres of Saint-Etienne.

57. *JO Chambre Débats*, 29 Décember 1903, 3445–3447.

58. *JO Sénat Documents*, 31 May 1904, annexe 144, 225–229.

59. *JO Sénat Débats*, 21 June 1904, 594.

60. *JO Sénat Débats*, 7 July 1904, 787–792. Defenders of free trade took up Milliès-Lacroix's arguments and pointed out that the Lyon mayor was complaining simultaneously about both competition and monopoly. They also disputed his claim that only a communal monopoly was equipped to defend the public interest and claimed that people were opposed to the "banality of the standard administrative box" for the "final sleep of their dead." A communal monopoly also threatened the privacy of the home, because it might try to restrict the decoration of the *maison mortuaire*, despite claims to the contrary by its proponents. But these appeals were tangential, and the major

issue remained the "liberty of commerce." *JO Sénat Débats*, 7 July 1904, 792–794, 829–831.

61. Laqueur, "Bodies, Death, and Pauper Funerals," 114.

62. Michael Miller, *The Bon Marché—Bourgeois Culture and the Department Store, 1869–1920* (Princeton: Princeton University Press, 1981), 166–189.

63. Rosalind Williams, *Dreamworlds: Mass Consumption in Late Nineteenth-Century France* (Berkeley: University of California Press, 1982). For a generally more positive interpretation of some of the same developments see Eugen Weber, *France—Fin de Siècle* (Cambridge: Harvard University Press, 1986). Jean Baudrillard, whose *La Société de consommation* (Paris: Denoël, 1970) is an influential critique of consumer society, argues that the integration of death into the modern political economy is both a symptom and a cause of the psychological and social repression that he sees as characteristic of contemporary France. Unfortunately, he makes this case with a prose that is so dense as to be virtually unintelligible. See Jean Baudrillard, *L'Échange symbolique et la mort* (Paris: Gallimard, 1976). For a useful guide to Baudrillard see Douglas Kellner, *Jean Baudrillard: From Marxism to Postmodernism and Beyond* (Stanford: Stanford University Press, 1989).

64. Reddy, *The Rise of Market Culture*, 1–18.

65. Viviana Zelizer, *Pricing the Priceless Child—The Changing Social Value of Children* (New York: Basic Books, 1985).

66. Anne Philipe, *Je l'écoute respirer* (Paris: Gallimard, 1984).

Epilogue

1. T. J. Clark, *Image of the People—Gustave Courbet and the 1848 Revolution* (Princeton: Princeton University Press, 1982), 136–138; Françoise Gaillard, "Gustave Courbet et le Réalisme—Anatomie de la réception critique d'une oeuvre: 'Un Enterrement à Ornans,' " *Revue d'histoire littéraire de la France* 80 (1980): 978–996; Georges Riat, *Gustave Courbet, peintre* (Paris, 1906), 86–88; *Exigences de réalisme dans la peinture française entre 1830 et 1870* (Chartres: Musée de Beaux-Arts, 1984), 978–996. Helène Toussaint lists contemporary references in her essay on the painting in *Gustave Courbet (1819–1877)* (Paris: Editions des musées nationaux, 1977), 98.

2. Clark, *Image of the People*, 114. For the social attitudes represented in French art see Raymond Grew, "Painting the People: Images of the Lower Orders in Nineteenth-Century French Art," *Journal of Interdisciplinary History* 17 (1986): 203–231.

3. Michael Fried, "The Structure of Beholding in Courbet's *Burial at Ornans*," *Critical Inquiry* 9 (1983): 636–637. This article has now been incorporated into Michael Fried, *Courbet's Realism* (Chicago: University of Chicago Press, 1990); see especially 116–118.

4. Fried, "Structure of Beholding," 636, 661. In *Courbet's Realism* Fried adopts a slightly different vocabulary; the "beholder" becomes the "painter-beholder," a shift that emphasizes Courbet's personal engagement with his project. See, for example, 124, where Fried alters the passage I cite so that it reads that "the open grave truncated by the bottom framing edge . . . is a

means . . . of resisting closure and therefore facilitating the quasi-corporeal merger of painter-beholder into the painting that I am arguing was an overarching and obsessive aim of Courbet's enterprise."

5. Clark, *Image of the People*, 83.

6. Linda Nochlin, "Innovation and Tradition in Courbet's *Burial at Ornans*," in *Essays in Honor of Walter Friedlander* (New York, 1965), 119–126. See also Linda Nochlin, *Realism* (New York: Penguin, 1971), 78–82. Nochlin's chapter "Death in the Mid-Nineteenth Century" in ibid., 57–102 places Courbet's painting in a broad context of artistic and literary treatments of death. Nochlin argues that "the nineteenth century artist or writer severs [death's] transcendental connections and posits the non-value of the dead person and the meaninglessness of his experience (65)." Nochlin's chapter is important both for its argument and for the extensive documentation that it provides on the theme of death. I argue, however, that the denial of transcendence that she cites as the crucial element in realist portrayals of death acquires its force only because it recalls the expectations and hopes that were still part of nineteenth-century culture.

7. *Du principe de l'art et de sa destination sociale*, in *Oeuvres complètes de P.-J. Proudhon*, ed. C. Bouglé et H. Moysset (Paris: Rivière, 1939), 15:175.

8. Ibid.

9. Courbet's knowledge of folk rituals can be seen in his 1855 painting *La Toilette de la mort*, which shows women from Franche-Comté preparing the corpse of a young woman for viewing and burial. See Toussaint, *Gustave Courbet (1819–1877)*, 107–109, where the author argues persuasively that this painting, formerly known as *La Toilette de la mariée*, is in fact a scene about the dead.

10. Meyer Schapiro, "Courbet and Popular Imagery: An Essay on Realism and Naiveté," *Journal of the Warburg and Courtault Institutes* 4 (1941): 164–191; Michael Marrinan, *Painting Politics for Louis-Philippe—Art and Ideology in Orléanist France* (New Haven: Yale University Press, 1988), 213–214, suggests that Courbet was building on a tradition established during the July Monarchy, when painting "addressed an audience versed in the pictorial grammar of popular prints, theater, and genre paintings." See also: Clark, *Image of the People*, 81, 138–140; Nochlin, "Innovation and Tradition"; Fried, *Courbet's Realism*, 114–115, 125–129.

11. David Troyansky, *Old Age in the Old Regime: Image and Experience in Eighteenth-Century France* (Ithaca: Cornell University Press, 1989), 20–23; Alain Charraud, "Analyse de la représentation des âges de la vie humaine dans les estampes populaires du XIXe siècle," *Ethnologie française* 1 (1971): 59–78; Jean Cuisenier, *French Folk Art* (New York: Kodansha, 1977), 161–162, 179–180. Barbara Ann Day, "Representing Aging and Death in French Culture," *French Historical Studies* 17 (1992): 688–724, appeared after my analysis.

12. Gabriel Weisberg, *The Realist Tradition: French Painting and Drawing, 1830–1900* (Cleveland: Cleveland Museum of Art, 1980), 109–110.

13. *French Painting, 1774–1830—The Age of Revolution*, Catalogue of Exhibit (Detroit and New York: Detroit Institute of Arts and Metropolitan Museum of Art, 1975), 257, 554–555. In many of the popular prints depicting the death

of Atala, based on Chateaubriand's novel, Père Aubry becomes the dominant figure; in administering communion and blessing the dying girl he provides Atala and her lover the reassurance of a Christian death. See Susan Delaney, " 'Atala' in the Arts," in *The Wolf and the Lamb: Popular Culture in France*, ed. Jacques Beauroy, Marc Bertrand, and Edward Gargan (Saratoga, Calif.: Anma Libri, 1977), 210–231.

14. Nochlin, "Innovation and Tradition in Courbet's *Burial at Ornans*."

15. "Le Fossoyeur," *Le Magasin pittoresque* 11 (1843): 215–216.

16. Of course, artists were not restricted to the expression of pious sentiments; Delacroix's *Death of Sardanapolous* is the most famous example of how romantics exploited the erotic possibilities available within the theme of death.

17. Claudette Mainzer, "Who is Buried at Ornans?" in *Courbet Reconsidered*, ed. Sarah Faunce and Linda Nochlin (New Haven: Yale University Press, 1988), 77–82. For a more detailed discussion of the transferral of the cemetery at Ornans see Claudette Mainzer, *Gustave Courbet, Franc-Comtois*, 49–74.

18. Clark, *Image of the People*, 127–128, refers precisely to the social context of death and burial as a context that informed Parisian viewers of the *Burial*; my argument here is that this element of his analysis deserves greater emphasis.

19. Toussaint, *Gustave Courbet (1819–1877)*, 100.

20. Max Buchon, Advertisement for Courbet's Exhibition in Dijon. Published in *Le Peuple*, 7 June 1850. T. J. Clark first called attention to the importance of Buchon's "Annonce" in "A Bourgeois Dance of Death: Max Buchon on Courbet," *Burlington Magazine* 111 (1969): 208–211, 286–290. Buchon's text is reprinted in Clark, *Image of the People*, 162–164.

21. If Helène Toussaint is right, the skull of the *Burial* may be a reference to the skull of Adam that the Gospel of Matthew reported as unearthed on Golgotha at the moment of Christ's death. She further proposes that it be read as a masonic symbol and that Courbet's intent in placing it in the scene was to suggest the possibility of universal reconciliation. This last point, however, seems difficult to justify given the ambivalence and detachment on the faces of the mourners. See Toussaint, *Gustave Courbet (1819–1877)*, 102.

22. For examples of Breton's paintings see *The Dedication of a Calvary* (1858), and *The Great Pilgrimage* (1869), in Weisberg, *The Realist Tradition*, 114, 121. For other examples of conventional scenes of death see *Exigences de réalisme*, 118

23. James Henry Rubin, *Realism and Social Vision in Courbet and Proudhon* (Princeton: Princeton University Press, 1980), 154–155 n. 17. Michael Fried, "The Structure of Beholding," 637, also makes this point, without developing it.

24. Rubin, *Realism and Social Vision*, 155. Nochlin, *Realism*, calls attention to the tendency among realist painters to represent death just after it has occurred, another way of considering death within a deritualized framework. Courbet's *Burial*, however, heightens the contrast between the nonritual and the ritual by bringing us so close to the moment when the prayers begin.

SELECT BIBLIOGRAPHY

PRIMARY SOURCES (UNPUBLISHED)

AN = National Archives (Paris)

BB 30 198	F2 2762
F19 5523	F15 3721
F19 5530	F19 2762
F19 5531	F19 4180
F19 5532	F19 4378
F19 5615	F19 4379
F19 5712	F19 5504
F19 5720	F19 5512
F19 5776	F19 5513
F19 6115	F19 5514
F19 10168	F19 5517
F19 10172	F19 5518
F19 11032	F19 5519
F20 573	F19 5520

ADS = Departmental Archives, Seine (Paris)

V D 4

D10, AZ 542

ADML = Departmental Archives, Maine-et-Loire (Angers)

1 M 1
1 M 6/48
46 M 1
1 N 39
1 N 48   2 V 2
5 V 30
5 V 32
5 V 34
7 V
7 V 6

AEA = Episcopal Archives, Angers

3 F 3
6 G 1
2 K 8
5 K 4
1 L 8
O—Baugé

O—Broc
O—Champtoceaux
O—Gennes
O—Montreuil-Bellay
O—St. Hilaire-St. Florent
OP   25
P   12
P   63
P   62
P   121

AMA – Municipal Archives, Angers
DD   16
37   M   1
37   M   5
37   M   7
37   M   10
37   M   12
37   M   47
Cimetières

Primary Sources (Published)

Administration des fabriques de la ville d'Angers—Règlement pour les concessions de terrains dans les cimetières. Angers: 1842.

Administration des fabriques de la ville d'Angers. Angers: [1862].

L'ami de la religion.

L'ami du clergé.

Aulard, F. A., ed. *La Société des Jacobins—Recueil des documents*. Vol. 6. Paris: Cerf, 1897.

Balard, M. *Aperçu sur quelques améliorations importantes à introduire dans le service des pompes funèbres de la ville de Paris et de ses dépendances*. Paris: Stahl, 1845.

———. M. *Les Mystères des pompes funèbres de la ville de Paris dévoilés par les entrepreneurs eux-mêmes*. Paris: Allard, 1856.

Balzac, Honoré de. *Cousin Pons*. Baltimore: Penguin, 1968.

———. *Old Goriot*. Baltimore: Penguin, 1971.

Baratte, Léon. *Rapports de l'autorité civile et de l'autorité religieuse en matière de sépulture*. Le Mans: Drouin, 1904.

Barry, Paul de. *Pensez-y bien, réflexions sur les quatre fins derniers*. Paris and Troyes: Société de Saint-Victor pour la propagation des bons livres, 1857.

Barthez, Dr. E. *The Empress Eugénie and Her Circle*. New York: Brentano's, 1913.

Baudelaire, Charles. *Oeuvres complètes de Charles Baudelaire—Traductions: Histoires extraordinaires par Edgar Poe*. Paris: Conard, 1932.

Bausset-Roquefort, Baptiste-Gabriel-Ferdinand. *Etude sur le mouvement de la population depuis le commencement du XIXe siècle*. Marseilles: Roux, 1862.

Bergson, Henri. *Mélanges*. Paris: Presses universitaires de France, 1972.

Bigot, Louis-Auguste. *Reclamation par Louis-Auguste Bigot, marchand tapissier-décorateur, premier entrepreneur des cérémonies religieuses et pompes funèbres à Paris . . . contre le prétendu privilège de Sieur Bobée concernant les pompes et ornements des inhumations dans la ville de Paris*. Paris: n.d.

Blanqui, Auguste. *L'Eternité par les astres*. Paris: Baillière, 1872.

Blot, Pierre, S.J. *Au ciel on se reconnaît*. 38th ed. Paris: 1902.

Bolo, Abbé Henry. *Nos communications avec les morts*, 6th ed. Paris: Haton, 1903.

Bontoux, Paul-Benoît-François. *Des devoirs á rendre aux morts*. Paris: Imprimerie Nationale, Prairial, an IV [1796].

Boutroue, Denis. *Journal de Denis Boutroue, curé-cultivateur (1783–1817)*. In *Le Folklore de la Beauce*, edited by Charles Marcel-Robillard and René Rivet. Vol. 12. Paris: Maisoneuve et Larose, 1978.

Bouvier, Jean. *Traité dogmatique et pratique des indulgences, des confréries, et du Jubilé*. Le Mans: Monnoyer, 1826.

Brouardel, Dr. Paul. *Sépultures—Projet de revision du décret du 23 prairial an XII*. Paris: Melun, 1896.

Brydaine, Jacques. *Sermons du Père Brydaine*. 5 vols. 4th ed. Paris: Lecoffre, 1867.

Cahagnet, Louis Alphonse. *Arcanes de la vie future dévoilés*. Paris: Baillière, 1848.

Cahier de charges de l'entreprise générale du service des inhumations. Paris: 1811.

Camp, Maxime du. *Le Salon de 1861*. Paris: Bourdilliat, 1861.

Camp, Maxime du. *Paris—Ses organes, ses fonctions, et sa vie*. Vol. 6. Paris: Hachette, 1875.

Cantiques à l'usage de la mission donnée dans l'Eglise Cathédrale en décembre 1807. Angers: Pavie, 1807.

Cantiques à l'usage des missions et des retraites. Angers: Mame, 1828.

Catechisme du diocèse d'Angers. Angers: Pavie, 1815.

Chants pieux ou choix de cantiques. Paris: Poussielgue, 1861.

Chardouillet, J.F.E. *Les Cimetières de Paris—Sont-ils foyers d'inféction?* Paris: 1881.

Chateaubriand, René de. *Génie du christianisme*. 2 vols. Paris: Flammarion, 1966; first published 1802.

Chevé, C. F. *Dictionnaire des conversions ou Essai d'Encyclopédie Historique des conversions au Catholicisme depuis le dix-huitième siècle*. Paris: Migne, 1852.

Clemenceau, Georges. *In the Evening of My Thought*, 2 vols. New York: Houghton-Mifflin, 1929.

Cloquet, Abbé Célestin. *Les Plus Faciles Indulgences à gagner*. 4th ed. Lyons: n.d.

Cognat, Abbé Joseph. "De l'évocation des esprits." *L'ami de la religion* 163 (14 January 1854): 109–115.

Collet, Abbé Pierre. *Traité des saints mystères où l'on résout les principales difficultés que se rencontrent dans leur célébration.* 2 vols. 10th ed. Paris: Méquingnon, 1828.

Comte, Auguste. *Auguste Comte and Positivism—The Essential Writings.* Edited by Gertrude Lenzer. New York: Harper, 1975.

———. *Catéchisme positiviste.* Paris: Garnier-Flammarion, 1966.

———. *Testament avec les documents qui s'y rapportent.* Paris: 1896.

Cormeau, Henry. *Terroirs mauges. Miettes d'une vie provinciale.* 2 vols. Paris: Georges Crès, 1912.

Cormenin, Louis-Maire. *Défense de l'évêque de Clermont, traduit pour cause d'abus devant les révérends Pères du Conseil d'Etat.* 2d ed. Paris: Pagnerre, 1839.

Coulanges, Fustel de. *The Ancient City.* Garden City, N.Y.: Anchor Doubleday, 1955; first published 1864.

Coupé, Jacques-Michel. *Des sépultures en politique et en morale.* Paris: Imprimerie Nationale, Thermidor an IV [1796].

Coupé, Jacques-Michel. *De la moralité des sépultures et de leur police.* Paris: Vallant, an IX [1801].

Cousin, Victor. *Du vrai, du beau, et du bien.* Paris: Didier, 1856.

———. *Philosophie populaire.* Paris: Didot, 1848.

Craisson, Abbé D. *De la sépulture ecclésiastique.* 2d ed. Poitiers: Oudin, 1868.

Daudet, Alphonse. *Lettres de mon moulin.* Paris: Livre de Poche, 1982.

Debreyne, Pierre. *Etude de la mort.* Paris: Poussielgue, 1845.

———. *La Théologie morale et les sciences médicales.* 6th ed. Paris: Poussielgue, 1884.

Delamalle, Gaspard. *Réflexions sur l'enterrement de ma mère.* 2d ed. Paris: Librairie Chrétienne, an IV [1796].

Delandre, Adrien. "La Magie et les magiciens au XIXe siècle." *Revue contemporaine* 32 (1857): 5–32, 251–284.

Demonferrand, J.B.F. *Essai sur les lois de la population.* Paris: 1838.

Duché, Emile. *Quelques particularités sur le mouvement de la population dans le département de l'Yonne.* 1864.

Dulaure, Jacques A. *Histoire physique, civile et morale de Paris.* Paris: Furne, 1838.

Durkheim, Emile. *Moral Education.* New York: Free Press, 1973.

———. *Suicide: A Study in Sociology.* Translated by J. A. Spaulding and G. Simpson. New York: Free Press, 1951.

Esquiros, Alphonse. "Les Cimetières de Paris." *Revue de Paris.* Feb.-March 1844: 261–266.

———. *De la vie future au point de vue socialiste.* Paris: Comon, 1850.

Fernand, Jacques. *Les Cimetières supprimés.* Paris: Vanier, 1873.

Figuier, Louis. *Le Lendemain de la mort, ou la vie future selon la science.* Paris: Hachette, 1871.

Flammarion, Camille. *Haunted Houses.* New York: Appleton, 1924.

———. *L'Inconnu et les problèmes psychiques: manifestations des mourants, apparitions, télépathie, communications psychiques, suggestion mentale, vue à distance; le monde des rêves, la divination de l'avenir.* Paris: Flammarion, 1900.

———. *La Mort et son mystère.* 3 vols. Paris: Flammarion, 1920–1922.

———. *La Pluralité des mondes*, 33d ed. Paris: Flammarion, 1885.

———. *Les Habitants de l'autre monde*. Paris: Ledoyen, 1862.

———. *Mémoires*. Paris: Flammarion, 1911.

———. *Récits de l'infini*. 11th ed. Paris: Flammarion, 1885.

Flaubert, Gustave. *Bouvard et Pécuchet*. Paris: Gallimard, 1979.

———.*Correspondance*. Vol. 2, *1852*. Paris: Conard, 1926–1954.

Fleury, Jules. *Souvenirs et portraits de jeunesse*. Paris: 1872.

Fontaine, Jean de la. *The Complete Fables of Jean de la Fontaine*. Edited and translated by Norman B. Spencer. Evanston: Northwestern University Press, 1988.

Fourier, Charles. *Oeuvres complètes*, Vol. 3. Paris: 1841.

Fraysse, Camille. *Le Folk-Lore du baugeois*. Baugé: Dangin, 1906.

G. G. *Promenade sérieuse au cimetière du Père Lachaise, ou de Mont-Louis près de Paris*. Paris: 1826.

Gasparin, Agenon de. *Science vs. Modern Spiritualism: A Treatise on Turning Tables, the Supernatural in General, and Spirits*. Translated by E. W. Robert. New York: Kiggins and Kellogg, 1858.

Gaudry, Joachim. *Traité de la législation des cultes*. 3 vols. Paris: Durand, 1856.

Gaume, Jean-Joseph Monseigneur. *The Christian Cemetery in the Nineteeth Century; or The Last War-Cry of the Communists*. Translated from the French by Rev. Richard Brennan. New York: Benziger, 1874.

Gautier, Théophile. *Abécédaire du salon de 1861*. Paris: Dentu, 1861.

———. *La Morte amoureuse, avatar, et autre récits fantastiques*. Paris: Gallimard, 1981.

Graffenauer, Jean-Philippe. *Topographie physique et médicale de la ville de Strasbourg*. Strasbourg: Levrault, 1816.

Gramont, Comte F. de. *Comment on vient et comment on s'en va*. Paris: Lévy, 1858.

Guépin, Ange, and Eugène Bonamy. *Nantes au XIXe siècle*. Nantes: Sebire, 1835.

Guillard, Achille. *Eléments de statistique humaine; ou Démographie comparée, où sont exposés les principes de la science nouvelle, et confrontés d'après les documents les plus authentiques, l'état, les mouvements généraux et les progrès de la population dans les pays civilisés*. Paris: Guillaumin, 1855.

Guillaumin, Emile. *The Life of a Simple Man*. Hanover, N.H.: University Press of New England, 1983.

Hamon, Père Edouard. *Au delà du tombeau*. 3d ed. Paris: Tequi, 1912.

Head, Sir Francis. *A Faggot of French Sticks or, Paris in 1851*. New York: Putnam, 1852.

Hugo, Victor. *Les Contemplations*. Paris: Gallimard, 1973; first published 1856.

———. *Les Misérables*. Translated by Charles Wilbour. New York: Random House Modern Library, n.d.

———. *Oeuvres complètes*. Vol. 9. Pt. 2. Edited by Jean Massin. Introduction by Jean and Sheila Gaudin. Paris: Le Club Français du Livre, 1971.

Huguet, Père Jean-Joseph. *Mois consolateur des âmes du Purgatoire*. Paris: Perisse, 1864.

Janet, Paul. *Victor Cousin et son ouevre*. Paris: Calmann-Lévy, 1885.

————*Le Journal de Maine-et-Loire.*

————*Journal Officiel* (referred to as *JO*).

Juin, Abbé Jean-Augustin. *Lettre au clergé français, ou conseils touchant les refus de sépulture.* Paris: Leclerc, n.d.

Kardec, Allan. *Le livre des esprits.* 15th ed. Paris: Didier, 1865.

Kardec, Allan. *Qu'est-ce que le Spiritisme?* 19th ed. Paris: Librairie des sciences psychologiques, n.d.

Lachaise, Claude. *Topographie médicale de Paris.* Paris: 1822.

Lacordaire, Henri de. *Conférences de Notre Dame.* 3 vols. Paris: Poussielgue, 1861.

Lagneau, Gustave. "Population de Paris; remarques démographiques sur l'habitat urbain." *Bulletin de l'Academie de Médecine* (1893): 740–760.

Lamartine, Alphonse de. *Opinions sur Dieu, le bonheur, et l'éternité d'après les livres sacrés de l'inde.* Paris: Sand, 1984; first published 1856.

Laurentin, René, and Bernard Billet, eds. *Lourdes—Documents authentiques.* Vol 1. Paris: Lethielleux, 1957.

Le médecin des pauvres. Rouen: Surville, 1851.

Le moyen d'aller droit au ciel. 4th ed. Lyons: Rougier, 1870.

Le Vavasseur, Père Léon-Michel. *Cérémonial selon le Rit Romain.* 5th ed. Paris: Lecoffre, 1876.

Legoyt, Alfred. *La France et l'étranger: études de statistique comparée.* 2 vols. Paris: Berger-Levrault, 1870.

Lelandais, Abbé Pierre. *Choix de la prédication contemporaine.* 4 vols. 7th ed. Paris: Bloud et Barral, 1885.

Lenormand, Marie-Anne-Adélaïde. *Arrêt suprème des dieux d'Olympe.* Paris: chez l'auteur, 1833.

————. *Les oracles sibyllins.* Paris: chez l'auteur, 1817.

Lépicier, Alexis. *Les indulgences—Leur origine, leur nature, leur développement.* 2 vols. Paris: Lethielleux, 1903.

Leroux, Pierre. *De l'humanité, de son principe, et de son avenir.* 2 vols. Paris: Perrotin, 1840.

Lettres familières de l'Impératrice. 2 vols. Paris: Le Divan, 1935.

Levasseur, Emile. *La Population française.* 3 vols. Paris: Rousseau, 1889–1892.

Littré, Emile. "Du tables parlantes, des esprits frappeurs et autres manifestations de ce temps-ci." *Revue des Deux Mondes* 1 (1856): 847–872.

Louvet, Abbé Louis-Eugène. *Le Purgatoire d'après les révélations des saints.* 3rd ed. Albi: 1899.

Le Magasin pittoresque.

Le Magasin catholique illustré.

Marthe. Paris: Seuil, 1982.

Martin du Gard, Roger. *Jean Barois.* New York: Bobbs-Merrill, 1969.

Matignon, Père Ambroise, S.J. *Les Morts et les vivants.* Paris: Le Clere, 1863.

Maupassant, Guy de. *Contes fantastiques complets.* Paris: Marabout, 1983.

————. *Contes de jour et de la nuit.* Paris: Garnier/Flammarion, 1977.

Mauriac, François. *The Inner Presence.* New York: Bobbs-Merrill, 1968.

Ménétra, Jacques-Louis. *Journal of my Life.* Introduction and commentary by Daniel Roche. New York: Columbia University Press, 1986.

Méric, Elie. *Le Merveilleux et la science—Étude sur l'hypnotisme*. Paris: Letouzey, 1887.

Mérimée, Prosper. *Carmen*. Paris: Flammarion, 1973.

Michelet, Jules. *Histoire de la Révolution française*. Vol. 2. Paris: Laffont, 1979.

Michelet, Jules. *Mother Death—The Journal of Jules Michelet, 1815–1850*. Translated and edited by Edward Kaplan. Amherst: University of Massachusetts Press, 1984.

Mirville, Jules Eudes de. *Pneumatologie: Des esprits et de leurs manifestations fluidiques*. 6 vols. Paris: Vrayet de Surcy, 1863–1864.

Nodier, Charles. *La Fée aux Miettes, Smarra, Trilby*. Paris: Gallimard, 1982.

Notice historique sur l'ancien grand cimetière et sur les cimetières actuels de la ville d'Orléans. Orléans: 1824.

Nus, Eugène. *Choses de l'autre monde*. 5th ed. Paris: Librairie des sciences psychologiques et spirites, n.d.

Observations présentées au nom des fabriques sur les modifications à apporter aux conditions prochaines de l'adjudication du service des pompes funèbres. Paris: Gros, n.d.

Offices de l'église du matin et du soir suivant le rit romain. Paris: Lecoffre, 1858.

Office des Morts. Laval: Godbert, 1859.

Parfait, Paul. *L'arsénal des dévotions*. Paris: Decaux, 1876.

Pector, Anatole. *Exposé des causes qui ont influé sur la situation de l'entreprise des pompes funèbres de la ville de Paris*. Paris: Bénard, 1849.

———. *Précis sur le service des inhumations et des pompes funèbres de la ville de Paris*. Paris: Duberger, 1842.

Perdiguier, Agricol. *Mémoires d'un compagnon*. Paris: Maspero, 1977.

Philipe, Anne. *Je l'écoute respirer*. Paris: Gallimard, 1984.

Prieur, Jean. *Les témoins de l'invisible*. Paris: Fayard, 1972.

Proudhon, Pierre-Joseph. *Du principe de l'art et de sa destination sociale*. In *Oeuvres complètes de P.-J. Proudhon*, edited by C. Bouglé et H. Moysset. Vol. 15. Paris: Rivière, 1939.

Quetelet, Lambert A. J. *A Treatise on Man*. Translated by Solomon Diamond. Edinburgh: William and Robert Chambers, 1842.

Ranvier, H. *Rapport sur la municipilisation du service des pompes funèbres de la ville de Paris*. Paris: 1905.

Ravignan, Gustave de. *Conférences du Révérend Père de Ravignan de la compagnie de Jésus prêchées à Notre-Dame de Paris*. 4 vols. Paris: Poussielgue, 1860.

Recherches statistiques sur la ville de Paris et sur le département de la Seine. Vol. 1. Paris: Ballard, 1821.

Recherches statistiques sur la ville de Paris. Paris: 1826.

Recherches statistiques sur la ville de Paris. Paris: 1860.

Recueil des scapulaires. Paris: Agence ecclésiastique et religieuse de Rome, 1862.

Réfutation de la Calomnie dirigée contre M. Pector par le Sieur Charles Baudouin. Paris: Duverger, 1842.

Renan, Ernest. *Oeuvres complètes*. Vol. 3. Paris: Calmann-Lévy, 1949.

———. *Souvenirs d'enfance et de jeunesse*. Paris: Gallimard, 1983.

Renouvier, Charles. *Essais de critique générale: Deuxième essai*. Paris: Ladrange, 1859.

———. *Les Derniers Entretiens*. Paris: Vrin, 1930.

Reynaud, Jean. *Réponse au concile de Périgueux*. Paris: Furne, 1858.

———. *Terre et ciel*. Paris: Furne, 1854.

Richard, N. *Conducteur de l'étranger dans Marseilles*. Marseilles: 1840.

———. *Le véritable conducteur aux cimetières du Père Lachaise, Montmartre, et Vaugirard*. Paris: 1836.

Richet, Charles. "Du somnambulisme provoqué." *Revue philosophique de la France et de l'étranger* 5 (1880): 337–374, 462–484.

Riobé, Xavier. *Note à consulter pour l'établissement d'un mode régulier d'inhumuation et de pompes funèbres*. Paris: Entreprises des Pompes Funèbres Générales, n. d.

Rituel du diocèse d'Angers. 3 vols. Angers: Mame, 1828.

Rouzic, Louis. *Le Purgatoire—Pour nos morts et avec nos morts*. 3d ed. Paris: Tequi, 1922.

Sand, George. *The Haunted Pool*. San Lorenzo, Calif.: Shameless Hussy Press, 1976.

Sanson, Abbé. *Purgatoire et ciel*. Paris: Bray et Retaux, 1875.

Schneider, Josephus, S.J. *Rescripta authentica sacrae congregationis indulgentiis sacrisque reliquiis*. Rome: 1885.

Schouppe, F. X. *Purgatory*. Rockville, Ill.: Tan, 1973; first published in France, 1893.

———. *Short Sermons for the Low Masses of Sunday*. Translated. New York: Benziger, 1883.

Ségala, Père Alexis. *Le Purgatoire—Dogme, suffrages, pratiques*. 2d ed. Paris: Poussielgue, 1880.

Simon, Jules. *La Religion naturelle*, 4th ed. Paris: Hachette, 1857.

———. *Le Devoir*. Paris: Hachette, 1854.

———. *Victor Cousin*. Paris: Hachette, 1887.

Soland, Aimé de. *Proverbes et dictons rimés de l'Anjou*. Angers: Lainé, 1858.

Swedenborg, Emmanuel. *Arcanes célestes*. 7 vols. Translated by J.F.E. Le Boys des Guays. St. Amande and Paris: 1841–1854.

———. *L'Apocalypse réveilée*. Translated by J. P. Moet and J.A.T. Tull. Paris: Treuttel et Wurtz, 1823.

———. *L'Apocalypse réveilée*. Translated by J.F.E. Le Boys des Guays. Saint Amande and Paris: 1856.

Le Temps.

Thiers, Jean-Baptiste. *Traité des superstitions qui regardent les sacremens*. 4 vols. Paris: 1751.

Tocqueville, Alexis de. *Oeuvres complètes*. Vol. 14. Paris: Gallimard, 1983.

Vafflard, Léon. *De l'intérêt que le public a ce que le bail actuel des pompes funèbres peut expirer depuis 3 ans*. Paris: Lacombe, 1842.

———. *Notice sur les champs des sépultures anciennes et modernes de la ville de Paris*. Paris: Librairie Internationale, 1867.

———. *Observations sur le service des inhumations et pompes funèbres de la ville de Paris*. Paris: 1847.

Velgre, R.P.A. *Cours élémentaire de liturgie sacrée*. 6th ed. Paris: Lethielleux, 1896.

Villermé, Louis-René. "De la mortalité dans les divers quartiers de Paris." *Annales d'hygiène publique et de médecine légale* 3(1830): 334.

——. "Des sociétés de prévoyance ou de secours mutuels." *Annales d'hygiène publique* (1845): 94–111.

——. *Tableau de l'état physique et moral des ouvriers employés dans les manufactures de coton, de laine, et de soie*. 2 vols. Paris: Renouard, 1840.

Vivent, Abbé Louis. *Petit manuel du pèlerinage de Lourdes*. Paris: Chance, 1874.

Yourcenar, Marguerite. *Souvenirs pieux*. Paris: Gallimard, 1974.

Zola, Emile. *L'Assommoir*. Baltimore: Penguin, 1970.

——. *Oeuvres complètes*. Vol. 9. Paris: Cercle du Livre Précieux, 1968.

Secondary Sources

Ackerman, Evelyn B. *Health Care in the Parisian Countryside, 1800–1914*. New Brunswick: Rutgers University Press, 1990.

——. *Village on the Seine: Tradition and Change in Bonnières, 1815–1914*. Ithaca: Cornell University Press, 1978.

Agulhon, Maurice. *La République au village*. Paris: Seuil, 1970.

——. "La 'statumanie' et l'histoire." *Ethnologie française* 8 (1978): 145–172.

Albaric, Michel, Barnard Ardura et al. *Histoire du missel français*. Paris: Brepols, 1986.

Amundsen, Darrel, and Ronald Numbers, eds. *Caring and Curing—Health and Medicine in Western Religious Traditions*. New York: Macmillan, 1986.

Ariès, Philippe. *Centuries of Childhood*. Translated by Robert Baldick. New York: Vintage, 1962.

——. *Essais sur l'histoire de la mort en Occident*. Paris: Seuil, 1975.

——. *Images of Man and Death*. Translated by Janet Lloyd. Cambridge: Harvard University Press, 1985.

——. *The Hour of Our Death*. Translated by Helen Weaver. New York: Knopf, 1981.

——. *Western Attitudes toward Death: From the Middle Ages to the Present*. Translated by Patricia Ranum. Baltimore: Johns Hopkins University Press, 1974.

Armengaud, André. *La Population française au XIXe siècle*. 2d éd. Paris: Presses Universitaires de France, 1976.

Armengaud, André. "Un siècle délaissé: le XIXe siècle (1815–1914)." *Annales de démographie historique* (1971): 299–310.

Auspitz, Katherine. *The Radical Bourgeoisie—The Ligue de l'Enseignement and the Origins of the Third Republic, 1866–1885*. Cambridge: Cambridge University Press, 1982.

Badone, Ellen, ed. *Religious Orthodoxy and Popular Faith in European Society*. Princeton: Princeton University Press, 1990.

——. *The Appointed Hour: Death, Worldview, and Social Change in Brittany*. Berkeley: University of California Press, 1989.

Barber, Paul. *Vampires, Burial, and Death—Folklore and Reality.* New Haven: Yale University Press, 1988.

Barrow, Logie. *Independent Spirits—Spiritualism and English Plebians, 1850–1910.* New York: Routledge and Kegan Paul, 1986.

Bascom, William. "The Forms of Folklore: Prose Narratives." In *Sacred Narrative—Readings in the Theory of Myth,* edited by Alan Dundes. Berkeley: University of California Press, 1984.

Beaver, M.V. "Population, Infant Mortality, and Milk." *Population* 25 (1970): 243–255.

Becker, Ernest. *The Denial of Death.* New York: Free Press, 1973.

Beecher, Jonathan. *Charles Fourier—The Visionary and His World.* Berkeley: University of California Press, 1986.

Bée, Michel. "La révolte des confréries de charité de l'Eure en 1842–1843." *Annales de Normandie* 24 (1972): 89–115.

———. "Les cimetières de Calvados en 1804." In *Mentalités religieuses dans la France de l'ouest aux XIXe et XXe siècles.* Caen: 1976.

Ben-Amos, Avner. *Molding the National Memory: The State Funerals of the French Third Republic.* Ph.D. diss., University of California, Berkeley, 1988.

Benichou, Paul. *Le Temps des prophètes: Doctrines de l'âge romantique.* Paris: Gallimard, 1977.

Berenson, Edward. *Populist Religion and Left-Wing Politics in France.* Princeton: Princeton University Press, 1984.

Berlanstein, Lenard. *Working People of Paris, 1870–1914.* Baltimore: Johns Hopkins University Press, 1984.

Bertocci, Phillip. *Jules Simon: Republican Anticlericalism and Cultural Politics in France (1848–1886).* Columbia: University of Missouri Press, 1978.

Bertrand, Régis, and Michel Vovelle. *La Ville des morts—Essai sur l'imaginaire urbain contemporain d'après les cimetières provençaux.* Paris: CNRS, 1983.

Bertrand, Régis. "Cimetières marseillais aux XVIIIe et XIXe siècles." *Provence Historique* 92 (1973): 217–246.

Bettelheim, Bruno. *The Uses of Enchantment—The Meaning and Importance of Fairy Tales.* New York: Vintage, 1977.

Bideau, Alain, Guy Brunet, and Roger Desbos. "Variations locales de la mortalité des enfants: L'Exemple de la Chatellenie de Saint-Trivier-en-Dombes (1730–1869)." *Annales de démographie historique* (1978): 7–29.

Bollème, Geneviève, ed. *La Bible bleue: Anthologie d'une littérature populaire.* Paris: Flammarion, 1975.

Borel, Jacques. *Séraphita et le mysticisme balzacien.* Paris: Corti, 1967.

Borsa, Serge, and C.-R. Michel. *La Vie quotidienne des hôpitaux en France au XIXe siècle.* Paris: Hachette, 1985.

Bossut, Nicole. "Aux origines de la déchristianisation dans la Nièvre: Fouché, Chaumette, ou les Jacobins?" *Annales Historiques de la Révolution française* 264 (1986): 181–202.

Bourdelais, Patrice, and Jean-Yves Raulot. *Une Peur bleue—Histoire du choléra en France, 1832–1854.* Paris: Payot, 1987.

Bourgeois-Pichat, J. "The General Development of the Population of France Since the Eighteenth Century." In *Population in History*, edited by D. V. Glass and D.E.C. Eversley. Chicago: Aldine Publishing Company, 1965.

Boutry, Philippe, and Michel Cenquin. *Deux pèlerinages au XIXe siècle: Ars et Paray-le-Monial*. Paris: Beauchesne, 1980.

Boutry, Philippe. *Prêtres et paroisses au pays du Curé d'Ars*. Paris: Cerf, 1986.

Bowman, Frank Paul. "Illuminism, Utopia, Mythology." In *The French Romantics*, edited by D. G. Charlton. Vol. 1. Cambridge: Cambridge University Press, 1984.

Brandon, Ruth. *The Spiritualists*. New York: Knopf, 1983.

Briggs, Robin. *Communities of Belief—Cultural and Social Tension in Early Modern France*. Oxford: Clarendon Press, 1989.

Britten, Emma Hardinge. *Nineteenth-Century Miracles*. New York: Lovell, 1884.

Brouard, Janine. *La Naissance, le mariage, la mort en Anjou dans la première moitié du XXe siècle*, Cahiers de l'I.P.S.A., no. 8. Angers: Université Catholique de l'Ouest, 1984.

Brown, Frederick. *Père Lachaise—Elysium as Real Estate*. New York: Viking, 1973.

Buckley, Michael J. *At the Origins of Modern Atheism*. New Haven: Yale University Press, 1988.

Burke, Peter. *Popular Culture in Early Modern Europe*. New York: Harper and Row, 1978.

Bynum, Caroline. "Bodily Self and the Resurrection of the Body in the High Middle Ages." In *Belief in History—Innovative Approaches to European and American Religion*, edited by Thomas Kselman. Notre Dame: University of Notre Dame Press, 1991.

Bynum, Caroline. *Holy Feast and Holy Fast—The Religious Significance of Food to Medieval Women*. Berkeley: University of California Press, 1987.

Cabanis, José. *Michelet, le prêtre, et la femme*. Paris: Gallimard, 1978.

Calbo, P. "Médecins en Sarthe dans la seconde moitié du XIXe siècle." *Annales de Bretagne et du pays de l'Ouest* 92 (1985): 209–224.

Camporesi, Piero. *The Fear of Hell—Images of Damnation and Salvation in Early Modern Europe*. University Park: Pennsylvania State University Press, 1991.

Capéran, Louis. *Histoire contemporaine de la laïcité française*. 2 vols. Paris: Rivière, 1957–1960.

———. *Histoire de la laïcité républicaine: La Laïcité en marche*. Paris: Nouvelle Editions Latines, 1961.

Castaldo, Clive. *La Foi Laïque and Its Critics: Secular Humanism After the Dreyfus Affair*. Ph.D. diss., Cambridge University, 1985.

Castellan, Yvonne. *Le spiritisme*. 5th ed. Paris: Presses Universitaires de France, 1974.

Castex, Pierre-Georges. *Le Conte fantastique en France de Nodier à Maupassant*. Paris: Corti, 1982.

Chaline, Jean-Pierre. *Les Bourgeois de Rouen: Une Elite urbaine au XIXe siècle*. Paris: Presses de la Fondation Nationale des Sciences Politiques, 1982.

Charbit, Yves. *Du malthusianisme au populationnisme—Les Economistes français et la population, 1840–1870.* Paris: Presses Universitaires de France, 1981.

Charlton, D. G. *Secular Religions in France, 1815–1870.* New York: Oxford University Press, 1963.

Charraud, Alain. "Analyse de la représentation des âges de la vie humaine dans les estampes populaires du XIXe siècle." *Ethnologie française* 1 (1971): 59–78.

Chassagne, Serge. "Une Ville provinciale à l'heure de la croissance (1815–1901)." In *Histoire d'Angers*, edited by François Lebrun. Paris: Privat, 1975.

Chaunu, Pierre. *La Mort à Paris 16e, 17e, 18e siècles.* Paris: Fayard, 1978.

Chevalier, Louis, ed. *Le Choléra: La Première Epidémie du XIXe siécle.* La Roche-sur-Yon: Imprimerie Centrale de l'Ouest, 1958.

Chevalier, Louis. *The Laboring Classes and Dangerous Classes.* Princeton: Princeton University Press, 1981.

Chevallier, Pierre. *La Séparation de l'église et de l'école.* Paris: Fayard, 1981.

Cholvy, Gérard. *Religion et société au XIXe siècle: Le Diocèse de Montpellier.* 2 vols. Lille: 1973.

Clark, Stuart. "French Historians and Early Modern Popular Culture." *Past and Present* 100 (August 1983): 62–99.

Clark, T. J. *Image of the People—Gustave Courbet and the 1848 Revolution.* Princeton: Princeton University Press, 1982.

Cohen, William. "Symbols of Power: Statues in Nineteenth-Century Provincial France." *Comparative Studies in Society and History* 31 (1989): 491–513.

Coleman, William. *Death Is a Social Disease: Public Health and Political Economy in Early Industrial France.* Madison: University of Wisconsin Press, 1982.

Comte-Sponville, André, et al., eds. *Tombeau de Victor Hugo.* Paris: Quintette, 1985.

Corbin, Alain. *The Foul and the Fragrant—Odor and the French Social Imagination.* Cambridge: Harvard University Press, 1986.

Crowe, Michael. *The Extraterrestrial Life Debate, 1750–1900.* Cambridge: Cambridge University Press, 1986.

Cuisenier, Jean. *French Folk Art.* New York: Kodansha, 1977.

Dallas, Gregor. *The Imperfect Peasant Economy: The Loire Country, 1800–1914.* New York: Cambridge University Press, 1982.

Danforth, Loring, and A. Tsiaras *The Death Ritual of Rural Greece.* Princeton: Princeton University Press, 1982.

Darmon, Pierre. *La Longue Traque de la variole.* Paris: Perrin, 1986.

Darnton, Robert. *The Great Cat Massacre.* New York: Basic Books, 1984.

———. *The Kiss of Lamourette.* New York: Norton, 1990.

———. *Mesmerism and the Enlightenment in France.* New York: Schocken, 1970.

Daumard, Adeline. *La Bourgeoisie parisienne de 1815 à 1848.* Paris: SEVPEN, 1963.

Delaney, Susan. " 'Atala' in the Arts." In *The Wolf and the Lamb: Popular Culture in France*, edited by Jacques Beauroy, Marc Bertrand, and Edward Gargan. Saratoga, Calif. : Anma Libri, 1977.

Delaporte, François. *Disease and Civilization: The Cholera in Paris, 1832.* Translated by A. Goldhammer. Cambridge: MIT Press, 1986.

Delarue, Paul. *Le Conte populaire français.* 3 vols. Nouvelle ed. Paris: Maisonneuve et Larose, 1976.

Delpal, Bernard. *Entre paroisse et commune—Les Catholiques de la Drôme au milieu du XIXe siècle*. Valence: Editions Peuple Libre, 1989.

Delumeau, Jean. *La Peur en Occident (XIVe-XVIIIe siècles)*. Paris: Fayard, 1978.

———. *Le Catholicisme entre Luther et Voltaire*. Paris: Presses Universitaires de France, 1971. Translated as *Catholicism between Luther and Voltaire*. Philadelphia: Westminster Press, 1977.

———. *Le Péché et la peur—La Culpabilisation en Occident (XIIIe-XVIIIe siècles)*. Paris: Fayard, 1983. Translated as *Sin and Fear—The Emergence of a Western Guilt Culture, 13–18th Centuries*. New York: St. Martin's Press, 1990.

Deniel, Reymond, and Louis Henry. "La Population d'un village du Nord de la France." *Population* 20(1965): 563–602.

Desan, Suzanne. *Reclaiming the Sacred: Lay Religion and Popular Politics in Revolutionary France*. Ithaca: Cornell University Press, 1990.

Devlin, Judith. *The Superstitious Mind: French Peasants and the Supernatural in the Nineteenth Century*. New Haven: Yale University Press, 1987.

Dijkstra, Bram. *Idols of Perversity—Fantasies of Feminine Evil in Fin-de-Siècle Culture*. New York: Oxford University Press, 1986.

Dole, George F., ed. *Emmanuel Swedenborg—The Universal Human and Soul-Body Interaction*. New York: Paulist Press, 1984.

Dommanget, Maurice. *Les Idées politiques et sociales d'Auguste Blanqui*. Paris: Rivière, 1957.

Dougherty, Patricia M., O.P. "Constitutional Bishops and the Catholic Press During the Early July Monarchy: Grégoire and Talleyrand." *Proceedings of the Annual Meeting of the Western Society for French History* 17 (1991): 305–314.

Dowbiggin, Ian. "French Psychiatry and the Search for a Professional Identity: The Société Médico-Psychologique, 1840–1870." *Bulletin of the History of Medecine* 63 (1989): 331–355.

Doyle, Arthur Conan. *The History of Spiritualism*. New York: Doran, 1926.

Dupâquier, Jacques, and Michel Dupâquier. *Histoire de la démographie*. Paris: Perrin, 1985.

Dupâquier, Jacques, ed. *Histoire de la population française*. Vol. 3. Paris: Presses Universitaires de France, 1988.

Dupâquier, Michel. "La Famille Bertillon et la naissance d'une nouvelle science sociale: La Démographie." *Annales de démographie historique* (1983): 293–311.

Ellenberger, Henri. *The Discovery of the Unconscious: The History and Evolution of Dynamic Psychiatry*. New York: Basic Books, 1970.

Etlin, Richard. *The Architecture of Death—The Transformation of the Cemetery in Eighteenth-Century Paris*. Cambridge: MIT Press, 1984.

Evans, David Owen. *Le Socialisme romantique—Pierre Leroux et ses contemporains*. Paris: Rivière, 1948.

Evans, Richard. "Blue Funk and Yellow Peril: Cholera and Society in Nineteenth-Century France." *European History Quarterly* 20 (1990): 111–125.

———. *Death in Hamburg: Society and Politics in the Cholera Years, 1830–1914*. New York: Penguin, 1990.

Exigences de réalisme dans la peinture française entre 1830 et 1870. Chartres: Musée des Beaux-Arts, 1984.

Faugeras, M. "Les Fondations dans le diocèse de Nantes de 1800 à 1850." In *Histoire de la messe, XVIIe–XIXe siècles*. Angers: Presse de l'Université d'Angers, 1980.

Faunce, Sarah, and Linda Nochlin, eds. *Courbet Reconsidered*. New Haven: Yale University Press, 1988.

Faure, Olivier. *Genèse de l'hôpital moderne—Les Hospices civils de Lyons de 1802 à 1845*. Lyons: Presses Universitaires de Lyons, 1982.

———. "The Social History of Health in France: A Survey of Recent Developments." *Social History of Medicine* 3 (1990): 437–451.

Favre, Robert, ed. *La Fin dernière*. Paris: Montalba, 1984.

———. *La Mort au siècle des lumières*. Lyons: Presses Universitaires de Lyons, 1978.

Flinn, Michael W. *European Demographic System, 1500–1820*. Baltimore: Johns Hopkins University Press, 1981.

Fosil, Madeleine. "Les Attitudes devant la mort au XVIIIe siècle: Sépultures et suppressions de sépultures dans le cimetière parisien des Saint-Innocents." *Revue historique* 510 (1974): 303–330.

Franklin, R. W. *Nineteenth-Century Churches—The History of a New Catholicism in Württemberg, England, and France*. New York: Garland, 1987.

Freeman, John, and Roger Williams. *How Modernity Came to a Provençal Town—Citizens and Clergy of Grasse*. Lewiston, N.J.: Mellen, 1988.

French Painting, 1774–1830—The Age of Revolution. Detroit and New York: Detroit Institute of Arts and Metropolitan Museum of Art, 1975.

Fried, Michael. *Courbet's Realism*. Chicago: University of Chicago Press, 1990.

———. "The Structure of Beholding in Courbet's *Burial at Ornans*." *Critical Inquiry* 9 (1983): 635–683.

Fuchs, Rachel. *Abandoned Children: Foundlings and Child Welfare in Nineteenth-Century France*. Albany: State University of New York Press, 1984.

Gadille, Jacques. "On French Anticlericalism: Some Reflections." *European Studies Review* 13 (1983): 127–144.

Gaillard, Françoise. "Gustave Courbet et le réalisme—Anatomie de la réception critique d'une oeuvre: 'Un Enterrement à Ornans.' " *Revue d'histoire littéraire de la France* 80 (1980): 978–996.

Gaillard, Lucien. "La Misère et l'assistance à Marseilles sous la second Empire et les premières années de la IIIe République." *Provence historique* 27 (1977): 341–363.

Garrett, Clark. *Respectable Folly—Millenarianism and the French Revolution in France and England*. Baltimore: Johns Hopkins University Press, 1975.

———. *Spirit Possession and Popular Religion: From the Camisards to the Shakers*. Baltimore: Johns Hopkins University Press, 1987.

Gayot, Gérard. *La Franc-Maçonnerie française*. Paris: Gallimard, 1980.

Gelfand, Toby. "Medical Nemesis, Paris, 1894: Léon Daudet's *Les Morticoles*." *Bulletin of the History of Medicine* 60 (1986): 155–176.

Germain, Elizabeth. *Parler du salut? Aux origines d'une mentalité religieuse*. Paris: Beauchesne, 1967.

Gervais, Karen Grandstrand. *Redefining Death*. New Haven: Yale University Press, 1986.

Gibson, Ralph. "De la prédication de la peur à la vision d'un dieu d'amour—La Prédication en Périgord aux XVIIe-XIXe siècles." In *Le Jugement, le ciel, et l'enfer dans l'histoire du christianisme*, Actes de la douzième rencontre d'histoire religieuse tenue à Fontevraud les 14 et 15 octobre 1988, 153–167. Angers: Presse de l'Université d'Angers, 1989.

———. "Hellfire and Damnation in Nineteenth-Century France." *Catholic Historical Review* 74 (1988): 383–402.

———. *A Social History of French Catholicism, 1789–1914*. New York: Routledge, 1989.

Giesey, Ralph. *The Royal Funeral Ceremony in Renaissance France*. Geneva: Droz, 1960.

Ginzburg, Carlo. *The Cheese and the Worms: The Cosmos of a Sixteenth-Century Miller*. Baltimore: Johns Hopkins University Press, 1980.

———. *Night Battles—Witchcraft and Agrarian Cults in the Sixteenth and Seventeenth Centuries*. New York: Penguin, 1985.

Girard, A., and J. Stoetzel. "Les Français et les valeurs du temps présent." *Revue française de sociologie* (January-March 1985): 3–31.

Goldstein, Doris. "Official Philosophies in Modern France: The Example of Victor Cousin." *Journal of Social History* 1 (1968): 259–279.

Goldstein, Jan. *Console and Classify: The French Psychiatric Profession in the Nineteenth Century*. New York: Cambridge University Press, 1987.

Gorovitz, Samuel. *Drawing the Line: Life, Death, and Ethical Choices in an American Hospital*. New York: Oxford University Press, 1991.

Gouhier, Henri. *La Vie d'Auguste Comte*. Paris: N.R.F., 1931.

Grew, Raymond. "Picturing the People: Images of the Lower Orders in Nineteenth-Century French Art." *Journal of Interdisciplinary History* 17 (1986): 203–232.

Guerber, Jean. *Le Ralliement du clergé français à la morale liguorienne*. Rome: Università Gregoriana, 1973.

Guillaume, Pierre. *Du désespoir au salut: les tuberculeux aux 19e et 20e siècles*. Paris: Aubier, 1986.

———. *La population de Bordeaux au XIXe siècle*. Paris: Presses Universitaires de France, 1972.

———. *Médecins, église et foi, XIXe-XXe siècles*. Paris: Aubier, 1990.

Gusdorf, Georges. *Du néant à Dieu dans le savoir romantique*. Paris: Payot, 1983.

Hecht, Jacqueline. "Johann Peter Süssmilch: Point alpha ou omega de la science démographique naive?" *Annales de Démographie Historique* (1979): 101–134.

Hélias, Pierre-Jakez. *The Horse of Pride—Life in a Breton Village*. New Haven: Yale University Press, 1978.

Hertz, Robert. *Death and the Right Hand*. Translated by Rodney and Claudia Needham. Glencoe, Ill.: Free Press, 1960; first published 1907, 1909.

Hess, David. *Spirits and Scientists: Ideology, Spirits, and Brazilian Culture*. University Park: Pennsylvania State University Press. 1991.

Hilaire, Yves-Marie. *Histoire religieuse de la France contemporaine, 1800–1880*. Paris: Privat, 1985.

———. *Une Chrétienté au XIXe siècle?* 2 vols. Villeneuve-d'Ascq: Université de Lille, 1977.

Hintermeyer, Pascal. *Politiques de la Mort.* Paris: Payot, 1981.

Houdaille, J. "La Population de Boulay (Moselle) avant 1850." *Population* 22(1967): 1055–1084.

Huntington, Richard, and Peter Metcalf. *Celebrations of Death—The Anthropology of Mortuary Ritual.* Cambridge: Cambridge University Press, 1979.

Hutton, Patrick. *The Cult of the Revolutionary Tradition: The Blanquists in Politics, 1864–1893.* Berkeley: University of California Press, 1981.

L'Image de piété en France, 1814–1914. Paris: Musée Galerie de la Seita, 1984.

Isambert, François. *Christianisme et classe ouvrière.* Paris: Castermann, 1961.

———. "Les Transformations du rituel catholique des mourants." *Archives de sciences sociales des religions* 39 (1975): 89–100.

Isherwood, Robert. *Farce and Fantasy: Popular Entertainment in Eighteenth-Century Paris.* New York: Oxford University Press, 1986.

Isser, Natalie. "Protestants and Proselytization During the Second French Empire." *Journal of Church and State* 30 (1988): 51–70.

Jaki, Stanley. *Science and Creation—From Eternal Cycles to an Oscillating Universe.* New York: Science History Publications, 1974.

Johnson, Christopher. *Utopian Communism in France—Cabet and the Icarians, 1839–1851.* Ithaca: Cornell University Press, 1974.

Jones, P. M. "Parish, Seigneurie and the Community of Inhabitants in Southern Central France During the Eighteenth and Nineteenth Centuries." *Past and Present* 91 (1981): 74–108.

———. *Politics and Rural Society.* Cambridge: Cambridge University Press, 1985.

Juin, Hubert. *Victor Hugo, 1844–1870.* Paris: Flammarion, 1984.

Kantorowicz, Ernst. *The King's Two Bodies—A Study in Medieval Political Theology.* Princeton: Princeton University Press, 1957.

Kearl, Michael. *Endings—A Sociology of Death and Dying.* New York: Oxford University Press, 1989.

Kelly, Armstrong George. *Mortal Politics in Eighteenth-Century France.* Waterloo: University of Waterloo Press, 1986.

Kennedy, Emmet. *A Cultural History of the French Revolution.* New Haven: Yale University Press, 1989.

Kligman, Gail. *The Wedding of the Dead: Ritual, Poetics, and Popular Culture in Translyvania.* Berkeley: University of California Press, 1988.

Kloppenberg, James. *Uncertain Victory: Social Democracy and Progressivism in European and American Thought, 1870–1920.* New York: Oxford University Press, 1986.

Kselman, Thomas. "Death in Historical Perspective." *Sociological Forum* 2 (1987): 591–597.

———. "Funeral conflicts in nineteenth-century France." *Comparative Studies in Society and History* 30 (1988): 312–332.

———. *Miracles and Prophecies in Nineteenth-Century France.* New Brunswick: Rutgers University Press, 1983.

Kübler-Ross, Elisabeth. *On Death and Dying.* New York: Macmillan, 1970.

Küng, Hans. *Eternal Life? Life After Death as Medical, Philosophical, and Theological Problem.* Garden City, N.Y.: Doubleday, 1984.

La Berge, Ann F. "Mothers and Infants, Nurses and Nursing: Alfred Donné and the Medicalization of Child Care in Nineteenth-Century France." *The Journal of the History of Medicine and Allied Sciences* 46 (1991): 20–43.

La Capra, Dominick, and Steven Kaplan, eds. *Modern European Intellectual History.* Ithaca: Cornell University Press, 1982.

La Capra, Dominick. *History and Criticism.* Ithaca: Cornell University Press, 1985.

Lagrange, F. *Vie de Mgr Dupanloup.* 3 vols. Paris: Poussielgue, 1884.

Lalouette, Jacqueline. "Les Enterrements civils dans les premières décennies de la Troisième République." *Ethnologie française* 13 (1983): 111–128.

Lambert, Yves. "Crise de la confession, crise de l'économie de salut: Le Cas d'une paroisse bretonne de 1900 à 1982." In *Pratiques de la confession—Des Pères du désert à Vatican II.* Paris: Cerf, 1983.

———. *Dieu change en Bretagne.* Paris: Cerf, 1985.

Laqueur, Thomas. "Bodies, Death, and Pauper Funerals." *Representations* 1 (1983): 109–131.

Lasserre, Madeleine. "La Loi et les morts: La Difficile Création du cimetière général de Tours au XIXe siècle." *Annales de Bretagne et des Pays de l'Ouest.* 98 (1991): 303–312.

Launay, Marcel. "Le Cimetière comme élément de la nouvelle sensibilité funèbre au XIXe siècle: Un Exemple nantais." *Bulletin de la Société archéologique et historique de Nantes et de Loire-Atlantique* 119 (1983): 179–190.

———. *Le Diocèse de Nantes sous le Second Empire.* 2 vols. Nantes: Cid, 1982.

Leach, Edmund. *Claude Lévi-Strauss.* New York: Penguin, 1976.

Le Braz, Anatole. *La Légende de la mort chez les bretons armoricains.* 5th ed. 2 vols. Paris: Champion, 1928.

Lebrun, François, ed. *Histoire des catholiques en France du XVe siècle à nos jours.* Paris: Privat, 1980.

Lebrun, François. *Les Hommes et la mort en Anjou au 17e et 18e siècles.* Paris: Mouton, 1971.

———. *Parole de Dieu et Révolution—Les Sermons d'un curé angevin avant et pendant la guerre de Vendée.* Paris: Imago, 1988.

Lécuyer, B. P. "Démographie, statistique et hygiène publique sous la monarchie censitaire." *Annales de démographie historique* (1977): 215–245

Le Goff, Jacques. *The Birth of Purgatory.* Chicago: University of Chicago Press, 1986.

Lehning, James. "Death and the Republic: Political Funerals in the Early Third Republic." *Proceedings of the Annual Meeting of the Western Society for French History* 18 (1991): 205–214.

———. *The Peasants of Marlhes.* Chapel Hill: University of North Carolina Press, 1980.

Leleux, Marie-Claude. "Les Prédicateurs jésuites et leur temps—à travers les sermons prononcés dans le Paris religieux du XVIIIe siècle, 1729–1762." *Histoire économique et sociale* 8 (1989): 21–44.

Le Mée, René. "La Statistique démographique officielle de 1815 à 1870 en France." *Annales de démographie historique* (1979): 252–279.

Léonard, Jacques. *La France médicale au XIXe siècle.* Paris: Gallimard, 1978.

————. *La Médecine entre les savoirs et les pouvoirs.* Paris: Aubier Montaigne, 1981.

————. *La vie quotidienne du médecin de province au XIXe siècle.* Paris: Hachette, 1977.

Le Roy Ladurie, Emmanuel. *Love, Death and Money in the Pays d'Oc.* New York: Penguin, 1984.

Levaillant, Maurice. *La Crise mystique de Victor Hugo (1843–1856).* Paris: Corti, 1954.

Licht, Fred. "Tomb Sculpture." In *The Romantics to Rodin: French Nineteenth-Century Sculpture from North American Collections,* edited by Peter Fusco and H. W. Janson. Los Angeles: Los Angeles County Museum of Art, 1980.

Lieberman, Lisa. *Une Maladie Epidémique: Suicide and its Implications in Nineteenth-Century France.* Ph.D. diss., Yale University, 1987.

Ligou, Daniel. "L'Évolution des cimetières." *Archives de sciences sociales des religions* 39 (1975): 61–77.

Locke, Ralph. *Music, Musicians, and the Saint-Simonians.* Chicago: University of Chicago Press, 1986.

Lottin, Alain. "Les Morts chassés de la cité—'Lumières et Préjugés': Les Emeutes à Lille et à Cambrai lors du transfert des cimetières." *Revue du Nord* 60 (1978): 73–117.

Loupès, Philippe. "Le Casuel dans le diocèse de Bordeaux aux XVIIe et XVIIIe siècles." *Revue d'histoire de l'église de France* 57 (1972): 19–52.

Lukes, Steven. *Emile Durkheim: His Life and Work.* New York: Penguin, 1973.

Mabire, Jean. "Marie Lenormand, devineresse—Les habiletés d'une 'grosse normande.' " *Historia* 466 (October 1985): 90–96.

MacDonald, Michael. "The Secularization of Suicide in England, 1660–1800." *Past and Present* 111 (May 1980).

Mainzer, Claudette. *Gustave Courbet, Franc-Comtois: The Early Personal History Paintings.* Ph.D. diss., Ohio State University, 1982.

Manuel, Frank. *The Prophets of Paris.* New York: Harper and Row, 1965.

Marcilharcy, Christianne. *Le Diocèse d'Orléans au milieu du XIXe siècle.* Paris: Sirey, 1964.

————. *Le diocèse d'Orléans sous l'épiscopat de Mgr Dupanloup, 1849–1878.* Paris: Plon, 1962.

Margadant, Ted. *French Peasants in Revolt.* Princeton: Princeton University Press, 1979.

Markale, Jean. *Contes de la mort.* Etrépilly: Presses du village, 1986.

Marrinan, Michael. *Painting Politics for Louis-Philippe—Art and Ideology in Orléanist France.* New Haven: Yale University Press, 1988.

Marrus, Michael. "Folklore as an Ethnographic Source: A 'Mise au Point.' " In *The Wolf and the Lamb—Popular Culture in France from the Old Regime to the Twentieth Century,* edited by Jacques Beauroy, Marc Bertrand, and Edward Gargan. Saratoga, Calif.: Anma Libri, 1977.

Massignon, Geneviève. *Folktales of France*. Chicago: University of Chicago Press, 1968.

Mathiez, Albert. *La Théophilanthropie et le culte décadaire*. Geneva: Slatkine-Margolis Reprints, 1973; first published 1903.

McDannell, Colleen, and Bernhard Lang. *Heaven—A History*. New Haven: Yale University Press, 1988.

McDougall, Mary Lynn. "Protecting Infants: The French Campaign for Maternity Leaves, 1890s-1913." *French Historical Studies* 13 (1983): 79–105.

McIntosh, Christopher. *Eliphas Lévi and the French Occult Revival*. New York: Weiser, 1974.

McKeown, Thomas. *The Modern Rise of Population*. New York: Academic Press, 1976.

McManners, John. *Church and State in France, 1870–1914*. New York: Harper Torchbooks, 1972.

———. *Death and the Enlightenment*. New York: Oxford University Press, 1981.

McMillan, James. *Housewife or Harlot—The Place of Women in French Society, 1870–1940*. New York: St. Martin's Press, 1981.

McNeill, William H. *Plagues and Peoples*. Garden City, N.Y.: Anchor Books, 1976.

Mellor, Alec. *Histoire de l'anticléricalisme français*. Paris: Veyrier, 1978.

Méry, Marcel. *La Critique du christianisme chez Renouvier*. 2 vols. Paris: Ophrys, 1963.

Miller, Michael. *The Bon Marché—Bourgeois Culture and the Department Store, 1869–1920*. Princeton: Princeton University Press, 1981.

Mitchell, Allan. "Obsessive Questions and Faint Answers: The French Response to Tuberculosis in the Belle Epoque." *Bulletin of the History of Medicine* 62 (1988): 215–235.

———. "Philippe Ariès and the French Way of Death." *French Historical Studies* 10 (1978): 684–695.

Moch, Leslie. *Paths to the City: Regional Migration in Nineteenth-Century France*. Beverly Hills: Sage Publications, 1983.

Monnin, Abbé Alfred. *Le Curé d'Ars*. 2 vols. Paris: Douniol, 1863.

Moody, Raymond. *Life after Life*. Atlanta: Mockingbird Press, 1975.

Moore, R. Laurence. *In Search of White Crows—Spiritualism, Parapsychology, and American Culture*. New York: Oxford University Press, 1977.

Moss, Bernard. *The Origins of the French Labor Movement: The Socialism of Skilled Workers, 1830–1914*. Berkeley: University of California Press, 1976.

Muchembled, Robert. *Culture populaire et culture des élites dans la France moderne (XVe–XVIIIe siècles)*. Paris: Flammarion, 1978.

Muray, Philippe. *Le 19e Siècle à travers les âges*. Paris: Denoel, 1984.

Nathan, Michel. *Le Ciel des Fouriérists—Habitants des étoiles et réincarnations de l'âme*. Lyons: Presses Universitaires de Lyons, 1981.

Nathan, Michel. "Les Métamorphoses de la féminité dans l'oeuvre de Camille Flammarion." In *La Femme au XIXe siècle*, 123–136. 2d ed. Lyons: Presses Universitaires de Lyons, 1979.

Nochlin, Linda. "Innovation and Tradition in Courbet's *Burial at Ornans.*" In *Essays in Honor of Walter Friedlander*. New York, 1965.

———. *Realism*. New York: Penguin, 1971.

Nora, Pierre, ed. *Les Lieux de mémoire*. 2 vols. Paris: Gallimard, 1984–1986.

Nye, Robert A. *Crime, Madness, and Politics in Modern France—The Medical Concept of National Decline*. Princeton: Princeton University Press, 1984.

Oppenheim, Janet. *The Other World—Spiritualism and Psychical Research in England, 1850–1914*. New York: Cambridge University Press, 1985.

Owen, Alex. *The Darkened Room: Women, Power and Spiritualism in Late Victorian England*. London: Virago, 1989.

Ozouf, Mona. *La Fête révolutionnaire*. Paris: Gallimard, 1976.

Paul, Harry. *The Edge of Contingency*. Gainesville: University of Florida Press, 1979.

Penin, Marc. "Les Questions de population au tournant du siècle à travers l'oeuvre de Charles Gide (1847–1932)." *Histoire, économie, et société* 5 (1986): 137–158.

Pérouas, Louis. *Refus d'une religion, religion d'un refus*. Paris: Ecole des hautes etudes en sciences sociales, 1985.

Perrot, Michelle, ed. *From the Fires of Revolution to the Great War*. Vol. 4 of *A History of Private Life*. Cambridge: Harvard University Press, 1990.

Phayer, Michael. "Politics and Popular Religion: The Cult of the Cross in France, 1815–1840." *Journal of Social History* 11 (1978): 346–365.

Pierrard, Pierre. *La Vie quotidienne du prêtre français au XIXe siècle*. Paris: Hachette, 1986.

Pinies, Jean-Pierre. *Figures de la sorcellerie languedocienne*. Paris: CNRS, 1983.

Pinkney, David H. *Napoleon III and the Rebuilding of Paris*. Princeton: Princeton University Press, 1958.

Poitou, Christian. "La Mortalité en Sologne orléanaise de 1670 à 1870." *Annales de démographie historique* (1978): 235–264.

Polain, Eugène. *Il était une fois. . . . Contes populaires entendus en français à Liège et publiés avec notes et index*. Paris: Droz, 1942.

Porter, Theodore M. *The Rise of Statistical Thinking, 1820–1900*. Princeton: Princeton University Press, 1986.

Postic, François. "Des antiquaires aux folkloristes: Découverte et promotion des littératures orales." In *Histoire littéraire et culturelle de la Bretagne*, edited by Jean Balcou and Yves Le Gallo. Vol. 2, 355–365. 2 vols. Paris: Champion, 1987.

Potel, Jacques. *Mort à vain, mort à vendre*. Paris: Desclée, 1970.

Praz, Mario. *The Romantic Agony*. New York: Meridian, 1956.

Ragon, Michel. *The Space of Death: A Study of Funerary Architecture, Decoration, and Urbanism*. Charlottesville: University Press of Virginia, 1983.

Ramsey, Matthew. *Professional and Popular Medicine in France, 1770–1830*. New York: Cambridge University Press, 1988.

Reardon, B.M.G. *Religion in the Age of Romanticism*. Cambridge: Cambridge University Press, 1985.

Rearick, Charles. *Beyond the Enlightenment: Historians and Folklore in Nineteenth-Century France*. Bloomington: Indiana University Press, 1974.

Reddy, William. *The Rise of Market Culture: The Textile Trade and French Society, 1750–1900.* New York: Cambridge University Press, 1984.

Rémond, René. *L'Anticléricalisme en France de 1815 à nos jours.* Brussels: Comlexe, 1985; first published 1976.

Renard, Hélène. *L'Après-Vie.* Paris: Philippe Lebaud, 1985.

Riat, Georges. *Gustave Courbet, peintre.* Paris: 1906.

Richardson, Ruth. *Death, Dissection, and the Destitute.* New York: Penguin, 1989.

Rogé, Joseph. *Le Simple Prêtre.* Paris: Casterman, 1965.

Rollet, Catherine, and Agnès Souriac. "Epidémies et mentalités: Le Choléra de 1832 en Seine-et-Oise" *Annales—Economies, sociétés, civilisations* 29 (1974): 935–965.

Rowell, Geoffrey. *Hell and the Victorians—A Study of the Nineteenth-Century Theological Controversies Concerning Eternal Punishment and the Future Life.* Oxford: Clarendon Press, 1974.

Rubin, Henry James. *Realism and Social Vision in Courbet and Proudhon.* Princeton: Princeton University Press, 1980.

Ruyssen, Théodore. "La Religion dans la vie de Proudhon." In *Ouevres complètes de P.-J. Proudhon—Ecrits sur la religion.* Paris: Rivière, 1959.

Sangoï, Jean-Claude. *Démographie paysanne en Bas Quercy, 1751–1872.* Paris: C.N.R.S., 1988.

Savart, Claude. *Les Catholiques en France au XIXe siècle—Le Témoignage du livre religieux.* Paris: Beauchesne, 1985.

Schapiro, Meyer. "Courbet and Popular Imagery: An Essay on Realism and Naiveté." *Journal of the Warburg and Courtault Institutes* 4 (1941): 164–191.

Schwab, Raymond. *The Oriental Renaissance—Europe's Discovery of India and the East, 1680–1880.* New York: Columbia University Press, 1984.

Sébillot, Paul. *Le Ciel, la nuit, et les esprits de l'air.* Paris: Imago, 1982.

Segalen, Martine. *Les Confréries dans la France contemporaine.* Paris: Flammarion, 1975.

———. *Love and Power in the Peasant Family.* Chicago: University of Chicago Press, 1983.

Sevrin, Ernest. *Les Missions religieuses en France sous la Restauration.* 2 vols. Saint Mandé et Paris: Vrin, 1948–1959.

Sewell, William H. *Structure and Mobility: The Men and Women of Marseille, 1820–1870.* Cambridge: Cambridge University Press, 1985.

———. *Work and Revolution in France—The Language of Labor from the Old Regime to 1848.* Cambridge: Cambridge University Press, 1980.

Singer, Barnett. *Village Notables in Nineteenth-Century France.* Albany: SUNY Press, 1983.

Smith, Bonnie. *Ladies of the Leisure Class—The Bourgeoises of Northern France in the Nineteenth Century.* Princeton: Princeton University Press, 1981.

Soboul, Albert. "Sentiment religieux et cultes populaires pendant la révolution: Saintes, patriotes et martyrs de la liberté." *Archives de sociologie des religions* 1 (1956): 73–87.

Spengler, Joseph. *France Faces Depopulation.* 2d ed. Durham, N.C.: Duke University Press, 1979.

Spitzer, Alan. *The French Generation of 1820*. Princeton: Princeton University Press, 1981.

Stannard, David. *The Puritan Way of Death—A Study in Religion, Culture, and Social Change*. New York: Oxford University Press, 1977.

Stock-Morton, Phyllis. *Moral Education for a Secular Society*. Albany: State University of New York Press, 1988.

Stout, Harry S. *The New England Soul—Preaching and Religious Culture in Colonial New England*. New York: Oxford University Press, 1986.

Sussman, George David. *From Yellow Fever to Cholera: A Study of French Government Policy, Medical Professionalism and Popular Movements in the Epidemic Crises of the Restoration and July Monarchy*. Ph.D. diss., Yale University, 1971.

Sussman, George D. *Selling Mother's Milk: The Wet-Nursing Business in France, 1715–1914*. Urbana: University of Illinois Press, 1982.

Tackett, Timothy. "The West in France in 1789: The Religious Factor in the Origins of the Counterrevolution." *Journal of Modern History* 54 (1988): 715–745.

Taylor, Lawrence. "The Uses of Death in Europe." *Anthropological Quarterly* 62 (1989): 149–154.

Thibaut-Payen, Jacqueline. *Les Morts, l'église, et l'état dans le ressort du parlement de Paris aux XVIIe et XVIIIe siècles*. Paris: Lanore, 1977.

Thomas, Keith. *Religion and the Decline of Magic*. New York: Scribners, 1971.

Thomas, Louis-Vincent. *Rites de mort—Pour la paix des vivants*. Paris: Payot, 1985.

Thomé, Jacques. *Douceur angevine? Naître, vivre, et mourir à Avrillé, 1532–1980*. Maulévrier: Hérault, 1986.

Tilly, Charles. *The Contentious French*. Cambridge: Harvard University Press, 1986.

———. *The Vendée*. New York: Wiley, 1967.

Todorov, Tzvetan. *Introduction à la littérature fantastique*. Paris: Seuil, 1970.

Toews, John. "Intellectual History after the Linguistic Turn: The Autonomy of Meaning and the Irreducibility of Experience." *American Historical Review*. 92 (1987): 879–907.

Toussaint, Helène. *Gustave Courbet (1819–1877)*. Paris: Editions des musées nationaux, 1977.

Troyansky, David. "Monumental Politics: National History and Local Memory in French *Monuments aux Morts* in the Department of the Aisne since 1870." *French Historical Studies* 15 (1987): 121–141.

———. "The Monument Wars of Saint-Quentin in the Third Republic." In *La Cérémonie du pouvoir: Rituels politiques du pouvoir d'état en France de la Révolution à nos jours*, edited by Antoine de Baecque. Forthcoming.

———. *Old Age in the Old Regime: Image and Experience in Eighteenth-Century France*. Ithaca: Cornell University Press, 1989.

Uzureau, Abbé F. "Les Cimetières d'Angers." *L'Anjou historique* 24 (1924): 132–136.

———. "Mort chrétienne de Benaben." *Andegaviana*. 3d series. Angers, 1905.

Vallin, Jacques. "La Mortalité en Europe de 1720 à 1914: Tendances à long terme et changements de structure par sexe et par âge." *Annales de démographie historique* (1989): 31–54.

Van Der Linden, P. J. *Alphonse Esquiros, de la bohème romantique à la république sociale*. Paris: Nizet, 1948.

Van de Walle, Etienne. *The Female Population of France in the Nineteenth Century*. Princeton: Princeton University Press, 1974.

Van Engen, John. "The Christian Middle Ages as an Historiographical Problem." *American Historical Review* 91 (1986): 519–552.

Van Gennep, Arnold. *Manuel de folklore français contemporain*. Vol. I. Paris: Picard, 1943.

Van Kley, Dale. *The Damiens Affair and the Unraveling of the Ancien Régime (1750–1770)*. Princeton: Princeton University Press, 1984.

Varagnac, André. *Civilisation traditionelle et genres de vie*. Paris: Albin Michel, 1948.

Vartier, Jean. *Allan Kardec—La Naissance du spiritisme*. Paris: Hachette, 1971.

Vedrenne-Villeneuve, Edmonde. "L'Inégalité sociale devant la mort dans la première moitié du XIXe siècle." *Population* 16(1961): 665–679.

Verrier, A. J., and Onillon. *Glossaire etymologique et historique des patois et des parlers de l'Anjou*. Angers: Germain et Grassin, 1908.

Viard, Jacques. "Les Origines du socialisme républicain." *Revue d'histoire moderne et contemporaine* 33 (1986): 133–147.

———. *Pierre Leroux et les socialistes européens*. Paris: Actes Sud, 1982.

Viatte, Auguste. *Les Sources occultes du Romantisme*. 2 vols. Paris: Champion, 1965.

———. *Victor Hugo et les illuminés de son temps*. Montréal: Les Editions de l'Arbre, 1942.

Viguerie, Jean de. "Les Fondations et la foi du peuple chrétien—Les Fondations des messes en Anjou aux XVIIe et XVIIIe siècles." *Revue Historique* 156 (1977): 289–320.

Vincent, Steven. *Pierre-Joseph Proudhon and the Rise of French Republican Socialism*. New York: Oxford University Press, 1984.

Vovelle, Michel, and Gaby Vovelle. *Vision de la mort et l'au-delà en Provence d'après les autels des âmes du Purgatoire*. Paris: Colin, 1970.

Vovelle, Michel. *Histoires figurales—Des monstres médiévaux à Wonderwoman*. Paris: Sogedin, 1989.

———. *La Mort et l'Occident de 1300 à nos jours*. Paris: Gallimard, 1983.

———. *Mourir autrefois—Attitudes collectives devant la mort aux XVIIe et XVIIIe siècles*. Paris: Gallimard, 1974.

———. *Piété baroque et déchristianisation en Provence au XVIIIe siècle*. Paris: Seuil, 1978.

Walicki, Andrzej. *Philosophy and Romantic Nationalism: The Case of Poland*. Oxford: Clarendon Press, 1982.

Walker, D. P. *The Decline of Hell—Seventeenth-Century Discussions of Eternal Torment*. Chicago: University of Chicago Press, 1964.

———. *Spiritual and Demonic Magic—From Ficino to Campanella*. Notre Dame: University of Notre Dame Press, 1975.

Wanzer, Syndey. H., M.D., et al. "The Physician's Responsibility Toward Hopelessly Ill Patients," *New England Journal of Medicine* 310 (12 April 1989): 955–959.

Weber, Eugen. *France—Fin de Siècle*. Cambridge: Harvard University Press, 1986.

———. *Peasants into Frenchmen: The Modernization of Rural France*. Stanford: Stanford University Press, 1976.

———. "The Reality of Folktales." *Journal of the History of Ideas* 42 (1981): 93–113.

Weill, Georges. *Histoire de l'idée laïque au dix-neuvième siécle*. Paris: 1925.

Weisberg, Gabriel. *The Realist Tradition: French Painting and Drawing, 1830–1900*. Cleveland: Cleveland Museum of Art, 1980.

Whaley, Joachim, ed. *Mirrors of Mortality—Studies in the Social History of Death*. New York: St. Martin's Press, 1981.

Wheeler, Michael. *Death and the Future Life in Victorian Literature and Theology*. Cambridge: Cambridge University Press, 1990.

Williams, Rosalind. *Dreamworlds: Mass Consumption in Late Nineteenth-Century France*. Berkeley: University of California Press, 1982.

Winock, Michel. *Edouard Drumont et Cie: Antsémitisme et fascisme en France*. Paris: Seuil, 1982.

Wylie, Laurence, ed. *Chanzeaux: A Village in Anjou*. Cambridge: Harvard University Press, 1966.

Yourcenar, Marguerite. *Souvenirs pieux*. Paris: Gallimard, 1974.

Zaleski, Carol. *Otherworld Journeys*. New York: Oxford University Press, 1985.

Zelizer, Viviana. *Pricing the Priceless Child—The Changing Social Value of Children*. New York: Basic Books, 1985.

Zielonka, Anthony. *Alphonse Esquiros (1812–1876)—A Study of His Works*. Paris: Champion-Slatkine, 1985.

Zimdars-Swartz, Sandra L. *Encountering Mary—From La Salette to Medjugorje*. Princeton: Princeton University Press, 1991.

Zipes, Jack. *Breaking the Magic Spell—Radical Theories of Folk and Fairy Tales*. Austin: University of Texas Press, 1979.

Zonabend, Françoise. *The Enduring Memory—Time and History in a French Village*. Manchester: Manchester University Press, 1984.

———. "Les Morts et les vivants—Le Cimetière de Minot en Chatillonnais." *Etudes Rurales* 52 (1973): 7–23.